Promoting Party Politics in Emerging Democracies

This book offers a critical and comparative examination of international support to political parties and party systems in emerging and prospective new democracies in several world regions. It combines the insights of a strong international grouping of leading academics and pioneering doctoral studies, and draws on extensive new field work inquiries. The wide-ranging coverage pools evidence from countries in Europe, Africa, East Asia and Central America. The book shows how far international support still has to go if it is to achieve its aims of helping party politics make a constructive contribution to furthering democracy. It advances our understanding both of the role the political parties are playing in the different polities and the sometimes negative impact of democracy promotion actors from outside.

By contributing original theoretical perspectives and empirical findings, the book points the way forward to agendas for future research and new courses of action. It will be of interest to academics and the policy-making and practitioner communities alike.

This book was originally published as a special issue of *Democratizations*.

Peter Burnell is a Professor in the Department of Politics and International Studies, University of Warwick, England.

André W. M. Gerrits is Professor of Russian Studies at Leiden University, The Netherlands.

Promoting Party Politics in Emerging Democracies

Edited by
Peter Burnell and André W. M. Gerrits

LONDON AND NEW YORK

First published 2012
by Routledge
2 Park Square, Milton Park, Abingdon, Oxon, OX14 4RN

Simultaneously published in the USA and Canada
by Routledge
711 Third Avenue, New York, NY 10017

Routledge is an imprint of the Taylor & Francis Group, an informa business

First issued in paperback 2013

© 2012 Taylor & Francis

This book is a reproduction of *Democratizations*, vol. 17, issue 6. The Publisher requests to those authors who may be citing this book to state, also, the bibliographical details of the special issue on which the book was based.

All rights reserved. No part of this book may be reprinted or reproduced or utilised in any form or by any electronic, mechanical, or other means, now known or hereafter invented, including photocopying and recording, or in any information storage or retrieval system, without permission in writing from the publishers.

Trademark notice: Product or corporate names may be trademarks or registered trademarks, and are used only for identification and explanation without intent to infringe.

British Library Cataloguing in Publication Data
A catalogue record for this book is available from the British Library

ISBN13: 978-0-415-59423-3 (hbk)
ISBN13: 978-0-415-85020-9 (pbk)

Typeset in Times New Roman
by Taylor & Francis Books

Disclaimer
The publisher would like to make readers aware that some chapters in this book may be referred to as articles as they had been in the special issue. The publisher accepts responsibility for any inconsistencies that may have arisen in the course of preparing this volume for print.

Contents

Notes on Contributors   vii

1. Introduction
   Peter Burnell and André Gerrits   1

2. Party politics in Georgia and Ukraine and the failure of Western assistance
   Max Bader   21

3. Crossing the line: partisan party assistance in post-Milošević Serbia
   Marlene Spoerri   44

4. 'Why did they vote for those guys again?' Challenges and contradictions in the promotion of political moderation in post-war Bosnia and Herzegovina
   John W. Hulsey   68

5. An uneasy symbiosis: the impact of international administrations on political parties in post-conflict countries
   Maja Nenadović   89

6. 'Sons of war': parties and party systems in post-war El Salvador and Cambodia
   Jeroen de Zeeuw   112

7. Problems of party assistance in hybrid regimes: the case of Morocco
   Nicole Bolleyer and Lise Storm   138

8. Political party assistance in transition: the German '*Stiftungen*' in sub-Saharan Africa
   Kristina Weissenbach   161

9. In search of the impact of international support for political parties in new democracies: Malawi and Zambia compared
   Lise Rakner and Lars Svåsand   186

CONTENTS

10. Political party assistance and political party research: towards a closer encounter?
    Gero Erdmann   211

Index   233

Notes on Contributors

Max Bader is a Post-Doctoral Researcher and Lecturer at the Geschwister-Scholl-Institute for Political Science at the University of Munich, Germany.

Nicole Bolleyer is Lecturer in Politics at the Department of Politics, University of Exeter, United Kingdom.

Peter Burnell is a Professor in the Department of Politics and International Studies, University of Warwick, United Kingdom.

Jeroen de Zeeuw is a Programme Officer/Policy Advisor for Sudan at the Catholic Organisation for Relief and Development Aid (Cordaid) in The Hague, The Netherlands. The views expressed by him are personal opinions of the author and should not be attributed to Cordaid.

Gero Erdmann is with the GIGA German Institute of Global and Area Studies, Hamburg, where he heads the Research Programme on 'Legitimacy and Efficiency of Political Systems'. He is also Head of the GIGA Berlin Office, Germany.

André Gerrits is Professor of Russian Studies at Leiden University, The Netherlands.

John W. Hulsey is a visiting Assistant Professor in Political Science at James Madison University and a PhD candidate at Indiana University, Bloomington, United States of America.

Maja Nenadović is a PhD candidate in the Department of European Studies at the University of Amsterdam, The Netherlands.

Lise Rakner is Head of Department and Professor of Comparative Politics at the University of Bergen, and she is affiliated with the Chr. Michelsen Institute, Bergen, Norway.

Marlene Spoerri is a PhD candidate in the Department of European Studies at the University of Amsterdam, The Netherlands.

NOTES ON CONTRIBUTORS

Lise Storm is Senior Lecturer in Middle East Politics at the Institute of Arab and Islamic Studies, University of Exeter, United Kingdom.

Lars Svåsand is Professor of Comparative Politics, University of Bergen, Norway.

Kristina Weissenbach is Research Fellow and Lecturer at the Institute of Political Science and the NRW School of Governance at the University of Duisburg-Essen, Germany.

Introduction

Peter Burnell[a] and André Gerrits[b]

[a]Department of Politics and International Studies, University of Warwick, Coventry, UK; [b]Russian Studies, Leiden University, The Netherlands

This opening section briefly introduces international political party support, that is, assistance to political parties by international organizations, mostly from the US and Europe, to strengthen individual political parties, to promote peaceful interaction between parties and to help to create a more stable and democratic environment for political parties in new, struggling or flawed democracies. Before going on to introduce the contributions to this collection, this introduction discusses three major issues related to international support to political parties: the current 'party crisis' in young as well as in old democracies; the intrusive (political) nature of international party assistance; and the difficulties involved in assessing its effectiveness. Political parties seem much more difficult to work with than (other) political and civil society organizations. Subsequently, we will turn to the case studies, which focus on the former Soviet Union, the Balkans, and Africa, with excursions into Cambodia and El Salvador. Most of the contributions dwell on two contrasting country cases, and all of them combine attention to the state of political parties and party systems in their respective countries with the role played by international involvement and party support in particular. We will briefly present and discuss the major issues raised for international party support in the country studies, and try to formulate an answer to the question about where and when party support might make a meaningful contribution to supporting democratic transformation and consolidation.

Practically every publication on international support for political parties in new and emerging democracies starts from the same paradoxical observation: on the one hand political parties should be considered as essentially important for a well-functioning democracy, while on the other hand parties often function poorly and are generally held in low esteem. Political parties inadequately perform the functions they are expected to fulfil. These include interest articulation and aggregation, political participation, elite recruitment, and governance. Parties frequently suffer from such limited legitimacy that they tend to undermine rather than support the often feeble democratic order in many countries. Political parties are often seen as the 'weakest link' in democratic transformation.[1] Arguably, international support to political parties, one aspect of a larger democracy assistance effort, is designed to overcome this paradox, to bridge the gap between the crucial role of political parties in representative democracies and their generally poor performance and reputation among the citizens of many countries. Interestingly, the problematic state and standing of many political parties does not remain limited to new, struggling, or seriously flawed democracies. Many long-established democratic countries also have their own 'crisis of parties' too.

This raises two important questions: (1) why are political parties so problematic in many new (and old) democracies and (2) what have international actors been doing to support and strengthen them? While the introduction briefly addresses both issues, the country studies to this collection focus mainly on the second question: the experience of international cooperation with and support for political parties in emerging and sometimes flawed democracies, in particular in the Balkans, the former Soviet Union and in Africa. Which international actors are engaged in assistance to political parties? Which strategies do they follow? What are the effects, intended as well as unintended, of international support to political parties and party systems in different national and political contexts? When and where might international support to political parties make a meaningful contribution to the transformation and consolidation of democracy?

A party crisis?

There are two separate, partly overlapping literatures on international party assistance: a still small number of academic studies on international involvement in the strengthening of political parties and party systems in former authoritarian countries, and additionally, an equally limited but also increasing number of evaluative studies, mostly commissioned by international donor organizations.[2] These publications are pioneering and valuable, but as yet they fail to fill major gaps in relevant academic debates. Scholarly research on political parties generally does not mention the external or international dimension of party development, while the literature on international democracy promotion by and large neglects the subfield of party assistance. This introduction is primarily concerned with the scholarly and evaluative literature on international party assistance, which it discusses within the wider context of the current problematic of political parties, in struggling and emerging democracies as well as in established democratic countries.

The role and nature of political parties in most democracies is changing.[3] Opinions differ on whether we face yet another period of adaptation by political parties to circumstances that are, partially at least, of their own making, or whether we are being confronted with a more fundamental crisis: a crisis of political party, or even worse, of political representation. The evidence is mixed. 'Parties have always been in a process of change', as the editors of a recent *Handbook of Party Politics*, stress. Political parties are inherently dynamic, as democracies in general are, and it might be premature to assert that a 'different kind of change' has come about.[4]

Moreover, the perceived crisis of party is a complex, ambiguous, and often contradictory phenomenon, which despite commonly shared features, varies from one country to another. The popular critique of political parties has not (yet) translated into the rejection of parties per se and even less so in the denunciation of democracy, neither in established nor in most of the new democracies. The crisis of party should not be confused with a crisis of democracy, not yet at least. And finally, parties do not seem to fail equally on all counts. Stefano Bartolini and Peter Mair group the various party functions under two headings: their representative and their procedural or institutional functions. It is in the realm of representation (interest articulation, aggregation, and policy formulation) that the decline of political parties is most conspicuous, they argue.[5] In established as well as in emerging democracies, the crisis of party seems first and foremost a crisis of popular support and legitimacy. While the link with the state has largely remained intact, the link with society has significantly weakened. Political party organization in Western Europe has entered a new phase, as Katz and Mair argue, 'a new phase in which parties become increasingly dominated by, as well as most clearly epitomized by, the party in public office'.[6] Political parties are more and more defined by their relation with the state, and less by their links with society. This development is theoretically captured by characterizations of party organization as cartel parties, or electoral-professional or cadre parties – types of party which are not only increasingly important in mature democracies but which have dominated the party political scene in many newly emerging democratic countries from the very beginning, as various contributions to this volume show.

The dimension of the party crisis may be different between established and new democracies, due to the fragility of many recent democratization processes, but the symptoms are largely similar and they have led to an increasingly serious shortfall in political parties' popular legitimacy. Parties in established and newly-emerged democracies (many of which are subject to foreign support) suffer from comparable flaws and weaknesses: few(er) party members, shallow(er) organization, weak(er) links with society and strong(er) links with the state; feeble(r) party identification, low(er) election turnouts, less(er) developed policy platforms and (more) volatile party systems. Interestingly, parties in many new democracies do not seem to be following the patterns laid down by long-established ones, but rather the sequence is the other way round. Aspects of party life which are widespread in new and occasionally seriously flawed democracies appear increasingly prominent in some more mature ones too: party life is ever more elite-driven, party membership is small or non-existent; party volatility is increasing and electoral turnout is declining; political articulation becomes increasingly vague; party legitimacy and popularity are going down, while alienation and anti-party sentiment is increasing in society, all symptoms of a 'weakened sense of "partyness"' in society, of 'party crisis'.[7]

International party assistance

Despite similarities between the problematic of political parties and party systems in established and in new democracies, international party assistance remains essentially a one-way affair: from organizations in old democracies (which occasionally hire activists from other countries, including recently democratized countries) to political parties in new democracies. We define international party assistance as the organizational effort to support democratic political parties, to promote a peaceful interaction between parties, and to strengthen the democratic political and legal environment for political parties. Party assistance works with an ideal-typical organizational, financial, and ideological image of political parties, largely derived from Western European experiences. The extent to which this party image actually determines concrete activities is not so easy to establish. The universalistic notions that inspire party assistance do not necessarily exclude receptiveness to local circumstances and conditions. Party assistance covers all major aspects of party life. It may focus on the internal organization of political parties (strengthening of party organization, inclusion of women and youth, internal democracy, and transparency of party finances), on electoral capacity building (political profiling and campaigning), on the legislative and governance functions, and on the dialogue and cooperation among parties (particularly relevant in post-conflict situations). These aspects of party support translate into a range of concrete activities among which training exercises are prevalent.[8]

Party assistance is part of a wider environment of international democracy assistance or promotion.[9] In 2006 Thomas Carothers estimated the total annual amount of external party aid worldwide to be approximately US$200 million. This is a small part, 5 to 7%, of international democracy support in general (estimated at between US$3–4 billion), which again is only a fraction of Western aid for international development cooperation overall.[10] And with the exception of some global and regional multilateral institutions (United Nations, Organization for Security and Co-operation in Europe, and the European Union (EU)), practically all major donors and organizations in international party assistance come from Western European countries and the United States. The US government, individual EU member states and the European Commission provide the lion's share of democracy support funds, including international party assistance. All relevant organizations are formally autonomous, though wholly or partially sponsored by their own national or regional (EU) authorities. This applies to the major US institutions (the National Endowment for Democracy, the National Democratic Institute as well as the International Republican Institute) and it goes for practically all European organizations (the German, Swedish, British and Dutch party-related organizations and the Netherlands Institute for Multiparty Democracy (NIMD)).

Although the sums involved in international party support are far from insignificant, the controversial dimension of party aid is not primarily financial but political.

Intrusiveness and effectiveness

Foreign support for political parties is a controversial form of democracy assistance. International party support, even if it is done under fully legal circumstances, is being perceived by many in recipient *and* donor countries as a form of intervention into the domestic affairs of sovereign countries. Additionally, the effectiveness of party support is repeatedly questioned. We consider intrusiveness and (the lack of) effectiveness as the major problematic issues with regard to international party support.

Its strongly political dimension is the *raison d'être* as well as the basic weakness (in terms of legitimacy) of international party assistance. The recognition that every sustainable democracy is party-based and that well-institutionalized political parties and party systems enhance the quality and viability of democratic governance is why most international democracy promotion organizations decided to engage in party assistance activities. Democracy assistance needed to become more 'political', more explicitly aimed at the political process in recipient countries as well as at the crucial agents of democracy, which includes political parties. Many donor organizations remain cautious, though, if not hesitant with regard to this specific form of democracy assistance: the political nature of international party support makes it inevitably intrusive, a direct intervention into the political process of countries.[11]

During the Cold War when party support was a negligible aspect of international democracy assistance as well as during the first few years into the post-Cold War era, most support went to selected political parties or to various parties, on an individual basis. For the most part assistance to individual parties followed, and still follows, the so-called 'partisan' approach, which implies working with ideologically similar parties, mostly for the longer term. The German and most other European foundations work primarily with sister parties or with sister party-related civil society organizations; whilst the main US based institutions follow a more inclusive approach.

There are various options to enlarge the practical scope of party assistance. Donor organizations can support various parties simultaneously (the multiparty or cross-party approach) or they might address the legal and institutional context in which parties operate. Both options go beyond political parties per se and intend positively to affect the party system or the institutional setting which influences the party system. Multi- or cross-party assistance has the additional advantage of circumventing the overtly partisan and interventionist dimension of party support.

Evaluating the effectiveness of international party assistance comes with a series of complex questions, many of which will be pursued in the contributions gathered here. How to formulate the criteria of effectiveness, as donors' ambitions are generally formulated in broad terms (such as to contribute to the formation of stable, democratic and representative political parties, within a democratic environment) and lack a specific strategic dimension? How to distinguish the effects of international party aid from other external influences? And how to differentiate between the various 'levels' of party assistance, between support for individual parties, for the party system in general, or for the institutional context of party politics?

Cautiousness prevails among most researchers as well as among the donors that have commissioned evaluative studies of their party work. Carothers argues that there seems little evidence that party assistance has 'transformative effects'.[12] This observation is shared by Gero Erdmann,[13] and the contributors to this study draw conclusions that do not fundamentally deviate from these modest assessments.

Providers of party assistance generally have a more positive view of the significance and effectiveness of their activities, although they hardly ever claim results that go beyond small or indirect effects on individual parties. A recent report for the Department for International Development and the Foreign and Commonwealth Office on assistance by United Kingdom-based organizations criticizes the 'somewhat patchy and ad hoc nature' of political party support and the 'relatively little progress (that) has been made in moving systematically from understanding context to tailoring support to context'.[14] Another evaluation, commissioned by the Ministry of Foreign Affairs of Denmark, draws comparable conclusions.[15]

Three major factors seem to be responsible for the limited effects of party assistance: first, the specific method of party aid by most donors and international non-governmental organizations; secondly, the unfriendly political environment or regime context for the development of viable parties and robust party systems; and finally the specific challenges in terms of ownership which political parties, different from other societal organizations, present to external and international involvement and engagement.

On the first, Carothers' critique of the 'standard method' of international party aid,[16] repeated by academic observers and donors' evaluators, contains two interrelated aspects: international party support is inspired by a 'mythic model' of political parties in established democracies, and international organizations often show a lack of knowledge and understanding of specific local circumstances.

Various contributions to this issue indicate that the crux in many cases is the misfit between the party model or norm which guides international donors and aid organizations and the type of party which serves the interests of many party leaders or political entrepreneurs in the recipient countries. Incentives provided by party assistance fail to induce party elites to comply, because doing so would not serve their personal or party-political interests. The case studies on Georgia and Ukraine, on Morocco and other African states as well as on the Balkans provide evidence that there is a major disconnect between what many of the politicians in these countries believe is in their own interests and what the international supporters of democracy think democratic progress requires. If relations with the state are the essential source of a party's influence, perhaps even of its viability, party leaders will principally invest in their contacts with those in power, not with society at large. If strong client-patron relations are a traditional aspect of political life in a given society, party leaders will show little interest in the 'impersonal', rational and policy-driven features of party life that are associated with the longer established democracies. And finally, if a political party mainly serves as a vehicle for the political or personal ambition of an individual, this individual will not show much enthusiasm for transparency, internal democracy, gender balance and other worthy aspects of the party model which international donors would be interested to support. In other words, the limited and sometimes even counterproductive effects of party assistance in struggling or flawed democracies may not so much be the result of a lack of strategy, toolkits, contextualization or other real or perceived deficiencies on the part of the donor organizations, but of the gap that exists between supply and demand, between what donors offer and what many recipients want. As a study of political party assistance submitted to USAID puts it: 'Regardless of how conducive to reform an environment may be and how well-designed foreign assistance programs are, the success of party assistance programs depends on individual actors, on the agency of people directly involved in promoting *and* preventing party development.'[17]

Regime context is the second crucially important variable of party assistance's efficacy. The role and relevance of political parties as well as the extent to which international party assistance efforts may be effective significantly depend on the institutional environment in a given country. And in many (formerly) democratizing countries, this political and legal infrastructure is not particularly conducive to democratic political parties. Strong executive power and weak legislatives, with domineering regime parties or 'parties of power' (i.e. parties which are founded by and principally act in the interests of those in power) leave little space for vibrant and meaningful competitive party politics. Mainstream theories on party systems, which take the interaction, the patterns of competition and cooperation between parties as the defining criteria of party systems, do not seem very helpful in many semi-democratic or authoritarian countries. Carothers suggests a different focus and introduces a 'power-oriented taxonomy of party systems', where the role and relevance of political parties is not so much determined by the power distribution among them as it is by the relationship of parties to the over-all exercise of power, that is to the state.[18] The Russian Federation offers a clear example. Multiple parties are allowed to organize, operate, and compete, but power resides outside of any single political party (including the so-called party/parties of power), and instead lies in the still largely non-party based bureaucracy and in the positions of president and/or prime-minister. This strongly affects the nature and the relevance of parties, and it also seriously limits the extent to which external, international actors can have a bearing on the organizational structure, the ideological make-up, and the political efficacy of parties.

Specific challenges in terms of ownership are the third major reason why the effectiveness of international party support proves to be rather limited. Political parties are principally domestic political actors. Neither the spatial context of party politics nor the research into political party and party system often go beyond the national state. It is either implicitly assumed or explicitly asserted by political scientists that political parties are domestic institutions par excellence, largely impervious to external or international influences. Yet, political parties *are* subject to external pressures, we would argue, three in particular: to the effects of globalization; to the association with trans-national parties and party networks; and in European accession countries to the consequences of EU enlargement. How much effect do trans-national party organizations, globalization and EU enlargement have on the nature and the functioning of parties?

Even if globalization may have no immediately discernable impact on political parties, aspects of globalization in the sphere of the economy and of information and communication do inevitably affect every party-based democracy.[19] More than other political and societal organizations (from governments to nongovernmental organizations and private enterprise) therefore, political parties seem to exemplify the growing discrepancy between ever increasing external, international influences and our still predominantly nationally organized polities.

International networks of political parties had and still have an impact on political parties, most conspicuously on those in the former communist countries of East Central Europe. In this part of the world party formation and development most closely resembles the West European pattern, including the ideological lines of division which separate the four major trans-national party networks: the social-democratic, liberal, Christian-democratic, and conservative internationals. Their involvement in party politics in East Central Europe mostly took the form of mutual consultations, while assistance generally took the form of seminars and visits. The four international networks are not major international policy actors, though. More important, therefore, is the presence of parties from the new member states of the European Union in European-level parties in the EU parliament – rare examples of supranational party formation, albeit still in an incipient stage, and a minor qualification of the predominantly 'national' nature of political parties. The critical issue here is the strong motivation by political parties to belong to and to be accepted by like-minded parties and party organizations in Western Europe.

Few external influences have impacted on political parties more strongly than the EU accession process, especially again in the countries of East Central Europe. Paradoxically, however, the influence of European integration on political parties in East Central Europe has been so 'pervasive and strong', that it becomes practically impossible to distinguish it from the overall process of change in the region.[20] Although EU enlargement has been presented as the most successful international democratization strategy ever, there is another side to it too: accession conditions seriously constrained governments' options, thereby limiting the choices and alternatives of office-seeking political parties. The Hungarian scholar Attila Ágh goes so far as to say the political parties in East Central Europe were 'programmed for transition and accession', and that once both ambitions are realized the parties and party leaderships in the region are left in a state of socio-political 'senilisation', 'aggravated by the unsettling effects of the EU membership'.[21] The painful measures involved were generally presented (by the EU as well as by the governing elites in most accession countries) as rational, necessary, even inevitable. Given the depoliticizing effect EU accession has had on parties and party politics in the newer member states of the EU, the *Demokratieunzufriedenheit* of which the rise of populist parties in East Central Europe may have attested to, look like a less agreeable feature of an otherwise healthy 'return to politics'.

Generally, donor organizations seem to have less leverage on political parties than on civil society organizations. Parties more than most civil society organizations have had to rely on local support, and depend on their local constituencies. In many countries parties secure local support through providing specific services to meet immediate material or financial needs, which may not have much in common with how donors perceive the role and relevance of parties, but which are crucially important to these parties and their electorates.

International party support operates under extremely challenging and difficult conditions. The political and institutional environment in many new democracies is not particularly conducive to solid and vibrant democratic parties and competitive party systems. And political parties and party-based democracy in most established democratic countries, the donors of international party support, face their own problems: situations of party uncertainty and change, if not crisis. How this all works out in practice, how it informs and affects international party support, is the focus of the country cases which this study brings together. We will now give a foretaste of the more substantive material in this collection, written not as some kind of imperfect substitute but in the spirit of encouraging readers to move swiftly on to the contributions themselves.

Turning to the country studies

The nine studies that follow form a strongly comparative collection. A majority of them dwell on two contrasting country cases to make their points. The coverage overall extends to the post-Soviet and post-communist space in Eastern Europe, the Caucasus and the Balkans, along with the North, East and Central-Southern regions of Africa, and selected countries in Central America and East Asia. Of course a fully comprehensive global coverage is not feasible here, and two of the regions that are not represented merit brief mention. These are the experience of (re)democratizing countries in South America, like for example Chile where there was international involvement with opposition politicians even during the time of military rule led by President Pinochet, and the countries of Central and Eastern Europe that have joined the European Union. Both regions are represented in the existing literature.[22] Nevertheless the original contributions made by this collection draw on primary data collection and field research carried out by the authors, in some cases over a period of several years. They pool the findings both of established scholars whose names are already prominent in the literature and the work of recently completed doctoral studies.[23] These last represent the first wave of new doctoral inquiries into international party support specifically, which forms part of a larger and rapidly growing body of doctoral-level and post-doctoral research on international democracy promotion more generally, in universities in North America and several European countries like Germany, the Netherlands and the UK.

All of the studies combine attention both to the state of the political parties and the party system in their respective countries with the role played by international involvement and party support in particular. Indeed, in order to fully appreciate the impact made by party support and how minimal or distorted its effects can be, some of the studies find it necessary to first paint in the details of the parties and party politics at some considerable length. The contributions by Bader and Hulsey are examples of this close attention to context.[24] But in the collection as a whole there is deliberate intent to integrate what political science can tell us about parties and party systems with what the democracy support industry – or that part which is engaged in working with political parties – actually does, and its experience to date and the lessons. This is a very novel undertaking. In some of the accounts the coverage emphasizes the domestic political and other conditions inside the countries that determine both the development of the political parties and party system and the impact that foreign support can have. In others the balance of attention focuses to a greater degree on what might be called the supply side, namely the external actors and especially the international organizations that specialize in offering party assistance. Prominent European examples can be found in the contributions by Rakner and Svåsand,[25] which highlight the Netherlands Institute for Multiparty Democracy, and Weissenbach[26] who hones in on Germany's political foundations.

Although the total number of international actors that have some involvement with party support is probably in excess of 30 (Table 1 in Weissenbach identifies the main organizations by name) Germany's political foundations (*Stiftungen*) have an especially long established presence in this field of activity, and their approach has some distinctive features. Despite having a reputation in the past for not disclosing very detailed information such as performance evaluations, recent years have seen them subject to probably more independent study, especially by academics, than most of the party support extended by other countries.[27] Weissenbach builds on and takes the existing studies further forward, by drawing on experience in two African countries to make the case for a new and more strategic approach to determining what party support should undertake.[28] Rakner and Svåsand's examination of the Netherlands Institute for Multi-party Democracy activities in two other countries in Africa focuses on an organization that has also carved out a distinctive reputation, for its engagement in cross-party work and strengthening inter-party dialogue, especially but not only in countries where there has been civil conflict.[29] This makes a welcome new extension to the few organizations that feature already in the very modest accumulation of academic literature on the topic in general.

The contributions in this collection by Bader,[30] Nenadović,[31] de Zeeuw[32] and others whose primary focus is more on the political actors and political conditions inside the countries than on the international partners per se are then fundamental to the overall balance in this integrated collection. Bolleyer and Storm[33] combine the two sides, the internal and the external, arguing convincingly that in a political system like Morocco's international party support is capable of exerting an effect, but the consequences for democratization can be the opposite of those intended. It helps freeze rather than transform the distribution of power that exists among the main political institutions and between the executive and the people. This dramatic finding draws on the important analytical distinction the authors make between how democratic institutions operate within a regime including one like Morocco that is not a fully fledged liberal democracy, and the contribution those institutions make to regime democratization. This distinction and the inevitable corollary of what the relationship between the two phenomena comprises look very significant, and is worth developing in future studies that reach well beyond the Moroccan case.[34]

At this point the reader will be struck by the possibility that the differences in approach between a strong focus on the countries, or alternatively a strong supply-side focus, will tend to be reflected in the findings the studies reach about where the main responsibility for party assistance failures and successes lies. Indeed this possibility seems to be born out here. On the one side there are for instance the accounts by Bader[35] on the impact of systemic political conditions – or what he calls constraints – in Georgia and Ukraine and by Bolleyer and Storm[36] on Morocco's monarchical regime. And on the other side there is Hulsey's claim[37] that external interventions in Bosnia have been responsible for strengthening rather than weakening the grip of ethno-nationalist tendencies. Weissenbach's comparison of the German foundations can also be included on this side: she finds that their decisions over party assistance strategy to South Africa contrast with their much less successful approach to Kenya.[38]

However, a close reading of all the contributions does not bear out a straightforward correspondence between where the authors focus the main thrust of their attention and where they ultimately assign responsibility for the effects of party support. In short, choice of approach does not necessarily dictate the findings. A part of the reason for this lies in the sensitivity the authors show to their task. But another undoubtedly lies in the obstacles to making confident statements about precise and firm causal connections concerning situations where the interplay of foreign and domestic factors can be so intimate that even attempting to make a sharp conceptual distinction between the two may distort the reality. In other words the situation on the ground may be messier or, in more prosaic language, the internal and the external involvements may to some degree become mutually constitutive of one another.[39]

Of course the situation on the ground may be messier in a different sense. A country like Morocco in many respects enjoys political continuity and the appearance of high political stability, the latter perhaps a beneficiary of the former and due to the absence of radical experimentation with full liberal democratic reform. In contrast, however a feature common to several, although not all the countries represented in this collection, is a recent history of violent civil conflict. Its relevance is noted in several places; and the studies by Hulsey, Nenadović, and de Zeeuw examine quite specifically the impact that violent conflict and its aftermath have had on the more recent development of party politics and on the achievements of international support.[40] Without going so far as to endorse theories of path dependence in their most extreme form, there does seem to be strong evidence here for treating civil conflict as a significant independent variable that influences the political parties and party system once conflict has ended, with implications for international party support. This does not mean we should abandon the entirely compatible proposition that says the democratic failings of political parties and such dangerous features as exclusionary ethic or nationalist competition between parties can actually trigger violent conflict, as happened in Kenya following the disputed presidential election of December 2007.

Yet even among cases where conflict has left a strong legacy there are some notable contrasts. Unlike either El Salvador or Cambodia which feature in de Zeeuw's study, both Bosnia-Herzegovina and Kosovo in the studies by Hulsey and Nenadović have experienced the effects of some form of international administration.[41] This adds a potent extra dimension to the mix of external influences. It complicates the role of party aid, and raises in stark form issues of ownership that are comparable to those that have long troubled the more mature industry of international aid for economic development. Also, it seems that the manner of their exit by international peace-builders can be as important to what happens next inside the country as are their peace-making and peace-keeping activities while still present on the ground. To what extent will the societies then be left to work out their own political future, the institutionalization of political parties and a suitable party system included? The sources of international influence of all sorts, indirect as well as direct, are of course much broader still, and they too can have implications for the parties that no one outside intended. For example as de Zeeuw's remarks on Cambodia suggest, the use of foreign aid meant for economic development may advantage the incumbent party in government, with consequences for the party system, especially where patronage is a prominent feature of the power relationships between and inside the parties individually.[42] Meanwhile in Europe tense relations between would-be accession states in the Balkans and the EU continue to matter to the political parties, and do not necessarily shape them in ways that are conducive to the societies' democratic development, as the accounts of Bosnia and Serbia seem to bear out.

The findings

Overall a number of major issues are raised for party support in new or emerging and prospective democracies, although the studies represented here cannot be expected to provide solutions to all of them. For example the material provides additional evidence of the limited ability of party assistance to achieve its stated objectives, whether these be the proximate ones relating to party politics or, more importantly, the contribution that party politics makes to democratic progress, or both of these. As discussed above: the parties themselves and especially their leaders simply may not want to go where their international partners are trying to lead them. Self-serving personal or particularistic and sectional or regional agendas may play a role, but parties and party leaders might also have legitimate concerns about the lack of expertise, the motives or the conduct of any foreign-based sources of advice and assistance, and these command respect.

Furthermore there is rather uncomfortable evidence from some of the accounts of perverse and unintended consequences of party support, in the likes of Serbia and Bosnia-Herzegovina, reinforcing the tendency of parties to root themselves in populist nationalist credentials, and Morocco, where helping the most politically successful parties to remain distant from society presents a contrasting perspective. There are also the more neutral cases of failed objectives, as for instance in Malawi or Kenya. Nenadović[43] adds for good measure the possibility that the international partners themselves acquire some bad habits from dealing with societies, even where correcting such traits is supposed to be part of what they are about, an example being the failure to seriously address dubious financial or other transactions. Spoerri[44] outlines the perils of partisanship in party assistance in the case of Serbia. In contrast Bolleyer and Storm[45] argue the corresponding limitations where international partners spread their efforts rather too widely and thinly, as well as noting the reluctance of for instance US partners to cultivate solid relationships with Islamist political groups and the suspicions these groups have about Western agencies, a finding that can stand for wider North African and Middle Eastern experience as well. The failure of party assistance in terms of its party objectives can have larger political system-level consequences, if the chances for party-based political competition to strengthen the democratic process and the long-term outlook for stable democracy are undermined or held back.

However, for international party support to have a good chance of success in helping to institutionalize parties and a party system that conform to the requirements of liberal democracy, it seems that certain conditions must be present first.[46] And as Bader almost goes so far as to argue, their absence – or the presence of overriding domestic constraints – may mean there is very little if anything constructive that party support can actually do. So, what do the international partners, especially those for whom party support is a flagship activity or whose commitment to a country goes back several years, do if they reach a similar conclusion? Irrespective of what the facts so far tell us, how should they react? The answers could well differ from case to case. So whereas a country like Ukraine can – and has taken steps to – rewrite the constitutional or other arrangements that formally distribute powers among the different political and governing institutions – improvements to the staging of free and fair elections being an example –, it is much less realistic to expect a country like Cambodia to banish the social and political cultural and other legacies of bitter civil conflict overnight. The differences will be reflected in the implications for changing the party politics.

So we are still left with the big questions about where and when party assistance by itself might make a truly meaningful contribution to supporting a complete transformation all the way to stable liberal democracy, although the studies do go some way towards providing answers. In regard to what the party assistance actors themselves can do to approach their task with better information and an appropriate strategic approach, the authors are not shy of offering clear advice. For example a stronger emphasis on distinguishing carefully not just the distinctive historical background of countries but, equally importantly, the stage of political system change that is under way comes through strongly in Weissenbach's imaginatively constructed 'phase model' of party assistance.[47] The importance of transferring appropriate norms rather than just participating in the construction of new and more formal institutions is another recommendation that is identified by Nenadović.[48]

This sits alongside the need to address thorny questions about how to render international partners more accountable when part of their stated mission is to help new or undemocratic political parties themselves become democratically accountable. What the accountability would look like and how it would work are matters left for future discussion. But as Rakner and Svåsand[49] indicate from Zambia – an example of a country that observers judge is still in transition[50] – if the international partners were more responsive to all the demands that political parties expressly make upon them then they might be led away from attempting to do what their own understanding of the situation tells them should be done. Bolleyer and Storm[51] also offer advice in the shape of concentrating party work on fewer and more carefully chosen partners, which is something that Bader[52] in his research into Georgia and Ukraine seems predisposed to agree with. But this could mean that in some countries there are few if any parties the international organizations should work with. And in any case the fact that in Ukraine the one party that has become most institutionalized is the party that has had least exposure to Western party aid seems to pose awkward questions for choices over where to concentrate support.

Still looming over everything then is the question what should the international partners do where there are strong grounds for believing that their chances of making a positive difference in the near to medium terms are rather slim? Some of the contributing authors might be thought to pull their punches on this, when others do provide concrete examples of party support organizations acting on lessons they have discovered for themselves. Nevertheless the international agencies that are involved in the highly specialized activity of party support could do much worse than spend time reading the contents of this collection, including the reflections in the final piece by Erdmann.[53]

Turning now to the parties and party systems, as distinct from party support, a few points must be made but only briefly. The material confirms that parties in new democracies may not resemble closely the idea, let alone the mythology, of mass parties enjoying strong linkages to society that are, or once were, present in some long established democracies in western and northern Europe. Revelations about the absence of strong ideological commitments or clear policy and programmatic dividing lines among the parties, and the importance that identity politics plays in structuring the party cleavages, may not be new. But what is striking from the material assembled here is how true these observations are of such a wide variety of societies, from those found in different regions of Africa to several countries in Europe and beyond.

Furthermore, the development of institutionalized versions of democratic parties and even more so democracy-favouring party systems remains extremely challenging in emerging and prospective new democracies. And as Randall and

Svåsand pointed out some time ago,[54] even the institutionalization of one or more political parties in accordance with the customary definitions adopted by contributions in this collection, may not mean that a well institutionalized and competitive system of democratic political parties will exist as well. Competition between parties might be present, but if it rarely crosses ethnic lines and if entering into interethnic compromises can actually harm a party's electoral chances, as Hulsey[50] claims for Bosnia, then the contribution to consolidating liberal democracy looks stunted, or at best mixed.

So, neither international party support nor the development of entities possessing party-like characteristics can guarantee the progress of democratization. This has troubling implications for how the performance of party support and its effectiveness should be evaluated, not least where the international partners' objectives for the parties and party system, their larger goal of democracy-building, and the desires of the parties themselves may have different time horizons and impose some different yardsticks. Thus the conflict between the preference that Zambia's parties appear to have for continuing bilateral party assistance and the NIMD's current preference for supporting inter-party dialogue and the party system is a typical illustration at one level of what could be larger and more widespread disagreements over goals and objectives, not just tactics and strategy. A plausible inference is that the political party and party-related challenges are at least as demanding – and possibly much more difficult to overcome – compared to some other major challenges of democratization, such as establishing the basis for relatively free and fair elections, improving state capacity and the quality of governance in particular, and, even, creating a vibrant civil society. Of course the ground encompassed by the studies is too restricted to prove this. Nevertheless, civil society is undoubtedly an area where endeavours to develop constructive long-term relations between political parties and civic groups could prove yet more challenging still. Rakner and Svåsand's[51] account of Malawi and the disputes in Zambia over the respective roles that politicians and civil society should play in advising on a new constitution for the country demonstrates the point vividly. Of course these and other challenges of democratization are incredibly hard to measure and to compare. But going by the evidence provided by the material in this collection, the political parties' dimension of developing a liberal democracy – not simply the contribution of international actors – merits continuing close attention. Needless to say this in itself may be a cause of concern to the party assistance organizations. And, perhaps, it helps explain why party support has tended to be only a minor part of the overall democracy promotion effort. But it does not have to be this way for ever.

Thus the concluding contribution by Erdmann on 'Party assistance and political party research'[52] can be read as a free-standing piece, but it also doubles as a very timely attempt to draw lessons from issues central to the material in this collection. There are lessons not just for party support but for research into parties and party support as well. There are reflections here that scholars as well as party assistance policy-makers and practitioners potentially can learn from. For although the collection as a whole adds substantially to our existing knowledge and demonstrates the value of doing comparative analysis in political science, it also shows up the limits to our understanding. It still leaves gaps in terms of the other societies where field research could pay dividends, which includes countries emerging from war which, as de Zeeuw convincingly argues,[53] have been unduly neglected in the study of party politics generally. If, as Rakner and Svåsand argue,[54] forming stable and amicable relations between parties on a basis that respects the rules of free and fair competition and encourages working together to improve the democracy's quality, is exacting, even where there has been no war, then the challenge is likely to remain that much more intriguing in conflict-prone and potentially post-conflict cases like Afghanistan and Iraq. In his concluding contribution however Erdmann goes well beyond the specific recommendations found in the country studies, and offers broader guidance on the directions that relevant research agendas should take in the future.[55]

Notes

1. Carothers, *Confronting the Weakest Link*. The weakest link metaphor does not go unchallenged. The record of political parties is not equally poor in all democratizing countries, and authors differ on the actual role that parties have played in specific democratic transitions.
2. In recent years evaluative studies on party assistance have been commissioned by, among others the United States Agency for International Development, International IDEA, the British Department for International Development and the Foreign and Commonwealth Office, the Netherlands Ministry of Foreign Affairs, the Danish Ministry of Foreign Affairs.
3. For the debate on party change and decline, covering new as well as old democracies: Dalton and Wattenberg, *Parties without Partisans*; Diamond and Gunther, *Political Parties and Democracy*; Gunther, Ramón-Montero and Linz, *Political Parties*; Katz and Crotty, *Handbook of Party Politics*.
4. Katz and Crotty, 'Introduction', 1–2.
5. Bartolini and Mair, 'Challenges to Contemporary Political Parties', 332–5.
6. Katz and Mair, 'The Ascendancy of the Party in Public Office', 122.
7. Webb, 'Political Parties and Democracy', 635.
8. Carothers, *Confronting the Weakest Link*; Catón, *Effective Party Assistance*; Wersch and de Zeeuw, *Mapping European Democracy Assistance*.
9. The distinction between democracy assistance and promotion is not without relevance. After the G.W. Bush presidency democracy *promotion* seems substituted by democracy *assistance*. This reflects the strong disillusionment with the rhetoric and practice of the democracy or freedom agenda in US foreign policies during the early 2000s. The change from promotion to assistance also illustrates a greater awareness of the relevance of a more gradual and encompassing and less impatient and politicized approach to the strengthening of democratic governance in other countries. This has also been defined in terms of a 'European' rather than an 'American' approach in international democracy support.
10. Carothers, *Confronting the Weakest Link*, 86. See for aggregate figures (mid-2000s); Catón, *Effective Party Assistance*, 12, table 2.
11. Amundsen, *Donor Support to Political Parties*, 1; Power, *Donor Support to Parliaments and Political Parties*, 12. A recent paper on democracy support in EU external relations by the European Union does not even mention political party assistance

(Commission of the European Communities, *Joint Paper Commission/Council General Secretariat on Democracy Building in EU External Relations*).
12. Carothers, *Confronting the Weakest Link*, 163.
13. Erdmann, 'Hesitant Bedfellows: The German *Stiftungen* and Party Aid in Africa'.
14. Wild and Hudson, *UK Support for Political Parties*, 5.
15. Power, *Donor Support to Parliaments and Political Parties*.
16. Carothers, *Confronting the Weakest Link*.
17. Democracy International, Inc., *A Study of Political Party Assistance in Eastern Europe and Eurasia*, 12.
18. Carothers, *Confronting the Weakest Link*, 69.
19. See Burnell, 'Political Parties, International Party Assistance and Globalisation'.
20. Ágh, 'East-Central Europe: Parties in Crisis and the External and Internal Europeanisation of the Party Systems'; Lewis and Mansfeldová, *The European Union and Party Politics in Central and Eastern Europe*; Pridham, *Designing Democracy*.
21. Ágh, 'East-Central Europe: Parties in Crisis and the External and Internal Europeanisation of the Party Systems', 89.
22. On Chile see Angell, 'International Support for the Chilean Opposition'; on Central-European accession states to the European Union, see note 18.
23. Various contributions to this volume are based on doctoral research. Jeroen de Zeeuw defended his PhD thesis on 'Political Party Development in Post-War Societies: The Institutionalization of Parties and Party Systems in El Salvador and Cambodia' at Warwick University (UK); Max Bader defended his thesis 'Against all Odds: Aiding Political Parties in Georgia and Ukraine' at the University of Amsterdam (the Netherlands).
24. Bader, 'Party Politics in Georgia and Ukraine and the Failure of Western Assistance'; Hulsey, '"Why did they Vote for these Guys Again?": Challenges and Contradictions in the Promotion of Political Moderation in Post-war Bosnia and Herzegovina'.
25. Rakner and Svåsand, 'In Search of the Impact of International Support for Political Parties in New Democracies: Malawi and Zambia Compared'.
26. Weissenbach, 'Political Party Assistance in Transition: The German *Stiftungen* in Sub-Saharan Africa'.
27. Previous accounts of the *Stiftungen's* party work include Mair, 'Germany's *Stiftungen* and Democracy Assistance' and Erdmann, 'Hesitant Bedfellows: The German Party *Stiftungen* and Party Aid in Africa'. The Westminster Foundation for Democracy has itself contributed to the party support literature (see for example Burnell, *Building Better Democracies*), as well as being the subject of independent reviews, commissioned by the Foreign and Commonwealth Office (River Path Associates, *Review*; Global Partners, *Review*). All the party support organizations from time to time publish material about themselves. The International Institute for Democracy and Electoral Assistance (IDEA) based in Stockholm is a further valuable source of independent commentary – see for example Catón, *Effective Party Assistance*.
28. Weissenbach, 'Political Party Assistance in Transition: The German *Stiftungen* in Sub-Saharan Africa'.
29. Rakner and Svåsand, 'In Search of the Impact of International Support for Political Parties in New Democracies: Malawi and Zambia Compared'.
30. Bader, 'Party Politics in Georgia and Ukraine and the Failure of Western Assistance'.
31. Nenadović, 'An Uneasy Symbiosis: The Impact of International Administrations on Political Parties in Post-conflict Countries'.
32. de Zeeuw, '"Sons of War": Parties and Party Systems in Post-war El Salvador and Cambodia'.
33. Bolleyer and Storm, 'Dilemmas of Party Aid in Hybrid Regimes: The Case of Morocco'.

34. A similar distinction was trailed in Burnell, 'Political Parties, International Party Assistance and Globalisation'. This argued for making a clearer, that is to say more selective, focus on what parties can do for the process of change known as democratization at the particular stage of political development a country is going through. This means refining or departing from the aggregate shopping list approach to the roles that parties are said to perform in, and for, well-established democracies.
35. 'Party Politics in Georgia and Ukraine and the Failure of Western Assistance'.
36. Bolleyer and Storm, 'Dilemmas of Party Aid in Hybrid Regimes: The Case of Morocco'.
37. Hulsey, '"Why did they Vote for these Guys Again?": Challenges and Contradictions in the Promotion of Political Moderation in Post-war Bosnia and Herzegovina'.
38. Weissenbach, 'Political Party Assistance in Transition: The German *Stiftungen* in Sub-Saharan Africa'.
39. For elaboration see Leininger, '"Bringing the Outside In"'.
40. Hulsey, '"Why did they Vote for these Guys Again?": Challenges and Contradictions in the Promotion of Political Moderation in Post-war Bosnia and Herzegovina'; Nenadović, 'An Uneasy Symbiosis: The Impact of International Administrations on Political Parties in Post-conflict Countries'; de Zeeuw, '"Sons of War": Parties and Party Systems in Post-war El Salvador and Cambodia'.
41. Ibid.
42. de Zeeuw, '"Sons of War": Parties and Party Systems in Post-war El Salvador and Cambodia'.
43. Nenadović, 'An Uneasy Symbiosis: The Impact of International Administrations on Political Parties in Post-conflict Countries'.
44. Spoerri, 'Crossing the Line: Partisan Party Assistance in Post-Milošević Serbia'.
45. Bolleyer and Storm, 'Dilemmas of Party Aid in Hybrid Regimes: The Case of Morocco'.
46. Measuring success is not easy, however, for reasons that Gero Erdmann explains in his contribution to this collection, 'Political Party Assistance and Political Party Research: Towards a Closer Encounter'.
47. Weissenbach, 'Political Party Assistance in Transition: The German *Stiftungen* in Sub-Saharan Africa'.
48. Nenadović, 'An Uneasy Symbiosis: The Impact of International Administrations on Political Parties in Post-conflict Countries'.
49. Rakner and Svåsand, 'In Search of the Impact of International Support for Political Parties in New Democracies: Malawi and Zambia Compared'.
50. Freedom House for instance rated Zambia only 'partly free' in its most recent assessment; see: http://www.freedomhouse.org/template.cfm?page=22&year=2010&country=7951 (accessed August 15, 2010).
51. Bolleyer and Storm, 'Dilemmas of Party Aid in Hybrid Regimes: The Case of Morocco'.
52. Bader, 'Party Politics in Georgia and Ukraine and the Failure of Western Assistance'.
53. Erdmann, 'Political Party Assistance and Political Party Research: Towards a Closer Encounter'.
54. Randall and Svåsand, 'Party Institutionalization in New Democracies'.
55. Hulsey, '"Why did they Vote for these Guys Again?": Challenges and Contradictions in the Promotion of Political Moderation in Post-war Bosnia and Herzegovina'.
56. Rakner and Svåsand, 'In Search of the Impact of International Support for Political Parties in New Democracies: Malawi and Zambia Compared'.
57. Erdmann, 'Political Party Assistance and Political Party Research: Towards a Closer Encounter'.
58. de Zeeuw, '"Sons of War": Parties and Party Systems in Post-war El Salvador and Cambodia'.

59. Rakner and Svåsand, 'In Search of the Impact of International Support for Political Parties in New Democracies: Malawi and Zambia Compared'.
60. Erdmann, 'Political Party Assistance and Political Party Research: Towards a Closer Encounter'.

Bibliography

Ágh, Attila. 'East-Central Europe: Parties in Crisis and the External and Internal Europeanisation of the Party Systems', in *Globalising Democracy. Party Politics in Emerging Democracies*, ed. Peter Burnell, 88–103. London and New York: Routledge, 2006.

Amundsen, Inge. *Donor Support to Political Parties: Status and Principles*. Bergen: Chr. Michelsen Institute, 2007.

Angell, Alan. 'International Support for the Chilean Opposition, 1973–1989: Political Parties and the Role of Exiles', in *International Dimensions of Democratization*, ed. Laurence Whitehead, 175–200, 2nd ed. Oxford: Oxford University Press, 2001.

Bader, Max. 'Party Politics in Georgia and Ukraine and the Failure of Western Assistance', *Democratization* 17, no. 6 (2010): 1085–107.

Bartolini, Stefano, and Peter Mair. 'Challenges to Contemporary Political Parties', in *Political Parties and Democracy*, ed. Larry Diamond and Richard Gunther, 328–43. Baltimore, MD and London: The John Hopkins University Press, 2001.

Bolleyer, Nicole, and Storm, Lise. 'Problems of Party Assistance in Hybrid Regimes: The Case of Morocco', *Democratization* 17, no. 6 (2010): 1202–24.

Burnell, Peter. *Building Better Democracies: Why Political Parties Matter*. London: Westminster Foundation for Democracy, 2004, http://www.wfd.org (accessed August 15, 2010).

Burnell, Peter. 'Political Parties, International Party Assistance and Globalisation', in *Globalising Democracy. Party Politics in Emerging Democracies*, ed. Peter Burnell, 16–45. London and New York: Routledge, 2006.

Carothers, Thomas. *Confronting the Weakest Link. Aiding Political Parties in New Democracies*. Washington, DC: Carnegie Endowment for International Peace, 2006.

Catón, Matthias. *Effective Party Assistance. Stronger Parties for Better Democracy*. Stockholm: International IDEA, November 2007.

Commission of the European Communities. *Joint Paper Commission/Council General Secretariat on Democracy Building in EU External Relations*. Brussels: Commission of the European Communities, 27 June 2009.

Dalton, Russell J, and Martin P. Wattenberg, eds. *Parties Without Partisans. Political Change in Advanced Industrial Democracies*. Oxford: Oxford University Press, 2002.

Democracy International, Inc. *A Study of Political Party Assistance in Eastern Europe and Eurasia*. Bethesda, MD: Democracy International, Inc., 2007.

Diamond, Larry, and Richard Gunther, eds. *Political Parties and Democracy*. Baltimore, MD and London: The John Hopkins University Press, 2001.

Erdmann, Gero. 'Hesitant Bedfellows: The German Stiftungen and Party Aid in Africa', in *Globalising Democracy. Party Politics in Emerging Democracies*, ed. Peter Burnell, 181–99. London and New York: Routledge, 2006.

Erdmann, Gero. 'Political Party Assistance and Political Party Research: Towards a Closer Encounter?', *Democratization* 17, no. 6 (2010): 1275–97.
Global Partners and Associates. *Review of the Westminster Foundation for Democracy*, February 2010, http://www.parliament.uk/deposits/depositedpapers/2010/DEP2010-0836.doc (accessed August 15, 2010).
Gunther, Richard, José Ramón Montero, and Juan J. Linz, eds. *Political Parties. Old Concepts and New Challenges*. Oxford: Oxford University Press, 2002.
Hulsey, John W. "Why did they Vote for Those Guys Again?' Challenges and Contradictions in the Promotion of Political Moderation in Post-war Bosnia and Herzegovina', Democratization 17, no. 6 (2010): 1132–52.
Katz, Richard, and William Crotty, eds. *Handbook of Party Politics*. London: Sage Publications, 2006.
Katz, Richard, and William Crotty. 'Introduction', in *Handbook of Party Politics*, ed. Richard Katz and William Crotty, 1–4. London: Sage Publications, 2006.
Katz, Richard, and Peter Mair 'The Ascendancy of the Party in Public Office: Party Organizational Change in Twentieth-Century Democracies', in *Political Parties. Old Concepts and New Challenges*, ed. Richard Gunther, José Ramón Montero and Juan J. Linz, 113–36. Oxford: Oxford University Press, 2002.
Leininger, Julia. '"Bringing the Outside In". Illustrations from Haiti and Mali and the Reconceptualisation of Democracy Promotion'. *Contemporary Politics* 16, no. 1 (2010): 65–81.
Lewis, Paul, and Zdenka Mansfeldová, eds. *The European Union and Party Politics in Central and Eastern Europe*. Houndmills: Palgrave Macmillan, 2007.
Mair, Stefan. 'Germany's Stiftungen and Democracy Assistance: Comparative Advantages, New Challenges', in *Democracy Assistance. International Co-operation for Democratization*, ed. Peter Burnell, 128–49. London and Portland, OR: Frank Cass, 2000.
Nenadović, Maja. 'An Uneasy Symbiosis: The Impact of International Administrations on Political Parties in Post-conflict Countries', *Democratization* 17, no. 6 (2010): 1153–75.
Power, Greg. *Donor Support to Parliaments and Political Parties: An Analysis Prepared for DANIDA*. Global Partners and Associates, March 2008, http://www.um.dk.
Rakner, Lise, and Svåsand, Lars. 'In Search of the Impact of International Support for Political Parties in New Democracies: Malawi and Zambia Compared', *Democratization* 17, no. 6 (2010): 1250–74.
Randall, Vicky, and Lars Svåsand. 'Party Institutionalization in New Democracies'. *Party Politics* 8, no. 1 (2002): 5–29.
Pridham, Geoffrey. *Designing Democracy: EU Enlargement and Regime Change in Post-communist Europe*. Houndmills: Palgrave Macmillan, 2005.
River Path Associates. *Review of the Westminster Foundation for Democracy. Final Report*, 2005, http://www.riverpath.com/library/highlight/review-of-westminster-foundation-for-democracy (accessed August 15, 2010).
Spoerri, Marlene. 'Crossing the Line: Partisan Party Assistance in Post-Milošević Serbia', *Democratization* 17, no. 6 (2010): 1108–31.
Webb, Paul. 'Political Parties and Democracy: The Ambiguous Crisis'. *Democratization* 12, no. 5 (2005): 633–50.
Weissenbach, Kristina. 'Political Party Assistance in Transition: The German '*Stiftungen*' in Sub-Saharan Africa', *Democratization* 17, no. 6 (2010): 1225–49
Wersch, Jos van, and Jeroen de Zeeuw. 'Mapping European Democracy Assistance', *Working Paper No. 36*. Netherlands Institute of International relations, The Hague, 2005.
Wild, Leni, and Alan Hudson. *UK Support for Political Parties: A Stock-Take*. London: Overseas Development Institute, October 2009.
de Zeeuw, Jeroen. 'Sons of War': Parties and Party Systems in Post-war El Salvador and Cambodia', *Democratization* 17, no. 6 (2010): 1176–201.

Party politics in Georgia and Ukraine and the failure of Western assistance

Max Bader

Geschwister-Scholl-Institute for Political Science, University of Munich, Munich, Germany

> Despite a sustained effort, international assistance to political parties has failed to make a significant impact on parties in Georgia and Ukraine: political parties in these countries have remained far removed from the type of stable, democratic, and representative organisation that is commonly aimed for by party assistance. This study argues that domestic constraints on the development of stable and democratic parties have invalidated the assistance effort to such an extent that the assistance has become highly ineffectual. A large degree of volatility in party politics, reflected primarily in a high turnover rate of parties, has rendered much of the assistance provided throughout the years futile. The less-than-democratic political context in Ukraine (until 2005) and in Georgia moreover produced political parties that were inherently unsuitable to receive party assistance, because essentially they were not interested in transforming into stable democratic parties. Since the domestic constraints on party development which have spoiled assistance to political parties in Georgia and Ukraine – weak party (system) institutionalisation and a less-than-democratic political context – are present in many countries where party assistance is provided today, there is reason for concern about the overall effectiveness of party assistance.

Introduction

Among the states that were once part of the 'third wave' of democratization, political party development has taken on very different forms. The vast difference in outcomes of party development in the two halves of the post-communist world is instructive in this regard. Whereas party politics in Central and Eastern Europe (CEE) is seen as gradually converging with party politics in Western Europe,[1] in the member states of the Commonwealth of Independents States (CIS) most relevant parties are anything but institutionalized, democratic forces. In these latter states, regime-initiated or regime-sponsored parties often distort the level playing field of party politics at the expense of opposition parties. Parties also play a much less significant role in politics in these states than they do in CEE, unless they are a central instrument of authoritarian rule. In part due to the dearth of credible incentives for most potential political party 'entrepreneurs', volatility in the supply of parties generally has also been higher than in CEE. In this inhospitable climate for party development, political party assistance by Western political foundations has been provided to parties in almost all CIS states, and for most of the period since 1991, as it has been in large parts of the 'third wave' world.

This study demonstrates how domestic constraints on the development of stable, democratic, and representative parties can spoil the chances of party assistance to make the desired impact. Specifically, the study highlights three ills of party development which tend to undermine the effectiveness of assistance: first, the distortion of the electoral playing field by regime-supported parties with broad access to state resources; secondly, the relative inconsequentiality of political parties in countries with a strong presidency and elections through single-member districts; and finally, the dominance in parties of a narrow leadership with little input from below. In states where these ills come together, most political parties are either inherently unstable or undemocratic, or both, leaving no or few parties that would be suitable, according to the directives of most assistance providers, to receive party support. Consequently, when considered on its own external assistance to political parties in these states is likely to turn out ineffective.

The study draws on evidence from Georgia and Ukraine, two states which have attracted considerable levels of party assistance and where the occurrence of 'electoral revolutions' has raised questions about the role and impact of Western democracy promotion. Georgia and Ukraine present two cases where political party assistance has proven broadly ineffective, as most parties that have received external assistance subsequently disappeared, while the parties that have received assistance and are still there suffer from much the same flaws that parties suffered from 10 or 15 years ago. The data in this study are derived from nearly 100 interviews with recipients and providers of party assistance, and have been supplemented by internal documentation of the funders and providers of party assistance.

The account first presents a brief overview of party assistance in Georgia and Ukraine. The second section explicates the main constraints on the development of stable and democratic parties in Georgia and Ukraine for most of the post-communist period. The next three sections show how party assistance in Georgia and Ukraine has related to these domestic constraints on party development in Georgia and Ukraine. A conclusion reiterates the main argument and discusses its broader implications.

Party assistance in Georgia and Ukraine

As can be gleaned from a collection of policy-setting documents issued by the funders and providers of assistance, party assistance principally aims to contribute to the development of stable, representative, and democratic parties.[2] Despite a relatively sustained effort ranging back as far as to the early 1990s, party assistance in Georgia and Ukraine has fallen short of attaining this basic goal. Due to a high degree of party turnover in both Georgia and Ukraine, much assistance, in practical terms, throughout the years has been rendered futile. Of the five forces – that is to say political parties and electoral coalitions – that were elected to the current convocation of the Ukrainian legislature, only one – the Communist Party of Ukraine – was also present 10 years ago, and ironically, this party has barely received assistance from Western organizations. In Georgia, none of the forces present in the 2008 parliament was in parliament 10 years earlier. The smaller Georgian parties which have survived as well as new parties are said to suffer from largely the same flaws that parties suffered from in the 1990s.[3]

The weakness of parties in Georgia, in terms of unstable and poorly developed organization, has also been noted by donors and providers of political party assistance. An evaluation of USAID-funded democracy and governance programmes in Georgia in 2002 remarked that 'Georgia's party system remains weak, inchoate and unstable. Parties and parliamentary factions form, transform, and quickly disintegrate ...'.[4] A 2006 evaluation of party assistance by Dutch party institutes commented: 'Political parties actually hardly exist in Georgia. Political movements are in fact more or less loyal clans around individuals'.[5]

In Ukraine, a modicum of continuity in political party development has become discernable in the new century, especially since the Orange Revolution.[6] Still, a noted expert on Ukraine speaks of 'the incredible weakness of political parties in Ukraine',[7] and in a recent scholarly study it is argued that 'Ukraine's party system is undeveloped and fluid'.[8] In 2009, Our Ukraine, the political force that emerged initially as an electoral bloc and later as a party and had been the biggest recipient of party assistance since the beginning of the decade, was on the brink of disintegration.[9] The negative assessment of Ukrainian parties is echoed in writings by the donors and providers of political party assistance. A work plan for 2006 of the International Republican Institute remarks: 'Though almost 100 political parties are registered in Ukraine, few are anything more than personality-driven organisations'[10] and '...few political parties have developed into well-defined ideological forces that could guide the country's path'.[11] A 2008 publication by the Konrad Adenauer Stiftung argued that, prior to the Orange Revolution, parties in Ukraine had only 'peripheral significance'. Moreover, '[t]he parties of Ukraine still contain many features of projects. They are first and foremost personality-centred networks, which are strongly interwoven with the economic interests of their leaders'.[12]

Principal providers of assistance

The three main actors in party assistance in Georgia over the last decade have been the National Democratic Institute (NDI) and the International Republican Institute (IRI), affiliated with the US Democratic and Republican Parties respectively, and funded by the United States Agency for International Development (USAID); and the Netherlands Institute for Multiparty Democracy (NIMD) with funding from the Office for Democratic Institutions and Human Rights (ODIHR) of OSCE. In Ukraine, the main actors have been, again, NDI and IRI, in addition to the Konrad Adenauer Stiftung (KAS) and Friedrich Ebert Stiftung (FES), which are affiliated with the Christian-Democratic Union and Socialist Party of Germany, respectively, and whose work with parties is mostly funded by the German Federal Ministry for Economic Cooperation and Development. NDI, IRI, KAS, and FES all took up work in Ukraine in the first half of the 1990s. In Georgia, NDI started providing party assistance in 1996, followed two years later by IRI. The NIMD programme ran in Georgia from 2005 until 2008. Exact figures of funding for party assistance are not made available. From information that has been disclosed in interviews it can be inferred that individual providers of assistance have each worked with budgets for party assistance of several hundreds of thousands of US dollars, but never more than half a million dollars, per year and per country.

The implementation of party assistance programmes in Georgia and Ukraine has been in line with what has been described as the 'standard method'[13] in party assistance: it has consisted primarily of educational seminars, whether for individual parties or for several parties at once, and in addition, and to a much smaller degree, of counsel to individual parties and study visits for party elites. All substantial party assistance programmes in Georgia and Ukraine have emphasized such issues as the strengthening of regional party organizations, message development, voter outreach, and internal democracy. In Georgia, assistance has been provided to the consecutive ruling parties: Citizens' Union of Georgia of President Shevardnadze and the United National Movement of current President Saakashvili, as well as to at least a few dozen of the typically small and poorly organized opposition parties. Before the Orange Revolution in Ukraine, assistance was provided both to parties favourable to the Kuchma presidency, and parties in opposition to the regime. After the Revolution, assistance was provided to the political forces of the three main personae of Ukrainian politics Viktor Yushchenko (Our Ukraine), Viktor Yanukovich (Party of Regions) and Yulia Timoshenko (Yulia Timoshenko Bloc), as well as to a large number of less influential political forces and parties. The political force of Viktor Yushchenko, which, as People's Union Our Ukraine, became a party only in 2005, has received a disproportionately large share of assistance since its emergence at the beginning of the century and until years after the Orange Revolution. This was because it was viewed favourably by the providers of assistance and because it was more eager to receive the assistance than were other forces.

Characteristics of the parties

Many characterizations of political parties in Georgia mention 'a lack of clear ideology, values or vision; excessive role of leaders' personalities; heightened degree of political opportunism and populism; lack of internal democracy'.[14]

Instead of broad-based, institutionalized organizations with a serious degree of political clout, parties in Georgia have been 'more like political clubs with loose organisational structures, small memberships and no real influence'.[15] During the 2003–2004 parliamentary elections, 'none of the political parties presented a meaningful or more-or-less comprehensive election programme'.[16] Wheatley argues that parties were all 'highly centralised, top-down organisations', 'elite-led and leader-driven', with a 'complete subordination of ordinary party members to the leadership', lacking 'a clear policy profile', and failing to 'forge links with Georgian society'. In sum, 'Georgian political parties were fundamentally different sorts of organisations from their Western counterparts'.[17] Authors speak of the 'weakness of political parties' both at the outset of Ukraine's 'transition' in 1993 and 14 years onwards.[18] Indeed, 'the parties' status and role have been persistently and deliberately undermined for more than a decade and a half'.[19] Parties in Ukraine, at least until not long ago, were 'of marginal importance in Ukraine' and 'often vehicles for oligarchic interests'.[20] Moreover, '[p]arties, as it has turned out, are short of a broad social base, their ideology and programme inadequately reflect current problems, they do not have a vision on the development of society, and they lack the capacity to function properly'.[21]

While the names of the parties have frequently changed, there has been a considerable degree of continuity in party politics in Georgia since the early 1990s in terms of patterns of competition. Both before and after the 2003 Rose Revolution, a regime-sponsored 'party of power' with inordinate access to state resources competed against a flurry of smaller opposition parties. When the Citizens' Union of Georgia of president Eduard Shevardnadze vanished following the Rose Revolution, its position was taken by the United National Movement of new president Mikheil Saakashvili. On the side of the successive opposition movements, there has been a turnover of parties and electoral alliances such that every parliamentary election so far has featured a largely new set of contenders. The Ukrainian political party landscape was equally marked by excessive volatility until the 2006 and 2007 parliamentary elections.

The adoption in 2006 of a package of constitutional amendments, as a result of which parties have become more influential compared to the period before the Orange Revolution, as well as the introduction of party list voting for all seats in parliament starting with the 2006 parliamentary election, appear to contribute to a greater degree of party continuity in Ukraine. This makes the situation different from the period before 2005. It is, however, questionable whether this relative continuity marks an incipient stage of party system institutionalization, especially since most relevant parties are still barely rooted in society and instead function at the whim of their leaders and the powerful 'oligarchs' who provide financial backing for these parties. A second major change in Ukrainian party politics after 2005 is that executive authorities are no longer involved in the creation of political parties and in other forms of active manipulation of the playing field. The fuller degree of competition in party politics in Ukraine experienced now represents one of the democratic gains of the post-revolutionary period.

Less-than-democratic or semi-authoritarian politics in Ukraine until the revolution and in Georgia throughout the post-communist period have produced party types that are not found or that are rarely found in established democracies.

'Parties of power'

The Citizens' Union of Georgia and the United National Movement are typical examples of the 'party of power' type that is found widely in the former Soviet Union and in other less-than-democratic polities. Parties of power are established by representatives of the executive branch of government, benefit from access to state resources, either support the president or are run by the president, and, different than other parties that are created by the regime, are meant to become dominant forces in party politics. The immediate goal of parties of power in undemocratic regimes is to win votes and to bind elites. If a party of power succeeds in securing a large share of the vote, it sends out a signal of regime strength, which, if effective, persuades political contenders to give up on actively opposing the regime, and elites to seek affiliation with the regime, thereby securing their loyalty to the regime.[22] An additional desired side-effect of a large vote share is the legitimacy it (seemingly) confers on the regime. To make a big win in elections more likely and to bind elites, parties of power tap state resources, which include 'administrative resources' (mobilization of public servants, offices, supplies), financial resources that are utilized, among others, in election campaigns, and the distribution of jobs and other assets to loyalists.[23] Because parties of power tap state resources that are not available to other parties, they contribute to distort the playing field of party politics. In Ukraine, it has proven more difficult to bind elites to the regime than in Georgia. For most of the post-communist period, elites have opted to affiliate with regionally-based interest groups which often controlled one or more political parties, resulting essentially in the simultaneous existence of different regional party systems. The most concerted effort to organize a single party of power, the People's Democratic Party, collapsed as it trailed the winning Communist Party in the 1998 parliamentary election.

'Spoiler parties'

A party type that was found in Ukraine up until the 2002 elections was the so-called 'spoiler party'.[24] Like parties of power, spoiler parties were instigated by regime actors and were primarily interested in winning votes, rather than office or the chance to implement certain policies. The main purpose of these parties was to win votes that otherwise would probably have gone to existing opposition parties. To attain this goal, these parties typically imitated the name and the image of those opposition parties. The 2002 parliamentary elections in Ukraine, for instance, witnessed the sudden emergence of the Rukh for Unity party which copied the Rukh party, and a 'renewed' communist party which, so it was hoped by its creators, would drain away support from the Communist Party of Ukraine, the major communist successor party.[25]

Oligarchic parties

A third party type that thrives more readily in less-than-democratic settings than in democratic settings and that has been found widely in Ukraine and to a lesser extent in Georgia, is represented by parties tied up with the private interests of wealthy individuals, that is, 'oligarchic parties'. Examples include the Social Democratic Party of Ukraine (united) and the Green Party in Ukraine, and the new Rights Party and Industry Will Save Georgia in Georgia. Rather than the pursuit of votes per se or the implementation of certain policies, oligarchic parties seek votes primarily to win office, and then reap the benefits related to holding office. Although some parties in Ukraine are less obviously of an oligarchic nature than they used to be, the influence of the wealthy sponsors of all of Ukraine's main parties is still considered to be strong.[26]

Parties of power, spoiler parties, and oligarchic parties have made up a large share of relevant parties in Georgia and Ukraine during most of the post-communist period. Most of these parties have not survived. Few other parties have been influential, and even fewer have proven durable. Taken together, there have not been many parties in Georgia and Ukraine which satisfied the conditions that would make them suitable recipients of party assistance: few parties were, first, (potentially) relevant in political life, because real power resided with the president and his entourage, secondly, likely to turn out to be stable forces, and thirdly, not the product of less-than-democratic politics or a political vehicle for wealthy individuals. An alternative way to present this point is by drawing on an analogy to Strom's tripartite classification, originally conceived for parties in democratic settings, of policy-seeking, vote-seeking, and office-seeking models of party behaviour.[27] In the words of Steven Wolinetz, 'a policy-seeking party is one which gives primary emphasis to pursuit of policy goals, a vote-seeking party is one whose principal aim is to maximise votes and win elections, while an office-seeking party is primarily interested in securing the benefits of office – getting its leaders into government, enjoying access to patronage, etc.'[28] Put simply, the problem for political party assistance in Georgia and Ukraine was that most relevant parties from the beginning were primarily vote-seeking or office-seeking, and fundamentally uninterested in having their dominant incentive structure changed, while party assistance, reflected in the emphasis it puts on programmatic distinction, promotes a policy-seeking model of behaviour. The circumstance that most relevant parties were vote-seeking or office-seeking rather than policy-seeking was a consequence of the particular environment in which party politics were played out. The next two sections look in more detail at how the domestic constraints on the development of strong and democratic parties in Georgia and Ukraine have related to the practice of party assistance.

Volatility in party politics

Until several years ago, one of the more remarkable features of party development in Ukraine and in Georgia ever since 1991 has been the high replacement rate of parties. From one parliamentary election to the next, the range of parties that stood for election and was able to muster some degree of popular support typically underwent a wholesale transformation. Next to the emergence and disappearance of parties, volatility was also apparent in changing electoral alliances, and sometimes in within-party change. Occasionally, parties even changed beyond recognition, especially when the leadership was changed or when the party received a new sponsor. Existing parties were rarely disbanded by the authorities, or exposed to overt pressure to disband themselves. Instead, party turnover has been driven by the relative lack of incentives for real and potential political party 'entrepreneurs' to invest in the development of parties. The lack of incentives for party development is explained from the fact that parties generally had little gravity in political life, which in turn was in large part a consequence of institutional arrangements, especially regarding executive–legislative relations and electoral legislation, and probably aggravated by the realization among parties that they had fairly little perspective of making much headway in an uneven electoral playing field.[29]

Until the Rose Revolution, Georgia was a purely presidential republic, with the popularly elected president heading the executive while not being subject to the confidence or the formal approval of the legislative assembly. Ukraine has had a semi-presidential arrangement throughout the post-communist period, while Georgia turned semi-presidential shortly after the revolution following the introduction of a second locus of executive power in the person of a prime minister.[30] Until 2006, the semi-presidential system in Ukraine heavily favoured the president, putting Ukraine in the class of 'highly presidentialised semipresidential regimes'.[31] Highly presidentialized semipresidential regimes 'often suffer the same problems as their purely presidential counterparts',[32] and are sometimes more 'presidentialized' than purely presidential regimes, a situation which, with regard to the Former Soviet Union (FSU), is sometimes captured by the term 'superpresidentialism'.[33] The introduction of the post of prime minister in Georgia was accompanied by a simultaneous increase in presidential powers, so that, despite the fact that executive power was now formally shared, Georgia became even more 'presidentialised' after the revolution.

It has been argued that there is an 'inverse relationship' between presidentialism and party strength.[34] This is, first, and most evidently, because of the way powers are distributed. In a presidential system, the more influential political actors will be inclined to place their bets on winning the presidency rather than investing in parties. Moreover, it is mostly the president, rather than a parliamentary majority, who is in charge of forming government cabinets in a presidential system. Secondly, due to the centrality of the presidency, presidential systems are more affected by the 'politics of personality' than parliamentary systems. Thirdly, parties have been found to be less cohesive in presidential systems.[35] In less-than-democratic presidential regimes, finally, successful parties may be thwarted by the regime because they are seen as alternative centres of the aggregation of interests and therefore as threats to the regime.

All parliamentary elections in Georgia and two in Ukraine (1998 and 2002) have been conducted according to a mixed electoral system, combining PR and single-member districts (SMDs) in different proportions – equally divided in Ukraine and two-thirds to one-third in favour of SMDs in Georgia until 2008. The 1994 elections in Ukraine were all-majoritarian, while party list voting in a single nation-wide district was applied in the 2006 and 2007 parliamentary votes. The main reason why SMDs often have a debilitating effect on party development is straightforward: individuals instead of parties are elected. A second reason lies in the heightened risk of one-party dominance – one party tends to win a disproportionately large number of SMD races – and a consequential lack of perspective for other parties.

There are at least two reasons why a mixed electoral system has contributed to undermine robust party development in Georgia and Ukraine. The first one is similar to the one mentioned in relation to all-SMD elections: candidates in the majoritarian section of the vote often refrain from seeking party affiliation, and even if they are party members, they do not directly represent their parties. The second reason is that the majoritarian section provides an alternative route for individuals and parties to make it into parliament, holding parties back from coalescing with other parties, and individuals from seeking party affiliation. Small, essentially unviable parties may content themselves with winning a few seats in parliament through SMD elections while relinquishing nationwide campaigning and organizational development. Another provision in electoral legislation in Georgia and Ukraine that has hampered party development is the opportunity to form electoral coalitions. If parties are too insignificant to cross the electoral threshold on their own, they can still win mandates by banding together with other parties for elections. If they do so, these parties are likely to stick around and be part of a fragmented party system with many small and weak parties. Volatility in party development in Georgia and Ukraine has been facilitated by the lack of societal rootedness of most parties, reflected in low membership figures and levels of popular identification with parties.[36] Most parties operate at the whim of a single leader or a limited group of leaders. Consequently, it takes only these individuals for a party to be disbanded, as it takes only several individuals to instigate a new political organization.

The response of party assistance

The excessively high replacement rate of political parties was apparent in Ukraine until recent years and in Georgia has not yet been halted. Throughout these years, there was no convincing reason to assume that volatility was a thing of the past. Providers of assistance have mainly worked with inherently unviable and unstable parties despite their claim, made in policy-setting documents that they would only work with viable parties. Viability is almost invariably mentioned as a core criterion of eligibility to receive assistance.[37] A party is considered viable when it has a relatively large base of support and has been successful in previous elections, or when it has representation in parliament, or when it is seen as having chances to win representation in parliament, or simply assessed qualitatively.

Two of the three core recipients of NDI party assistance in Georgia before 1999 – the Citizens' Union of Georgia and the People's Party – have disappeared, while the third, the National Democratic Party, has at best turned into a marginal force. The three other parties with which NDI worked in Georgia until 1999 – the Socialist Party, the Traditionalist Party, and the Green Party – have all withered away. Of the six parties that received the bulk of NDI and IRI assistance between 1999 and 2003, two have withered (Citizens' Union of Georgia and National Democratic Party); the Labour Party and the New Rights Party, which rose to prominence around the turn of the century, are marginal, but still active; and the National Movement and the United Democrats have merged to become the ruling United National Movement, a very different type of party than its original constituents were, from 2003. Shortly after the Rose Revolution, NIMD initiated a large party assistance programme comprising six parties that had parliamentary representation at the time – United National Movement, Labour Party, Conservative Party, Industry Will Save Georgia, Republican Party, and New Rights Party. Despite the suggestion that these parties except the Labour Party were largely indistinguishable in terms of programme, NIMD expected that these six parties would constitute the core of an incipient party system.[38] A few years into the project, however, it was no longer evident that these parties were more relevant or viable than some of the many other opposition parties, such as Georgia's Way, the Freedom Party, of For a United Georgia. Moreover, it can be questioned whether these parties were relevant political forces at all, given the degree of fragmentation among the opposition and the highly uneven playing field in which the ruling United National Movement, the sixth participating party in the ODIHR-NIMD project, towered over all other parties in terms of representation in parliament and accessible resources.

The three parties that received most of NDI's assistance in Ukraine during the 1990s – the People's Democratic Party, Rukh, and the Party of Reform and Order have lost much of their relevance, if they ever had much relevance. While the People's Democratic Party has subsided, both the Party of Reform and Order and the successors of Rukh are reduced to the role of 'junior partner' in electoral coalitions, and in that role have little autonomous potential. The same can be said of almost all 'junior partners' in electoral coalitions, including the large number of small parties from the Our Ukraine bloc, many of which have eagerly participated in assistance programmes. The political force that has received far more assistance than any other force in Ukraine since 2000, the 'presidential' People's Union Our Ukraine, which formally exists as a party only since 2005, obviously has been a highly relevant force. In 2008, however, splits occurred within the party, and it is unclear whether the party will be sustained with President Yushchenko no longer in the presidency since the presidential elections of 2010. The sustainability of Batkivshchyna is believed to hinge entirely on the political future of its leader, Yulia Tymoshenko. The Socialist Party of Ukraine, long-time partner of FES, is at risk of becoming marginal after failing to cross the electoral threshold in the 2007 parliamentary elections. Two other nominally social-democratic parties, the Social-Democratic Party of Ukraine and the Social-Democratic Party of Ukraine (united), which have previously received assistance from several actors, have already become marginal.

Ironically, the Communist Party of Ukraine, the one party that has been continuously represented in parliament since the early 1990s and by that token has proven to be the most durable political party in Ukraine, has barely received foreign assistance. The party was often not invited to assistance programmes; when it was, the party turned down the invitation.[39] Moreover, the most relevant party of recent years in terms of electoral support and political leverage, the Party of Regions, has received relatively little assistance, and admits not to have made any changes in the party following the little assistance it has received.[40] All taken together, most of the assistance that has been provided to political parties in Georgia and Ukraine since the late 1990s has gone to parties which did not turn out to be relevant for the longer term, or even disappeared entirely.

Undemocratic politics and party assistance

Ukraine (until 2005) and Georgia have been among the large group of 'transitional' states which in the years after the initial move away from politically closed autocracy did not consolidate to become liberal democratic regimes. Both states have for the most time lingered in the 'partly free' category of the widely used Freedom House Freedom in the World comparative assessment of political liberties and civil rights.[41] Manifestations of the less-than-democratic nature of Georgia and Ukraine (until 2005) include, as in many other places, an uneven political playing field, inadequate safeguards of civil and political rights, and weak horizontal accountability due to a concentration of power in the executive branch of government. In assessments of Ukraine under Kuchma, the focus is most often on the corruptive entanglement of the political and economic domains and on the frequent prevalence of informal practices over formal institutions.[42]

Much analysis of the 'façade democracy' or 'Potemkin democracy' of Shevardnadze-era Georgia stresses the impact of all-pervasive corruption and weak state capacity on how the country was governed. Wheatley argues that Georgia essentially was a 'contested oligarchy', where a number of influential groups vied for political and economic power, while the state was largely incapable of providing for the common good.[43] According to King, 'Georgia is a chronically weak state. In a region of only minimally successful countries, however, the Georgian case is particularly dire.... Indeed, it is worth asking whether a state called "Georgia" even exists today in any meaningful sense'.[44] Since the Rose Revolution, corruption is no longer all-pervasive and government has become more effective, while political competition is as circumscribed as before the revolution. According to Freedom House, Georgia now scores as poorly on political and civil rights as it did under Shevardnadze.[45]

As outlined above, many of the more relevant parties in Georgia and Ukraine have been products of undemocratic politics. In their policy-setting documents, providers of assistance rule out cooperation with undemocratic parties. To be eligible for receiving party assistance, parties presumably need to be democratic both in terms of attitude and of actual behaviour in respect to their internal operation, and with respect to their operation in the party system and in society. Attitudinally, parties are deemed democratic when they, among other things, embrace political and civil liberties and accept the holding of elections as the sole legitimate means of obtaining power.[46] Behaviourally, recipient parties, especially when they are in power, should respect competing parties and act responsibly and constructively in government and in parliament.[47] Furthermore, parties, in their internal functioning, should maintain 'an acceptable level of internal democracy or a stated aspiration to achieve this'.[48]

Undemocratic practices in party politics have been most evidently embodied in the parties of power which benefited extensively from state resources and patronage. Although the Citizens' Union of Georgia of President Shevardnadze contained most features of a party of power, the party counted as one of NDI's main recipients of assistance until not long before the Rose Revolution. NDI's lack of inhibition to work with the Citizens' Union of Georgia squares with the generally favourable opinion of Western governments towards the Shevardnadze regime until at least 1999. Since the Rose Revolution, all providers of assistance have been eager to work with the United National Movement. Even after the 2008 parliamentary elections, which have been generally seen as suffering from serious flaws, NIMD maintained that the United National Movement is a 'democratic' party and an appropriate partner for party assistance.[49]

As in Georgia, a party of power, albeit in this case the unsuccessful People's Democratic Party, was one of the main recipients of assistance of NDI in Ukraine during the 1990s. Other parties that have received assistance in Ukraine, such as the Social Democratic Party of Ukraine (united) and the Labour Party have been equally associated with the exploitation of state resources for electoral gain. Providers of assistance generally have held back from offering assistance to parties that ostentatiously were virtual projects. Since IRI in Ukraine, however, as part of a very inclusive approach, has only declined assistance to a few extremist parties among the parties that took part in parliamentary elections,[50] some 'virtual' and 'oligarchic' parties have inevitably been offered assistance.

Several arguments could be put forward why the Party of Regions would not pass the test of being a democratic force and therefore should not be eligible to receive assistance. Among other things, its leaders sought to steal the presidential election in 2004. In addition, the party contains features of a dominant party of power on a regional level in the southern and eastern regions of the country and is propped up by donations from the country's wealthiest businessman, Rinat Akhmetov.[51] Still, all major providers of party assistance do not refrain from offering assistance to the party. The democratic credentials of the Socialist Party of

Ukraine, one of the political parties which actively supported the Orange Revolution and for this reason was seen as a democratic and reliable force, were shattered in the eyes of many when the party entered a government coalition with the Party of Regions and the Communist Party of Ukraine in 2006. The example of the Socialist Party of Ukraine illustrates that external providers of assistance often harbour unrealistic expectations concerning the parties they work with. Another example of this is the Citizens' Union of Georgia. A work plan of NDI in Georgia for the years 2001–2002 stated that NDI 'would try to help the Citizens' Union of Georgia remain true to its original democratic ideals'.[52] Given that the Citizens' Union of Georgia was a party of power which served the interests of a less-than-democratic regime, as became clear, for example, in the complicity of the Citizens' Union of Georgia in the large-scale fraud during the 1999 parliamentary election, it is far from evident that there was much sincerity to the 'original democratic ideals' of the Citizens' Union of Georgia.

Parties in Georgia and Ukraine have been notoriously undemocratic concerning their inner functioning. In Georgia, '[a]cross the political spectrum, political parties lack internal democracy and meaningful distribution within the party'.[53] With regard to Ukrainian parties it has been remarked that 'all serious decisions are often made by a "club" of about one or two dozen individuals'.[54] Most parties have the formal trappings of internally democratic parties (several elected bodies, regional branches, regular party congresses) but few have implemented meaningful procedures of internal democracy. Tellingly, in just a few parties in Georgia and Ukraine has there been a change of leadership, and if there was one, it was typically orchestrated by the outgoing leaders. Parties are often described as the personal fiefdoms of their leaders: a single party leader or a small group of leaders are the only ones with enough leverage to carry through reform within the party.

A problem for party assistance in Georgia and Ukraine is that most of its direct recipients – participants in the many educational seminars organized by providers of assistance – lack the power to initiate reform. Making things worse, since reform may undermine their hold on power, party leaders often have an explicit interest in blocking it. An example of a leader-dominant party is the Georgian Labour Party: 'In a country where parties were often dominated by their leaders, Labour was extreme even by Georgian standards'.[55] Still, the Labour Party has received assistance from both NDI and IRI and has participated in the NIMD project. An example of a party of which the overly dominant position of its leader has been detrimental to the goals of party assistance, is the Socialist Party of Ukraine. According to former and current staff members of the party, years of receiving party assistance have not led to any changes within the party because its leader, Oleksandr Moroz, ruled the party as a dictator and did not allow change.[56] The Socialist Party of Ukraine is a participant in assistance programmes by all major providers of assistance, and is the 'sister party' of FES.

In sum, a significant share of parties that have received assistance in Georgia and Ukraine have not met the criteria of viability and democracy that the providers of assistance impose on themselves with regard to the selection of parties. Decisions to include certain parties in assistance programmes have been driven by misguided perceptions of those parties. Parties were often considered viable and/or democratic when they were clearly not. The problems with the selection of unviable and undemocratic parties for the effectiveness of party assistance are obvious: the possible effect of assistance on unviable parties is lost when these parties disappear, while inherently undemocratic parties are by default unreceptive to the message of party assistance. The reason why these parties were selected in the first place seems obvious: very few parties, if any would have qualified for assistance if the only parties who were deemed eligible were parties who were both credibly viable and democratic already.

The parties in the aftermath of the colour revolutions

The 2003 Rose Revolution in Georgia and 2004 Orange Revolution in Ukraine were widely regarded as opportunities for democratic breakthrough and, concomitantly, for the belated emergence of an institutionalized democratic party system. The conditions for the development of viable and democratic parties in Georgia, however, did not visibly improve. As before, the ruling powers precluded a full degree of political competition.[57] The political force of the new president, Saakashvili, the United National Movement, took over from the Citizens' Union of Georgia as the party of power. In the 2008 parliamentary election, the United National Movement gained 80% of the seats in parliament in a contest in which the ruling party was alleged to have benefited from access to state resources and electoral rules to have been modified to elevate the result of the ruling party.[58] The emergence of viable parties in Georgia after the revolution was further impeded by the continuous limited role of political parties. Even more than before the revolution, parliament wielded little influence. The mixed electoral system has furthermore remained in place.

In Ukraine, by contrast, the foremost constraints on the development of viable and democratic parties were removed. A 'presidential' party, People's Union Our Ukraine, was founded, but besides the administration of the new president was unable or unwilling to manipulate the political playing field. Conducted in an atmosphere of fierce and open competition, the 2006 and 2007 parliamentary elections were praised by international observers. The institutional setting for party development improved as a result of a package of amendments to the constitution that was agreed upon at the time of the revolution and that entered into force in 2006. From a 'highly presidentialised' semipresidential regime Ukraine acquired a regime with a more even balance of presidential and prime-ministerial powers. The weight of parties increased mainly because cabinets of ministers were henceforth formed by parliamentary majorities, consisting of party coalitions, and because approval by parliament was now needed for a larger number of crucial appointments both in and outside government.

The role of parties in Ukraine also grew stronger as a result of new electoral legislation, adopted in 2005, which introduced party list voting for all seats in the national parliament, replacing the mixed electoral system that had been used in 1998 and 2002. Despite the fact that the main constraints on party development were removed, party assistance did not succeed in having a significant impact on parties. Of the five most relevant parties since the Orange Revolution – the Party of Regions, Batkivshchyna, the People's Union Our Ukraine, the Socialist Party of Ukraine, and the Communist Party of Ukraine – none was notably affected by participation in party assistance programmes. The Party of Regions has been hesitant to work with the providers of assistance. As representatives of the party have admitted, moreover, the limited participation of their party in assistance programmes did not lead to any change within the party.[59] The Communist Party as before has declined to receive assistance. On the orders of the US embassy, NDI and IRI halted party assistance for several months in 2007 after the Party of Regions and the Communist Party accused the US of support for Yushchenko's decision to disband parliament in which the Party of Regions formed a coalition with the Communist Party and Socialist Party.[60]

The 'dictator-like' position of the party leaders of Batkivshchyna (Tymoshenko) and the Socialist Party (Moroz) has, according to party representatives, inhibited reform within these parties.[61] Activists from these parties have frequently participated in party assistance programmes. Because these programmes, however, tend to only reach lower-ranking party activists without the leverage to instigate reform in their parties, the possible effects of party assistance are not translated into party reform. The biggest recipient of party assistance, the People's Union Our Ukraine, finally, was progressively weakened as the popularity of its honorary chairman president Yushchenko dwindled in the years after the Orange Revolution and the party, as the main constituent of the ten-party Our Ukraine – People's Self-Defense won only 14% of the vote in the 2007 elections, far behind the Party of Regions and the Yulia Tymoshenko Bloc. There have been few indications of tangible impact from the various forms of assistance that the People's Union Our Ukraine has received.[62] In the words of a former Konrad Adenauer Foundation representative in Ukraine, the leaders of the party persistently proved 'immune to counsel'.

Conclusions and implications

Party assistance can generate effects outside parties proper. Particularly young party activists have indicated in interviews that participation in educational seminars has had a formative impact on them.[63] Party assistance can contribute to bigger political outcomes as well. Representatives from both NDI and KAS in Ukraine, for example, claim that party assistance by their organization was instrumental in the emergence of the Our Ukraine bloc, the political vehicle of Viktor Yushchenko in the 2004 presidential elections which led to the Orange Revolution.[64]

Party assistance in Georgia and Ukraine, however, has failed to contribute to the development of substantially more democratic, more stable, and more representative parties. It has not been uncommon to realize this. For example, in 2001 it was advised, in an independent evaluation, to scale back US party assistance in Georgia primarily because 'limited interest exists within the major political parties to transform themselves into well-structured democratic organizations presenting the public with credible, differentiated policy platforms'[65] and 'limited political will seems to exist within the parties to overcome their many institutional weaknesses, particularly among the national leadership who hold most of the authority within the party'.[66] Party assistance in Georgia by NDI and IRI was nonetheless continued.

Similar grim assessments of party assistance can be found in the other few independent evaluations of party assistance in the CIS states. A 2007 evaluation of US party assistance in Kyrgyzstan points out that institutional arrangements and the political context have long blocked opportunities for successful party assistance.[67] An earlier evaluation of party assistance by NDI in Kyrgyzstan equally saw little effect from the assistance and proposed that NDI scale back its party assistance programme for two years.[68] With respect to party assistance in Armenia, it has been plainly commented that 'the political environment in Armenia is not conducive to political party building assistance'[69] and that '[t]he assessment found little impact from donor assistance to political parties. Parties characterized USAID-funded assistance as well-meaning but better suited for a more democratic context'.[70]

Assessments of the effectiveness of party assistance, and of democracy promotion in general, tend to concentrate on the quality of the input of the assistance while overlooking constraints at the recipient-side of the assistance equation. It is exactly domestic constraints on party development which have invalidated the party assistance effort in Georgia and Ukraine. This study suggests that the local setting of party development needs to be freed from at least three ills for party assistance to have a chance at making a serious impact.

First, the distortion of the playing field by regime-supported parties with broad access to state resources can lead to a situation, as in Georgia under Saakashvili, in which regime-supported parties are the only relevant forces, stunting the development of alternative parties.

Secondly, a setting in which parties are relatively inconsequential organizations due to specific institutional arrangements – especially regarding executive-legislative relations and electoral legislation – or whichever other factors make it more likely that parties are highly unstable forces which are often replaced by new forces at the next election. This has been the case in Georgia and Ukraine for most of the post-communist period.

Thirdly, where parties tend to be top-down organizations entirely dominated by a narrow leadership effectively holding the party hostage, as is often the case in Georgian and Ukrainian parties, is it unlikely that meaningful reform can be implemented. The implication is that parties that are selected for party assistance should meet some minimal requirements; for, as the study has argued, parties that were created to help sustain a less-than-democratic regime, as well as parties that appear as ephemeral 'projects' and that are 'owned' by their leadership, are unlikely to be ever receptive to Western assistance. Providers of party assistance themselves refer to the need to work only with parties that meet these minimal requirements. In Georgia and Ukraine, however, they have often failed to apply the requirements in the selection of parties.

Party assistance in Georgia and Ukraine, despite the absence of notable effects in Georgia and Ukraine, has not been halted or drastically revised, which seems to suggest that assistance programmes have not been carefully scrutinized, and that providers of assistance have not been held accountable for the ineffectiveness of their programmes.[71] Party assistance in individual countries is seldom and irregularly evaluated in a comprehensive manner, and there are few indications that the conclusions of evaluations that have been carried out for Georgia and Ukraine have led to substantial revisions of existing programmes. At different moments, an honest and informed assessment of the party landscape in Georgia and Ukraine could either have forestalled the selection of unsuitable parties, or have persuaded the funders and providers of assistance to suspend assistance until more receptive parties would appear in a more conducive environment for stable and democratic party development.

It is alarming that the ills of and for party development surveyed in this study of Georgia and Ukraine are present, albeit in different degrees and combinations, in many countries where party assistance is still offered today. When party assistance was launched in the post-communist states, an implicit assumption was that there was a genuine interest in those countries in democratization, and a genuine interest among recipient parties to transform into truly representative and democratic forces. Recipient parties were seen as constituents of a stable and democratic party system that would crystallize in the not too distant future as the transition to democracy would progress into consolidation. In much of the post-communist world as well as in many other countries outside the post-communist world where party assistance is still carried out, however, regimes are not in a state of transition toward democracy, and it is doubtful that most parties which receive assistance are really interested in internal reform. As the third wave of democratization has ground to a halt, most third wave states are stuck in a political grey zone: they are neither liberal democracies nor closed autocracies, and most are neither becoming significantly more democratic nor are they moving backwards.[72]

Whether in Africa, South East Asia, or Latin America, political parties are often characterized by weak institutionalization, as parties have been in Georgia and Ukraine.[73] In the majority of 'gray zone' countries with weakly institutionalized parties, international actors are involved in providing assistance to parties.[74] They have in recent years moved out of Central and Eastern Europe, the region with most of the successful transitions to liberal democracy in the past two decades. Now that those 'easy' cases of transition have been completed, providers overwhelmingly work in countries with less sanguine prospects for democratization and stable party development. Confronted with adverse conditions for party assistance in so many recipient countries, a reconsideration of the purpose and the strategies of party assistance now seems an imperative.

Notes

1. Lane and Ersson, 'Party System Instability in Europe: Persistent Differences in Volatility between West and East?'.
2. See, for instance, Netherlands Institute for Multiparty Democracy, *A Framework for Democratic Party-Building*; Saxer, 'Parteiförderung als Element der Demokratieförderung'; United States Agency for International Development, *Political Party Development Assistance*; United States Agency for International Development, *USAID Political Party Assistance Policy*.
3. Dolidze, 'Political Parties and Party Development in Georgia'.
4. ARD, *Democracy and Governance Assessment of Georgia*, v.
5. Author's translation of 'Politieke partijen bestaan eigenlijk nauwelijks in Georgië. Politieke bewegingen zijn feitelijk min of meer loyale clans rondom individuen.' Verheije et al., *Van partij naar partij: Nederlandse ondersteuning van politieke partijen in Europese landen in transitie*, 59.
6. Wilson and Birch, 'Political Parties in Ukraine. Virtual and Representational'.
7. D'Anieri, *Understanding Ukrainian Politics. Power, Politics, and Institutional Design*, 43.
8. Slomczynski, Shabad and Zielinski, 'Fluid Party Systems, Electoral Rules and Accountability of Legislators in Emerging Democracies: The Case of Ukraine', 93.
9. Topolyanskiy, *Nukonets. Partiia Yushchenko tikho umiraet*.
10. International Republican Institute, *Ukraine Work Plan 2006*, 4.
11. Ibid., 2.
12. Author's translation of: 'Die Parteien der Ukraine tragen noch immer starken Projektcharakter. Sie sind in erster Linie personenzentrierte Netzwerke, die stark mit ökonomischen Interessen ihrer Betreiber verflochten sind'. Konrad Adenauer Stiftung, *International Parteienzusammenarbeit der KAS. Globales Engagement für Frieden und Demokratie*, 32.
13. Carothers, *Confronting the Weakest Link*, 112–41.
14. Tarkhan-Mouravi, 'Politicheskie Partii v Gruzii. Zatiunuavsheesia Stanovlenie', 243.
15. Dolidze, 'Political Parties and Party Development in Georgia', 2.
16. Usupashvili, 'An Analysis of the Presidential and Parliamentary Elections in Georgia: A Case Study, November 2003–March 2004', 98.
17. Wheatley, *Georgia from National Awakening to Rose Revolution: Delayed Transition in the Former Soviet Union*, 155–9.
18. Wilson and Bilous, 'Political Parties in Ukraine', 693; D'Anieri, *Understanding Ukrainian Politics. Power, Politics, and Institutional Design*, 43.
19. Riabchuk, 'Ukraine: Lessons Learned from Other Postcommunist Transitions', 44.
20. Van Zon, 'Neo-Patrimonialism as an Impediment to Economic Development: The Case of Ukraine', 17.
21. Author's translation of: Політичні партії, як виявилося, позбавлені широкої соціальної бази, їх ідеологія та програми неадекватно відбивають поточну ситуацію і не відповідають завданням розвитку суспільства, партії не мають у своєму розпорядженні механізмів реалізації притарк манних їм функцій та завдань. Romaniuk and Shveda, *Partii ta Elektoralna Politika*, 239.
22. Gel'man, 'Party Politics in Russia: From Competition to Hierarchy'.
23. Greene, *Creating Competition: Patronage Politics and the PRI's Demise*.
24. For a discussion of the phenomenon of spoiler parties, see Wilson, 'Ukraine's New Virtual Politics'.
25. Birch, 'The Parliamentary Elections in Ukraine', 526.
26. Kubicek, 'Problems of Post-post-communism: Ukraine after the Orange Revolution'.
27. Strom, 'A Behavioral Theory of Competitive Political Parties'.

28. Wolinetz, 'Beyond the Catch-All Party: Approaches to the Study of Parties and Party Organisation in Contemporary Democracies', 149–50.
29. Geddes, 'Why Parties and Elections in Authoritarian Regimes?'.
30. For a discussion of semi-presidentialism, see Shugart, 'Semi-Presidential Systems: Dual Executive and Mixed Authority Patterns'.
31. For a classification of semi-presidential systems, see Elgie, 'Variations on a Theme', 102–5.
32. Ibid., 102.
33. For example, Fish, *Democracy Derailed in Russia: The Failure of Open Politics*; Ishiyama and Kennedy, 'Superpresidentialism and Political Party Development in Russia, Ukraine, Armenia and Kyrgyzstan'.
34. Shugart, 'The Inverse Relationship Between Party Strength and Executive Strength: A Theory of Politicians' Constitutional Choices'.
35. Croissant, *Electoral Politics in Southeast and East Asia: A Comparative Perspective*, 354; Kitschelt and Smyth, 'Programmatic Party Cohesion in Emerging Postcommunist Democracies: Russia in Comparative Context'.
36. Membership of Georgian parties has been recorded at 2.6%. See Nodia and Pinto Scholtbach, *The Political Landscape of Georgia*, 105. Only 1% of Ukrainians were members of a political party in 2000 according to Carson, *Attitudes toward Change, the Current Situation, and Civic Action in Ukraine*, 38. On levels of identification with parties in Georgia, see IRI, The Gallup Organisation and IPM, 'Georgian National Voter Study', 67; On levels of identification with parties in Ukraine, see Kubicek, 'The Limits of Electoral Democracy in Ukraine', 126.
37. For example, Doherty, *Promoting Democracy in Difficult Settings*, 4; USAID, *OECD/DAC Peer Review of the United States*, 27.
38. Author's interview, NIMD, The Hague, April 2007.
39. Author's interview, IRI Ukraine, Kyiv, March 2008.
40. Author's interview, Party of the Regions, Kyiv, March 2008.
41. Freedom House Freedom in the World reports can be consulted at http://freedomhouse.org/template.cfm?page=15 (accessed December 13, 2009).
42. D'Anieri, *Understanding Ukrainian Politics. Power, Politics, and Institutional Design*, 69; Way, 'Kuchma's Failed Authoritarianism', 4.
43. Wheatley, *Georgia from National Awakening to Rose Revolution: Delayed Transition in the Former Soviet Union*, 218.
44. King, 'Potemkin Democracy: Four Myths about Post-Soviet Georgia', 100.
45. See http://freedomhouse.org/template.cfm?page=47&nit=452&year=2008 (accessed November 11, 2009).
46. United States Agency for International Development, *USAID Political Party Assistance Policy*, 9.
47. United States Agency for International Development, *Political Party Development Assistance*, 1.
48. See Doherty, *Promoting Democracy in Difficult Settings*, 4; Konrad Adenauer Stiftung, *International Parteienzusammenarbeit der KAS. Globales Engagement für Frieden und Demokratie*, 76.
49. Author's telephone interview, NIMD, January 2009.
50. Author's interview, IRI Ukraine, Kyiv, May 2007.
51. See '"Tsina" vyborchoi kampanii-2007: xto finansuie ukrainskii partii', http://www.newsru.ua/arch/ukraine/03jul2007/lapsha.html (accessed December 9, 2009).
52. National Democratic Institute, *USAID Workplan Georgia August 1, 2001–July 31, 2002*, 8.
53. Black, Jay and Keshishian, *USAID/Caucasus/Georgia Civil Society Assessment*, iii.

54. Barca, Skoczylas and Ingraham, *Transforming Elections in Ukraine. An Assessment of Progress Made in Elections Administration and the Challenges Ahead*, 25.
55. Mitchell, *Uncertain Democracy. U.S. Foreign Policy and Georgia's Rose Revolution*, 58.
56. Author's interviews with former and current Socialist Party of Ukraine activists, Kyiv, 2007–2008.
57. Mitchell, *Uncertain Democracy. U.S. Foreign Policy and Georgia's Rose Revolution*, 94.
58. See OSCE/ODIHR Election Observation Mission Final Report. Available from http://www.osce.org/documents/odihr/2008/09/32898_en.pdf (accessed December 19, 2009).
59. Author's interviews, Party of Regions, Kyiv, March 2008.
60. Author's interview, IRI Ukraine, Kyiv, March 2008.
61. Author's interviews with Batkivshchyna and Socialist Party of Ukraine activists, Kyiv, 2007–2008.
62. Author's interview, People's Union Our Ukraine, October 2007.
63. Author's interviews with representatives from several Georgian and Ukrainian parties, 2007–2008.
64. Author's interview, KAS Germany, Berlin, May 2007; Author's interview, NDI Ukraine, March 2008.
65. Black, Jay and Keshishian, *USAID/Caucasus/Georgia Civil Society Assessment*, iii.
66. Ibid., 2.
67. United States Agency for International Development, *A Study of Political Party Assistance in Eastern Europe and Eurasia*, x.
68. Roberts, *Evaluation of the National Democratic Institute (NDI) in Kyrgyzstan, February 23–March 10, 2001*, 30.
69. Nelson and Katulis, *Armenia Political Party Assessment*, 27.
70. Ibid., vii.
71. Only the NIMD programme in Georgia has been halted, in 2008. The decision to halt this programme, however, had to do primarily with a shift of priorities of the OSCE, which had provided funding for the programme.
72. Carothers, 'Stepping Back From Democratic Pessimism'.
73. On parties in Africa, see Basedau and Stroh, 'Measuring Party Institutionalisation in Developing Countries'. On parties in South East Asia, see Ufen, 'Political Party and Party System Institutionalisation in Southeast Asia'. On parties in Latin America, see Sanchez, 'Transformation and Decay'.
74. The countries where party assistance is carried out are listed on the websites of the main providers. See http://www.fes.de/sets/s_fes_i.htm, http://www.kas.de/wf/en/71.4782/, http://www.iri.org/, http://ndi.org/wherewework, http://nimd.org/page/nimd_programmes (accessed December 15, 2009). Most of these countries are associated with weak party system institutionalization and are characterized by a less-than-democratic political context (see http://www.freedomhouse.org/template.cfm?page=363&year=2009 (accessed December 9, 2009)).

Bibliography

ARD, Inc. *Democracy and Governance Assessment of Georgia*. Washington, DC: ARD, Inc., 2002.
Barca, Peter, Elehie Natalie Skoczylas, and Jeson Ingraham. *Transforming Elections in Ukraine. An Assessment of Progress Made in Elections Administration and the Challenges Ahead*. Arlington, VA: Development Associates, 2006.
Basedau, Matthias, and Alexander Stroh. 'Measuring Party Institutionalisation in Developing Countries: A New Research Instrument Applied to 28 African Political Parties', *Working Paper No. 69*. Hamburg: GIGA German Institute of Global and Area Studies, 2008.
Birch, Sarah. 'The Parliamentary Elections in Ukraine, March 2002'. *Electoral Studies* 22, no. 3 (September 2003): 524–31.
Black, David, Susan Jay, and Michael Keshishian. *USAID/Caucasus/Georgia Civil Society Assessment*. Burlington, VT: 2001.
Carothers, Thomas. *Confronting the Weakest Link: Aiding Political Parties in New Democracies*. Washington, DC: Carnegie Endowment for International Peace, 2006.
Carothers, Thomas. 'Stepping Back From Democratic Pessimism', *Carnegie Paper no. 99*. Washington, DC: Carnegie Endowment for International Peace, 2009.
Carson, Thomas P. 'Attitudes toward Change, the Current Situation, and Civic Action in Ukraine'. Paper prepared for the International Foundation for Electoral Systems, Kyiv, 2000.
Croissant, Aurel. *Electoral Politics in Southeast and East Asia: A Comparative Perspective*. Singapore: Friedrich Ebert Stiftung, 2002.
D'Anieri, Paul. *Understanding Ukrainian Politics. Power, Politics, and Institutional Design*. Armonk, NY: M.E. Sharpe, 2007.
Doherty, Ivan. 'Promoting Democracy in Difficult Settings'. Paper presented at CEPPS Roundtable, Washington, DC, 29 April 2002.
Dolidze, Valerian. 'Political Parties and Party Development in Georgia'. *Central Asia and the Caucasus* 2 (2005): 49–59.
Elgie, Robert. 'Variations on a Theme'. *Journal of Democracy* 16, no. 3 (July 2005): 98–112.
Fish, M. Steven. *Democracy Derailed in Russia: The Failure of Open Politics*. Cambridge, MA: Cambridge University Press, 2005.
Geddes, Barbara. 'Why Parties and Elections in Authoritarian Regimes?'. Revised version of a paper prepared for presentation at the annual meeting of the American Political Science Association, Washington, DC, 2005 (2006).
Gel'man, Vladimir. 'Party Politics in Russia: From Competition to Hierarchy'. *Europe-Asia Studies* 60, no. 6 (August 2008): 913–30.
Greene, Kenneth F. 'Creating Competition: Patronage Politics and the PRI's Demise', *Working Paper No. 345*. Notre Dame, Kellogg Institute for International Studies, The Kellogg Institute Working Papers, 2007.
International Republican Institute. *Ukraine Work Plan 2006*. Washington, DC: International Republican Institute, 2005.
International Republican Institute, The Gallup Organisation and IPM, 'Georgian National Voter Study', *USAID, Baltic Surveys*. International Republican Institute, The Gallup Organisation, IPM, 2007. http://www.iri.org/eurasia/georgia/pdfs/2007-05-09-Georgia-Poll3.pdf (accessed December 18, 2009).
Ishiyama, John T., and Ryan Kennedy. 'Superpresidentialism and Political Party Development in Russia, Ukraine, Armenia and Kyrgyzstan'. *Europe-Asia Studies* 53, no. 8 (2001): 1177–91.
King, Charles. 'Potemkin Democracy. Four Myths about Post-Soviet Georgia'. *The National Interest* 64 (Summer 2001): 93–104.

Kitschelt, Herbert, and Regina Smyth. 'Programmatic Party Cohesion in Emerging Postcommunist Democracies: Russia in Comparative Context'. *Comparative Political Studies* 35 (2002): 1228–56.

Konrad Adenauer Stiftung. *International Parteienzusammenarbeit der KAS. Globales Engagement für Frieden und Demokratie*. Berlin: Konrad Adenauer Stiftung, 2008.

Kubicek, Paul. 'The Limits of Electoral Democracy in Ukraine'. *Democratization* 8, no. 2 (Summer 2001): 117–39.

Kubicek, Paul. 'Problems of Post-post-communism: Ukraine after the Orange Revolution'. *Democratization* 16, no. 2 (April 2009): 323–43.

Lane, Jan E., and Svante Ersson. 'Party System Instability in Europe: Persistent Differences in Volatility between West and East?' *Democratization* 14, no. 1 (February 2007): 92–110.

Mitchell, Lincoln A. *Uncertain Democracy. U.S. Foreign Policy and Georgia's Rose Revolution*. Philadelphia, PA: University of Pennsylvania Press, 2008.

National Democratic Institute. *USAID Workplan Georgia August 1, 2001–July 31, 2002*. Washington, DC: National Democratic Institute, 2001.

Nelson, Sue, and Brian Katulis. *Armenia Political Party Assessment*. Washington, DC: United States Agency for International Development, 2005.

Netherlands Institute for Multiparty Democracy. *A Framework for Democratic Party-Building*. The Hague: Netherlands Institute for Multiparty Democracy, 2004.

Nodia, Ghia, and Álvaro Pinto Scholtbach. *The Political Landscape of Georgia*. Delft: Eburon Academic Publishers, 2006.

Riabchuk, Mykola. 'Ukraine: Lessons Learned from Other Postcommunist Transitions'. *Orbis* 52, no. 1 (Winter 2008): 41–64.

Roberts, Sean R. *Evaluation of the National Democratic Institute (NDI) in Kyrgyzstan, February 23–March 10, 2001*. Washington, DC, 2001.

Romaniuk, Anatolii, and Yurii Shveda. *Partii ta Elektoralna Politika*. Lviv: Astrolyabiya, 2005.

Sanchez, Omar. 'Transformation and Decay: the De-Institutionalisation of Party Systems in South America'. *Third World Quarterly* 29, no. 2 (March 2008): 315–37.

Saxer, Marc. 'Parteiförderung als Element der Demokratieförderung'. Berlin, 2006.

Shugart, Matthew S. 'The Inverse Relationship Between Party Strength and Executive Strength: A Theory of Politicians' Constitutional Choices'. *British Journal of Political Science* 28 (1998): 1–29.

Shugart, Matthew S. 'Semi-Presidential Systems: Dual Executive and Mixed Authority Patterns', *Working Paper*. San Diego: Graduate School of International Relations and Pacific Studies, University of California, 2005.

Slomczynski, Kazimierz M., Goldie Shabad, and Jakub Zielinski. 'Fluid Party Systems, Electoral Rules and Accountability of Legislators in Emerging Democracies: The Case of Ukraine'. *Party Politics* 14, no. 1 (2008): 91–112.

Strom, Kaare. 'A Behavioral Theory of Competitive Political Parties'. *American Journal of Political Science* 34, no. 2 (1990): 565–98.

Tarkhan-Mouravi, Giorgi. 'Politicheskie Partii v Gruzii. Zatiunuvsheesia Stanovlenie'. *Political Science Quarterly* 1 (2006): 243–67.

Topolyanskiy, Aleksandr. 'Nukonets. Partiia Yushchenko tikho umiraet'. INTV, March 3, 2009, http://www.intv-inter.net/ru/news/study/?id=57761747.

Ufen, Andreas. 'Political Party and Party System Institutionalisation in Southeast Asia: A Comparison of Indonesia, the Philippines, and Thailand', *GIGA Working Papers No. 44*. Hamburg: German Institute of Global and Area Studies, 2007.

United States Agency for International Development. *Political Party Development Assistance*. Washington, DC: USAID, 1999.

United States Agency for International Development. USAID *Political Party Assistance Policy*. Washington, DC: USAID, 2003.

United States Agency for International Development. *OECD/DAC Peer Review of the United States*. Washington, DC: USAID, 2006.

United States Agency for International Development. *A Study of Political Party Assistance in Eastern Europe and Eurasia*. Washington, DC: USAID, 2007.

Usupashvili, David. 'An Analysis of the Presidential and Parliamentary Elections in Georgia: A Case Study, November 2003–March 2004'. *Election Assessment in the South Caucasus, 75–100*. Stockholm: IDEA, 2004.

Van Zon, Hans. 'Neo-Patrimonialism as an Impediment to Economic Development: The Case of Ukraine'. *The Journal of Communist Studies and Transition Politics* 17, no. 3 (September 2001): 71–95.

Verheije, Marga, André Krouwel, Dessy Gavrilova, and Theo van Koolwijk. *Van partij naar partij: Nederlandse ondersteuning van politieke partijen in Europese landen in transitie. Evaluatie Matra Politieke Partijen Programma 2000–2005*. Wormerveer, 2006.

Way, Lucan. 'Kuchma's Failed Authoritarianism'. *Journal of Democracy* 16, no. 2 (2005): 131–45.

Wheatley, Jonathan. *Georgia from National Awakening to Rose Revolution: Delayed Transition in the Former Soviet Union*. Aldershot: Ashgate, 2005.

Wilson, Andrew. 'Ukraine's New Virtual Politics'. *East European Constitutional Review* 10 (2001): 60–8.

Wilson, Andrew, and Artur Bilous. 'Political Parties in Ukraine'. *Europe-Asia Studies* 45, no. 4 (1993): 693–703.

Wilson, Andrew, and Sarah Birch. 'Political Parties in Ukraine. Virtual and Representational. In Political Parties in New Democracies', in *Trajectories of Development and Implications for Democracy*, ed. Paul Webb and Stephen White, 53–84. Oxford: Oxford University Press, 2007.

Wolinetz, Steven B. 'Beyond the Catch-All Party: Approaches to the Study of Parties and Party Organisation in Contemporary Democracies', in *Political Parties. Old Concepts and New Challenges*, ed. Richard Gunther, José Ramón Montero, and Juan J. Linz, 136–65. Oxford: Oxford University Press, 2002.

Crossing the line:
partisan party assistance in post-Milošević Serbia

Marlene Spoerri

Department of European Studies, University of Amsterdam, Amsterdam, the Netherlands

This contribution explores one of the most widely discussed examples of pro-democracy international intervention: regime change in Serbia. It takes the contemporary scholarship on regime change one step further, however, examining not only the international effort leading up to Milošević's ouster, but also, and most importantly, that which followed. As is explained, despite the widely cited premise that democracy aid to political parties does not seek to determine electoral outcomes, political party assistance in Serbia has often been designed to do precisely that. The study examines how partisan party aid has detracted from donors' larger efforts to promote democracy abroad. In so doing, it demonstrates that a partisan approach to party aid has the potential not only to compromise the legitimacy of democracy's promotion abroad, but also to undermine fledgling democratic processes in post-authoritarian states. In such circumstances, partisan party assistance may very well be less desirable than no party assistance at all.

The close of the twentieth century saw the rise of a new breed of regime change: the 'Electoral Revolution'.[1] With the help of a large swathe of opposition forces and a deeply unpopular incumbent, disgruntled masses stretching from Croatia to Georgia pushed the bounds of semi-authoritarianism to bring about democratic breakthroughs. In each of these instances, external actors played a behind-the-scenes role: providing trainings in electoral monitoring, sponsoring massive Get-Out-The-Vote (GOTV) campaigns, aiding independent media, and in several instances, offering opposition forces both material and financial assistance. Overtly partisan – albeit not always explicitly geared towards regime-change – these external interventions were widely hailed as a contributing, if not determinative, factor in the unseating of semi-authoritarian leaders throughout post-communist Europe.[2] Eager to ensure that such efforts did not go to waste in the wake of revolution, democracy promoters created elaborate aid programmes designed to strengthen and further democratize these countries' newly elected political systems. No doubt caught up in the post-revolutionary euphoria, many in the aid community believed the forces of the *ancien régime* to have been so thoroughly discredited that their exclusion from such programmes was a mere *fait accompli*.

Yet in the years that have followed electoral revolution, donors have been forced to confront an uncomfortable reality: in countries from Serbia to Ukraine, the public's antipathy towards newly-elected authorities has breathed new life and legitimacy into the forces of the old regime. As they win back votes and in some cases governments and presidencies, external actors seeking to promote democracy are faced with a stark choice: to incorporate these actors into their democratization programmes or to castigate them as mere authoritarian strongholds. How donors should respond to these new developments is far from obvious.

On the one hand, these revamped forces of the old regime are hardly carbon copies of their predecessors. They by and large play by the rules of the democratic game, support democratic policies and constitutions, and pledge their allegiance to democratic principles. On the other hand, they are far from endearing characters. Their leaders often espouse anti-Western rhetoric and their policy preferences tend to flout liberal values. As the aid community recalibrates its strategy in the aftermath of electoral revolution, it thus finds itself enmeshed in a Catch-22: work with the de facto forces of the *ancien régime* and risk bolstering the very actors that brought hardship (and in some cases, bloodshed) upon their societies; work without them (and thus, in effect, against them) and risk unduly influencing fledgling democratic processes. For no segment of the aid community is this issue more pressing than for those working with political parties.

Tasked with bolstering the capacities of actors in the forefront of the democratic process, party aid providers are more susceptible than most to charges of unwarranted meddling. In democratic contexts, their formal mandates thus often prescribe that they act in accordance with principles of non-partisanship. Yet the decision *not* to work with parties of the old regime in the wake of electoral revolution raises important – but hitherto unexplored – questions as to the veracity of partisan party assistance in these newly democratic settings. This study takes a first step towards answering these questions. It seeks, in particular, to understand the potential consequences of partisan party aid as they pertain to the democratic process in post-authoritarian states. In other words, does a partisan approach to party aid help or hinder fledgling democratic processes? Assuming a combination of the two, is there reason to believe that the benefits of the former outweigh the latter, or vice versa? To answer these questions, this analysis explores instances in which donors have opted for a distinctly partisan approach to party aid. Using post-Milošević Serbia as a case in point, the account elucidates how party aid has evolved in the aftermath of Serbia's 'Bulldozer' Revolution. As we shall see, the Serbian case suggests that when implemented in newly democratic contexts, partisan party assistance has the potential both to compromise the legitimacy of external democracy promotion abroad and to undermine indigenous democratic processes. Under such circumstances, partisan party assistance may thus be less desirable than no assistance at all.

In making this case, the contribution proceeds by discussing the rationale underlying political party assistance, with specific emphasis on the largely unexplored terrain of partisanship in party aid programmes and policies. The consequences of such partisanship are then examined through an in-depth case study of foreign assistance to political parties in post-Milošević Serbia. As shall be seen, Serbia was the recipient of a wave of highly partisan political party assistance both prior to and following its transition to democracy in late 2000. Having made great strides in the midst of semi-authoritarianism, the effects of party aid were more ambiguous in the democratic context that followed. Rather than embrace a nonpartisan approach in the wake of electoral revolution, donors replicated the tactics initially designed to facilitate Milošević's ouster. In so doing, they may have exacerbated some of the problems still afflicting Serbian democracy, most notably by increasing political polarization, deepening foreign dependencies, and raising suspicions of aid recipients.

Party aid and partisanship

Of all the images conjured up by external interventions into the affairs of sovereign democratic states, few are more unsettling than those that threaten to derail the democratic process. Where such intrusions target political parties – the chief interlocutors between citizens and their governments – they raise even greater suspicions. It is thus incumbent upon those seeking to influence the work and conduct of political parties abroad to clarify the nature and aims of their activities. And so they have. As a subset of the larger democracy promotion agenda, party assistance is heralded as strengthening – rather than weakening – the democratic process. Its aim is one of assisting in the development of political parties and party systems abroad.[3]

Strong, democratic parties, it is said, help connect citizens to their governments, not only by aggregating and representing the public's diverse range of interests before decision-making bodies, but also by holding those bodies accountable to the electorate.[4] In addition, they fulfil such necessary functions as disseminating political information, recruiting leaders and representatives, and socializing citizens as to the norms and practices of democratic politics. Parties' ability to perform such functions efficiently and effectively is widely seen as critical to the democratic process.[5]

All too frequently, however, the demand for competent, democratic parties in new democracies is met by a devastating lag in supply. Parties in new democracies are often unresponsive to citizens' interests, playing little role outside of the electoral arena and inspiring little confidence in fledgling democratic processes. More often than not, they suffer from a so-called 'standard lament': they are perceived as self-interested, programmatically indistinct, leadership-centric, and incapable of governing effectively.[6] It is the proclaimed aim of party assistance to help remedy such ills. Thus the arsenal of party aid – including workshops, trainings, public opinion polling, cultural exchanges, and financial and in-kind contributions – is targeted at helping parties to develop their functions more effectively and democratically. If this is achieved, aid providers believe, countries will be better equipped to support the forms of (liberal) democratic practice to which donors aspire.

Despite such ambitions, 'doubts and suspicions about underlying objectives and intentions are particularly acute regarding party aid'.[7] Indeed, given its potential to affect political parties' electoral prospects, many question the motives underpinning party aid, assuming such assistance to be but an instrument through which foreigners seek to manipulate electoral outcomes to further their own interests.

Donors have sought to address such qualms by pointing to the widespread practice of non-partisanship. By spreading their assistance along a range of political contenders, party assisters maintain that their efforts avoid crossing the line into the more dubious terrain of electoral meddling. Thus, American donors insist that party assistance 'be provided without reference to specific policy positions taken by competing candidates or parties' and be 'offered equitably to all groups committed to the democratic process, regardless of their specific platforms or programmes'.[8] Over the years, other donors have followed suit. The Netherlands Institute for Multiparty Democracy, for example, boasts that it 'supports political parties in young democracies, regardless of their political colour'.[9] And while many European party foundations have embraced the so-called 'fraternal' approach to party assistance – with mother parties in Germany or Great Britain establishing exclusive partnerships with ideological sister-parties in, say, Bulgaria or Albania – they too insist that the cumulative effects of such aid is nonpartisan, in so far as it ultimately benefits democratic pluralism rather than any single ideological variant.

Thus, the Westminster Foundation for Democracy (WFD) highlights its cross-party approach to party aid as indicative of what is ultimately a nonpartisan agenda. In a former Chief Executive's words, WFD member parties develop 'party-to-party relationships across the political spectrum in the interests of promoting thriving, multi-party democracies'.[10] The six German *Stiftungen* (the Friedrich Ebert Stiftung (FES), Konrad Adenauer Stiftung (KAS), the Friedrich Naumann Stiftung, the Heinrich Böll Stiftung, the Rosa Luxemburg Stiftung, and the Hanns Seidel Stiftung) make similar claims. As one representative of the FES argued, the 'single party approach of FES is justified by the fact that the simultaneous activity of the other German political foundations ensures pluralism'.[11] The German government is in fact so sensitive to accusations of unwarranted political interference abroad that the *Stiftungen* are all but barred from providing overt financial and material assistance to foreign political parties (see the contribution by Weissenbach to this special issue[12]). Instead, they often work with party-affiliated non-governmental organizations (NGOs) or youth wings. As one interviewee noted, we 'want to avoid any impression that we meddle into electoral issues or campaigns'.[13]

Nonpartisan ideals are, however, often unattainable in practice. Perhaps the most prevalent exception to non-partisanship is that of party viability. In many emerging democracies it is not uncommon for dozens, even hundreds, of groups to be registered as political parties. Many are no more than so-called 'sofa' parties, boasting only a handful of members and little popular appeal. Given their limited means, donors are unable to work with such parties. Instead, donors limit their assistance to those they define as 'viable' and 'relevant' (that is, those that are 'able to compete in elections, sustain themselves independently, and have a significant impact or influence on the political system').[14]

Party aid providers are similarly partisan with respect to what they define as 'anti-democratic' parties. To qualify as democratic, National Democratic Institute (NDI) insists, parties must demonstrate a proven commitment to: human rights, legitimate elections, free competition; as well as non-violence and responsible governance.[15] In addition, such parties must communicate principles, policy proposals, accomplishments, and encourage political participation. Yet what this means in practice is not always self-evident. In discussions with practitioners, competing definitions of 'anti-democratic' abound: some cite a lack of internal party democracy[16] and others the absence of commitment to ruling democratically.[17]

Even then, however, there are several additional examples in which the party assistance community has flouted its nonpartisan mandate. Carothers points to two such instances: in the immediate aftermath of communism and in semi-authoritarian contexts. As communist governments fell across Central and Eastern Europe in the early 1990s, party aid providers largely ignored the needs of successor communist parties, opting instead to support their opponents in an effort to promote political pluralism.[18] So too with parties beholden to semi-authoritarian regimes. In the Slovak Republic, Croatia, and Georgia – to name but a few – party aid providers supported representatives of the 'democratic bloc' in a bid to level the political playing field. Kumar adds a third caveat to Carothers' list: post-conflict contexts. In societies exiting a period of sustained violence, party aid providers frequently target their assistance so as 'to influence the outcome of elections by supporting favourite parties'.[19] Thus, in post-war Bosnia, for example, party aid providers channelled their assistance to parties they saw as bucking the trend of ethnic nationalism.[20]

However indirectly, scholars concerned with political party assistance have generally condoned such exceptions. Partisanship employed in the run-up to electoral revolutions has, for example, been hailed as a positive factor in enabling democratic breakthrough. And while Kumar admits that partisanship has the capacity to 'blur the distinction between assistance and political manipulation' he also maintains that 'partisan assistance can promote peace and democracy'.[21] Burnell reaches a similar conclusion in the context of post-conflict environments, where he says 'democracy foundations can contribute to peace-building and reconciliation by refusing to support parties whose leaders were involved in the recently ended violence or alleged human rights violations'.[22]

Yet the exceptions to non-partisanship raise several important questions that demand further consideration. While partisanship in the midst of semi-authoritarianism may indeed work in democracy's favour, it is difficult to make the same case with respect to newly democratic settings, particularly when excluded parties are no longer overtly 'anti-democratic' or 'marginal'. Unfortunately, few have examined how partisanship in newly democratic contexts impacts upon local processes of democratization. This study takes a first step in this direction. It relies on 150 interviews with party aid practitioners and recipients, as well as thousands of pages of internal documents hitherto unreleased to the public.[23] In so doing, this study examines one case: that of post-Milošević Serbia. As the following pages explain, political party assistance in Serbia has, without exception, been a partisan affair. The dual legacy of ethnic conflict and semi-authoritarianism that tormented the former Yugoslavia throughout the 1990s was taken to legitimate such partisanship. Understanding how this has affected domestic democratic processes in the aftermath of Milošević's rule may shine light on the viability of such an approach in similar settings.

Partisan party aid in a changing Serbia

When party aid providers first set foot in Serbia's capital in the winter of 1996/1997, they were confronted not only by a war-torn, impoverished nation, but also by a non-democratic regime-type reminiscent of what Levitsky and Way have entitled 'competitive authoritarianism'.[24] At the forefront of Serbia's non-democratic regime-type lay two political parties: Milošević's Socialist Party of Serbia (SPS) and Vojislav Šešelj's Serbian Radical Party (SRS). Where the former claimed to seek the middle ground of Serbian politics, the latter was brash and demagogic. Together, the SPS and SRS oversaw Serbia's descent into a bloodbath of civil war, a decade of international isolation, and the grips of authoritarianism.

As is now well known, the ousting of Slobodan Milošević in October 2000 opened the door to electoral democracy.[25] Lesser known is that this transition away from semi-authoritarianism was also met by a transition of sorts for the parties of the *ancien régime*. No longer at the helm of power, the SPS and SRS were forced to adapt to their roles as oppositional parties in a newly democratic Serbia. Over the years, they presented themselves as the standard-bearers of Serbia's poor and disenchanted. As frustrations with Serbia's new authorities mounted, public opinion worked in the *ancien régime's* favour. By late 2003 the SRS had established itself as the largest party in Serbia, occupying one in three of Serbia's 250-seat parliament.

From 2004 onwards, the anti-democratic credentials of the *ancien régime* grew increasingly questionable. Although still directly affiliated with their controversial leaders,[26] the SRS and SPS consistently played by the rules of the democratic game. They participated in free and fair elections and respected the results of these elections, even when doing so meant accepting defeat. Both parties also supported the ratification of Serbia's first post- Milošević constitution. In 2006, they went so far as to help pass legislation *increasing* ethnic minority representation in parliament. By the following year, William Montgomery, a former US Ambassador to Serbia, publicly dismissed the notion that either party was 'anti-democrat'.[27]

According to Montgomery, the SRS's Vice President, Tomislav Nikolić, 'actually came across in a better light than many of the "democrats"' in Serbia's parliament. Indeed, when in 2008 Nikolić narrowly lost a presidential bid to Boris Tadić of the DS, Nikolić not only conceded his defeat that same night, but also became Serbia's first politician to publicly congratulate his adversary.[28]

Despite such feats, it was only in late 2009 – after the SPS has joined a pro-EU government and the bulk of the SRS had splintered off into the pro-EU Serbian Progressive Party (SNS) – that the international community took steps to adopt a nonpartisan approach to party aid. Although doubts regarding the veracity of such partisanship had long plagued practitioners working in Serbia,[29] the decision to exclude the SRS and SPS from their assistance was in many respects a *fait accompli*.

Party aid in Milošević's Serbia 1997–2000

Party aid to Serbia first began in the aftermath of a series of local-level victories won by the pro-democratic coalition, *Zajedno* (Together) in late 1996.[30] Yet it was only after the cessation of the Kosovo war two years later that party assistance truly proliferated. It was then that a policy based on overt partisanship developed, with one clearly defined aim: regime change.[31] The Coordinator of US assistance to Europe and Eurasia explains: 'Normally we're there to level the playing field, but [in Serbia] we were there trying to get rid of [Milošević].'[32] The same was true for European aid providers. As a former Resident Director of FES's Serbia office explains, the goal of regime change was 'very explicit – huge amounts were involved in this, all with the objective to overthrow Milošević'.[33]

And so, in a bid to unseat Milošević the party aid community deviated from its nonpartisan mandate. Not only did it help anti-Milošević parties identify potential supporters, it worked to forge a coalition – the Democratic Opposition of Serbia (DOS) – of 18 anti-Milošević parties. In addition to training DOS parties in the techniques of campaigning and mass mobilization, party aid providers – both European and American alike – paid for the coalition's media campaign, funded DOS infrastructure, and hired top-notch political consultants to help lead DOS parties to victory.[34] Party assistance was in fact one facet of a calculated donor effort designed not only to facilitate Milošević's electoral defeat in presidential elections held in September 2000, but also to galvanize public sentiment against his subsequent electoral theft and to secure the opposition's victory in parliamentary elections staged just two months thereafter. By the eve of 2001, with oppositional parties in command of both the executive and legislative branches, there was a broad consensus that they had succeeded.[35]

Party aid post-Milošević 2001–2003

From the perspective of the party aid community, post-Milošević Serbia offered unprecedented opportunities for the successful promotion of democracy.

According to the FES's Michael Weichert, it was a 'very optimistic, forward-looking atmosphere – everybody wanted to do something'.[36] Rob Benjamin, Director of NDI programming for Central and Eastern Europe, agrees: 'We thought the Balkan powder keg had finally been resolved'.[37] As a result, 'a lot of resources' stemming from both sides of the Atlantic were poured into the country in the following months (see Figure 1).[38]

Having abruptly transitioned from a much-oppressed opposition to a majority-led government, Serbia's new authorities found themselves wielding enormous power. Because DOS lacked both executive and legislative experience, donors initially targeted their assistance not at individual member parties, but at the government as a whole. Within several months, however, the fissures in the DOS alliance had grown too large to ignore. Personal animosities, policy disagreements, and rivalry drove a wedge between competing parties, most notably Zoran Djindjić's Democratic Party and Vojislav Koštunica's Democratic Party of Serbia. By late 2001, it was apparent that DOS's days were numbered, leaving donors with little recourse but to seek out the allegiances of individual DOS-member parties.

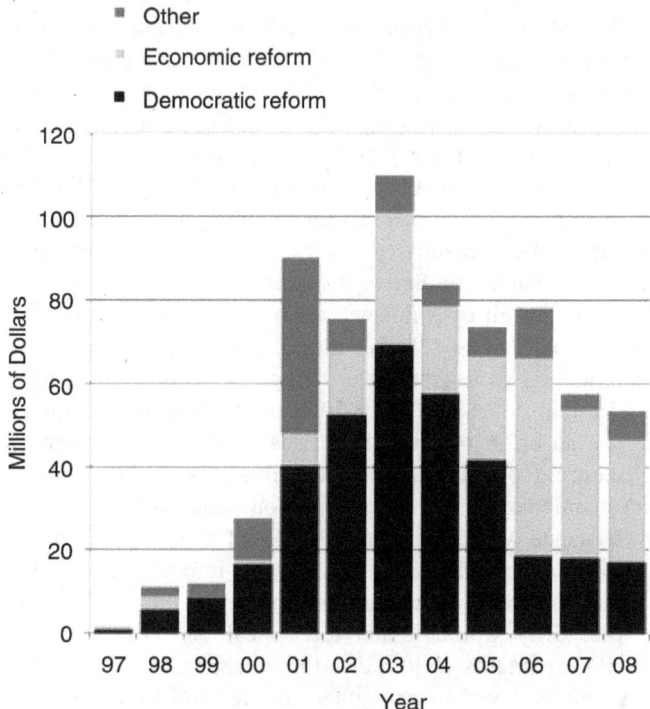

Figure 1. Breakdown of US SEED spending on Serbia 2001–2008.
Source: Compiled by author on the basis of SEED Annual Reports FY 2001–2008.
Note: 'Other' includes SEED funds dedicated towards humanitarian assistance; security, regional, stability and law enforcement assistance; as well as cross-sectoral assistance.

For the next two years, party aid focused on the standard array of party aid programmes, incorporating trainings spanning from local branch development to coalition building. Yet even in this period, the overwhelming focus lay on helping Serbia's first post-Milošević government remain united and pro-reform. It was in fact only after the first series of setbacks – Prime Minister Djindjić's assassination in March of 2003, the fall of the DOS government several months later, and the strong electoral performance of the SRS in December 2003 – that party aid providers seriously reconsidered this coalition-based approach.

Partisan party aid post-Djindjić 2004–2009

The Serbia of January 2001 bore little resemblance to the Serbia of January 2004. The combination of Djindjić's murder and the subsequent rise of Vojislav Šešelj's SRS, profoundly altered the political landscape. For party aid providers, Djindjić's assassination was a particularly unwelcome blow: 'We were completely shell-shocked', recalls NDI's Rob Benjamin.[39] Indeed, Djindjić's death left a vacuum not only in the power structure of what had hitherto been the party aid community's closest ally – the Democratic Party (DS) – but also on the national political stage. Serbia post-Djindjić lacked a strong forward-looking leader capable of making the necessary, and often unpopular, decisions required of reform. Having pinned their hopes on Djindjić's capacity to initiate such changes, donors were unsure of how to proceed.

Uncertainties were further aroused following December 2003's parliamentary elections. To the disbelief of many in the international community,[40] Serbia's far right had staged a major comeback, winning over a third of the national vote. Yet rather than respond to these events by reaching out to nationalist parties and their supporters, donors dismissed their comeback as the product of post-revolutionary disenchantment. Serbs, it was thought, were not so much attracted by the serenade of Šešelj or Milošević as they were repelled by the failings of Djindjić's successors.[41] The solution thus lay in ensuring that DOS successor parties would mount a more credible challenge in the years to come.

The policies that developed from 2004 onwards were two-fold. On the one hand, there was an effort to raise the standard of living for Serbia's 'losers of transition'. Enduring public support for Serbia's far right forces was seen as underscoring democracy assistance's limitation: whatever its past achievements, democracy assistance was deemed an insufficient antidote to Serbia's nationalist persuasions. To moderate Serbia's masses, the foreign aid community would seek recourse elsewhere. It soon found solace in the notion that rising levels of wealth and prosperity would lessen the appeal of Serbia's radical elements. Increasing Serbs' standards of living – through jobs, trade, and foreign investments – was thus believed to strengthen the demand for stability and political moderation. US Ambassador to Serbia, Michael Polt, therefore reallocated US foreign aid spending, effectively turning the ratio of economy-to-democracy aid spending on its head[42] (see Figure 1). As a facet of democracy aid, funding for political party assistance decreased significantly (Figure 2).

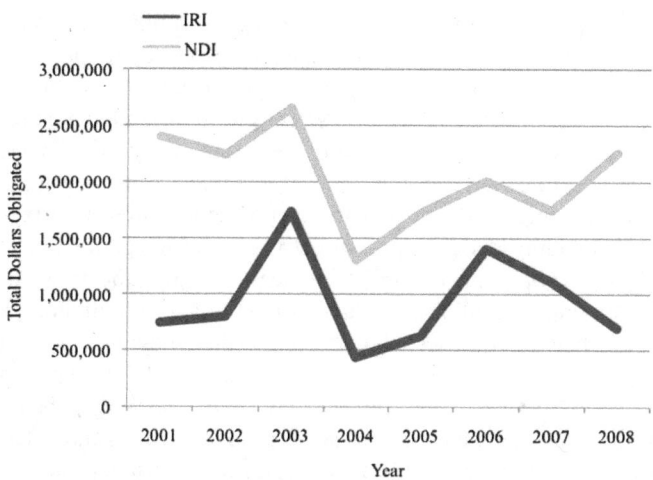

Figure 2. USAID funding for US party institutes.
Source: Compiled by the author on the basis of IRI/NDI grant agreements with USAID.
Notes: Figures do not include a $31,684 grant NDI obtained from the National Endowment for Democracy in support of its 'Demographic Analysis for Voter Targeting' database. Also not included are the budgets of the European party foundations. Less transparent than their American counterparts, they have been reluctant to share such detailed information with the public. That said, the Serbia budget of NDI by all accounts exceeds that of any single European party foundation. Interviews with FES representatives – the most prominent of the European foundations operating in Serbia – confirm that their budget for the post-2000 period is roughly €1 million, one third of which is devoted to party work.

Although economic development was thought to be an antidote to Serbia's nationalist upswing, political party assistance was not entirely forsaken. By enhancing the capacities of DOS successor parties, party aid providers believed Serbs would be less inclined to vote the *ancien régime* back into office. From 2004 onwards, party aid providers thus lay renewed emphasis on helping DOS successor parties strengthen their internal structures and modernize their electoral machinery. Trainings and seminars focused on skills building and local branch development. Youth and women's wings were encouraged and cultivated. Conferences on party ideology were sponsored and advice given on platform development.[43]

Yet at the heart of the post-2004 party aid effort stood a programme designed to bolster parties' campaign performances. Intended to help aid recipients outperform Serbia's so-called 'anti-democratic' bloc, the programme was first developed in the run-up to the June 2004's presidential elections, pitting Boris Tadić of the DS against Tomislav Nikolić of the SRS.[44] Critical to this effort was a new campaign strategy: voter targeting on the basis of demographic analysis. In the months before June 2004, party aid providers established a fully functional voter-targeting database, the first of its kind in Serbia. By connecting past electoral results in polling stations throughout Serbia to current census data, the database was capable of producing highly-detailed lists of individual voters' addresses, political preferences, economic statuses, gender, and age – polling station by polling station.[45] The location, voting habits, and socio-economic profiles of voters across Serbia was thus contained in a single database and, thanks to the American party institutes, placed in the hands of a select group of aid recipients.

From the perspective of party aid providers, the utility of the voter-targeting database was two-fold. On the one hand, it enabled partner parties to pinpoint those areas harbouring likely or potential supporters. Using an array of GOTV techniques – including door-to-door, direct mail, and telephone banks – parties could rally their supporters to the ballot box. At the same time, the targeted nature of their campaigns allowed partner parties to avoid motivating individuals who favoured their adversaries, thus ensuring that they did not inadvertently increase voter turnout on their opponents' behalf. As NDI's Quarterly Report from April–June 2004 explains, the database was 'tailored to help individual parties identify and target their potential supporters (abstainers and voters sympathetic to parties with similar platforms) and positive supporters (voters currently or formerly loyal to the party), while avoiding areas likely to be loyal to opponents'.[46]

But the voter-targeting database served another purpose as well. As the International Republican Institute (IRI) reported in mid-2004, the outcome of the presidential election of 27 June 'depended heavily on voter turnout'.[47] 'Low turnout', IRI believed 'would have favoured Nikolić'.[48] Indeed, the consensus at the time (and for some years thereafter) was that support for the SRS was unwavering: 30% of the population – no more, no less – could be relied upon to vote in favour of the SRS, rain or shine. By contrast, support for DOS successor parties was considered far more fickle. Despite their larger numbers, potential DOS supporters often abstained from the electoral process, choosing not to exercise their voting rights.[49] In 2004 the worry for the foreign aid community was that if too many voters chose to stay home on Election Day, Nikolić would take the presidency. From the perspective of party aid practitioners, the solution was clear: increase voter turnout and increase the likelihood of a Tadić victory.[50] 'The key', as one former Resident Director of NDI noted, lay in 'identifying segments of the electorate who were moving into and out of abstention' and targeting them accordingly.[51] If placed in the hands of (ostensibly) nonpartisan NGOs, the voter targeting database thus presented the ideal tool through which to accomplish this.

Thus from 2004 onwards, party aid providers sponsored parliamentary and presidential GOTV campaigns headlined by the Centre for Free Elections and Democracy (CeSID), an NGO specializing in electoral monitoring and public opinion polling. On the basis of demographical analysis drawn from NDI's voter targeting database, CeSID employed an extensive door-to-door outreach and a direct mailing campaign designed to encourage suspected (DOS) abstainers to vote. As IRI explained, the hope was that CeSID's campaign 'would reach the largest number of potential *reform* voters'.[52] The effort was targeted at the young and women aged 25–40 – two demographics, IRI noted, that 'generally have low rates of turnout and are considered essential to *reform*-party victories'.[53] In addition, FES sponsored a large, albeit low profile, voter outreach campaign of its own, funding the efforts of partner NGOs to send out thousands of text messages to their supporters in the run-up to elections.[54]

June 2004's presidential election marked the start of a new breed of party assistance programming. Rather than focus merely on bolstering democratic forces, party institutes formulated 'strategies to convert Radical votes to democratic votes', while actively 'striving to stem the tide of radical political support'.[55] Increasingly, the voter targeting database was used not simply as a standard GOTV device, but as a partisan tool strategically designed to encourage some, but not all, of the Serbian electorate to partake in the democratic process. As party aid providers subsequently reported, the aim was to support voter turnout exclusively in 'reform-oriented' households. Thus, when in 2008's parliamentary elections many so-called 'anti-reform' voters chose to stay home, their lack of participation in the electoral processes was widely applauded. As Serbia's NDI Resident Director reported to his Board in May 2008, anti-reform 'voters supported their own best interests by not voting' – this, he said, was 'good news'.[56]

The consequences of partisan party aid in post-Milošević Serbia

The foregoing discussion laid out the dynamics of party aid in Serbia, both prior to and following regime change. As was demonstrated, partisanship prevailed in both these periods, as practitioners worked not merely to exclude the SRS and SPS from their activities, but also to undermine their electoral prospects by strengthening those of their opponents. Such partisanship, it was shown, abounded irrespective of the changing attitudes these parties exhibited towards the democratic process. The following section explores the consequences of partisanship in party aid as they pertain to Serbia's domestic democratic processes.

Crossing the line into electoral meddling

Perhaps the most glaring problem associated with partisanship lies in party aid's capacity to sway electoral outcomes. If selectively targeted, foreign contributions may leave some parties better equipped than others, putting them at an electoral advantage. According to Bussey, however well intended, these interventions risk undermining the free market of ideas by providing individuals external to the democratic process with undue influence over voters' electoral preferences.[57] In Serbia, party aid providers sought to do precisely that. In the late 1990s and 2000 party aid aimed at uniting and equipping Serbia's democratic opposition, paying for media spots and high-profile campaign consultants – all in a bid to unseat Milosevic. Similarly, in the post-Milošević period, donors selectively targeted their assistance at those parties they deemed worthy of support – this time in a bid to ward off a nationalist revival. They thus not only excluded the SRS from their activities, but they actively sought to undermine their electoral prospects by launching targeted GOTV campaigns on 'democrats'' behalf.

At no point was the desire to sway electoral outcomes in post-Milošević Serbia more clearly underlined than in the run-up to the parliamentary elections of January 2007. Wary of the DOS-successor government's perceived failings, a growing portion of the electorate flirted with abstention. Thus, when in July 2006 an IRI poll 'indicated that widespread apathy...will likely result in a low-turnout election, greatly benefiting the Radical elements in the country', many in the international aid community took note. Within weeks of the poll's release, USAID received signals from their Washington, DC headquarters to gear up for a GOTV campaign. Over the course of the following months, USAID pledged $2 million – funds hitherto withheld due to Serbia's failure to comply with the International Criminal Tribunal for the Former Yugoslavia (ICTY) – for GOTV activities.[58] In the coming months, IRI and NDI launched a campaign capacity building programme linking public opinion research, party communications programming, and direct voter targeting. In December, they co-sponsored a multipronged voter outreach campaign aimed at boosting democratic voter turnout. The party assistance that subsequently commenced was, according to the former Director of Democracy and Governance at USAID's Mission to Belgrade, 'as close to overt political involvement as we've ever come'.[59]

While it is impossible to determine the precise degree to which partisan party aid in fact swayed electoral results in Serbia, it is clear that donors and practitioners are reasonably confident regarding their own achievements. As IRI reported shortly after 2004's presidential elections, 'Democratic turnout out in targeted areas was significantly higher than in past elections'.[60] Indeed, post-election analysis for those elections revealed that Tadić's support nearly doubled in the 1500 polling stations targeted by CeSID. According to IRI, it was thus 'Largely due to [its] voter turnout efforts, [that] DS candidate Boris Tadić defeated Nikolić'.[61] NDI has been similarly confident, arguing that its assistance changed the nature of electoral campaigning in Serbia and 'made the difference in maintaining *democratic* voters at the polls'.[62]

Such findings are no doubt overstated. However impressive voter turnout has proven in recent years, rising voter participation has not always exclusively favoured aid recipients (see Figure 3). In 2007's parliamentary elections, for example, strong voter turnout (61%) failed to dispel the SRS's impressive electoral performance. To the contrary, the forces of the *ancien régime* won close to 40% of the national vote – far more than aid providers predicted. A similar development was witnessed in 2007's presidential race. Despite the unprecedented voter turnout of nearly 70%, Tadić's margin of victory hinged on a mere 107,312 votes. 'Until the 2008 presidential elections', IRI noted, 'the SRS' ability to grow beyond a certain percentage of the electorate was limited', however, 'the 2008 presidential elections proved that a flood of voters participating in the election tended to benefit the SRS at least as much as it did the DS'.[63] Such results suggest that despite aid providers' best efforts, they have had less influence than they suggest.

But even if one assumes that party aid providers were successful and thus that the DS and a host of other aid recipients came to power or remained in power as a

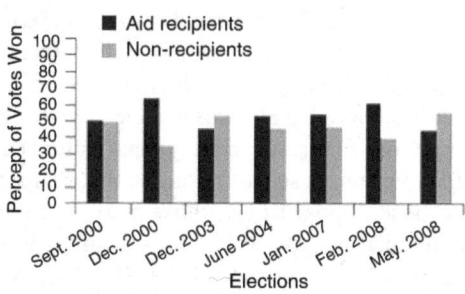

Figure 3. Electoral performance of aid recipients vs. non-recipients.
Source: Author.
Notes: All figures pertain to the total percentage of votes won. September 2000, June 2004, and February 2008 refer to the final rounds of successful presidential elections.

result of foreign aid, it is unclear that this would have worked in democracy's favour. What is clear is that partisan party assistance raises important questions about the integrity of such assistance in democratic contexts – questions that many more established democracies would be reticent to entertain within their own polities. Indeed, when in the late 1990s word spread that the Chinese authorities were covertly financing the US Democratic Party, a national uproar ensued culminating in a series of high-profile Congressional investigations and 22 convictions of fraud.[64] Similarly, when in 2003 allegations surfaced that Swedes and Canadians had funnelled money to Moveon.org in the hopes of undermining the re-election of the Republican Party's presidential nominee, George W. Bush, the group took immediate steps to ban foreign contributions.[65]

Not, of course, that the US is alone in harbouring such misgivings. Just about half of all democracies boast some form of legislation explicitly forbidding foreigners from donating to domestic political parties. Given their potential to influence and thus obstruct the will of the people, such donations are believed to be at odds with the democratic process. In light of its own democratic status, there is little reason to believe that other standards should apply to post-Milošević Serbia.

Exacerbating political polarization

A second consequence of partisan party aid in post-Milošević Serbia has been that of intensifying pre-existing political cleavages. As this section demonstrates, by favouring one set of political parties over another while simultaneously supporting activities that work to the latter's disadvantage, donors have at times aggravated tensions between the two, thereby further deepening political polarization.

Serbia's political system has long suffered from polarization. Fierce disagreements concerning the nature of the regime characterized Serbia's political landscape throughout the 1990s, dividing democrats from anti-democrats and nationalists from anti-nationalists. The nature but not the magnitude of such cleavages changed as Serbia's transition got underway in the early 2000s. Initially, a clear line divided the *ancien régime* from the new, with the former questioning the legitimacy of the October 2000 changes and demanding a reconstitution of the old order. Yet by the mid-2000s, this cleavage was less clear. In its place, new divisions emerged, differentiating those for versus those against European integration, those heralding the free market versus those lambasting it, those supporting cooperation with the ICTY versus those opposed to it, those bearing the mantle of Serbia's saviours versus those derided as national traitors. Until at least 2009 (at which point the SRS had largely disintegrated and the SPS had joined forces with a DS-led government), polarization was widely regarded as amongst the foremost inhibitors of democratic consolidation in Serbia.[66] This was because polarization had shifted the political discourse away from a more nuanced policy discussion and towards the more inflammatory 'pre-political' issues of the day, such as Serbia's so-called 'national question'. According to Pavlović and Antonić, the continued predominance of these cleavages is in fact 'the major reason for the slow consolidation' of democracy in Serbia'.[67]

Despite this, party aid providers deliberately sought to compound such divisions. In seeking to bolster the electoral prospects of Serbia's 'democratic' bloc, practitioners sought to pit the forces of the new regime against those of the old, encouraging aid recipients to accentuate (and arguably, exaggerate) the very differences that have long polarized the political scene. The presumption was is that voters' fear of a radical resurgence would propel 'reformist' voters to the ballot box.[68]

Thus, in the run-up to 2006's parliamentary elections, IRI advised aid recipients to 'focus on the Radicals and Nikolić', since 'campaigning that targets the SRS makes 'reform' minded voters more likely to participate' come election day.[69] Similarly, when polls showed public support for Nikolić exceeding that of Tadić in the run-up to 2008's presidential elections, IRI advised Tadić to launch a number of hard-hitting commercials featuring footage of Šešelj and Nikolić making incendiary remarks. Such messages, IRI explained, should be designed to remind Serbia's voters 'who Nikolić actually is and what his real politics are'.[70] Likewise, in parliamentary elections held several months later, IRI encouraged members of the 'For a European Serbia' (ZES) coalition to distinguish their own pro-EU platform from those of their opponents, whom, IRI warned, 'paid lip service to the [EU] but would not be able to lead Serbia towards Europe'.[71] To this end, the Institute advocated yet another series of contrast ads featuring SRS candidates condemning European integration. Such ads, IRI noted, would force 'voters to re-evaluate which political options were truly open to EU integration'.[72]

Polarization has been further augmented by donors' advocacy of coalition formation. Despite their acknowledgment that 'voters sympathetic to reformist parties increasingly complain that it is unclear to them what any of the parties believe in, or how any of the parties differ from one another'[73] party aid providers have been strong advocates of electoral alliances such as ZES, believing they are better posited to challenge the SRS. In so doing, however, aid providers have encouraged aid recipients to focus exclusively on the ties that bind them – in ZES' case, members' support for EU integration – while playing down their own programmatic differences. ZES thus united parties as ideologically disparate as Vuk Drašković's Serbian Renewal Movement and Mladjan Dinkić's G17 Plus – the former an advocate of the restoration of the Serbian monarchy, and the latter a staunch opponent thereof. However strategically auspicious such advice is it still contradicts party aid providers' self-stated goals of enabling partner parties 'to develop and communicate clear, coherent platforms that…are uniquely and ideologically identifiable'.[74] Indeed, today's parties are no more ideologically defined or programmatically distinct than they were at the outset of transition.[75] Surely, the formation of coalitions such as ZES does little to offset this.

Increased suspicions of aid recipients

A third consequence of partisanship in party aid has been an inadvertent one. Because aid providers support some – but not all – of Serbia's parties, those falling under the rubric of aid recipients have made themselves vulnerable to charges of divided loyalties. Such charges have the potential to erode public confidence in recipient parties.

This was certainly Milošević's line of thinking throughout much of the 1990s, during which he decried Serbia's democratic opposition as mercenaries and traitors. Indeed, many suspect Milošević's electoral loss in October 2000 to have come, at least in part, as a consequence of Koštunica's perceived 'untaintedness' by foreign aid. In fact, Koštunica condemned the foreign aid community for doing more harm than good in Serbia and publicly denied having received external assistance. Ironically, it was his ability to distance himself from foreign aid that ultimately made Koštunica the ideal DOS front man.

Post-Milošević, aid recipients' close relations to the international community –namely, the US and countries of the EU – have proven no less contentious. In a country that still flaunts the scars of bombing by North Atlantic Treaty Organisation (NATO) forces, suspicions regarding the international community's intentions towards Serbia are particularly acute. A 2008 survey conducted by CeSID found that 47% of respondents believed 'the new world order wants to turn [Serbia] into a colony' and a further 55% believed 'the world and Europe do not let us remain 'ourselves on our own'.[76] Parties have proven enormously sensitive to such fears, wishing to avoid any appearance of indiscretion.

Not surprisingly, the SRS was quick to assume the mantle of Serbia's solely 'independent' party. Noted one SRS member, 'other parties will do anything, make any alliance, just to work against the SRS because this is a dictate from the West. Western countries spent so much money in order to have October 5, 2000 occur. They have their marionettes here. We don't want to be marionettes.'[77] Such accusations clearly resonate with many Serbian voters. Until 2009, polling data regularly showed party aid recipients to suffer from higher unfavourable ratings than their SRS counterpart, with the SRS widely perceived as amongst the least corrupted of Serbia's parties and Nikolić as amongst the most trusted of the country's politicians.[78] Although this cannot solely – or even mostly – be attributed to partisanship in party aid, the fact that donors selectively target their assistance has emboldened aid's non-recipients and added further credence to their claims of 'independence'.

Creating dependencies amongst party aid recipients

As the American party institutes, and to a lesser extent, the European party foundations, have worked to bolster Serbian aid recipients' electoral prospects, they have more than merely aided parties in their electoral campaigns – they have actually done the work for them. This, in turn, has fostered relationships of dependency that raise questions as to parties' electoral capacities once aid providers cease operations in Serbia.

No doubt the most questionable of such activities has been conducted by NDI. In the run-up to elections from 2004 onwards, the Institute commissioned CeSID to do what parties in every democratic polity are expected to do on their own: bring out their voters. NDI not only instructed CeSID to target only reform-oriented voters, but it *paid* CeSID 'volunteers' to go door-to-door on partner parties' behalf. In June 2004 paid 'volunteers' visited some 35,000 homes where tentative supporters of Boris Tadić were thought to reside.

The direct electoral involvement of NGOs such as CeSID has meant that party aid recipients have not relied solely on their own resources to bring out their own vote: Institute-paid 'volunteers' have done it for them. Ostensibly nonpartisan, NGOs have worked actively on behalf of party aid recipients: targeting their voters while avoiding those areas and individuals deemed loyal to recipients' opponents. Such activities have raised concerns even amongst party aid providers. In its own evaluation of the 2004 GOTV effort, IRI noted that despite its success 'IRI has some concerns about the manner in which the campaign was designed and implemented and about the viability of such efforts in the future'.[79] In a memo sent to the US Embassy, IRI reiterated its conviction that parties – not NGOs – 'are the most appropriate and effective vehicles for GOTV' given that they have 'an immediate self-interest in getting out the vote, making parties much more likely to mobilize and commit the resources to sustain GOTV in the long-term'.[80]

Particularly worrying for IRI was CeSID's reluctance to partake in door-to-door efforts without financial enticement. CeSID, IRI explained, 'admitted they would not have been able to mobilize enough activists to carry out that portion of the programme had IRI and the other implementers not agreed to pay CeSID's door-to-door activists a stipend'.[81] Future assistance, IRI pleaded, should thus 'be directed at enhancing the capacity of political parties...to conduct GOTV utilizing their own resources, to ensure the sustainability of GOTV long after international donors depart Serbia'.[82] Despite such concerns, however, IRI's complaints went unheeded. Over the course of the following five years, CeSID was paid to do what parties should otherwise do for themselves.

Conclusion

As the dust settled following Milošević's overthrow in October 2000, foreign aid donors working in Serbia were faced with a stark choice: to work with the representatives of the *ancien régime* or to continue a policy of the isolating them. As they did throughout much of the post-communist world, donors opted for the latter. This account has argued that it is not, however, entirely clear that partisanship was the strategy best suited to meet the evolving challenges confronting a newly democratic Serbia. Whereas democratic ends undoubtedly necessitated partisan means in the run-up to Milošević's overthrow, little evidence suggests that a similar trade-off was necessary, let alone beneficial, in the period that followed. To the contrary, partisanship in a democratic context has encouraged party aid providers to veer into the dubious terrain of electoral meddling. It has encouraged advice that further exacerbates political polarization. And it has fostered dependencies that undermine the sustainability of current electoral practices. The Serbian case suggests that partisanship in party aid is not only undesirable in newly democratic settings, but that it may ultimately undermine the nascent democratic processes that emerge in the aftermath of electoral revolution.

Such findings are troubling for several reasons. Most importantly, the Serbian case suggests that donors are slow to respond to evolving political dynamics that effectively reshape the political landscape. In Serbian post-regime change, there was a clear tendency on the part of party aid providers to view political developments through the same polarized lens that served so well under Milošević. Rather than seek to identify and address contemporary impediments to democracy, they sought to ensure that those of the past did not resurface. Thus, many of the same (now passé) dichotomies which once marred Serbia's democratic transition – anti-democrat vs. democrat, nationalist vs. anti-nationalist, pro-European vs. anti-European – continued to dictate a strategy of partisanship, despite the fact that such lines had long since blurred.

Yet the Serbian case suggests not only that party providers may fail to acknowledge an evolving political landscape, but that even when they do, they may have little incentive to adapt their strategies accordingly. Indeed, in the early 2000s voices warning of a possible nationalist upturn were repeatedly stifled amidst the initial post-Milošević euphoria. Recalls a former officer of the US Embassy in Serbia, his insistence that 'we take the Radical Party seriously' in early 2001 was repeatedly dismissed: 'people laughed at me, because the Radicals and Socialists were gone'.[83] Michael Weichert of the FES, agrees. He admits that the Stiftungen 'didn't care very much' about deciphering the rising support for Serbia's nationalist parties: 'we just labelled the other side as "non-democratic", as if this was the "other side", the "dark side".... Somehow it was not even a thought to consider, let alone even to debate, about the other side.'[84] But when in 2004 the SRS became the largest party in parliament, party aid providers were forced to confront an uncomfortable reality: 'you realized that you had somehow overlooked something, that the other side is not just the darkness, not just the security forces, the military, or the gray sector – no, they are people who are frustrated, without any orientation, who feel lost in the process'. And yet despite this realization, party aid providers responded not by recalibrating their relationship to the *ancien régime*, but by hardening their opposition to it. As they did, they crossed the line into electoral meddling, the benefits of which are still far from certain.

Notes

1. Acronyms frequently employed throughout this contribution include: CeSID – Center for the Free Elections and Democracy; DOS – Democratic Opposition of Serbia; DS – Democratic Party; DSS – Democratic Party of Serbia, FES – Friedrich Ebert Stiftung; GOTV – Get Out the Vote; IRI – International Republican Institute; KAS – Konrad Adenauer Stiftung; NDI – National Democratic Institute; NGO – non-governmental organization; SNS – Serbian Progressive Party; SPS – Socialist Party of Serbia; SRS – Serbian Radical Party; ZES – For a European Serbia.
2. C.f. Bunce and Wolchik, 'Favourable Conditions and Electoral Revolutions', 12–14; Carothers, 'Ousting Foreign Strongmen', 1–7; Kuzio, 'Civil Society, Youth and Societal Mobilization in Democratic Revolutions, 365–86.
3. Kumar, 'Reflections on International Political Party Assistance', 506.
4. Burnell, *Building Better Democracy: Why Parties Matter*, 6–8.
5. C.f. Lipset, 'The Indispensability of Political Parties', 48–55; Schmitter, 'Twenty-Five Years, Fifteen Findings', 23–24.
6. Carothers, *Confronting the Weakest Link*, 3–20.
7. Ibid., 142.
8. USAID, *USAID Policy Paper: Democracy and Governance*, Section III, 12–13.
9. NIMD, *NIMD: Partner in Democracy*, 1.
10. As quoted by WFD Chief Executive David French in: WFD, *Annual Review 2002/3*, 5.
11. Author's interview with FES representative, conducted on 10 May 2007 in Berlin, Germany.
12. Weissenbach, 'Political Party Assistance in Transition: The German '*Stiftungen*' in Sub-Saharan Africa'.
13. Author's interview with former FES Director for Serbia, conducted on 22 September 2009 (phone).
14. NDI, *A Guide to Political Party Development*, 19.
15. NDI, *Minimum Standards for Democratic Functioning of Political Parties*, 12.
16. Interview with USAID officer in Washington, DC conducted on 12 April 2007.
17. Interview with US State Department officer in Washington, DC conducted on 20 April 2007.
18. There are exceptions to this rule. The Alfred Mozer Stichting, for example, worked with communist successor parties in Poland and Hungary almost immediately after regime change.
19. Carothers, *Confronting the Weakest Link*, 153–6.
20. Please refer also to the studies by Hulsey ('"Why Did They Vote for Those Guys Again?"') and Nenadović ('An Uneasy Symbiosis') in this collection. There are, however, exceptions to this rule. In Kosovo, for example, party aid providers have worked freely with the Alliance for the Future of Kosovo, despite the party's strong links to the Kosovo Liberation Army.
21. Kumar, 'Reflections on International Political Party Assistance', 520.
22. Burnell, *Building Better Democracy: Why Parties Matter*, 11.
23. Such documents include the Quarterly Reports, Annual Workplans, and grant agreements issued by NDI and IRI to their chief donor, USAID. Such data was obtained primarily through the US Freedom of Information Act.

24. Levitsky and Way, 'Elections without Democracy: The Rise of Competitive Authoritarianism'. For more on Serbia, see also: Gordy, *The Culture of Power in Serbia*; Thomas, *The Politics of Serbia in the 1990s*; Bieber, 'The Serbian Opposition and Civil Society: Roots of the Delayed Transition in Serbia'; Batt, 'The Question of Serbia'.
25. By 2001, Freedom House had labelled Serbia an electoral democracy (Freedom House, 2003). By 2009, Serbia was considered 'free' according to Freedom House's Freedom in the World Survey.
26. This is in spite of the fact that both Slobodan Milošević and Vojislav Šešelj were extradited to The Hague in 2001 and 2003, respectively, on charges of war crimes.
27. William Montgomery, 'Let's Stop Talking about a Democratic Block in Serbia', *b92*, 21 May 2007, http://www6.b92.net/eng/news/in_focus.php?id=152&start=0&nav_id=41324 (accessed October 21, 2010).
28. The speed of Nikolić's concession is all the more surprising when one takes into account the close nature of 2008's electoral contest. Nikolić lost by just two percentage points, after having won the first round of presidential elections held several weeks earlier. By contrast, it took Ukraine's Yulia Tymoshenko six days to concede her defeat to Victor Yanukovych after it was determined that she had lost 2010's presidential race by more than three percentage points.
29. In my interviews from 2007 onwards, many practitioners privately confided their own doubts concerning the partisan approach to party aid. Yet all felt powerless to bring about a change in policy, citing the issue as being 'above one's pay-grade'. In fact, the decision seems to have been largely driven by the US Embassy, with Ambassador Polt barring all American engagements with SRS and SPS officials. For more on this, please refer to: Spoerri, 'US Policy Towards Ultranationalist Political Parties in Serbia: The Policy of Non-Engagement Examined'.
30. The party aid community made several initial ventures into Serbia during the very early 1990s. Given, however, that Yugoslavia was then embroiled in a violent civil war, no large-scale assistance programs were developed until the second half of the decade.
31. Regime change is understood here to mean the transfer for rule from one form of government to another, in this case from semi-authoritarian to electoral democratic rule. Though in Serbia's case regime change has been treated synonymously with Milošević's ouster, in fact, regime change need not require the unseating of a given leader, but rather the unseating of a given form of government.
32. Author's interview with Thomas C. Adams, Coordinator of US Assistance to Europe and Eurasia, conducted on 19 April 2007 in Washington, DC.
33. Author's interview with former FES Director of Serbia, opting to remain anonymous, conducted 22 September 2009.
34. C.f. Carothers, 'Ousting Foreign Strongmen'; Bunce and Wolchik, 'Favourable Conditions and Electoral Revolutions'; Birch, 'The 2000 Elections in Yugoslavia: The 'Bulldozer Revolution''; Schoen, *The Power of the Vote*.
35. In the aftermath of the political change the distributors of US aid credited their assistance for having played a 'key role' in this by providing Serbia's citizens 'the tools [they] needed to liberate themselves' (SEED, *SEED Act Implementation Report Fiscal Year 2000*, 1, 149). Similarly, the Office of Transition Initiative (OTI) identified its assistance as one of but three factors accounting for the 'surprising and extraordinary defeat of Milošević (OTI, *Final Evaluation of OTI's Program in Serbia-Montenegro*, 2). Scholars have offered similar, if less hyperbolic, praise of the foreign aid effort. C.f. McFaul, *The National Endowment for Democracy's Program in Serbia Surrounding the Breakthrough Elections of 2000*; Carothers, 'Ousting Foreign Strongmen'; Bunce and Wolchik, 'Favourable Conditions and Electoral Revolutions'; Birch, 'The 2000 Elections in Yugoslavia: The 'Bulldozer Revolution'.

36. Author's interview with Michael Weichert, former FES Director Serbia, conducted on 22 September 2009 (phone). This enthusiasm is also reflected in: FES, *10 Godina u Srbiji*.
37. Author's interview with Robert Benjamin, NDI Director of Central and Eastern Europe, conducted on 19 April 2007 in Washington, DC.
38. Ibid.
39. Ibid.
40. In the months leading up to December 2003's elections, NDI reported that the 'parties of the Milošević regime are clearly on the wane' (NDI, *Quarterly Report April–June 2003*). The SPS, it predicted, would fail to pass the electoral threshold, while its ultra-nationalist counterpart, the SRS, was 'losing support' (NDI, *Quarterly Report April–June 2003*).
41. As one party aid practitioner remarked, DOS 'parties fell victim to a phenomenon you've seen just about everywhere in Central and Eastern Europe and the former Soviet Union, which is to say that expectations were higher than they could deliver once they were in government'. Author's interview with former IRI Serbia Resident Director, 6 April 2008 in Washington, DC.
42. If in 2003 for every $1 spent on economic development, $2.2 was spent on democratic development; by 2006 those numbers were reversed: for every $1 spent on democracy, $2.5 was dedicated to the economy.
43. This is evident in NDI and IRI Quarterly Reports, the evaluations of the Stiftungen, as well as the author's conversations with party aid practitioners.
44. In semi-presidential systems such as Serbia's, party aid is frequently directed both at political parties as well as presidential candidates, who, more often than not, are political party leaders. By virtue of these candidates' close affiliation with their respective parties, party aid to presidential candidates often directly influences parties themselves. Party members are not only the beneficiaries of their presidential candidates' success, but are directly involved in their campaigns – mounting GOTV efforts, providing the necessary electoral infrastructure, and bearing the financial burden.
45. NDI, *Serbia: Demographic Analysis for Voter Targeting*.
46. NDI, *Quarterly Report April–June 2004*.
47. IRI, *Quarterly Report April–June 2004*.
48. Ibid.
49. This was confirmed in interviews with US aid providers and political party aid practitioners. As one party aid practitioner commented, 'The "surge" for SRS was more apparent than real, when viewed from this perspective. Voters were seldom persuaded to switch from ex-DOS parties to SRS or SPS. However, voters did move in quite large numbers into and out of abstention.' Author's interview with former party aid practitioner (by email), 16 March 2009.
50. Author's interview with former NDI Resident Director of Serbia (by email), 16 March 2009. This point was also reiterated in NDI's evaluation of its NED-sponsored 'Demographic Analysis for Voter Targeting' project. In its words, 'since turnout among democratic voters wavers more than support for the nationalist parties, targeting practices that address absenteeism provide a fundamental advantage for the democratic parties' (NDI, *Serbia: Demographic Analysis for Voter Targeting*).
51. Author's interview with former party aid practitioner (by email), 16 March 2009.
52. IRI *Quarterly Report July–September 2004*, emphasis added.
53. IRI *Quarterly Report January–March 2004*, emphasis added.
54. Author's interview with Ana Manojlović, FES Programme Coordinator for Serbia, conducted on 6 March 2007 in Belgrade.
55. IRI *Quarterly Report January–March 2006* and NDI, *Workplan – Country: Serbia June 1, 2004–May 31, 2005*. In its annual work plan for 2004–2005, NDI pledged

to concentrate on the following three areas: 'assisting democratic political parties in contesting presidential, municipal and possible early parliamentary elections, *striving to stem the tide of radical political support*, while bolstering democratic forces before and after elections (NDI, *Workplan – Country: Serbia June 1, 2004–May 31, 2005*, emphasis added).

56. Tom Kelly, as quoted in: NDI, 'Review of Parliamentary Elections in Serbia', 2.
57. Bussey, 'Campaign Finance Goes Global', 75.
58. IRI, *Quarterly Report July–September 2006 Serbia*; see also NDI, *Quarterly Report October–December 2006*.
59. Author's interview with former Director of Democracy and Governance, USAID Serbia, conducted on 2 March 2007, in Belgrade, Serbia.
60. IRI, *Quarterly Report April–June 2004*.
61. IRI, Associate Award No. 169-A-00-06-00103-00, 24.
62. NDI, *Workplan – Country: Serbia June 1, 2006–May 31, 2007*.
63. IRI, *Quarterly Report April–June 2008*.
64. C.f. Bob Woodward, 'Findings Link Clinton Allies to Chinese Intelligence', *Washington Post*, February 10, 1998, A01.
65. Moveon.org now lists US citizenship or US permanent residency as a requirement for all donations. See: https://pol.moveon.org/donate/email.html (accessed October 21, 2010).
66. Goati, *Partije i Partijski Sistemi u Srbiji*, 182–4; Pavlović and Antonić, *Konsolidacija Demokratskih Ustanova u Srbiji Posle 2000 Godine*, 275; Orlović, *Politićki život Srbije*, 402–3; Stojiljković, *Partijkski Sistem Srbije*.
67. Pavlović and Antonić, *Konsolidacija Demokratskih Ustanova u Srbiji Posle 2000 Godine*, 279.
68. This was confirmed in interviews with US party aid practitioners.
69. IRI, *Serbia June 2006*, 60.
70. IRI, *Quarterly Report January–March 2008*.
71. IRI, *Quarterly Report April–June 2008*.
72. Ibid.
73. USAID, Letter to Mr Craner Associate Award No. 169-A-00-06-00103-00.
74. IRI, *Quarterly Report January–March 2007*.
75. C.f. Djurković, *Srbija 2000–2006*, 55.
76. The public opinion poll, conducted on 13–20 April 2008, included 2732 respondents. CeSID, *Public Opinion Survey*, 12.
77. Author's interview with SRS member wishing to remain anonymous, conducted on 15 March 2007 in Belgrade.
78. C.f. CeSID, *Public Opinion Survey*; and IRI, *Serbia June 2006*.
79. IRI, *Quarterly Report April–June 2004*.
80. Ibid.
81. Ibid.
82. Ibid.
83. Author's interview with former officer of the US Embassy Belgrade conducted on 25 April 2009.
84. Author's interview with Michael Weichert, former FES Director of Serbia, conducted 22 September 2009.

Bibliography

Batt, Judy. 'The Question of Serbia', *Chaillot Paper No. 81*. Paris: Institute for Security Studies, 2005.
Bieber, Florian. 'The Serbian Opposition and Civil Society: Roots of the Delayed Transition in Serbia'. *Journal of Politics, Culture, and Society* 17, no. 2 (2003): 73–90.
Birch, Sarah. 'The 2000 Elections in Yugoslavia: The 'Bulldozer Revolution''. *Electoral Studies* 21, no. 3 (2002): 499–511.
Bunce, Valerie, and Sharon Wolchik. 'Favourable Conditions and Electoral Revolutions'. *Journal of Democracy* 17, no. 4 (2006): 5–18.
Burnell, Peter. *Building Better Democracy: Why Parties Matter*. London: Westminster Foundation for Democracy, 2004.
Bussey, Jane. 'Campaign Finance Goes Global'. *Foreign Affairs* 118 (2000): 74–84.
Carothers, Thomas. *Confronting the Weakest Link: Aiding Political Parties in New Democracies*. Washington, DC: Carnegie Endowment for International Peace, 2007.
Carothers, Thomas. 'Ousting Foreign Strongmen: Lessons from Serbia'. *Carnegie Endowment for International Peace* 1, no. 5 (2001): 1–7.
CeSID. *Public Opinion Survey*. Belgrade: CeSID, April 2008.
Djurković, Miša. *Srbija 2000–2006: Država, Društvo, Privreda*. Belgrade: Institute for European Studies, 2007.
FES. *10 Godina u Srbiji*. Belgrade: Friedrich Ebert Stiftung, 2007.
Freedom House. 'Yugoslavia (Serbia and Montenegro)', in *Freedom in the World 2002*. Washington, DC: Freedom House, 2003.
Freedom House. 'Serbia', in *Freedom in the World 2009*. Washington, DC: Freedom House, 2010.
Goati, V. *Partije I Partijski Sistemi u Srbiji*. Belgrade: Ogi Centar, 2004.
Gordy, Eric. *The Culture of Power in Serbia: Nationalism and the Destruction of Alternatives*. Pennsylvania: University of Pennsylvania, 1999.
Hulsey, John W. "Why did they vote for those guys again?' Challenges and contradictions in the promotion of political moderation in post-war Bosnia and Herzegovina'. *Democratization* 17, no. 6 (December 2010): 1132–52.
IRI. Associate Award No. 169-A-00-06-00103-00, May 31, 2006.
IRI. *Quarterly Report January–March 2004 Serbia*. Washington, DC: IRI, 2004.
IRI. *Quarterly Report April–June 2004 Serbia*. Washington, DC: IRI, 2004.
IRI. *Quarterly Report July–September 2004 Serbia*. Washington, DC: IRI, 2004.
IRI. *Quarterly Report January–March 2006 Serbia*. Washington, DC: IRI, 2006.
IRI. *Quarterly Report July–September 2006 Serbia*. Washington, DC: IRI, 2006.
IRI. *Quarterly Report January–March 2007 Serbia*. Washington, DC: IRI, 2007.
IRI. *Quarterly Report January–March 2008 Serbia*. Washington, DC: IRI, 2008.
IRI. *Quarterly Report April–June 2008 Serbia*. Washington, DC: IRI, 2008.
IRI. *Serbia June 2006*. Salem: Williams and Associates Opinion Research and Consulting, 2006.
Kumar, Krishna. 'Reflections on International Political Party Assistance'. *Democratization* 12, no. 4 (2005): 505–27.
Kuzio, Taras. 'Civil Society, Youth and Societal Mobilization in Democratic Revolutions'. *Communist and Post-Communist Studies* 39 (2006): 365–86.
Levitsky, Steven, and Lucan Way. 'Elections without Democracy: The Rise of Competitive Authoritarianism'. *Journal of Democracy* 13, no. 2 (2002): 51–65.
Lipset, Seymour Martin. 'The Indispensability of Political Parties'. *Journal of Democracy* 11, no. 1 (2000): 48–55.
McFaul, Michael. *The National Endowment for Democracy's Program in Serbia Surrounding the Breakthrough Elections of 2000*. Washington, DC: National Endowment for Democracy, 2006.

NDI. *A Guide to Political Party Development*. Washington, DC: NDI, 2008.
NDI. *Minimum Standards for Democratic Functioning of Political Parties*. Washington, DC: NDI, 2008.
NDI. *Quarterly Report April–June 2003 – Serbia: Political Party Building and Civil Society*. Washington, DC: NDI, 2003.
NDI. *Quarterly Report April–June 2004 – Serbia: Political Party Building and Civil Society Development*. Washington, DC: NDI, 2004.
NDI. *Quarterly Report October–December 2006 – Serbia: Political Party Building and Civil Society Development*. Washington, DC: NDI, 2006.
NDI. *Review of Parliamentary Elections in Serbia*, May 15, 2008.
NDI. *Serbia: Demographic Analysis for Voter Targeting – Final Report, NED Core Grant 2004-036 (04029)*. Washington, DC: NDI, March 2006.
NDI. *Workplan – Country: Serbia June 1, 2004–May 31, 2005*. Washington, DC: NDI, 2004.
NDI. *Workplan – Country: Serbia June 1, 2006–May 31, 2007*. Washington, DC: NDI, 2006.
Nenadović, Maja. 'An uneasy symbiosis: The impact of international administrations on political parties in post-conflict countries'. *Democratization* 17, no. 6 (December 2010): 1153–75.
NIMD. *NIMD: Partner in Democracy*. The Hague: NIMD, 2008.
Orlović, Slaviša. *Politički Život Srbije: Između Partokratije i Demokratije*. Belgrade: Glasnik, 2008.
OTI. *Final Evaluation of OTI's Program in Serbia-Montenegro*. Arlington, VA: Development Associates, 2002.
Pavlović, Dušan, and Slobodan Antonić. *Konsolidacija Demokratskih Ustanova u Srbiji Posle 2000 Godine*. Belgrade: Službeni Glasnik, 2007.
Schmitter, Philippe C. 'Twenty-Five Years, Fifteen Findings'. *Journal of Democracy* 21, no. 1 (2010): 17–28.
Schoen, Douglas. *The Power of the Vote: Electing Presidents, Overthrowing Dictators, and Promoting Democracy Around the World*. New York: William Morrow, 2007.
SEED. *SEED Act Implementation Report Fiscal Year 2000*. Washington, DC: Department of State, March 2001.
Spoerri, Marlene. 'US Policy Towards Ultranationalist Political Parties in Serbia: The Policy of Non-Engagement Examined'. *CEU Political Science Journal*, no. 1 (2008): 25–48.
Stojiljković, Zoran. *Partijski Sistem Srbije*. Belgrade: Glasnik, 2006.
Thomas, Robert. *The Politics of Serbia in the 1990s*. New York: Columbia University Press, 1999.
USAID. *USAID Policy Paper: Democracy and Governance*, Section III: Objective and Scope of the Democracy Initiative, Handbook 1. Washington, DC: US Agency for International Development, 1991.
Weissenbach, Kristina. 'Political party assistance in transition: The German '*Stiftungen*' in sub-Saharan Africa'. *Democratization* 17, no. 6 (December 2010): 1125–49.
WFD. *Annual Review 2002/3*. London: WFD, 2003.

'Why did they vote for those guys again?' Challenges and contradictions in the promotion of political moderation in post-war Bosnia and Herzegovina

John W. Hulsey

Department of Political Science, James Madison University, Harrisonburg, VA, USA

> Party assistance in Bosnia and Herzegovina has focused on encouraging multi-ethnic and moderate mono-ethnic parties by placing funding and political restrictions on ethnonationalist parties while providing technical assistance and public support to those parties with less nationalist agendas. However, multi-ethnic parties have met with very limited electoral success and moderate mono-ethnic parties have found electoral success primarily by radicalizing their political discourse to match that of nationalist parties. This study provides evidence for the effect of international intervention drawn from patterns of electoral support for multi-ethnic and moderate mono-ethnic parties in canton, entity and national elections from the 2006 general elections in Bosnia and Herzegovina. The analysis shows that even voters who are predisposed to vote for multi-ethnic parties are much less likely to choose non-nationalist parties in elections where parties representing other ethnicities also compete. As a result, there is a clear trade-off between promoting Bosnia's integration and promoting parties and candidates who refrain from using often incendiary nationalist rhetoric.

Introduction

Bosnia and Herzegovina is now a classic case of party politics gone wrong. The first multiparty elections in Bosnia and Herzegovina[1] in 1990 resulted in the election of nationalist parties[2] who were among the protagonists in Bosnia's bloody war. Since the cessation of armed hostility in 1995, Bosnia and Herzegovina has been the target of intensive international intervention aimed at preventing a return to violence and normalizing (de-nationalizing) politics. Recently, the focus of intervention has shifted toward preparing Bosnia for the European Union (EU) accession process, with the possibility of changing Bosnia's consociational political system. A key goal of international intervention has been to foster the emergence of a significant non-nationalist alternative in Bosnian electoral politics. This study discusses the failure to reach that goal and examines the impact of Bosnia's constitutional structure on voter behaviour. International intervention plays a key role in shaping party politics in Bosnia and Herzegovina through the implementation of the electoral system included in the 1995 Dayton Peace Agreement and through active intervention against nationalist parties and on behalf of non-nationalist parties. These efforts have met with limited results because of the continued electoral salience of nationalist claims, but there is some evidence that the poor performance of non-nationalist parties is, in part, due to the effects on voter behaviour of Bosnia's constitutional and electoral arrangements.

This investigation examines evidence from voting patterns across various levels of Bosnian elections in order to gauge the degree to which elections based on ethnicity help or hinder the performance of moderate, non-nationalist parties at the expense of ethnonationalist parties. The results show that the ethnopolitical context of elections in Bosnia and Herzegovina has a substantial effect on voters' support for non-nationalist parties. Even voters who vote for non-nationalist parties in other elections will choose nationalist parties in electoral contexts that include an element of competition with other ethnic groups. This conclusion casts doubt on the possibility of simultaneously achieving two of the goals of international intervention in Bosnia and Herzegovina: the creation of a politically united Bosnia and the promotion of non-nationalist parties.

The account engages scholarly debates regarding the appropriateness of consociational political systems for promoting stability in deeply-divided societies, through a sophisticated examination of the impact on voting behaviour of mono-ethnic and multi-ethnic electoral constituencies. Consociational political systems seek to defuse ethnically-charged political environments by ensuring broad representation and creating institutional configurations that force power-sharing and require elites to govern by consensus. Stability is achieved by providing political security to voters and leaders of each ethnic group in the form of veto rights, a proportion of government positions, and the devolution of state competencies to ethnically homogenous federal sub-units.[3] The primary criticism of consociationalism argues that in ascribing rights to ethnic groups or parties it codifies and institutionalizes ethnic categories present at the time that the institutions are created, thereby reifying their political salience and discouraging the emergence of alternative dimensions of politics of multi-ethnic parties.[4] Some explanations of poor support for multi-ethnic parties in Bosnia and Herzegovina blame consociational aspects of Bosnia's system, particularly elected offices set aside for members of specific ethnic groups.[5] The analysis presented below shows the situation to be more complex in that mono-ethnic constituencies carved out by Bosnia's consociational system show greater support for multi-ethnic parties. While the long-term effect of consociationalism may be to solidify the role of ethnicity in politics, in Bosnia today the presence of ethnically homogenous electoral contexts is creating space for less nationalist parties.[6]

Finally, the study examines the effects of international intervention on party system development, with an emphasis on the effects of the internationally-imposed electoral system[7] on the performance of the Social Democratic Party of Bosnia and Herzegovina (SDP) and other non-nationalist parties. The core of the analysis is an exploration of the degree to which Bosnia's electoral system is influencing the success of non-nationalist parties. This is related to the deeper question of the potential support for non-nationalist or multi-ethnic politics in Bosnia given its recent experience with extreme ethnic violence. Taken as a whole, the performance of non-nationalist parties indicates that there is very little support for a move away from ethnonationalist politics in Bosnia and Herzegovina. In light of recent calls for changes in Bosnia's constitution,[8] the analysis seeks to evaluate the effects of Bosnia's current electoral system on voting behaviour. To do this, it compares the performance of the non-nationalist parties across election races within the same election. On a single ballot, voters are faced with elections that vary significantly in their nationalist context, creating a natural experiment that demonstrates the impact of those contexts on voter behaviour. The account proceeds by introducing Bosnia's constitutional structure and party system, developing hypotheses on the effect of different electoral contexts on non-nationalist voting behaviour, and testing the effect of electoral contexts by comparing the performance of non-nationalist parties across electoral contexts in the Federation of Bosnia and Herzegovina.

Party competition in Bosnia and Herzegovina

Party systems reflect political competition shaped by the interaction between cleavages in society and formal constitutional rules. The most visible cleavages in Bosnian society since the first multiparty elections are based on ethnicity, and the violence that followed the first multiparty elections in 1990 indicates the depth of ethnicity-based cleavages while reinforcing those same cleavages. Being a Bosniak (Bosnian Muslim), Croat or Serb clearly has political meaning in Bosnia, but ethnicity is not the only relevant dimension of political competition. There is a significant ideological divide between nationalist and non-nationalist parties, as well as region-based cleavages distinct from ethnicity that have been weakened but not made irrelevant by ethnic cleansing and other population transfers accompanying and following the war and subsequent political division of Bosnia. However, in the electoral arena, these regional and ideological dimensions have largely been subsumed into the ethnonationalist party system.

Since the war, only one multi-ethnic party has enjoyed significant electoral success, the Social Democratic Party (SDP).[9] The SDP incorporates Titoist symbols and arguments in its campaigns, pushing an explicitly anti-nationalist agenda. The SDP grew out of the non-nationalist bloc of parties that contested Bosnia's first multiparty elections, which resulted in victories for the nationalist parties (SDA, SDS, HDZ) that became chief protagonists in the Bosnian war.[10] The SDP's greatest success resulted from a modest increase in electoral support during the 2000 parliamentary elections. In order to exclude the wartime nationalist parties from government, international organizations put pressure on the more moderate ethnic parties to form coalitions with the SDP, which had also received direct electoral support, in forming state and entity level governments.[11] SDP leader Zlatko Lagumdžija served as chairman of the council of ministers, a position equivalent to prime minister in a presidential system. The resulting 'Alliance for Change' was unstable and is widely viewed as a failure.[12] The 2002 general elections saw a reversal for the members of the 'Alliance for Change', and particularly for the SDP.

In the 2006 elections for the Croat member of the three-member, state-level presidency, the SDP candidate, Željko Komšić was elected, but his means of election is controversial and open to interpretation. What is clear is that a significant number of Bosniak voters chose to vote for Komšić in the race for the Croat member of the presidency rather than vote in the race for the Bosniak member. These cross-over voters, combined with a split between moderate and more extreme Bosnian Croat nationalist parties, resulted in a narrow victory for Komšić. How one interprets that victory depends on what one reads into the intentions of those Bosniak voters, specifically, whether they sought to weaken the Croat side by electing a non-nationalist or wished to see a non-nationalist elected regardless of nationality.[13] Beyond this aberration, the SDP's success has been limited to Bosniak voters and particularly Bosniak voters in larger cities as well as in the Tuzla Canton. The SDP's ideology is strongly multi-ethnic, but they have made few inroads in Croat or Serb-dominated areas.

Leaving aside the SDP and other multi-ethnic parties, the Bosnian party system is best viewed as three separate party systems, one for each ethnicity (see Table 1). In each, the nationalist party that won the pre-war elections continued in power through the initial post-war elections. The Serbian Democratic Party (SDS), Party for Democratic Action (SDA), and the Croatian Democratic Union (HDZ) were the dominant parties among Serbs, Bosniaks and Croats, respectively. Early elections were characterized by a lack of political competition within ethnic groups and intense competition between groups, which is to be expected in the immediate post-war period. With international intervention, changes in the

Table 1. Bosnia's party system(s).

	Bosniak (Bosnian Muslim)	Croat	Serb
Wartime Ethnic Party (initially more nationalist)	SDA	HDZ	SDS
Challenger Ethnic Party (initially less nationalist)	SBiH	HDZ-1990	SNSD
Multi-ethnic/Non-nationalist	SDP, NSRzB, LDS		

Source: Adapted from the classification in Pugh and Cobble, 'Non-Nationalist Voting'.
Notes: In contrast to Pugh and Cobble, SNSD has been categorized as Serb Nationalist in order to reflect the change in its rhetoric since 2000. HDZ 1990, NSRzB and LDS each emerged after 2000 and have been categorized by the author.

political scene in Croatia and Serbia (chiefly the death of Franjo Tuđman in Croatia and the fall of Slobodan Milošević in Serbia), the death of the SDA leader (Alija Izetbegović), and general dissatisfaction with the performance of government, alternative parties emerged within the Bosniak, Serb and Croat blocs.[14]

Direct international intervention in Bosnian party politics took the form of preventing politicians who opposed the goals of the peace implementation process from participating in elections and removing elected politicians who opposed international efforts once in office. Annex 10 of the Dayton Peace Agreement created the Office of the High Representative (OHR) to coordinate civilian aspects of the agreement. However, lack of progress by the end of 1997 in implementing the agreement led the group of outside countries that had brokered the peace agreement to invest the Office of the High Representative with the power to enforce the agreement by removing public officials and enact legislation, all without due process.[15] Between 1998 and 2002, dozens of public officials were removed by the OHR for a variety of offences, including attempting to set up parallel structures to those indicated in the Dayton Agreement,[16] obstructing refugee return,[17] aiding indicted war criminals,[18] and general corruption.[19] International efforts were focused most strongly on the SDS and HDZ, which both had their sources of funding restricted and key members banned from public office, including party offices.[20] The Bosniak nationalist party, SDA, was less frequently in conflict with the international community, as the aspects of peace implementation that the SDS and HDZ resisted most strongly (such as refugee return and a strong central government) were consistent with the goals of the SDA. In most cases, the SDA advocated more aggressive international intervention. One result of international intervention was to strengthen parties that appealed to only one of the three nationalities but that presented themselves as more moderate alternatives. The Alliance of Independent Social Democrats (SNSD) led by Milorad Dodik, the Party for Bosnia and Herzegovina (SBiH) led by Haris Silajdžić and later the Croatian Democratic Union 1990 (HDZ-1990) each benefited from the weakening of the dominant ethnic party. SNSD and SBiH were junior partners, serving both as coalition partners and opponents of dominant ethnic parties during and after the war. During the 2000 general elections, when direct international intervention into party politics was strongest, SNSD and SBiH won enough votes and presented themselves as moderate enough to gain international support and join the 'Alliance for Change'. Both suffered setbacks after the collapse of the coalition, as the more nationalist parties were strengthened in the 2002 elections.

However, both also resurged in the 2006 elections, and Dodik and Silajdžić are now the most visible Serb and Bosniak politicians and are dominant figures within their respective parties. The resurgence of SNSD and SBiH coincides with a nationalist turn in both parties. SDS and SDA reacted to international pressure by moderating their stances, which created opportunities for SNSD and SBiH. SNSD and SBiH differ in the degree to which their parties have been successful in translating the electoral success of their leaders at lower levels of government. SBiH remains the junior partner to SDA in most cantonal and municipal governments in the

Federation of Bosnia and Herzegovina, whereas SNSD has been much more successful in supplanting the SDS. SDA was not weakened to the degree of SDS by OHR sanctions, so SBiH has not supplanted SDA in the way that SNSD has supplanted SDS. While SBiH's Silajdžić is the most visible Bosniak politician, SBiH continues to run second to SDA in most lower-level elections.

The situation among the Bosnian Croat parties differs because of the role played by the HDZ in Croatia. During and after the war, Tuđman's HDZ in Croatia supported and sometimes controlled the HDZ in Bosnia and Herzegovina. However, the death of Tuđman, the emergence of strong moderate parties in Croatia, and the prospect of EU accession has put pressure on the HDZ in Croatia to moderate its stances and frequently put it in conflict with harder-line elements of the HDZ in Bosnia and Herzegovina. The result in 2006 was a split in the HDZ in Bosnia and Herzegovina between HDZ and HDZ-1990. The more moderate HDZ-1990 then formed an electoral coalition, Croatian Togetherness, with several smaller Bosnian Croat parties. It remains to be seen whether HDZ-1990 will follow a path similar to SNSD and SBiH. The connection to Croatia is likely to remain important, but will also be complicated by the fact that so many Bosnians also have Croatian citizenship and can therefore vote in Croatian elections. HDZ in Croatia relies on voters living in Bosnia, as they disproportionally support the HDZ in Croatian elections.[21]

Bosnian patterns of party competition in theoretical perspective

The pattern of party competition in Bosnia and Herzegovina since the end of the war and the signing of the Dayton Accords shows both the capacity of external intervention to bring about change as well as the limits of international intervention in the face of the power of nationalist electoral rhetoric in Bosnia's charged political atmosphere. One common explanation of the effectiveness of nationalist rhetoric states that, because of historic or more recent events, Bosnian voters are predisposed to respond to nationalist claims, making them an inevitable part of politics in Bosnia.[22] Such an explanation clearly has some truth to it, but the pattern of Bosnian voting can be explained without relying heavily on such claims about the mentality of Bosnians, which sometimes uncomfortably echo Orientalism (as understood by Edward Said and others) and Balkanism[23] in their attribution of Bosnian failures to non-Western values. At the very least, it is important to leave open the possibility for mentalities to change.[24] An explanation for the pattern of party competition emerges when we synthesize broader discussions of post-communist party systems with those that focus on ethnic party politics.

Comparing Bosnia's electoral system to other post-communist states is complicated by Bosnia's constitutional structure and its effects on political competition. The constitution enacted as part of the Dayton Accords that ended the war, as well as the Washington Agreement (1994) that had previously ended fighting between Bosnian Croat and Bosnian Muslim (Bosniak) forces, put in place a consociational government structure.[25] That aims to achieve security by devolving most power to mono-ethnic units and forcing consensus in inter-ethnic decision-making. The result is an unwieldy and complex constitutional structure with a weak, state-level government made up of a rotating three-member presidency with one seat allocated to each ethnic group, an upper chamber of the assembly with seats allocated by ethnicity and lower chamber of the assembly elected according to a proportional system. Most important domestic tasks are the responsibility of the two entities: the Federation of Bosnia and Herzegovina and Republika Srpska. Republika Srpska is overwhelmingly Serb, and is further divided into 62 municipalities, almost all of which have at least an absolute majority of Serbs.[26] The Federation of Bosnia and Herzegovina's constitutional structure was laid out in the Washington Agreement and is itself a consociational system that allows power sharing primarily between Croats and Bosniaks. This is accomplished largely by further devolving power to a system of ten cantons, seven of which are mono-ethnic. There is a special provision for multi-ethnic cantons, whereby additional responsibilities are devolved to the municipal level when the dominant ethnicity in the municipality differs from the dominant ethnicity of the canton.[27]

Broad comparisons of party systems tend to focus on the degree of party system fragmentation (that is, the number of effective parties) and the degree of party stability over time. The number and continuity of parties influences the capacity for voters to make electoral choices, since a system with fewer parties who are present from election to election is more likely to give voters both a manageable number of choices and make it easier for voters to hold incumbents accountable. In other post-communist cases, the problem has been fluctuation in the party system from election to election or extreme fragmentation.[28] Standard means of measuring political competition and instability in party systems like the effective number of parties and party volatility have the advantage of being relatively comparable over a large number of cases, but suffer from their failure to predict desirable political outcomes like good governance. Grzymala-Busse argues for measures of political competition that are more strongly correlated with lower levels of corruption, such as her own measures of robust competition.[29]

However, Bosnia and Herzegovina's party system has not suffered from instability; instead, it is the persistence of wartime nationalist parties that has concerned the organizations that seek to promote democracy in Bosnia and Herzegovina.[30] It also cannot be said that there is a lack of political competition; however, political competition in Bosnia rarely crosses ethnic lines. Competition takes place between parties of one ethnicity, frequently within electoral constituencies that are ethnically homogeneous. This pattern has been highly resistant to small electoral rule changes.[31] Bosnia's party system is well-consolidated and competitive in its own way. It is, however, still largely based on ethnicity.

International intervention and Bosnia's party system

As discussed in the party system narrative above, international organizations, such as the Office of the High Representative and European Union Special

Representative, USAID, and the National Democratic Institute, have influenced party competition in Bosnia primarily by supporting multi-ethnic and less-nationalist parties while sanctioning wartime nationalist parties.[32] This intervention has not brought about widespread support for multi-ethnic parties, and parties that initially seemed to be less nationalist are now impossible to differentiate from wartime nationalist parties. The shift from the use of the OHR's powers to remove politicians and enact legislation toward EU-style conditionality means that Bosnia's relationship to Europe shares many characteristics with East European countries that have gone through or are going through the EU accession process.[33]

Grzymala-Busse and Innes' examination of the domestic political impact of EU accession in East Central Europe shows that the process of EU accession itself may play a role in encouraging the emergence of extremist parties. Broad domestic consensus on the desirability of EU accession, as well as the technical nature of the process, shapes the space in which political parties can compete. Reform and the direction of reform are not up for debate, resulting in minimal policy differences among mainstream parties. Worse, domestic politicians find themselves caught between the interests of voters and the requirements of the accession process, with severe consequences for neglecting either. Inevitably, the popularity of accession and the prospects of mainstream parties associated with it decrease. The result is a strengthening of populist parties on the right and left.[34]

Although Bosnia is in the earliest stages of actual EU accession, the dynamics between the international community and domestic politics are similar. The agenda for reform is provided by the High Representative or some other international office, and domestic politicians are called upon to enact that reform within some acceptable framework. The policy options are too limited to allow for meaningful political competition, which foments populist politics. In Bosnia, populist politics means nationalist politics. With many bread-and-butter issues off the table, the issues available for campaigning include constitutional changes, the corrupt actions of other politicians, and the role of international organizations in Bosnia. Such an environment is decidedly hostile to the development of non-nationalist and multi-ethnic parties, whose performance suffers when elections take on an explicitly ethnic dimension.

Studies on ethnic parties and politics also give reason for doubt that a truly multi-ethnic, non-nationalist political space could emerge in Bosnia and Herzegovina.[35] The definition of parties along ethnic lines serves to limit the choices available to voters, as party and group membership are a matter of birth as opposed to choice, thereby channelling political competition through pre-defined routes.[36] Furthermore, parties defined along ethnic lines inevitably focus on ensuring support of their own group as opposed to winning the support of members of other groups.[37] The existence of non-ethnic or multi-ethnic parties alongside ethnic parties is only possible in cases where there is a strong issue dimension in addition to ethnicity.[38] The degree to which such a dimension exists is an open and much debated question in the study of Bosnian politics, but most electoral evidence suggests that ethnicity is and will remain the dominant dimension.

The narrative of party system development in Bosnia and Herzegovina presented above shows one important way that international actors have shaped ethnic politics in Bosnia. Whereas party systems based on non-ethnic parties tend to produce competition over centrist votes (centripetal competition), ethnic party systems result in political competition that is centrifugal, as party leaders seek to ensure control over the party by focusing on the demands of group members as opposed to attempting to pry voters away from other parties, as is the case in non-ethnic systems.[39] Intense international pressure[40] during the 2000 general elections in Bosnia opened space for parties that were more moderate as well as the SDP, a multi-ethnic party. For a time, party competition within ethnic groups pulled both the war-time and more moderate parties toward the centre; however, the centrist, moderate parties did not stay moderate but took advantage of the opportunities available in order to out-nationalist the nationalists, resulting in the return to centrifugal competition and greater divergence in ethnic party demands. For a brief period surrounding the 2000 elections, international pressure was able to work against the prevailing ethnic tendency in Bosnian politics by strengthening less nationalist and multi-ethnic parties at the expense of wartime nationalist parties, but the perceived poor performance of those parties in office served to undercut their future electoral prospects. The SDP's share of the seats in the state-level parliament fell from 22% in 2000 to 9% in 2006.[41]

Electoral systems like Bosnia's are designed to ensure representation of opposing groups and create institutions through which the elected leaders of those groups can negotiate and reach compromises while ensuring the security of their group. This perspective relies on elites who are willing to make hard compromises in order to implement common projects.[42] Consociational systems rely on the ability and willingness of elites to create consensus.[43] The Dayton constitution has been criticized for not creating incentives for politicians to engage in compromise and reach consensus.[44] The experience of Bosnia suggests that interethnic compromise can be very costly to parties that attempt it. Bosnia's constitution does not include provisions that explicitly encourage cross-ethnic campaigning. In fact, for the most part it discourages such behaviour. However, the same electoral system structures that make cross-ethnic competition unlikely may also be creating pockets at lower government levels where ethnicity is de-emphasized.[45]

Ethnopolitical electoral contexts

A large proportion of elected positions are either *de jure*, allocated to one of the three ethnic groups (referred to as constituent peoples in the constitution), or *de facto*, single ethnicity competitions because of the homogeneous makeup of the constituency in question. The three members of Bosnia's presidency, as well as seats in the upper house of parliament, are explicitly allocated to a Bosniak, a Croat, or a Serb. The lower house of parliament is elected according to a proportional representation formula. At the entity and canton levels, there is a similar mix between positions explicitly allocated based on ethnicity and those that depend on the constituency, but elections below the state level are much more likely to take place within a constituency that is ethnically homogeneous. The vast majority of municipalities effectively are mono-ethnic constituencies. Only one party, the SDP, has successfully fielded candidates of more than one constituent group, but almost all of the SDP's support is among Bosniaks.

This institutional configuration calls into question whether Bosnia has one electoral system or several. It is useful to think of political competition in Bosnia taking place in three types of contexts depending on the demographic content of the constituency and the expected nature of the positions. Mono-ethnic, non-competitive contexts are positions where a constituency either *de facto* or *de jure* represents only one ethnic group and in which elected representatives are not in direct competition for resources with elected representatives of other ethnic groups. An example is a member of a municipal council from a municipality where only Bosniaks live. Mono-ethnic, competitive contexts are positions in which the constituency is mono-ethnic and in which the elected representative is in direct competition with representatives of other ethnic groups. For example, the members of the presidency are allocated to each ethnic group but sit on a presidential council and vote with the other two members of the presidency. Multi-ethnic constituencies are those where the representation of any particular group is not fixed and is an open competition involving voters of more than one ethnic group. The context in which an election is held has an effect on the role that ethnicity plays in the voting process; however, the contexts are also not in isolation from one another, as elections reflecting all three contexts occur simultaneously, with individual voters casting votes in more than one type of context. For example, a Bosniak voter from a canton with a majority Bosniak population in the Federation votes for the Bosniak member of the state-level presidency (a mono-ethnic, competitive context), the state-level parliament (multi-ethnic), the Federation parliament (multi-ethnic) and the Cantonal Assembly (mono-ethnic, non-competitive) all during the same visit to the ballot box. Consequently, campaigns and impressions associated with one context have an impact across contexts.

Table 2. Ethnopolitical electoral contexts.

	'Mixed-ethnicity' constituency	'Mono-ethnic' constituency
Political office is in a body in which more than one ethnicity is represented.	Multi-ethnic, competitive: example is BiH Assembly. Leads to 'ethnic census' behaviour.	Mono-ethnic, competitive: example is BiH Presidency. Rewards nationalist rhetoric.
Political office is in a body in which only one ethnicity is represented.	Multi-ethnic, non-competitive: no corresponding office (except perhaps OHR, which is not an elected position).	Mono-ethnic, non-competitive: examples include mono-ethnic municipalities, mono-ethnic cantons. Downplays ethnic dimension.

Despite the noise created by simultaneous elections in multiple contexts, the electoral context of specific elections plays a significant role in voter behaviour simply because ethnicity plays a different role in each context, as summarized in Table 2. The mono-ethnic, non-competitive constituencies should have the best chance of producing non-nationalist parties, as there is no ethnic 'other' against whom to campaign. Evidence from Northern Ireland has shown indications that mono-ethnic constituencies created under consociationalism have given parties the incentive to moderate.[46] The other two contexts are less fertile ground for non-nationalist parties, although for slightly different reasons. Mono-ethnic, competitive contexts encourage nationalist rhetoric and ethnic outbidding precisely because there is competition between those who are elected, even if there is no direct electoral competition between them. Electoral campaigns for such positions are more likely to be framed according to which candidate or party can best promote the interests of the constituent ethnicity relative to the other ethnic groups, in what has been described as an 'ethnic tribune' effect.[47] This kind of framing rewards ethnonationalist rhetoric and encourages ethnonationalist parties. Multi-ethnic contexts are also unlikely to produce non-nationalist parties because of their tendency to become an 'ethnic census', whereby the electoral strength of each group depends on the number of voters from that group who participate.[48] In both of the latter contexts, voting for non-nationalist or multi-ethnic parties may be construed as weakening one's own side.

Non-nationalist voting by context

Examining the patterns of non-nationalist voting in Bosnia and Herzegovina provides an opportunity to examine the plausibility of some of these explanations, and particularly those tied to the relationship between non-nationalist voting and electoral contexts. The clearest pattern to emerge regarding the performance of the SDP is that the SDP, with the exception of the election of Komšić as the Croat member of the BiH presidency, has performed better in mono-ethnic, non-competitive contexts such as ethnically homogenous cantons and at the municipal level. This may result in part from the fact that support for SDP is not distributed uniformly across Bosniak-dominated areas. At the cantonal level, SDP is strongest in Tuzla Canton, where they also have several mayors. At the municipal level, the SDP is strongest in urban areas, in the municipalities of Tuzla Canton, and in a few scattered rural municipalities. SDP has succeeded in electing mayors in 11 municipalities across Bosnia, which is about a third as many as SDA, but dramatically more than SBiH, which was then and continues to be a party that performs best at the state level.

Nationalist/non-nationalist ticket splitting – a natural experiment

The division between mono-ethnic and multi-ethnic cantons within the Federation half of Bosnia and Herzegovina offers the opportunity for a natural experiment by focusing on differences in the number of votes cast for the non-nationalist parties in the cantonal and Federation elections in 2006.[49] Much like identical twins separated at birth and raised by different families, Federation voters with a predilection to vote for multi-ethnic parties find themselves in either mono-ethnic or multi-ethnic cantons. Whereas studies on identical twins make it possible to control for genetic factors and focus on environmental factors, the natural experiment used in this study makes it possible to control for differences in level of election and support for multi-ethnic parties in order to focus on the impact of electoral context. The analysis here takes advantage of votes cast during the same election and aggregated at the precinct level. Differences in the proportion of votes cast for non-nationalist parties across elections represent voters who split their tickets across elections.[50]

The natural experiment, illustrated in Table 3, occurs when comparing the results in mono-ethnic cantons against multi-ethnic cantons in order to test the effect of different electoral contexts discussed above. In terms of electoral context, multi-ethnic cantonal elections, the Federation Assembly elections and BiH Assembly elections all fall under the multi-ethnic, competitive context. So, there should be no electoral context effect on those municipalities. The mono-ethnic cantonal elections fall under the mono-ethnic, non-competitive context. Accordingly, we expect mono-ethnic cantonal elections to have greater support for the SDP and other parties in the cantonal election than in the Federation or Assembly elections. The natural experiment controls for other factors, such as inherent differences in cantonal and Federation elections and focuses on the impact of the ethnonationalist electoral context. Figure 1 shows the proportion of voters who split their ticket by voting nationalist in Federation and BiH Assembly election while voting for non-nationalist parties in canton elections. The estimates are generated and analysed at the precinct level but aggregated to the municipality level in the map. The map excludes Republika Srpska, as Republika Srpska does not have cantons and is therefore outside the natural experiment.

Table 4 shows the results of two weighted least-squares regressions, which take as their dependent variable the proportion of voters who split their tickets by voting non-nationalist[51] in cantonal elections and nationalist in FBiH or BiH elections. The explanatory variables are a set of dummy variables for different types of

Table 3. Ethnopolitical electoral contexts across mono-ethnic and multi-ethnic cantons: a natural experiment.

	Voter in mono-ethnic canton	Voter in multi-ethnic canton
Cantonal Assembly	Mono-ethnic, non-competitive electoral context	Multi-ethnic, competitive electoral context
Federation Assembly	Multi-ethnic, competitive electoral context	Multi-ethnic, competitive electoral context
BiH Assembly	Multi-ethnic, competitive electoral context	Multi-ethnic, competitive electoral context

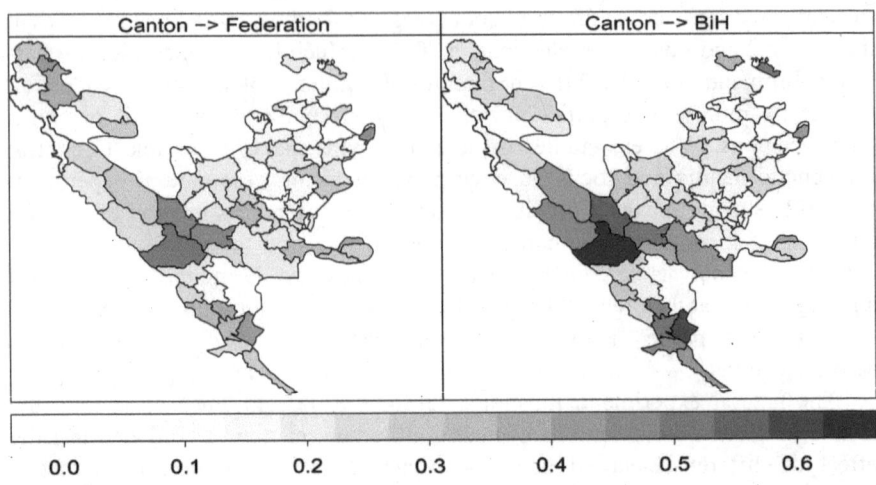

Figure 1. Proportion of non-nationalist voters in cantonal elections who voted nationalist in Federation and BiH Assembly elections.
Source: EZI estimates from precinct-level election results for the 2006 General Elections available from the Election Commission of Bosnia and Herzegovina (http://www.izbori.ba). Precinct-level estimates have been aggregated to the municipality-level for mapping purposes. The map was generated in R using the packages SP and Maptools.

cantons, differentiated by the ethnopolitical electoral context of each canton, and the proportion of seats won by non-nationalist parties in the 2004 municipal elections. The baseline category for the set of dummy variables represents those precincts within mono-ethnic, Bosniak-dominated cantons, and the three included dummy variables correspond to precincts within multi-ethnic, Bosniak-dominated cantons, mono-ethnic, Croat-dominated cantons and multi-ethnic, Croat-dominated cantons.

The most direct test is in the results for the dummy variable for precincts in mixed, Bosniak-dominated cantons. Since mixed Bosniak cantons, the BiH Assembly and the FBiH Assembly are all multi-ethnic, competitive electoral contexts, any difference in the amount of ticket splitting cannot be due to electoral context. Mono-ethnic, Bosniak cantons are mono-ethnic, non-competitive districts, so the effect of electoral context will be visible in the difference between the two types of Bosniak-dominated cantons, and in a similar way between the two types of Croat-dominated cantons. Simply stated, there should be more voters who chose non-nationalist at the canton level who split their tickets to vote nationalist at the FBiH or BiH level in mono-ethnic cantons than in multi-ethnic cantons.

Table 4 shows weighted least-squares results for both BiH Assembly and FBiH Assembly elections in 2006. The coefficient for those precincts within mixed Bosniak cantons is negative and statistically significant at or below the .01 level. For BiH Assembly elections, precincts in mono-ethnic, Bosniak-dominated

Table 4. WLS regression of non-nationalist > nationalist ticket splitters.

	Log proportion of voters who voted non-nationalist in cantonal elections and BiH Assembly elections	Log proportion of voters who voted non-nationalist in cantonal elections and nationalist in FBiH Assembly
Mixed Bosniak canton	−0.15191** (0.05525)	−0.52739*** (0.05806)
Mixed Croat canton	1.21242*** (0.15678)	0.8206*** (0.09963)
Mono-ethnic Croat canton	0.25632 (0.17921)	−0.1883 (0.16272)
Proportion of municipal council seats held by non-nationalist parties	−3.70263*** (0.16973)	−4.12853*** (0.18289)
Intercept	−1.19116*** (0.06751)	−0.9054*** (0.07228)
R-Squared	.27	0.26
N	2001	2001

Notes: Signif. codes: '***' = 0.001, '**' = 0.01, '*' = 0.05. Standard errors in parentheses.
Source: Weighted Least Squares (WLS) analysis of EZI estimates from precinct-level election results for the 2006 General Elections available from the Election Commission of Bosnia and Herzegovina (http:www.izbori.ba). WLS analysis performed in R (R Development Core Team, *R: A Language and Environment for Statistical Computing*).

cantons had 16% more ticket splitters among voters who chose non-nationalists in cantonal elections than multi-ethnic, Bosniak-dominated cantons. The effect was even more dramatic for FBiH Assembly elections, where precincts in mono-ethnic, Bosniak-dominated cantons had 69% more ticket splitters than multi-ethnic, Bosniak-dominated cantons. The results for the Bosniak cantons contain strong evidence in favour of the prediction based on electoral contexts.

Interpreting the coefficients for the Croat-dominated cantons is somewhat more complex, as they do not directly relate to the reference category. The large and statistically-insignificant coefficients for precincts in mono-ethnic, Croat-dominated cantons indicate that, after controlling for the proportion of municipal council seats held by non-nationalist parties, it is not possible to say with certainty that there is a difference in the proportion of ticket-splitters among those who voted non-nationalist in cantonal elections between Bosniak- and Croat-dominated, mono-ethnic cantons. The large, positive, statistically significant coefficients for precincts in mixed Croat cantons indicate that those precincts have dramatically higher proportions of ticket splitters than either mono-ethnic, Croat cantons or mono-ethnic, Bosniak-dominated cantons.

On the surface, the results for the Croat cantons run contrary to the predicted effect of the ethnopolitical electoral context. However, once the difference in overall performance of non-nationalist parties across Bosniak and Croat voters is taken into account, then the results fall into line with theoretical predictions. Bosniak voters are two to three times more likely to be non-nationalist voters than Croats, and multi-ethnic, Croat cantons are multi-ethnic because they have a significant number of Bosniaks; however, the overall level of support for non-nationalist parties is similar for multi-ethnic, Croat cantons and mono-ethnic

Croat cantons. This is a result of two tendencies cancelling one another out, with the higher proportion of Bosniak voters driving up the level of support for non-nationalist parties and the effect of a multi-ethnic electoral context suppressing support for non-nationalist parties by both Croats and Bosniaks. There is also evidence of strategic voting on the part of Bosniaks and Serbs living in Croat-dominated cantons, whereby Bosniaks and Serbs who are inclined to vote nationalist pool their votes in canton elections by voting for non-nationalist parties but then revert to voting for their nationalist parties in Federation and BiH Assembly elections. This suggests that the predictions related to ethnopolitical electoral context hold in relation to voters who are a majority within a particular canton but fail to capture all of the incentives facing voters who find themselves in the minority at the canton level.

Conclusion

Party assistance favouring multi-ethnic, non-nationalist parties in Bosnia and Herzegovina has met with very limited success, as shown by the persistence and even resurgence of political parties that espouse nationalist rhetoric. The domestic factors working against multi-ethnic, non-nationalist parties are very strong. The rise of the SNSD and SBiH as moderate parties and their subsequent leap to success when they embraced more extreme rhetoric strongly suggests that nationalist parties that moderate do so at the risk of losing their core constituency. As a result, it may not be possible in the current climate and under the current constitution to promote moderation from the outside. This is particularly true in multi-ethnic constituencies because competition between ethnic blocs in multi-ethnic constituencies is likely to lead to more extremism and not less.

There is a tension between the goals of democracy promotion in Bosnia and Herzegovina and the tools available to democracy promoters. The ideal end state for democracy promoters is a Bosnia that is both politically integrated and no longer under the grip of ethnonationalist politics. However, the tools available to bring about integration, including direct support for non-nationalist and multi-ethnic parties, constitutional reform away from consociationalism, and progress toward EU accession, serve to inflame nationalist sentiment and increase the likelihood of continued electoral success for Bosnia's ethnonationalist parties. As the results of the empirical section of this chapter also illustrate, attempts to promote non-nationalist parties are least successful in political contexts with more than one ethnicity.

Given this trade-off, attempting to promote non-nationalist parties under the current electoral system likely does more harm than good. As shown in this account, the electoral rules in place actively discourage parties that appeal across ethnic lines, except at the local level. However, having constitutional and electoral change constantly on the agenda may also have significant costs, as such issues fall into the wheelhouse of the nationalist view of Bosnia. Uncertainty about the final constitutional status of Bosnia and its electoral system plays into the hands of nationalists, as does the current electoral system.

PROMOTING PARTY POLITICS IN EMERGING DEMOCRACIES

The EU accession process is unlikely to be a panacea for Bosnia's problems. The rise of radical populism in other EU candidates, as well as its rise among the original EU members, suggests that moving forward with EU accession may reinforce populist identity politics in Bosnia, even as other aspects of EU accession, including reduced emphasis on national borders and additional infrastructure investment, may help with issues underlying Bosnia's political problems.

The ideals behind party assistance in Bosnia have come up against harsh political realities. While continued external support for multi-ethnic, non-nationalist parties may still play a positive role by helping to give voice to perspectives on politics that downplay the role of ethnicity and push for multi-ethnic solutions to Bosnia's problems, the evidence presented in this study suggests strongly that party assistance will be unable to bring about a dramatic change in the way Bosnian politics works. Furthermore, attempts to unify Bosnia politically by creating more multiethnic electoral contexts are likely to make the task of assisting multi-ethnic, non-nationalist parties even more difficult.

Acknowledgements

Earlier versions of this analysis were presented at a workshop on International Dimensions of Party (System Development) held at the University of Amsterdam, the Annual Meeting of the Midwest Political Science Association as well as the Working Group on the Political Economy of Democratic Sustainability at the Workshop on Political Theory and Policy Analysis, Indiana University. I would like to thank the participants in each for their valuable feedback. I am particularly thankful to Peter Burnell, André Gerrits and two anonymous reviewers for their contributions to improving both the content and delivery. The funding for field work supporting this research was provided by IREX-IARO.

Notes

1. For convenience, this account uses 'Bosnia and Herzegovina' and 'Bosnia' interchangeably. Where appropriate, 'Bosnia and Herzegovina' or 'BiH' is used to denote state-level institutions as opposed to those of Bosnia's entities or cantons.
2. The analysis is concerned primarily with the performance of multi-ethnic and non-nationalist parties. These differ from ethnic and nationalist parties in the composition of their leadership, the breadth of voters to which they appeal and their use of incendiary rhetoric that explicitly or implicitly threatens members of other nations. The task of categorizing parties is made more difficult by the fact that party behaviour changes over time and that there is a frequent disconnect between the official party platforms and statements by party leaders. Few parties in Bosnia would describe themselves as nationalist parties, but most engage in rhetoric that can clearly be categorized as such. The wartime, nationalist parties SDA, HDZ and SDS make up one natural group of parties, in that they were the chief protagonists of the war in Bosnia that accompanied the collapse of Yugoslavia. Each explicitly represents one ethnic group. Radovan Karadzic's SDS stands out from this group for its ultranationalist rhetoric before, during and after the war as well as its initiation of ethnic cleansing in Bosnia. SBiH, SNSD and HDZ-1990 are also ethnic parties, but they emerged after the war and initially presented a more moderate alternative to the wartime, nationalist parties. This paper defines the SDP, NSRzB, and LDS as non-nationalist, multi-ethnic parties because

of their rejection of nationalist rhetoric and attempts to build constituencies from voters of more than one ethnic group. However, even this characterization of the SDP can be challenged based on the fact that the preponderance of its support comes from urban Bosniak voters. Despite this fact, the SDP is included as a multi-ethnic party because its leadership is multi-ethnic and it clearly seeks and receives votes beyond its core constituency of Bosniaks. Future research will be expanded to include newer parties with non-nationalist, multi-ethnic profiles (chiefly Naša Stranka) that have emerged since the last general election.

3. The classic piece on consociationalism is Lijphart, *Democracy in Plural Societies*. For discussions of Bosnia as a consociational system see Bose, *Bosnia after Dayton*; Belloni, *State Building and International Intervention in Bosnia*; Bieber, *Post-War Bosnia*.

4. For a discussion of criticisms of power-sharing and consociational regimes, see Norris, *Driving Democracy*, 27–31. See also the lively debate on the behavioural effects of consociationalism in Northern Ireland, especially Tilley, Evans and Mitchell 'Consociationalism and the Evolution of Political Cleavages in Northern Ireland, 1989–2004'; Mitchell, Evans and O'Leary, 'Extremist Outbidding in Ethnic Party Systems is Not Inevitable: Tribune Parties in Northern Ireland'; Garry, 'Consociationalism and its Critics'.

5. For example, the three members of the presidency of Bosnia and Herzegovina, each of whom explicitly represent and are elected by members of one of Bosnia's three 'constituent peoples'. Specifically, Belloni, *State Building and International Intervention in Bosnia*, 74 argues that electoral engineering aimed at encouraging multi-ethnic parties failed because of Bosnia's consociational system.

6. Other analyses of support for non-nationalist and multi-ethnic parties in Bosnia found support for political attitudes as well as prewar ethnic distribution as explanatory factors favouring support for non-nationalist parties. Pickering, 'Explaining Support for Non-nationalist Parties', finds that, among Bosniaks, left-leaning survey respondents were much more likely to support non-nationalist parties than right-leaning respondents. Pugh and Cobble, 'Non-Nationalist Voting', find that support for non-nationalist parties depends on the pre-war demographic distribution, especially the presence of a Bosniak majority in multi-ethnic municipalities.

7. Bosnia's electoral system is complex and defies simple categorization. The elections used in the empirical section of this paper use proportional representation with open party lists. Their salient characteristic for the purpose of this analysis is whether their geographically-defined constituency contains one or more than one of Bosnia's three 'constituent peoples'. The most detailed and current account of attempts at electoral engineering in Bosnia can be found in Belloni, *State Building and International Intervention in Bosnia*.

8. See, for example the *New York Times* editorial 'Bosnia Unravelling', 22 January 2009.

9. The empirical portion of this study includes the National Work for Betterment Party (*Narodna Stranka Radom za Boljitak* or NSRzB) as well as the Liberal Democratic Party (*Liberalna Demokratska Stranka* or LDS). NSRzB and LDS are much smaller parties and of more recent provenance but they share the SDP's resistance to the use of nationalist electoral rhetoric and policy of putting forward candidates from multiple ethnic groups. NSRzB especially enjoys support in Croat areas of Bosnia and Herzegovina. It is the combination of refraining from using nationalist electoral rhetoric and putting forward candidates from multiple ethnic groups that differentiates SDP, NSRzB and LDS from the other parties.

10. For an account of non-nationalist parties' attempts to contest the elections, see Pejanović, *Through Bosnian Eyes*. In pre-war elections, the most significant political divide was between nationalist parties from all ethnicities on the one side and the

non-nationalist, socialist parties on the other. SDA, SDS and HDZ cooperated in attacking non-nationalist parties during the election campaign. This nationalist coalition collapsed once in office, after successfully cooperating to defeat the non-nationalist coalition.

11. The tenuous nature of this victory is apparent in the titles of the two International Crisis Group reports detailing the election results, *Bosnia's November Elections: Dayton Stumbles*, December 2000 and *Bosnia's Alliance for (Smallish) Change*, August 2002.
12. International Crisis Group, *Bosnia's Alliance for (Smallish) Change*.
13. Author interviews with Bosniak SDP members suggest the former interpretation: that Bosniak SDP supporters preferred to use their vote to elect an SDP of any ethnicity rather than choose between an SDA and SBiH candidate in the Bosniak election.
14. This paper addresses only the most significant Bosniak, Croat and Serb parties in Bosnia, as well as the three parties that are most clearly multi-ethnic parties. The SDA (*Stranka demokratske akcije*) is the most established Bosniak (Bosnian Muslim) party and was led by Alija Izetbegović during and after the war. The next largest Bosniak party is SBiH (*Stranka za Bosnu i Hercegovinu*) which is led by Haris Silajdžić, currently the most prominent Bosniak politician. HDZ-BiH (*Hrvatska demokratska zajednica*) is the dominant Croat party in Bosnia, but a more moderate splinter party, HDZ 1990, has emerged to challenge it in recent election cycles. The dominant Serb party after the end of the war was the SDS (*Srpska demokratska stranka*), which continues to be powerful in many municipal governments in Republika Srpska; however, SDS has largely been replaced by SNSD (*Savez nezavisnih socialdemokrata*), led by Milorad Dodik at higher levels of the state. The most significant multiethnic party is the SDP-BiH (*Socijaldemokratska partija Bosne I Herzegovina*). Two smaller multi-ethnic parties NSRzB (*Narodna stranka Radom – Za boljitak*) and LDS (*Liberalna demokratska stranka*) are also included in the analysis, primarily to better extend the analysis to Croat-dominated areas where SDP does not perform well.
15. These 'Bonn Powers' of the OHR understandably are controversial. Belloni, *State Building and International Intervention in Bosnia*, 20–5 gives a balanced overview. For a critique see Knaus and Martin, 'Travails of the European Raj'.
16. Office of the High Representative, 'Decision removing Ante Jelavic from his position as the Croat member of the BiH Presidency', 7 March 2001, http://www.ohr.int/decisions/removalssdec/default.asp?content_id=328 (accessed August 15, 2010).
17. Office of the High Representative, 'Decision removing Ivan Damjanovic from his position as Mayor of Glamoc', 7 September 2001, http://www.ohr.int/decisions/removalssdec/default.asp?content_id=304 (accessed August 15, 2010).
18. Office of the High Representative, 'Decision to remove Mr. Dragomir Vasic from his position as member of the Republika Srpska National Assembly and as councilor in the Zvornik Municipal Assembly', 7 March 2003, http://www.ohr.int/decisions/removalssdec/default.asp?content_id=30263 (accessed August 15, 2010).
19. Office of the High Representative, 'Decision removing Mr. Bosko Lemez from his position in the Management Board of Elektroprivreda Republika Srpska', 26 February 2003, http://www.ohr.int/decisions/removalssdec/default.asp?content_id=29338 (accessed August 15, 2010).
20. For a more detailed analysis of international efforts and the limits of their effects see Manning and Antic, 'The Limits of Electoral Engineering'. Information on specific actions of the Office of the High Representative was obtained from its official website, http://www.ohr.int. Data on the distribution of OHR decisions were compiled by the author.
21. This situation did not hold for the Croatian presidential election in 2009 in which an independent candidate, Milan Bandić received more diaspora votes than the HDZ

candidate. Republic of Croatia Election Commission, http://www.izbori.hr/2009Predsjednik/indexr.html (accessed August 15, 2010).
22. See International Crisis Group, *Bosnia's November Elections: Dayton Stumbles*, 18–19.
23. See Todorova, *Imagining the Balkans*.
24. For an even-handed discussion of the debate over Bosnian mentality as it relates to interethnic cooperation, see Bose, *Bosnia after Dayton*.
25. For the seminal discussion of consociational democracy see Lijphart, *Democracy in Plural Societies*. For a discussion of the application of consociationalism to the Bosnian case see Mujkic, 'Bosna i Herzegovina i izazovi konsocijacije'.
26. This homogeneity is in many cases the direct result of successful ethnic cleansing. Serbs were a minority in the following municipalities (percentage of Serbs in 1981 is in parentheses): Bosanski Brod (33% of Serbs), Bosanski Šamac (41%), Bratunac (40%), Čajniće (48%), Derventa (40%), (Doboj 39%), Foča (42%), Kotor Varoš (41%), Modriča (38%), Prijedor (42%), Rogatica (37%), Srebrenica (28%), Višegrad (33%), Vlasenica (44%), Zvornik (41%). Source: Bertić, *Veliki atlas Jugoslavije*, 228–30.
27. Washington Agreement, 1994, Section II, http://www.usip.org/files/file/resources/collections/peace_agreements/washagree_03011994.pdf (accessed August 15, 2008).
28. See Bielasiak, 'The Institutionalization of Electoral and Party Systems in Post-Communist States'.
29. Grzymala-Busse, 'Encouraging Effective Democratic Competition'.
30. Davidson, 'Ambassador Douglas Davidson's Remarks at Prof. Dr. Mirko Pejanović's Book Presentation'.
31. Manning, 'Elections and Political Change in Post-War Bosnia and Herzegovina'.
32. USAID and NDI restrict their party assistance, consisting primarily of technical support for campaigning, to multiethnic parties. Center for Democracy and Governance, *USAID Political Party Development Assistance*. See note 20 for attempts to hinder nationalist parties.
33. While Bosnia is in the earliest stages of the EU accession process, the Office of the High Representative is also the EU Special Representative in Bosnia and Herzegovina. Following the heavy use of the High Representative's power to remove officials and enact legislation through 2003, there was a shift toward conditionality as a means of exercising influence over Bosnian politicians. For example, police reform and constitutional reform have been put forward as pre-requisites for steps toward EU accession.
34. Grzymala-Busse and Innes, 'Great Expectations: The EU and Domestic Political Competition in East Central Europe'.
35. In fact, most studies question whether such a divided yet stable society is possible at all, notably Rabushka and Shepsle, *Politics in Plural Societies*.
36. Horowitz, *Ethnic Groups in Conflict*.
37. Ibid., 318.
38. Ibid.
39. Ibid., 347.
40. This pressure took the form of party assistance to the SDP, sanctions on the nationalist parties, and media campaigns targeted at nationalist incumbents (see International Crisis Group *Bosnia's November Elections: Dayton Stumbles*, 2–3). Pressure continued after the election, as the American and British ambassadors to Bosnia and Herzegovina engaged in 'energetic lobbying and arm-twisting' in order to create a coalition that excluded the war-time nationalist parties. International Crisis Group, *Bosnia's Alliance for (Smallish) Change*.
41. For results see http://www.izbori.ba, the website of the electoral commission for Bosnia and Herzegovina.
42. See Lijphart, *Democracy in Plural Societies*.

43. In Lijphart's later work, consociational systems are grouped under a broader set of consensus-based systems, Lijphart, *Patterns of Democracy.*
44. See Mujkic, 'Bosna i Herzegovina i izazovi konsocijacije'.
45. Norris, *Driving Democracy: Do Power-Sharing Institutions Work?*
46. Garry, 'Consociationalism and its Critics: Evidence from the Historic Northern Ireland Assembly Election 2007'.
47. Mitchell, Evans and O'Leary, 'Extremist Outbidding in Ethnic Party Systems is Not Inevitable: Tribune Parties in Northern Ireland'.
48. Horowitz, *Ethnic Groups in Conflict.*
49. All precinct-level election data was obtained by the author from the Electoral Commission of Bosnia and Herzegovina (http://www.izbori.ba).
50. Since neither individual-level electoral return data nor suitable individual-level survey data are available, the data analysis here makes use of aggregate, precinct-level returns, which are subject to ecological inference (EI) problems. Ecological inference problems emerge when attempting to draw individual-level conclusions based on aggregate data. In this case, it is necessary to estimate the proportion of voters who split their tickets while not directly observing individual votes. Rather, it is only possible to observe the aggregate proportion of non-nationalist voters in each election. This study makes use of EZI (Benoit and King, *EZI: An Easy Program for Ecological Inference*) to generate estimates of the proportion of voters who split their votes between non-nationalist parties in cantonal elections and nationalist parties in FBiH Assembly or BiH Assembly elections. The results used in this analysis follow the recommendations in Adolph et al., 'A Consensus on Second Stage Analyses in Ecological Inference Models', in that the covariates for the second stage analysis have been included in the extended EI model, and observations are weighted according to the standard errors of the EI point predictions (whereby less certain predictions are devalued in the analysis relative to more certain predictions).
51. The combined totals for SDP, National Party – Work for Betterment, and the Liberal Democratic Party.

Bibliography

Adolph, Christopher, Gary King, Michael C. Herron, and Kenneth W. Shotts. 'A Consensus on Second Stage Analyses in Ecological Inference Models'. *Political Analysis* 11, no. 1 (2003): 86–94.

Benoit, Kenneth, and Gary King. *EZI: An Easy Program for Ecological Inference*, 1999. Cambridge, MA: Department of Government, Harvard University, http://gking.harvard.edu/stats.shtml.

Bertić, Ivan. *Veliki Atlas Jugoslavije.* Zagreb: Liber, 1987.

Belloni, Roberto. *State Building and International Intervention in Bosnia.* New York: Routledge, 2007.

Bieber, Florian. *Post-War Bosnia: Ethnicity, Inequality and Public Sector Governance.* New York: Palgrave, 2006.

Bielasiak, J. 'The Institutionalization of Electoral and Party Systems in Post-Communist States'. *Comparative Politics* 34, no. 2 (2002): 189–210.

Bose, Sumantra. *Bosnia after Dayton: Nationalist Partition and International Intervention.* London: Hurst, 2002.

Center for Democracy and Governance. *USAID Political Party Development Assistance*, Technical Publication Series. Washington, DC: USAID, 1999, http://www.usaid.gov/our_work/democracy_and_governance/publications/pdfs/pnace500.pdf (accessed August 15, 2010).

Davidson, Douglas, 'Ambassador Douglas Davidson's Remarks at Prof. Dr. Mirko Pejanović's Book Presentation', 2007, http://www.oscebih.org/public/print_news.asp?id=2132 (accessed August 15, 2010).

Garry, John. 'Consociationalism and its Critics: Evidence from the Historic Northern Ireland Assembly Election 2007'. *Electoral Studies* 28 (2009): 458–66.

Grzymala-Busse, Anna. 'Encouraging Effective Democratic Competition'. *East European Politics and Societies* 21, no. 1 (2007): 91–110.

Grzymala-Busse, Anna, and Abby Innes. 'Great Expectations: The EU and Domestic Political Competition in East Central Europe'. *East European Politics and Societies* 17, no. 1 (2003): 64–73.

Horowitz, Donald. *Ethnic Groups in Conflict*. Berkeley: University of California Press, 2000.

International Crisis Group. *Bosnia's November Elections: Dayton Stumbles*, Europe Report. Sarajevo/Brussels: International Crisis Group, December 2000.

International Crisis Group. *Bosnia's Alliance for (Smallish) Change*, Europe Report. Sarajevo/Brussels: International Crisis Group, August 2002.

Knaus, Gerald, and Felix Martin, 'Travails of the European Raj'. *Journal of Democracy* 14, no. 3 (2003): 60–74.

Lijphart, Arend. *Democracy in Plural Societies: A Comparative Exploration*. New Haven, CT: Yale University Press, 1977.

Lijphart, Arend. *Patterns of Democracy: Governmental Forms and Performance in Thirty-Six Countries*. New Haven, CT: Yale University Press, 1999.

Manning, C. 'Elections and Political Change in Post-War Bosnia and Herzegovina'. *Democratization* 11, no. 2 (2004): 60–86.

Manning, Carrie, and Miljenko Antic. 'The Limits of Electoral Engineering'. *Journal of Democracy* 14, no. 3 (2003): 45–59.

Mitchell, Paul, Geoffrey Evans, and Brendan O'Leary. 'Extremist Outbidding in Ethnic Party Systems is Not Inevitable: Tribune Parties in Northern Ireland', *Political Studies* 57, no. 2 (2009): 397–421.

Mujkic, Asim. 'Bosna i Herzegovina i izazovi konsocijacije', *Odjek* (2007): 6–12.

Norris, Pippa. *Driving Democracy: Do Power-Sharing Institutions Work?* New York: Cambridge University Press, 2008.

Pejanović, Mirko, *Through Bosnian Eyes: The Political Memoir of a Bosnian Serb*. West Lafayette: Purdue University Press, 2004.

Pickering, Paula. 'Explaining Support for Non-nationalist Parties in Post-conflict Societies in the Balkans'. *Europe-Asia Studies* 61, no. 4 (2009): 565–91.

Pugh, Michael, and Margaret Cobble. 'Non-Nationalist Voting in Bosnian Municipal Elections: Implications for Democracy and Peacebuilding'. *Journal of Peace Research* 38, no. 1 (2001): 27–47.

R Development Core Team. *R: A Language and Environment for Statistical Computing*. Vienna, Austria: R Foundation for Statistical Computing, 2009.

Rabushka, Alvin, and Kenneth A. Shepsle. *Politics in Plural Societies: A Theory of Democratic Instability*. Columbus, OH: Merrill, 1972.

Tilley, James, Geoffrey Evans, and Claire Mitchell. 'Consociationalism and the Evolution of Political Cleavages in Northern Ireland, 1989–2004'. *British Journal of Political Science* 38, no. 4 (2008): 699–717.

Todorova, Maria, *Imagining the Balkans*. New York: Oxford University Press, 1997.

An uneasy symbiosis: the impact of international administrations on political parties in post-conflict countries

Maja Nenadović

Department of European Studies, University of Amsterdam, Amsterdam, The Netherlands

This study examines the impact of international administrations on the development and functioning of political parties in post-conflict settings, using Bosnia-Herzegovina and Kosovo as case studies. These cases show how, next to the establishment of a functioning institutional framework, the development and maturity of local political elites are crucial factors of post-conflict democratization, as a genuine handover of power has yet to take place in both countries. Notwithstanding the international political relevance attached to the establishment of democratic governance in post-conflict areas, the local dimension of (enforced) democratization, especially the role and relevance of political parties, has been largely overlooked in academic research. This analysis therefore explores the institutional and cultural dimensions of 'external' democratization and international administrations' influence on political parties and politics in Bosnia-Herzegovina and Kosovo.

Glossary of abbreviations

Alliance for the Future of Kosovo	AAK
Alliance of Independent Social Democrats	SNSD
Bosnia-Herzegovina	BiH
Croatian Democratic Party	HDZ
Dayton Peace Agreement	DPA
Democratic League of Dardania	LDD
Democratic League of Kosovo	LDK
Democratic Party of Kosovo	PDK
International Criminal Tribunal for former Yugoslavia	ICTY
Kosovo Liberation Army	KLA
New Kosovo Alliance	AKR
Office of the High Representative	OHR

PROMOTING PARTY POLITICS IN EMERGING DEMOCRACIES

Organization for Security and Cooperation in Europe	OSCE
Party for Bosnia-Herzegovina	SBiH
Party of Democratic Action	SDA
People's Party Work for Betterment	NSRzB
Reformist Party ORA	ORA
Serbian Democratic Party	SDS
Social Democratic Party	SDP
Special Representative of the Secretary General	SRSG
United Nations Mission in Kosovo	UNMIK
United Nations Security Council Resolution	UNSCR

Introduction

The building of functional democratic states in the aftermath of conflicts has been a growing preoccupation of Western countries since the 1990s. The increase in the number of conflicts and peace-building operations has led to a parallel increase in both policy and scholarly literature analysing state- and peace-building strategies, tools and the outcomes they yield in the field of post-conflict reconstruction. In the aftermath of conflict, the 'international community' intervenes in many ways, the most extensive of which is 'literally taking over the governance function from local actors'.[1] Two prime examples of such countries are Bosnia-Herzegovina (hereafter: BiH) and Kosovo.[2] Currently (mid-2010), the former is in its 15th and the latter in its 11th year under international administration since the cessation of the conflicts. They show how, next to the establishment of a functioning institutional framework, the development of local political parties and elites is a crucial factor of post-conflict stabilization and democratization. In both cases, the handover of governance responsibility has yet to take place, and the international community officials often lament the apparent lack of 'local ownership' of the political elites over the democratization and state-building processes. Moreover, local political elites in BiH are generally considered the principal culprits for the country's political stalemate which is blocking its reform and progress towards EU integration.[3]

The international and local actors are inevitably intertwined in their interactions in post-conflict environments. As creation of functional and democratic states is the final mission objective of international administrations in both BiH and Kosovo,[4] local political elites play a key role in the eventual fulfilment of this goal. While the international actors have received ample attention from the scholarly community,[5] local political actors have been largely overlooked as subjects of analysis.[6] This study is an attempt to redress this imbalance. The aim of this study is to examine the ways in which international administrations influenced political parties and their development in BiH and Kosovo.

Several parts form this investigation. The first defines the key terms and synthesizes the literature on post-conflict reconstruction, more specifically on post-conflict political parties' development. The second section briefly explores the setup of international administrations in BiH and Kosovo. The third part presents an overview of the dominant parties in the BiH and Kosovo political party systems. The analysis of international administrations' influence on political parties in BiH and Kosovo is divided in two dimensions: institutional and cultural. The institutional impact is distinguished through the analysis of direct influence on parties in the form of party laws and regulations, and the design of electoral systems. Given that 'political culture' is a broad term, the cultural-dimension analysis is addressed through evaluation of one particular democratic value directly relevant for the subject of political elites: accountability. This section thus consists of both establishing the presence and level of accountability of local political actors and discerning the international administrations' influence on the state of this particular democratic norm in BiH and Kosovo.

The international administrations in both cases, owing to their overarching governance powers, received a lot of bad press for their perceived extensive intervention in local politics.[7] In BiH, the international administration singled out ethnic nationalist parties as problem-makers and sought to undermine their power in order to pave the way for parties seen as moderate. In Kosovo, on the other hand, the international administration cooperated tightly with parties that emerged from the guerrilla Kosovo Liberation Army (KLA), even though they were involved in mass-scale retribution and violence against the remaining Serb minority members as well as against political opponents from other parties.[8] However, this investigation reveals in the concluding section that international administrations – despite their overarching governance powers – did not exert substantial democratizing impact on political parties and their development in either institutional or cultural dimension.

What do we (think we) know about politics after conflict?

Academic analyses as a rule lag behind actual developments in the post-conflict reconstruction field. The rise in international peacekeeping and peace building operations, the multiplicity of actors involved in the reconstruction effort and the often ad hoc nature of that response further complicate studying these cases. However, there are a growing number of observations based on 'lessons learned' in the past and current post-conflict reconstruction efforts. This section addresses some of those findings, dealing with questions such as: what is known about political parties and their development in the aftermath of conflicts? What are thought to be the best designs for post-conflict political systems?

Political parties after conflict

Political parties, as organizations that exist to run for positions of power through popular elections,[9] fulfil several important functions in a democratic system. As articulators, aggregators and representatives of social interests, they are in the position to shape public opinion and the perceptions of the society they inhabit. There is a consensus that political parties are a crucial element for the functioning of democracy: 'political parties created democracy and...modern democracy is unthinkable save in terms of parties'.[10]

Little has been written about political parties and their development in the aftermath of conflicts. In most of the analyses of post-conflict reconstructions, they receive a brief mention in discussions on (re)creating a working government and state institutions. These fleeting remarks can best be described as pieces of advice to the international administrations or intervening forces (that is, peace builders), rather than theories on post-conflict party development.

Despite this lack of attention, political parties are believed to have 'magnified importance' in post-conflict and conflict-prone societies.[11] They are seen as important post-conflict 'agents of democratization'.[12] Roland Paris advises that – before allowing a party to be registered and to function – 'parties should be obliged to have members from all of the formerly warring groups and to espouse cross-factional compromise and coexistence as a principal goal'.[13] Timothy D. Sisk concurs, saying that creating multiethnic parties and coalitions would serve 'to create incentives for political leaders to be moderate on divisive ethnic themes, and to enhance minority influence in majority decision making'.[14] Political parties can be influenced in various ways through 'using institutional incentives and constraints': party regulation (on party formation, financing, and distribution of members), electoral law design, strengthening parties in the parliament (top-down approach aimed at building greater intra-party discipline) and international party assistance interventions.[15]

Finally, another group of scholars points out that political parties may pose a threat to the peace process by having former military groups transform into political ones while not renouncing violence (for example, Democratic Party of Kosovo – PDK), or by establishing their identity and support base on divisive issues such as nationalism (for example, Party of Democratic Action – SDA, Serbian Democratic Party – SDS, Croatian Democratic Party – HDZ in BiH). They therefore hypothesize that, 'one way of avoiding these problems is to remove political parties from the process'.[16] In BiH and Kosovo, however, this move has not been contemplated. To the contrary, elections were one of the primary tools that international administrations used to introduce democracy in these two countries.

Post-conflict political system design

Reilly and Nordlund's book on party development in conflict-prone societies demonstrates that those in charge of designing political institutions have many options in front of them. They range from regulations that demand political parties to be nation-wide or have multi-ethnic composition of members in order to compete in elections, instituting high vote thresholds or gender quotas or providing financial or technical assistance to moderate or democratic parties as opposed to nationalist ones.[17] By now it is widely accepted that post-war elections should not be organized prematurely. Some see the danger of 'little more than a repackaging of the armed groups that fought the original conflict',[18] while others point out that under these circumstances, 'in societies divided along ethnic lines...unscrupulous leaders who "play the ethnic card" can be rewarded with electoral success'.[19]

Most of the authors on the subject of post-conflict governance reconstruction advocate the institution of a power-sharing system for ethnically divided societies. The model that has lately received a substantial amount of attention is consociationalism, first introduced by Arend Lijphart. It is based on power sharing, group autonomy and representational proportionality of different cleavages in society.[20] At the same time, Timothy D. Sisk and Anna K. Jarstad warn that, 'some types of power-sharing systems may contain the seeds of their own self-destruction as the search for consensus turns into deadlock by political leaders aware that they hold the power of veto over governmental action'.[21] This warning echoes strongly with assessments of BiH's consociational political system and its functional flaws.

Finally, in answering their own question – can democracy be designed? – Bastian and Luckham point out that 'Institutional design is an apparent oxymoron...because institutions...evolve, grow, become rooted.... And where attempts are made to design them, history, "accident and force" and political manipulation may turn them on their heads and produce perverse and unforeseen outcomes...'[22] Similarly, Fukuyama cautions against the limits of institutional design and stresses the importance of society's norms, traditions and values for shaping the (political) actors' behaviour.[23] In short, there is no theory to fall back on when it comes to creating or resurrecting political systems after war. Likewise, there seem to be more warnings than advice regarding the design of governance institutions.

International administrations and political systems of BiH and Kosovo

This section explores the peace agreements that laid the foundation for international administrations in BiH and Kosovo, and the political systems they gave birth to.

Bosnia-Herzegovina

The war in BiH ended with the negotiation of the Dayton Peace Agreement[24] (DPA) in Dayton, Ohio in the US in November 1995. Annex IV of the DPA, the Constitution, laid out the complex four-tier[25] power-sharing structure in the country between the three main ethnic groups. Bosniaks, Croats, Serbs and 'Others' living in BiH thus found themselves in a political system fashioned with consociational characteristics. The main characteristic of this system is the previously mentioned acute stalemate in decision-making and lack of cooperation between the groups: 15 years after the conclusion of the peace agreement, BiH's three main ethnic groups are still failing to agree on how to run the country. The DPA has provided peace, but it has also instituted a dysfunctional and ineffective governance system that has proven extremely difficult to dismantle.[26]

The chief institutions of the international administration in BiH are the Office of the High Representative (OHR)[27] and the Organization for Security and

Cooperation in Europe (OSCE). The OHR was mandated to carry out the civilian implementation of the DPA as laid out in its Annex X, whose Article V also left the High Representative (HR) with 'the final authority to interpret' the DPA. This led to a drastic expansion of the international administration mandate in BiH in December of 1997: the HR was given the power to dismiss obstructive public officials and impose legislation if BiH's legislative bodies failed to deliver.[28] Finally, the OSCE was tasked with the responsibility for elections, human rights, (regional) military stabilization and democracy-building.[29]

Kosovo

The North Atlantic Treaty Organization (NATO)-led Operation Allied Force conducted from March until June 1999 was launched in the name of stopping grave violations of human rights and crimes against humanity. Its purpose was to expel the Serbian forces from Kosovo and prevent Serbian President Milošević from continuing the oppression of Kosovar Albanians.

The international administration in Kosovo began with United Nations Security Council Resolution 1244.[30] This 1999 document set out the basic framework of Kosovo's post-conflict reconstruction under the leadership of international officials. The issue that remained unresolved was the issue of Kosovo's status: the UNSCR 1244 (re)affirmed Serbia's territorial sovereignty while laying out the plan for creating autonomous self-governing institutions in Kosovo. However, the unresolved status issue proved to be a major obstacle to the post-conflict democratization, and on 17 February 2008 Kosovo went ahead and proclaimed independence, coordinating the move with its strongest Western allies.[31] The international administration in Kosovo was a division of labour between the United Nations Interim Administration Mission in Kosovo (UNMIK) headed by the Special Representative of the Secretary General (SRSG), and the OSCE.[32] While the OSCE is mandated with democratization, institution building, promotion of human rights and the rule of law, UNMIK was tasked with the establishment and monitoring of the development of provisional democratic self-government institutions.

Political parties in BiH and Kosovo: an overview

This section proceeds with an overview of major parties in BiH and Kosovo and it describes the political party systems that have been formed since the beginning of international administrations.

Political parties in Bosnia-Herzegovina

One of the main provisions in DPA was the immediate holding of elections in 1996. Though it was difficult to organize nation-wide elections at short notice alongside other tasks of post-conflict reconstruction, the international administration in BiH nevertheless delivered. This proved to be a pyrrhic victory:

The election project stalled the process of reforms for at least a couple of years because this very democratic measure, backed by no rule of law to speak of, simply allowed criminals to legitimize themselves by being elected to office all over the country. What this led to in September 1996 was not the launching of a democratic future for Bosnia, but allowing criminals and war profiteers to hijack the institutions of the state.[33]

The political parties that emerged as winners of the 1996 elections were the same mono-ethnic parties that led BiH into war in the early 1990s. This 'ethnicization' of the political landscape effectively resulted in a tripartite party system: Bosniak, Serb and Croat. This section discusses the main parties in all three ethnic groups, as well as the major intra-group changes that have taken place in the last 15 years. The final paragraph looks at the parties that declare themselves multi-ethnic.

Two parties dominate the Bosniak political scene. These are the SDA and Party for BiH (SBiH). SDA was a nationalist Muslim party founded in May 1990 and its founder and leader Alija Izetbegović was BiH's wartime president. Though in the beginning they were coalition partners (1998 elections), the SBiH soon established itself as SDA's chief competitor. Traditionally the Bosniak seat in the tripartite presidency has been occupied by SDA leaders, but in 2006 the leader of SBiH Haris Silajdžić won the bid for the post. Both SDA and SBiH are affiliated with an organization called the Islamic Community.[34] Following the failure of the constitutional reform talks in April 2006, President Silajdžić's clashes with Republika Srpska Prime Minister Milorad Dodik have dominated the political scene in BiH.

While in Federation BiH, Bosniak and Croat parties share power, Republika Srpska is a largely ethnically homogenous entity.[35] The Serbian political party system in BiH was in the first half of the post-Dayton period dominated by the SDS. Originally, the party was led by Radovan Karadžić, who is currently standing trial for war crimes at the International Criminal Tribunal for former Yugoslavia (ICTY) in The Hague. Widely perceived as the nationalist obstructers of the DPA implementation, the SDS was under direct assault from the international administration throughout most of its time in power. Its elected officials were systematically removed from power following indictments by the ICTY and corruption allegations. The political party that received ample international support was the initially moderate Alliance of the Independent Social Democrats (SNSD), led by Milorad Dodik. With international support,[36] SNSD has managed to win overwhelming support of the RS electorate and squeeze its former rival SDS into opposition. SNSD's tightening grip on power is a sign of dominant-party system emergence in the RS. Since 2006, Dodik has received increasing criticism from the international administration for his lack of cooperation with BiH state level institutions and threats of holding an RS referendum on independence.

Since the beginning of the multi-party system in BiH, the Croat ethnic group was represented by the nationalist HDZ. It had close links with both the HDZ party in Croatia and with the Catholic Church. Throughout its time in power, HDZ was troubled by internal factions that resulted in breakaway parties.

In 2006, the most serious split took place and a group of HDZ members who felt that the party no longer represented the interests of the Croat people living in BiH founded their own party, giving it the name HDZ-1990, to signal their commitment to the party's original nationalist goals. Finally, one Croat family business party has been on a steady rise since its formation in 2006 – People's Party Work for Betterment (NSRzB). The Croat party system, therefore, could be classified as a multi-party system.

The strongest multi-ethnic party is the Social Democratic Party (SDP), successor to the Communist League of BiH. The party opposes ethnic nationalism and runs on civic, bread-and-butter issue platforms. SDP was in power within the governing coalition Alliance for Change from 2000 until 2002 that was championed by the international administration at the time. The Alliance was a short-lived coalition of moderates and was beaten by nationalists in the 2002 elections. Since then, the SDP has been the main opposition party in BiH. The party's self-proclaimed multi-ethnic character is threatened by the general perception of it being a Bosniak-dominated party.

Political parties in Kosovo

The international administration in Kosovo was, among other things, tasked with the job of creating a political system, rather than resurrecting one as was the case in BiH: 'If political institution-building in BiH has been a process of design and reform, in Kosovo...it has been a more gradual one of staged development from consultation to co-government and finally to self-government...'[37]

Prior to the 1998–1999 Kosovo crisis, there were no officially organized political parties in the province. The late President Ibrahim Rugova organized and led the Democratic League of Kosovo (LDK), a peaceful resistance movement that organized parallel institutions of governance to the Serbian-dominated ones. Perhaps having learned a lesson from the events in BiH, the international administration waited before organizing the first general post-conflict elections – they held them in Kosovo two years after the intervention, in 2001.

From the very beginning, there seemed to be a parallel development of two multiparty party systems: one composed of Kosovar Albanian (the majority population), and the other of Serbian[38] and other minority parties. Reflecting the pre- and post-intervention division in the society, the Albanian and Serbian parties always had starkly different visions of Kosovo, its past, present and future. Whilst the former saw the post-1999 period as giving them the freedom of self-determination that they had been long hoping and fighting for, the latter saw the post-1999 developments as an illegal international intervention violating the territorial and national sovereignty of their home country, Serbia. The international administration has not been able to bridge the continuing divide between the two groups.

The majority multi-party system is composed of several parties. The oldest one, LDK, reformed into a political party after the 1999 foreign intervention. Its founder and leader, Ibrahim Rugova, was the first President of Kosovo, and he stayed in this position until his death in 2006. Following an internal faction struggle in 2007, LDK's breakaway splinter party LDD took some of the votes in the 2007 elections and thus ensured LDK's decline from the status of the strongest party in Kosovo. The Alliance for the Future of Kosovo (AAK) and the PDK both stem from the Kosovo Liberation Army (KLA), the former guerrilla/military group. AAK's leader Ramush Haradinaj was recently exonerated from charges during his trial at the ICTY for war crimes.[39] His counterpart, Hashim Thaçi, is currently the Prime Minister – his party PDK won the most votes in the 2007 general elections. Those elections saw two other major changes in the political scene – the Reformist Party ORA, previously represented in the Assembly, did not pass the 5% vote threshold, whilst the one-year-old New Kosovo Alliance (AKR), founded by the wealthy Kosovo diaspora businessman Behgjet Pacolli, surprised everyone by gaining 12% of the vote. The OSCE has been working through its Political Party Unit on party profilization, that is, steering them to dominant European party ideologies on the left–right spectrum. As a result, Kosovo parties have identified with various European-level parties or are leaning towards certain ideologies. Thus, LDK is affiliated with the Centrist Democrat International; LDD sees itself as Liberal Conservative; ORA and PDK are flirting with Social-democratic ideology; AAK and AKR seem to be leaning towards Liberal. However, this process of political party profilization is in its infancy and parties in Kosovo are still far from having clear ideological affiliation or well developed party programmes.[40]

The political landscape of the minority parties is less clear. In the Kosovo Assembly, minority parties are allocated 20 (out of 120) seats – 10 for the representatives of Serbian minority, four for the representatives of Roma, Ashkali and Egyptians, three seats for Bosniaks, two for Turks and one seat for the representative of the Gorani minority group. The political participation of Kosovar Serbs after 1999 has been highly problematic. Several political parties that are present in Serbia established or continued their branch involvement in Kosovo.[41] These parties boycott Kosovo institutions and elections, insisting that Kosovo is an integral part of Serbia. The international party assistance organizations in Kosovo, most notably the National Democratic Institute (NDI), have supported the development of Kosovar Serb parties independent from Belgrade. Examples include the Independent Liberal Party (SLS), Serbian People's Party (SNS), Kosovo Objective Party (KOS), Serbian Democratic Party (SDS), New Democracy (ND). The Serbian multi-party system in Kosovo is noticeably fragmented. Despite the supposed wide choice of political options, Serbs from Kosovo have largely boycotted the elections.

The institutional dimension impact

The international community establishes its administrations in post-conflict territories expecting that they can create the institutional structure conducive to democratic development of local political elites. This section explores the most important international administration regulations that have influenced the formation, functioning and behaviour of political parties. It does so through analysing the influence on parties through party regulation and electoral system designs.

Party regulation

As mentioned before, the political landscape in both BiH and Kosovo is composed of ethnically divided parties. The literature, on the other hand, suggests that it is more conducive for the development of stable democracies to have a few socio-ideologically broad-based political parties.[42] The international officials viewed the ethnicization of the political arena as one of the obstacles for the reform and effective local governance in BiH. At the same time, little was done in terms of party registration and organization laws to change the status quo. In BiH, the base of the party registration law is the pre-war 1991 Law on Political Organizations.[43] Basic in its provisions, this law fails to take into account the damaging ethnicization of the BiH political landscape. The only recognition of that special nature lies in the following provision:

> BiH Election Law...[states] that a political party or coalition will not meet the requirements for participating at elections for as long as a function or position in the party is held by a person who is serving a sentence delivered by the International War Crimes Tribunal for Former Yugoslavia, or is indicted by the Tribunal and has failed to appear before it when requested.[44]

Indictment by the ICTY has been used in BiH as a reason for HRs to remove dozens of elected officials from public office. In Kosovo, the Office of the Political Party Registration and Certification was initially set up and run by the OSCE. The ICTY provision is also a part of the Rule No.01/2008 on Registration and Operation of Political Parties.[45] In the same rule, article 5.1 (c) stipulates that, a party may be denied registration if it applies '...under a name, acronym, or symbol that is likely, in the judgment of the Office, to incite inter-communal, ethnic or religious hatred or violence'.[46] This seems to be the only reminder within the rule on party formation and organization that the society of Kosovo holds internal tensions which this provision is seeking to keep under control.

Regarding the laws on party financing, the international administrations were slow in their implementation in both BiH and Kosovo. In BiH the Law on Party Financing[47] was implemented in 2000 whereas in Kosovo it was incorporated within the rule No.01/2008 on Registration and Operation of Political Parties. In BiH the amount of both individual and corporate contributions to political parties is set at eight average salaries (currently it comes to about €2,500). In Kosovo, the limit is substantially higher, set at €20,000. At the same time, journalists point to the exuberant spending by the BiH political parties and the funds channelled into them from the state and entity budgets.[48] In Kosovo, the general perception holds that most, if not all political parties are linked to organized crime networks.[49] Ahead of the 2007 general and municipal elections, the candidates running for office were required to disclose their financial assets: the fact that several leaders and prominent members of the main political parties declared incomes over €1,000,000 in a country with a virtually non-existent economy seems to confirm that predominant perception.[50] Finally, an investigation in BiH has revealed that state budget funds are by far the biggest source of the financing of political parties: 'The funds put aside for some political parties were up to as high as a million EUR per year...these funds are progressively increasing, and the estimate is that public budgets on all levels of governance yearly distribute as much as 10 million Euros to political parties'.[51] This goes to show that the laws on party financing in BiH have not prevented 'the dominant predatory elite project in post-communism – extraction from the state'.[52]

Electoral system design

International administrations have a proven affinity for elections – in BiH they organized general elections in 1996, 1998, 2000, 2002 and 2006; in Kosovo, the electoral enthusiasm was still intact, with general elections taking place in 2001, 2004 and 2007.[53] According to an OSCE discussion brief, 'continuous elections, if held in as free and fair a manner as possible, have been viewed by the international community as a means to bring stability and recovery to a country divided by extreme nationalist political leaders...'[54]

This continuing faith of the international administrations in elections as an appropriate and effective tool for political change stemmed from their view that popularly represented local officials would pave the way for a quick exit strategy.[55] In BiH, this expectation proved to be based on a faulty premise – that the elected local political actors will be responsible, democratic and interested in working for the welfare of all the citizens. Instead, they ended up with political parties and their nationalist leaders who were pitching their own group's individual interests against the other groups, making the consociational power-sharing deadlocked at best and potentially violent at worst.

In BiH, the electoral law that was in power until 2000 was one of proportional representation and closed-party lists.[56] The international administration amended it in the hope of moderating the political space and allowing the moderate and non-nationalist/multiethnic parties to get to power: the lists were thus made open for the 2000 elections. The election system of BiH is now a combination of several elements:

> ...majority/plurality first-past-the-post principle for the Presidency elections...proportional representation principle for the Parliament... 3% electoral threshold, preferential voting, compensatory seats. ...This complex electoral system was implemented by the international administration in a very specific political moment...and it is a high time for it to be reconsidered.[57]

The fact that in BiH the High Representative so frequently resorted to his powers of removing elected officials perceived to be harmful to the peace process from power has made the original nationalist political parties sensitive to their candidate selection.[58] At the same time, this failed to influence the leading parties' nationalist ideologies. The 2006 general elections further discouraged the international administration mandated with the task of democratization of BiH: the electoral success of the so-called 'second-generation nationalist parties' (SBiH, SNSD, HDZ 1990) has further cemented the political and governance stalemate.

The multiparty system in Kosovo is elected through proportional representation, with a 5% vote threshold.[59] The party lists were closed in 2001 and 2004. Following the pressure by the international administration institutions, the decision to switch to open party lists was the result of a consultation with the major political parties. Kosovo's first elections with open party lists took place in 2007. This step was expected to bring the candidates closer to their constituencies. At the same time, the 2007 general elections had the lowest voter turnout yet – less than 45% of the eligible voters cast their vote, indicating the electorate's disillusionment and disappointment with politics in Kosovo.[60]

The impact of international administrations on political culture

Democracy is not just a technical, institutional form – it is also a cultural practice.[61] Scholars have observed that, 'culture is perhaps the greatest constraint on reconstruction efforts'.[62] One of the key studies on the international administration in Kosovo concludes that,

> ...it was the efforts to turn Kosovo into a multi-ethnic democracy subject to the rule of law that failed so spectacularly. After six years as an international protectorate, Kosovo's political culture remained largely unchanged. The OSCE was charged with democratization; as it contemplated its departure, parties were neither internally democratic nor distinguished by a political philosophy, the amount of grassroots activism was minute and political violence was commonplace.... In the realm of soft power, the mission barely dented the political culture underlying Kosovo's instability.[63]

The importance of instituting democratic values within post-conflict societies and the failure of norm transfer is therefore increasingly recognized.

This section focuses on one of the key dimensions of democratic governance: the accountability of political representatives. Accountability is central to democracy, because it 'makes the abuse of political power less likely, while at the same time helping to empower governments to serve the ends that democratically elected governments are legitimately asked to pursue'.[64] Andreas Schedler's definition of accountability as a multi-dimensional phenomenon is used here: 'answerability, the obligation of public officials to inform about and to explain what they are doing; and enforcement, the capacity of accounting agencies to impose sanctions on power-holders who have violated their public duties'.[65]

Therefore, accountability here is understood as a *value* that ideally exists among the political elites. Secondly, it stands for the existence of an enforcement mechanism of that value. The next section will look at the status quo of accountability of local political actors. The concluding part uncovers the ways in which the international administrations influenced the development of that accountability.

The level of accountability in BiH and Kosovo

In 2006 a group of researchers assembled by the Open Society Foundation carried out an extensive assessment of the level of democracy in Bosnia-Herzegovina.[66] The report states that elected representatives hold no accountability for the pace of reform in the country.[67] Conversely, the report suggests that the international administration and the HR in particular do not seem to be accountable to anyone.[68] Though values are difficult to establish and measure, certain events and the general atmosphere suggest that the people in BiH are a long way from holding their elected officials accountable. When the former Croat member of the Presidency Dragan Čović was removed from his post by the HR Paddy Ashdown in 2005 due to the allegations of fraud and corrupt activities, he returned to his constituency in the Herzegovina-Neretva canton and was the next day re-elected President of the HDZ party. This party continued to win the popular vote of the Croat ethnic group in BiH, while under his leadership. This indicates that corruption is *not* a deal breaker for political engagement in BiH. Furthermore, the public confidence in elected officials in BiH has continuously been assessed as low and the corruption is perceived as widely spread at all government levels.[69] Finally, the newspapers in BiH regularly publish investigative stories linking the elected officials with criminal activities. Yet, the same actors are rarely investigated by judicial organs or the police, which adds to the general feeling that politicians are untouchable by the law. Do accountability enforcement mechanisms exist in BiH? The Democracy Assessment report suggests that they do, but it fails to specify whether they are being used. The report does, however, discuss the inflated and intricately burdensome four-tier state apparatus of the country and states that it is not functional. The experience from the field suggests that the mechanisms for enforcement of accountability are drowned in that complex state apparatus and are hence being ignored.

The situation is not very different in Kosovo. The rich leaders of the main political parties and their perceived links with the organized crime networks make the political domain highly susceptible to a lack of democratic accountability. Despite the fact that the international administration has been present in Kosovo since the cessation of the conflict in 1999, the international and local actors realized only in 2006 that the country needed an action plan to fight corruption.[70] Is accountability of local political elites a value present in the Kosovar society? The evidence, just as in the BiH case, points to a negative answer. It is widely documented that Kosovo operates on a clan-based structure. This implies nepotism and disregard of meritocratic or transparent forms of governance, civil service and other appointments. Furthermore, Kosovo's problematic image as 'a country in which organized crime is the form of government'[71] suggests democratic accountability as yet to take root.

Are there accountability enforcement mechanisms in Kosovo? There are several local and international corruption fighting agencies active on the ground. Interviews with some of their officials however, point to the fact that only 'small fish' are being investigated. Also, these interviews confirmed that members of political parties, despite the allegations of corruption and criminal activities that exist in the press, are not under investigation by any of these agencies.[72] Finally, the Ombudsman reports in Kosovo have traditionally been critical of the international role there, blaming the international administration for violation of human rights, operating in the least transparent way and an apparent lack of accountability.[73]

International administrations' impact on accountability of local political actors

The previous section has established that the level of accountability of political elites in BiH and Kosovo can be found somewhere along the spectrum ranging from low to non-existent.[74] Though some accountability enforcement mechanisms exist in both of the cases, they constitute window-dressing implemented by the international administration, rather than a genuine, effective and applied instrument of good democratic governance. This section will investigate how the international administrations influenced the development of accountability in BiH and Kosovo's political elites.

First of all, the very existence of the international administrations provides for a convenient excuse for the local political actors when their policy making gets deadlocked due to their incapacity for consensus politics. In both countries, local political elites tend to blame the slow democratization and reform pace on the international administrations. Similarly, the four-tier structure present among the local governance institutions in BiH allows for avoidance of both responsibility and accountability by the political elites. The officials at the municipal, cantonal, entity and state levels are fond of shifting the blame amongst one another.

Secondly, holding local political actors accountable was not an international priority in the immediate post-conflict reconstruction and state building phase. Although accountability was always formally listed as one of the pillars of democracy and good governance, there was no concentrated effort for its institution. The international administrations in both BiH and Kosovo have both received a substantial amount of criticism for their lack of clear exit strategy.[75] A part of the response to that criticism was the lip service to issues of corruption fighting and fostering local ownership.

Thirdly, the lack of political will among the international community for enforcement of accountability standards is best illustrated by the fact that they failed to implement them within their own ranks. The paradox here is that even though one could expect that officials from the Western established democratic countries had a developed sense of accountability, the international administrations operating in BiH and Kosovo did not create any mechanisms for its enforcement. Whereas this has generated widespread criticism and allegations of corruption, there have been few cases of international officials who were investigated or prosecuted for their wrongdoings.[76] Anecdotal 'theory' from the field has it that instead of democratizing the Balkans, the international administrations ended up being 'Balkanized'.[77] As one interviewee put it, 'When the cat's away, the mice will play', pointing to the problematic lack of accountability mechanisms for the international administrations.[78]

Fourthly, the international community's lack of prioritization of accountability is also seen in their strategic approach to holding local actors to that standard. In other words, the local officials who demonstrate their willingness to cooperate with the international administrations[79] or those who become key players in the political processes by generating extensive popular support[80] elude investigation and prosecution, despite allegations of corruption or implication in war crimes. Those unwilling to cooperate but without strong political backing are more susceptible to being held up against an accountability standard by the international administrations. This strategically selective and self-interested approach by the international administrations harms the general value of holding local political actors accountable for their actions.

Finally, one has to wonder to what extent is the accountability of local actors enforced or promoted as a value, if the only mechanisms enforcing it – albeit selectively – are the international administrations? In this way, the voters who elected them do not get the chance to hold the same officials accountable, which poses problems for the building of democracy.[81] The international administrations did little to strengthen and protect genuinely domestic anti-corruption and accountability-enforcing institutions.

Conclusion

The reconstruction of post-conflict societies and the state building projects involved are based on the goal that the countries in question will one day become functional, democratic and viable states. The continuing international administrations in BiH and Kosovo, 15 and 11 years respectively post-conflict, stand as evidence that neither of the countries is ready for sovereign, democratic self-rule.

A stable political party system and effective and accountable governance are some of the vital conditions for conclusion of international administrations and handover of power from the international to the local political officials. It is a known weakness of transitional states that elites get to '...govern in the name of the people without having to be fully accountable to voters'.[82] In both BiH and Kosovo this seems to be the norm: the level of accountability of local actors is low. Furthermore, the political landscape continues to be ethnically divided, and BiH exemplifies the difficult if not impossible mission of democratizing a country in which the divisive ideology of nationalism equals votes.

The uneasy symbiosis between the international administrations and their local political counterparts stems from the blame game taking place between the two groups. Increasingly coming under pressure from both the academic and journalistic communities, as well as from the final funders of the reconstruction projects sitting in the capitals of various Western countries, in place of concrete results in the field they point to one another as the excuse for the lack of reform, the slow pace of democratization and a failure to meet expectations.

This investigation has revealed that international administrations – despite their overarching governance powers – did not exert substantial impact on political parties and their (democratic) development in either institutional or cultural dimensions. In terms of the institutional impact, the introduced party laws were basic: they did not create incentives for, nor did they demand the formation of cross-cleavage, multi-ethnic parties. Equally, the laws on party financing exist, but have not prevented the parties' extraction of funds from the state budget, nor do they effectively regulate or make party financing transparent.

Coyne identifies a potential cause behind the failure to develop liberal democracy in the aftermath of conflict: 'failure is not due to a lack of a clear end-goal, but instead, failure is due to the lack of knowledge of how to go about achieving the desired end. In other words, failure is due to the gap between the *know-what* and *know-how*'.[83] This analysis has shown that international administrations have paid insufficient effort to discovering the know-how of democratic norm diffusion. Furthermore, it has been documented that the transfer of norms might flow in both directions: although the work of international administrations is aimed to democratize the local political elites and institutions, the local political culture seems to penetrate its ways into the behaviour of the international administration officials. In the uneasy symbiosis between the two groups, the Balkan political culture may be winning the war of norm diffusion: the local political elites seem to have had more success in 'socializing' the international administration officials to 'the local way of doing things' than the latter have had in making the local elites more democratic and accountable in their work.

This analysis has shown that international administration aegis is not a guarantee for success for international democracy promotion in post-conflict societies. The international administrations' rather insipid impact on the institutional framework governing the formation and functioning of political parties has not brought either BiH or Kosovo closer to becoming democratic states. Also, the internationals' failure to transplant democratic norms to the local political elites, as illustrated by the example of accountability has only proven the resilience of the local political culture in the face of foreign norms. Ultimately, 'fractionalized and ethnically-exclusive party systems are inherently damaging for democratic prospects and are, consequently, found widely in failed democracies'.[84] Until the international administrations summon the political will to toughen their regulations on political parties in order to change the divisiveness and corruption dominating the political arena, and until they learn to lead by example in terms of introducing democratic norms into the societies of BiH and Kosovo, the task of the democratization of these two post-conflict Balkan states will continue to be Sisyphus work.

PROMOTING PARTY POLITICS IN EMERGING DEMOCRACIES

Acknowledgements

I would like to thank Marlene Spoerri, André Gerrits, Thomas Carothers, Peter Burnell and Jeff Haynes for their insightful comments on the earlier drafts of this contribution. I thank Laura Dauban for her invaluable proofreading. Note: All interviews were conducted in confidentiality, and the names of interviewees are withheld by mutual agreement.

Notes

1. Fukuyama, *State-Building: Governance and World Order in the 21st Century*, 93. International administrations are staffed by nationals of the countries footing the bill of the reconstruction and accompanied by local support staff. Their heads and top officials are appointed by foreign governments.
2. At the time of writing, Kosovo's independence was recognized by 65 of 192 United Nations (UN) member states. Kosovo will be referred to as 'country' throughout this account, owing to the fact that the author's institution (University of Amsterdam) is in the Netherlands, which is one of the states that has recognized it.
3. Many articles published on Bosnia-Herzegovina are warning about the deteriorating domestic political situation: Kulish, 'While Europe Sleeps, Bosnia Seethes'; McMahon and Western, 'The Death of Dayton: How to Stop Bosnia from Falling Apart'; Champion, 'Bosnia Risks Sliding Into Turmoil, Diplomat Says'.
4. The Dayton Agreement in Bosnia-Herzegovina prescribed, 'that democratic governmental institutions and fair procedures best produce peaceful relations within a pluralist society' (General Framework Agreement for Peace 1995, annex 4, preamble). In Kosovo, the UNSCR 1244 instituted, 'transitional administration while establishing and overseeing the development of provisional democratic self-governing institutions...' (S/Res/1244, 10 June 1999).
5. Two books are dedicated exclusively to the subject of international administrations: Caplan, *International Governance of War-Torn Territories*; Chesterman, *You, the People: The United Nations, Transitional Administration, and State-Building*. Some authors provided case-study evaluations of international administrations: Chandler, *Bosnia: Faking Democracy After Dayton*; *Peace Without Politics*; Bose, *Bosnia after Dayton*; King and Mason, *Peace at Any Price*.
6. Notable exception is the work of Manning: *The Making of Democrats*.
7. Most prominent example of such critique is: Knaus and Martin, 'Travails of the European Raj'.
8. Several authors document the damaging effect of this cooperation, and the sense of impunity it gave to these local warlords-turned-politicians: Wolfgram, 'When the Men with Guns Rule'; King and Mason, *Peace at Any Price*; O'Neill, *Kosovo: An Unfinished Peace*.
9. Sartori, *Parties and Party Systems: A Framework for Analysis*, 63.
10. Schattschneider, *Party Government*, 1.
11. Reilly, 'Introduction', 9. Also, Manning, *The Making of Democrats*, 5–7.
12. Jarstad and Sisk, *From War to Democracy*, 139–41.
13. Paris, 'The Faulty Assumptions of Post-Conflict Peacebuilding', 777.
14. Sisk, 'Democratization and Peacebuilding', 792.
15. Reilly, 'Introduction', 11–18.
16. Chesterman, Ignatieff and Thakur, *Making States Work*, 367–8.
17. Reilly, 'Introduction', 11–18.
18. Chesterman, Ignatieff and Thakur, *Making States Work*, 367.
19. Reilly, 'Political Engineering and Party Politics in Conflict-Prone Societies', 812.
20. Lijphart, 'Constitutional Design for Divided Societies', 96–109.

21. Jarstad, 'Power Sharing', 105–33.
22. Bastian and Luckham, *Can Democracy Be Designed?*, 304.
23. Fukuyama, 'Development and the Limits of Institutional Design'.
24. Full text of the DPA is available at http://www.ohr.int/dpa/default.asp?content_id=380 (accessed October 2, 2008).
25. 1. State-level; 2. Entity-level (Federation of Bosnia-Herzegovina – FBiH; Republika Srpska – RS); 3. Canton-level (10 cantons in FBiH); 4. Municipal-level (142 in total: 79 in FBiH, 62 in RS).
26. This is an often-made critique in international reports on BiH. Prominent local authors agree with this assessment, for example, Arnautović, *Ten Years of Democratic Chaos*.
27. The Peace Implementation Council (PIC) and its Steering Board are the international organs offering 'political guidance' to the Office of the High Representative: more on their composition and involvement at: http://www.ohr.int/pic/default.asp?content_id=38563.
28. The extension of the HR mandate is also referred to as 'the Bonn powers' because the decision to expand the OHR role was brought at the PIC conference held in Bonn, Germany, 9–10 December 1997.
29. OSCE Mission to Bosnia-Herzegovina official website, http://www.oscebih.org/overview/statement.asp?d=7.
30. The full text of United Nations Security Council Resolution 1244 can be accessed at the United Nations Mission in Kosovo (UNMIK) website, http://www.unmikonline.org/press/reports/N9917289.pdf.
31. Currently, the international administration in the country is undergoing restructuring and its future form is as of yet unclear. The European Union is expected to take on most of the governance role.
32. OSCE Mission in Kosovo, official website, http://www.osce.org/kosovo.
33. Pajić, 'State Building: From Transition to Transformation'.
34. Islamic Community ('Islamska zajednica') is the top religious institution for Muslims in Bosnia-Herzegovina. Led by Raisu-l-Ulama Dr Mustafa Cerić, it is closely affiliated with Bosniak political parties. The official website: http://www.rijaset.ba/en (accessed April 2, 2010).
35. This is the result of the ethnic cleansing committed during the 1992–1995 war when Croats and Bosniaks living in the RS territory were systematically expelled or killed.
36. The international support for SNSD-Milorad Dodik consisted of international administration removing SDS officials from power in order to pave the way for SNSD's rise in the elections. Furthermore, international political party assistance organizations, most prominently the US National Democratic Institute (NDI), provided SNSD with extensive aid and expert advice, culminating in the party's overwhelming victory over the SDS in the 2006 general elections.
37. Caplan, *International Governance of War-Torn Territories*, 114.
38. Both genuinely Kosovar Serb parties and parties with headquarters in Belgrade and branch offices throughout Kosovo are included here.
39. UNMIK's public support of an indicted war criminal left the Tribunal's prosecution team shocked as they, 'felt it gave Haradinaj international legitimacy and fostered a chilling effect that discouraged prosecution witnesses from testifying against him'. In: 'Haradinaj, a Forced Marriage between Politics and Justice', *International Justice Tribune*, March 17, 2008.
40. Author interviews with members from PDK, LDK and ORA parties, OSCE representatives and NDI staff members in Prishtina, Kosovo, November 2007 and May 2008.
41. The most notable ones are the Democratic Party of Serbia – DSS, Serbian Radical Party – SRS, Democratic Party – DS, and the Socialist Party of Serbia – SPS.

42. Diamond, Linz and Lipset, 'Introduction: What Makes for Democracy?', 35, in: Reilly and Nordlund, *Political Parties in Conflict-Prone Societies*, 10.
43. Law on Political Organisations, *Official Gazette SRBiH* No. 27/91.
44. Kotlo, 'Democratic Role of the Political Parties', 150.
45. On Registration and Operation of Political Parties Rule No.01/2008, based on Section 11, 12 and 63.7 of the Law nr.03/L-073 on General Elections in the Republic of Kosovo, http://www.cec-ko.org/en/legjislacioni/materiale/rregullatkqz/01-08_en.pdf (accessed October 3, 2008).
46. Ibid., Section 5: Grounds for Denying Registration, 4–5.
47. Bosnia-Herzegovina, the Law on Party Financing, available online through the Council of Europe website: http://www.venice.coe.int/docs/2000/CDL(2000)003-e.asp (accessed September 29, 2008).
48. 'Bosnian Parties Spending Millions', *B92 news*, http://www.b92.net/eng/news/region-article.php?yyyy=2008&mm=08&dd=15&nav_id=52733 (accessed October 13, 2008).
49. Strazzari, 'The Decade Horribilis'.
50. For the 2007 general elections, all candidates running for office had to declare their incomes. The database in which one can look up the records of all the candidates can be accessed from the OSCE Mission in Kosovo Elections website: http://kosovoelections.org/ (accessed November 27, 2007).
51. Martinović, 'Strogo Kontrolisana Anarhija: Financiranje političkih stranaka u BiH' [Strictly Controlled Anarchy: The Financing of Political Parties in BiH]. Note: the sums converted from BAM/KM to EUR currency.
52. 'In Search of Responsive Government: State Building and Economic Growth in the Balkans', 44.
53. The municipal and presidential elections were also held in this period.
54. Commission on Security and Cooperation in Europe (US), 'Elections in Bosnia-Hercegovina', 12–13 September 1998, http://www.house.gov/csce/bosniaelec.htm, 1, in: Manning, 'Elections and Political Change in Post-War Bosnia and Herzegovina'.
55. Manning, 'Elections and Political Change in Post-War Bosnia and Herzegovina', 62–3.
56. BiH Election Law, *Official Gazette BiH* No. 23/01, 7/02, 9/02, 20/02, 25/02, 4/04, and 20/04, 25/05. Text in full available at: http://www.aeobih.com.ba/documents/election%20law%20-%20eng%20language.pdf (accessed December 10, 2008).
57. Mijan, 'Volja Birača ili Algebra Bez Granica: Kakav izborni sistem treba BiH' ['The Will of Voters or Endless Algebra: What Kind of Electoral System BiH is Need Of'].
58. Manning, *The Making of Democrats*, 79–81.
59. Kosovo Electoral Law, available online at the Kosovo Electoral Commission website: http://www.cec-ko.org/en/legjislacioni/materiale/ligjetezgjedhjeve/zgjedhjetpergjiths hme_en.pdf (accessed November 22, 2007).
60. Author interviews with several OSCE election specialists disclosed that even this figure may have been inflated. Prishtina, Kosovo, November 2007.
61. Coles, *Democratic Designs*, 245.
62. Coyne, *After War*, 23.
63. King and Mason, *Peace at Any Price: How the World Failed Kosovo*, 260–2.
64. Burnell, 'The Relationship of Accountable Governance and Constitutional Implementation, with Reference to Africa', 10.
65. Schedler, Diamond and Plattner, *The Self Restraining State*, 14–17.
66. *Democracy Assessment in BiH*, Open Society Institute, 2006, http://www.soros.org.ba/images_vijesti/Istrazivanje%20demokratije/eng/01_democracy_assessment_in_bh.pdf (accessed June 17, 2008).
67. Ibid., 162.

68. Ibid., 186–7.
69. Ibid., 193.
70. The Anti-Corruption Action Plan: Social and Economic Necessity for Kosovo, October 2006, http://www.osce.org/kosovo/item_11_21712.html (accessed October 14, 2008).
71. High ranking German Secret Service official quoted in: 'BND Kosovo Affair: German Spy Affair Might Have Been Revenge'.
72. Interviews with directors and representatives of various anti-corruption agencies and international judiciary members, Prishtina, November 2007.
73. For more information, please refer to the reports listed on the Ombudsperson official website: http://www.ombudspersonkosovo.org (accessed December 18, 2008).
74. Several factors may be causing this low level of accountability: the legacy of the communist past and the conflicts in the 1990s; the links between military groups, organized crime and the local political actors; the problem of dual international/local governance structures; the lack of political will for eradication of corruption; lack of independent checks, i.e. weak civil society and rule of law and insufficiently independent and free media.
75. International Crisis Group and European Stability Initiative reports point to the dependency created between the international administrations and the countries they were supposed to emancipate to democracy.
76. A report warns about '…billions of dollars of reconstruction aid spent without accountability to its intended beneficiaries…' In: 'Postwar Reconstruction Aid Risks Fuelling More Conflict'. Furthermore, journalists often point to corruption cases in the ranks of international administration officials, which often end up with the implicated individuals losing their jobs or leaving to another mission. For an example of journalist reports pointing to corruption among the international officials in Kosovo: Zaremba, *Report From Unmikistan, Land of the Future*.
77. This 'theory' was proposed in several interviews with NGO representatives and journalists in both BiH and Kosovo. Norm diffusion can go both ways: interviewees ironically commented on internationals behaving more like locals, than locals themselves – when it comes to taking extensive coffee and lunch breaks, not delivering results, feeling immune to rule of law.
78. Author interview with an NGO activist in Sarajevo, BiH, 10 May 2008.
79. Examples: Dragan Čović, President of HDZ who, after his dismissal from the State Presidency post due to fraud, is rumoured to have struck a deal with the international community not to obstruct certain reforms in exchange for immunity. Kosovo Prime Minister Hashim Thaci's ICTY investigation dossier (containing evidence for indictment on war crimes) was shelved, indefinitely, following instructions from Washington, DC: author interview with ICTY official, The Hague, 12 April 2008.
80. Example: Milorad Dodik, RS Prime Minister. Though obstructive to the peace- and statebuilding reforms, his party SNSD has established itself as the absolute majority in the RS entity. This makes it impossible for the international administration to remove him (on several occasions threats have been made for his removal from power, to which he replied with counter threats of holding a referendum for independence of the RS).
81. Jarstad, 'Democratisation in Postconflict Societies: Lessons from the Balkans, Prospects for Iraq'.
82. Mansfield and Snyder, 'Democratization and the Danger of War', 5–38.
83. Coyne, *After War*, 21.
84. Huntington, *The Third Wave*, in: Reilly, 'Political Engineering and Party Politics in Conflict-Prone Societies', 813.

Bibliography

Arnautović, Suad. *Ten Years of Democratic Chaos: Electoral Processes in Bosnia and Herzegovina 1996 to 2006 – Essays, Analyses and Comments.* Sarajevo: Promocult d.o.o., 2006.

Bastian, Sunil, and Robin Luckham, eds. *Can Democracy Be Designed? The Politics of Institutional Choice in Conflict-Torn Societies.* London: Zed Books, 2003.

'BND Kosovo Affair: German Spy Affair Might Have Been Revenge'. *Welt Online*, translated by Jacob Comenetz, November 30, 2008, http://www.welt.de/english-news/article2806537/German-spy-affair-might-have-been-revenge.html (accessed October 18, 2010).

Bose, Sumantra. *Bosnia after Dayton: Nationalist Partition and International Intervention.* New York: Oxford University Press, 2002.

Burnell, Peter. 'The Relationship of Accountable Governance and Constitutional Implementation, with Reference to Africa'. *Journal of Politics and Law* 1, no. 3 (September 2008): 10–24.

Caplan, Richard. *International Governance of War-Torn Territories: Rule and Reconstruction.* New York: Oxford University Press, 2005.

Champion, Marc. 'Bosnia Risks Sliding Into Turmoil, Diplomat Says'. *The Wall Street Journal*, March 25, 2009.

Chandler, David. *Bosnia: Faking Democracy After Dayton.* London: Pluto, 1999.

Chesterman, Simon. *You, the People: The United Nations, Transitional Administration, and State-Building.* New York: Oxford University Press, 2004.

Chesterman, Simon, Michael Ignatieff and Ramesh Thakur, eds. *Making States Work: State Failure and the Crisis of Governance.* Tokyo: United Nations University Press, 2005.

Coles, Kimberly. *Democratic Designs: International Intervention and Electoral Practices in Postwar Bosnia-Herzegovina.* Ann Arbor: the University of Michigan Press, 2007.

Coyne, Christopher J. *After War: The Political Economy of Exporting Democracy.* Stanford, CA: Stanford University Press, 2008.

Democracy Assessment in BiH. Open Society Institute, 2006, http://www.soros.org.ba/images_vijesti/Istrazivanje%20demokratije/eng/01_democracy_assessment_in_bh.pdf (accessed June 17, 2008).

Diamond, Larry, Juan Linz, and Seymour Martin Lipset, 'Introduction: What Makes for Democracy?', in *Politics in Developing Countries*, ed. Larry Diamond, Juan Linz, and Seymour Martin Lipset, *Politics in Developing Countries: Comparing Experiences with Democracy.* Boulder, CO: Lynne Rienner Publishers, 1995.

Fukuyama, Francis. *State-Building: Governance and World Order in the 21st Century.* New York: Cornell University Press, 2004.

Fukuyama, Francis. 'Development and the Limits of Institutional Design'. *Global Development Network*, January 20, 2006.

Huntington, Samuel P. *The Third Wave: Democratization in the Late Twentieth Century.* Norman, OK: University of Oklahoma Press, 1991.

'In Search of Responsive Government: State Building and Economic Growth in the Balkans', *Policy Studies Series.* Budapest: Central European University, 2003.

Jarstad, Anna. 'Democratisation in Postconflict Societies: Lessons from the Balkans, Prospects for Iraq'. Paper prepared for delivery at the ISA Annual Convention in Honolulu, Hawaii, USA, March 2005.

Jarstad, Anna. 'Power Sharing', in *From War to Democracy: Dilemmas of Peacebuilding*, ed. Anna K. Jarstad and Timothy D. Sisk, 105–33. Cambridge: Cambridge University Press, 2008.
Jarstad, Anna K., and Timothy D. Sisk, eds. *From War to Democracy: Dilemmas of Peacebuilding*. Cambridge: Cambridge University Press, 2008.
King, Iain, and Whit Mason. *Peace at Any Price: How the World Failed Kosovo*. New York: Cornell University Press, 2006.
Knaus, Gerhard, and Felix Martin. 'Travails of the European Raj'. *Journal of Democracy* 14, no. 3 (July 2003): 60–74.
Kotlo, Rebeka. 'Democratic Role of the Political Parties: Does the Party System Assist the Working of Democracy?', in *Democracy Assessment in BiH*, 149–84. Sarajevo: Open Society Institute, 2006.
Kulish, Nicholas. 'While Europe Sleeps, Bosnia Seethes'. *The New York Times*, September 6, 2009.
Lijphart, Arend. 'Constitutional Design for Divided Societies'. *Journal of Democracy* 15 (2004): 96–109.
Manning, Carrie. 'Elections and Political Change in Post-War Bosnia and Herzegovina'. *Democratization* 11, no. 2 (April 2004): 60–86.
Manning, Carrie. *The Making of Democrats: Elections and Party Development in Postwar Bosnia, El Salvador and Mozambique*. New York: Palgrave Macmillan, 2008.
Mansfield, Edward D., and Jack Snyder. 'Democratization and the Danger of War'. *International Security* 20, no. 1 (1995): 5–38.
Martinović, Aleksandra. 'Strogo Kontrolisana Anarhija: Financiranje političkih stranaka u BiH' ['Strictly Controlled Anarchy: The Financing of Political Parties in BiH']. *Pulse of Democracy*, October 3, 2008, http://www.pulsdemokratije.ba/index.php?l=bs&id=1084 (accessed October 5, 2008).
McMahon, Patrice C., and Jon Western. 'The Death of Dayton: How to Stop Bosnia from Falling Apart'. *Foreign Affairs* 88, no. 5 (September 2009): 69–83.
Mijan, Zvonko. 'Volja Birača ili Algebra Bez Granica: Kakav izborni sistem treba BiH' ['The Will of Voters or Endless Algebra: What Kind of Electoral System BiH is Need Of']. *Pulse of Democracy* (September–October 2006): 1–3.
O'Neill, William G. *Kosovo: An Unfinished Peace*. London: Lyne Rienner Publishers, 2002.
Pajić, Zoran. 'State Building: From Transition to Transformation'. *Transitions Online*, February 12, 2007, http://www.tol/org/client/article/18305-from-transition-to-trans formation.html (accessed September 28, 2008).
Paris, Roland. 'The Faulty Assumptions of Post-Conflict Peacebuilding', in *Turbulent Peace: The Challenges of Managing International Conflict*, ed. Chester A. Crocker, Fen Osler Hampson, and Pamela Aall, 765–84. Washington, DC: United States Institute of Peace, 2001.
'Postwar Reconstruction Aid Risks Fuelling More Conflict'. TIRI Media Release, London, January 16, 2007.
Reilly, Benjamin. 'Political Engineering and Party Politics in Conflict-Prone Societies'. *Democratization* 13, no. 5 (December 2006): 811–27.
Reilly, Benjamin. 'Introduction', in *Political Parties in Conflict-Prone Societies*, ed. Benjamin Reilly and Per Nordlund, 3–24. Tokyo: United Nations University Press, 2008.
Sartori, Giovanni. *Parties and Party Systems: A Framework for Analysis*. Cambridge: Cambridge University Press, 1976.
Schattschneider, E. E. *Party Government*. New York: Rinehart, 1942.
Schedler, Andreas, Larry Diamond, and Marc F. Plattner, eds. *The Self Restraining State: Power and Accountability in New Democracies*. London: Lynne Rienner Publishers, 1999.

Sisk, Timothy D. 'Democratization and Peacebuilding', in *Turbulent Peace: The Challenges of Managing International Conflict*, ed. Chester A. Crocker, Fen Osler Hampson, and Pamela Aall, 785–800. Washington, DC: United States Institute of Peace, 2001.

Strazzari, Francesco. 'The Decade Horribilis: Organized Violence and Organized Crime along the Balkan Peripheries, 1991–2001'. *Mediterranean Politics* 12 (July 2007): 185–209.

Wolfgram, Mark A. 'When the Men with Guns Rule: Explaining Human Rights Failures in Kosovo since 1999'. *Political Science Quarterly* 123, no. 3 (2008): 461–84.

Zaremba, Maciej. 'Report From Unmikistan, Land of the Future', http://www.dn.se/DNet/jsp/polopoly.jsp?d=2502&a=664639 (accessed June 15, 2008).

'Sons of war': parties and party systems in post-war El Salvador and Cambodia

Jeroen de Zeeuw

Catholic Organisation for Relief and Development Aid (Cordaid), The Hague, The Netherlands

This study argues that individual parties and party competition in El Salvador and Cambodia today are still profoundly affected by the period of civil war that has long passed. The war-time origins of the main Salvadoran and Cambodian parties have left a deep imprint on their organizational structures and style of leadership, just as war-time political exclusion set the tone for unbalanced party competition after the war. Although El Salvador's party system is more institutionalized and pluralistic than Cambodia's, there have been clear cross-national patterns of unequal institutionalization and ruling party dominance that are a product of the war. International engagement ranging from election observation, election organization to party assistance has had some benefits, particularly for opposition parties. At the party system level, however, international support has only been of minor influence, with the possible exception of financial, economic and technical assistance to the government, which has served to accentuate the tendency towards dominance by the party in power.

Introduction

In recent years there has been growing scholarly and policy attention for the relationship between political party development and civil war.[1] Most of this attention has focused on the dangers of unfettered party competition in new democracies with the key argument being that electoral competition between weak and undemocratic political parties, unless carefully managed and/or regulated, can destabilize fragile political stability, exacerbate tensions and even lead to violent conflict.[2] Under some conditions, therefore, political parties are said to have a negative effect on conflict management in deeply divided and post-war societies. But questions such as 'what makes parties weak in post-war societies?' and 'why do parties in these contexts tend to raise tensions rather than peacefully cooperate?' are rarely asked. These questions point to the importance of the inverse relationship between parties and war, namely the effect that civil war and post-war context can have on political party development, which is the main focus of this account.[3]

The lack of attention for war's effect on party development is surprising considering the assertion by many authors in the (Western-oriented) party politics literature that parties do not form in a vacuum and are strongly influenced by the context in which they emerge and operate. Scholars focusing on Western Europe and the United States, for example, have shown that wars, authoritarian rule and legal provisions restricting organized political activities hindered early party development.[4] Studies concentrating on East- and Central Europe indicate that party development there was heavily shaped by the different varieties of communist rule.[5] Context also matters when we look beyond the 'heartlands' of party development. Recent investigations about party development in Africa, Asia and Latin America highlight colonial administration, periods of military rule and civil war as important factors shaping parties and party competition in these regions.[6]

By implication it seems fair to assume, therefore, that party development in countries ravaged by long and intense periods of civil war is, at least partly, shaped by such war. After all, when the adverse security and economic conditions as well as the complete lack of trust across different socioeconomic, political and ethnic groups affect all other forms of organization during and immediately after the war, they are not unlikely to affect political parties as well. By focusing on the development of parties and party systems in two very different post-war countries this inquiry demonstrates that war is indeed an important contextual factor. More specifically, it argues that the particular conflict history and the political conditions after civil war have a significant influence on the organization, functioning and interaction of individual parties in post-war societies.

A key question thus is whether, how and to what extent international involvement and in particular political party assistance makes a difference in these distinctive situations. Close examination of the cases of Cambodia and El Salvador will help provide answers, and show why any contribution that it might make towards the development of party politics will be highly contingent on the impact and legacy of war.

Methodology

One note of caution is in order here. Political parties in developing countries cannot easily be equated with parties in more established democracies. Although the elusive 'model political party' is increasingly difficult to find, the vast majority of parties in contemporary Western democracies are still based on some form of structure (elite/cadre, mass- or cartel-based) and have a definable group of party members and/or supporters that share a certain ideology or set of ideas.[7] Most parties in non-Western (post-war) societies lack a clear ideological profile, have a more fluid membership and operate on a pragmatic, clientelist basis.[8]

In Cambodia, and less so in El Salvador, ruling as well as opposition parties are first and foremost patronage networks that allow members to gain access to certain services and resources in return for loyalty, political support and, crucially, votes. Nevertheless, by using Sartori's minimalist definition of a political party – that is, 'any political group that presents at elections, and is capable of placing through elections, candidates for public office' – we can compare parties in very different contexts.[9]

The arguments presented in this study are based on findings from a broader doctoral research project, involving extensive interviews and in-depth field research conducted by this author between September 2007 and August 2008.[10] That project included an assessment of the institutionalization of parties and party systems in almost 30 post-war countries. It concentrated on studying a number of war-related factors explaining the variety in the degree of institutionalization in two (most different) cases, namely El Salvador and Cambodia.[11] The reasons for focusing on these two countries are fivefold.

First, El Salvador and Cambodia both have party systems that revolve around one highly institutionalized ruling party, which is the most prevalent type of party system in post-war societies.[12] Secondly, both countries have relatively stable party systems, with the main parties having had more than 15 years to develop between the end of the war in the early 1990s and recent national elections in 2009 (El Salvador) and 2008 (Cambodia). In most other post-war countries party systems are still too fluid to draw any meaningful conclusions. Thirdly, both El Salvador and Cambodia have had a particularly intense and long-lasting war, which brings out the influence of war-related factors more clearly than in cases where wars were less intense and shorter in duration. A fourth reason for choosing El Salvador and Cambodia is because both countries have received large-scale international assistance and support, including party assistance, which allows us to study the role of international actors in post-war party development. And finally the relatively limited scholarly attention for the post-war development of political parties and party systems in these two countries makes it an interesting pair for comparison.[13]

The account is divided into five sections. The first section provides a brief overview of the history of the war and early party development in El Salvador and Cambodia. The second section shifts attention towards the post-war period in El Salvador and Cambodia. It argues that although the peace process, post-war institutional design and the nature of international engagement provided opportunities for all parties, the particular outcome of these processes and initiatives mainly benefited the two ruling parties. The third section reviews some of the cross-national patterns, inclusive of key differences and similarities between the two cases, especially with regard to the institutionalization of individual parties and party systems. This section also contains a brief review of the role of international actors, inclusive of the provisions of international political party support. Section four deals with the lasting effects that war has had on the formation, development, behaviour and interactions of parties and party leaders in El Salvador and Cambodia. The concluding section discusses the scope of the findings, highlights some implications for theory, policy and practices, including for international party assistance, and summarizes the key points raised.

Early party development and war in El Salvador and Cambodia

El Salvador

Deep socioeconomic inequalities and political exclusion lie at the roots of much of the instability, civil war and criminal violence that El Salvador has experienced in the past half century. Concentration of land, labour and other economic resources in the hands of family oligarchies and business elites, in combination with market-oriented political regimes and an authoritarian military establishment, have led to a strongly polarized political system.

Early party development in El Salvador was hindered by an almost 50-year-long period (1932–1980) of direct and indirect military rule. Especially in the first part of that period, elections for the national assembly and presidency were held only occasionally and manipulated in such a way that opposition parties were unable to challenge the power of the 'official' parties.[14] The latter, such as the Revolutionary Party of Democratic Unification (PRUD) and its successor the National Conciliation Party (PCN) were controlled by the military-economic elite and mainly served to concentrate land and other sources of wealth in their hands.[15] During the 1960s and 1970s the political arena opened up somewhat, which led to the emergence of several progressive popular organizations and new left-wing opposition parties, such as the Christian Democratic Party (PDC). However, in the subsequent period party politics started to disintegrate again.

The fraudulent 1972 elections and the surrounding political tensions spawned a variety of popular mass organizations protesting against the unequal socioeconomic conditions and the increasing restrictions of political space. The military meanwhile set up or expanded already existing paramilitary organizations, some of which also doubled as 'death squads'.[16] This period also saw a quick succession of different military juntas, until eventually a new (civilian) government was elected in 1982. By that time political-military opposition groups had entered into a transition phase and started to prepare themselves for an armed revolution.

In October 1980, five guerrilla organizations decided to unite in the Farabundo Martí National Liberation Front (FMLN). The Democratic Revolutionary Front (FDR), established a few months earlier, acted as the FMLN's political voice. At the height of the war in the mid-1980s approximately 12,000 FMLN rebel fighters were pitted against an approximately 56,000 strong Salvadoran army force.[17] Despite these large disparities in force size, it soon became clear that neither side would be able to win the war militarily. However, the war dragged on and it would not be until 1989 that the first direct negotiations between the FMLN and the government – now controlled by the Nationalist Republican Alliance (ARENA) – would take place.

Cambodia

A weak state controlled by all-powerful leaders with a strong political machine features prominently in Cambodia's long conflict history. After independence in 1953, successive Cambodian regimes espoused different types of authoritarian leadership and single-party rule.

In the period 1953–1970, Cambodia's political, economic and socio-cultural life was dominated by King Norodom Sihanouk and his Sangkum Reastr Niyum (People's Socialist Community). By allowing only non-party affiliated supporters as members and co-opting the majority of prominent politicians, Sihanouk's Sangkum effectively halted the development of Cambodia's nascent elite-oriented political parties.[18] The predominantly left-wing parties that refused to merge into the Sangkum, such as the Pracheachon and the Khmer People's Revolutionary Party (KPRP), could only continue their activities clandestinely. However, by the end of the 1960s Sihanouk's paternalistic rule was no longer working and in March 1970 he was deposed by a group of conservative politicians led by General Lon Nol.

Almost immediately, the country's political system was changed from a parliamentary monarchy into a presidential Khmer Republic (1970–1975). But despite the adoption of a more democratic constitution and the allowance of opposition parties, Lon Nol's republic quickly turned repressive and morphed into a de facto single-party system.[19] Self-exiled in Beijing, Sihanouk meanwhile agreed to a secret alliance with the Chinese and Vietnamese governments to foster a national resistance front under his command in exchange for allowing North Vietnamese and Communist Party of Kampuchea (CPK) forces – also described as 'Red Khmer' or 'Khmer Rouge (KR)' – to expand their operations on Cambodian soil. Despite large-scale US military assistance, Lon Nol's poorly trained and badly coordinated troops failed to fight back the Khmer Rouge forces, which eventually took control of the capital Phnom Penh on 17 April 1975.[20]

With the subsequent establishment of the Democratic Kampuchea (DK) regime (1975–1979), the Khmer Rouge embarked on a nationwide project of radical political, economic and social transformation ostensibly aimed at creating a self-reliant communitarian peasant society at the cost of massive loss of human lives.[21] Competitive party politics – to the limited extent it had still existed under the Khmer Republic – was replaced with a communist party state. But after its early 'successes' in eliminating its political enemies, the CPK soon fell victim to factionalization. Internally weakened, KR forces were unable to defeat the more powerful Vietnamese army – despite the strong support of Maoist China. After Vietnamese forces invaded Cambodia at the end of 1978, the DK regime collapsed on 7 January 1979.

With the establishment of the People's Republic of Kampuchea (PRK) (1979–1989) the war in Cambodia did not end, however. Although the PRK's socialist policies were a far cry from the violent totalitarianism of the Khmer Rouge, the Vietnamese-backed regime was still perceived as very restrictive, among others because of its ban on the formation of political parties that could challenge the new ruling Khmer People's Revolutionary Party (KPRP). By the mid-1980s the PRK regime faced not only an international boycott but also opposition from three externally-supported armed groups, including the Khmer Rouge, opportunistically allied in the Sihanouk-led Coalition Government of Democratic Kampuchea (CGDK).

Only towards the end of the 1980s, with the Cold War slowly coming to an end and Vietnam withdrawing its troops from Cambodia, did the political situation start to change. The new situation forced the regime in Phnom Penh – now 're-branded' as the State of Cambodia (SOC) led by the Cambodian People's Party (CPP) – to finally look for a political solution to its conflict with the CGDK resistance.

Making peace and post-war party development

The Salvadoran peace process started in earnest in early 1990 after the Cold War. Under strong pressure from the United Nations and the United States and stimulated by the efforts of several neighbouring states to bring peace to the Central American region, the Salvadoran government and the FMLN finally signed the Chapultepec Accords on 16 January 1992. The purpose of the accords was 'to end the armed conflict by political means as speedily as possible, promote the democratization of the country, guarantee unrestricted respect for human rights and reunify Salvadoran society'.[22] The United Nations Observer Mission in El Salvador (ONUSAL) was established to supervise the implementation of the accords.

Apart from a broad range of provisions dealing with the reform of existing security and judicial institutions and the creation of new electoral institutions, one of the key clauses concerned the legalization of the FMLN as a legitimate political party. This core element of the peace agreement was not only important in pressuring the FMLN to disarm and demobilize its armed combatants, but also proved essential in transforming the former armed rebel group into a viable political party.[23]

The Cambodian civil war came to an end around the same time. With the Cold War over and the major powers seeking a normalization of their relations, the US, China, and Soviet Union started to put pressure on their respective Cambodian 'clients' to come to a negotiated solution to their conflict. After much wrangling, the four main warring parties finally signed the Paris Peace Accords on 23 October 1991.[24] To ensure implementation of the accords, a United Nations Transitional Authority in Cambodia (UNTAC) was mandated to supervise the various tasks. With an 18-month budget of USD2.8 billion, more than 15,000 troops and 7000 international civilian staff, UNTAC was the largest peacekeeping mission of the early 1990s.[25]

Key provisions of the Paris Accords focused on the withdrawal of foreign forces, the cessation of outside military assistance, the return of refugees and internally displaced persons, rehabilitation of basic infrastructure as well as the organization of free and fair elections to create a liberal democratic system.[26]

Significantly, however, the accords did not provide much clarity on how such a system would be achieved and remained silent about how to transform the various armed factions into political parties.

In both countries elections were organized soon after the peace accords were signed. The 1994 municipal, parliamentary and presidential elections in El Salvador were easily won by the ruling ARENA party, although a party coalition led by the FMLN managed to force ARENA into a second round of voting for the presidency. The 1993 parliamentary elections in Cambodia were won by the royalist National United Front for an Independent, Neutral, Peaceful and Cooperative Cambodia (FUNCINPEC), one of the former armed groups of the CGDK.

In both countries, the winners of the elections did not gain the required number of seats to form a government by themselves. In the case of El Salvador, ARENA did control the most important political institution in the country – i.e. the presidency – and struck a deal with the rightwing PCN to reach the necessary majority in parliament. In the case of Cambodia, however, a coalition between FUNCINPEC and its erstwhile enemy, the CPP, was considered as the only realistic option. At first, the CPP refused to accept the results, accusing UNTAC of anti-CPP bias.[27] But with the help of King Sihanouk a power-sharing deal between FUNCINPEC and the CPP was eventually reached, locking both parties into an unwieldy coalition government with two prime-ministers and parallel structures of authority throughout the state bureaucracy.

Despite the different outcomes, the first post-war elections had a generally positive effect on party development in both countries. El Salvador's party scene expanded beyond the three-party clique of the 'official' PCN, the opposition PDC and ARENA to include the rebel movement-turned-political party FMLN, as well as the new United Democratic Centre (CDU) (later Democratic Convergence, CD). In subsequent elections between 1997 and 2006 some of the new left-wing parties proved able to challenge the much older, 'traditional' parties, which led to the decline of the once-powerful PCN and PDC. ARENA consolidated, the CD/CDU entered as a small centre-left opposition party, and the FMLN became the strongest left-wing opposition party.

In Cambodia, the political arena now comprised not only the CPP and FUNCINPEC, but also the Buddhist Liberal Democratic Party (BLDP) and the National Liberation Movement of Kampuchea (MOLINAKA), two former armed groups. However, in subsequent elections between 1998 and 2008 the latter two disappeared and the only major new party to emerge was the Sam Rainsy Party (SRP). Moreover, the CPP managed to consolidate its political position, largely at the expense of FUNCINPEC which in 2008 became one of the smallest opposition parties in Cambodia's parliament.

These brief overviews show that the political histories of El Salvador and Cambodia are both characterized by major armed conflict, political instability and severely restricted forms of party competition. But obviously, there are stark differences in the duration and intensity of conflict as well as the nature of early party development between the two countries.

In Cambodia, the period of war was spread out over more than 30 years, claimed more than 1.5 million lives and brought party development almost to a complete stop. Under the one-party DK and PRK regimes political parties other than the ruling CPK and KPRP were banned and no competitive elections were held between 1972 and 1993. In El Salvador the war lasted for more than 10 years, claimed more than 75,000 lives and led to the electoral exclusion of almost all left-wing political parties. Surprisingly, however, in El Salvador electoral and political party competition continued during the 1980s, albeit in a rather artificial and severely restricted manner. Artificial because results did generally not reflect the will of the people; restricted because electoral competition excluded centre-left and extreme left parties.

Despite these differences, the conflict histories and the violent nature of early party development in both countries have had profound and quite similar effects on the institutionalization of their political parties and nature of party competition, as we will see below. In the post-war period, with the strong ruling Cambodian People's Party (CPP) dominating the country's political scene, Cambodia has become one of the clearest examples of a dominant party system. At first sight, El Salvador's party system seems slightly more balanced with two parties (ARENA and the FMLN) competing for power since 1992. In practice, however, ARENA has dominated El Salvador's political and economic spheres until early 2009.[28]

Cross-national patterns

Due to their unique historical, cultural and geographical backgrounds, Salvadoran and Cambodian political parties are quite different. Generally speaking, parties in El Salvador have a clearer ideological profile, are more policy- and interest-oriented and are therefore perhaps closer to the elusive 'model' of a Western political party than parties in Cambodia. Nevertheless, most Salvadoran and Cambodian political parties operate on a similar patrimonial logic and both perform essentially the same role in presenting candidates for public office during elections. In addition, there are a number of other interesting similarities.

Individual parties: different backgrounds, similar gaps in institutionalization

One of the most salient parallels between the two countries is the similar gap in the degree of institutionalization between the individual parties. The two (former) ruling parties of El Salvador and Cambodia are each politically and organizationally significantly stronger than the various opposition parties. ARENA's strength was a function of its organizational set-up as an alliance of influential societal sectors and its popular recognition as a symbol of anti-communist nationalism. The CPP derives much of its strength from its hierarchical and centralized (communist) party structure pervading all administrative levels and institutions in Cambodia. Because of its relatively open alliance structure, ARENA has been able to adapt more quickly to new challenges and allowed for the emergence of new leadership within the party, than the structurally more rigid CPP.

Despite these differences, however, the organizational strength and privileged position of ARENA and the CPP vis-à-vis other parties is in both cases related to how the ruling parties came to power. In El Salvador and Cambodia alike the ruling party won government authority and managed to take control over the state long before the end of the war. In El Salvador, ARENA obtained governing power by winning the elections in 1988. In Cambodia, the CPP attained governing power by forcing the Khmer Rouge out of government with the help of the Vietnamese army in 1979. This early capture of power enabled ARENA and the CPP not only to extend their political control over state policies but also over the state's administrative and security apparatus. In both cases this led to deep penetration of the party into the state; in Cambodia, it led to an almost complete merger of party and state structures.

With the institutionalization of the ruling parties has come a weakening of the opposition parties. Now more than 15 years after the wars ended, opposition parties in El Salvador and Cambodia are only weakly to moderately institutionalized. However, there are big differences in the organizational and political strength of the opposition parties. The PDC in El Salvador, for example, is stronger than the CD, just as the SRP in Cambodia is stronger than the relatively new Norodom Ranarridh Party (NRP).[29] But more important is the huge gap in institutionalization between the various opposition parties on the one hand and the two ruling parties on the other. In El Salvador and Cambodia, as perhaps in other post-war societies, this gap seems to be much bigger than in even the most asymmetrical party systems of more established democracies.

If we compare, for example, ARENA and CD in El Salvador on two rudimentary indicators of political and organizational strength – namely control over municipalities and estimated number of party members – ARENA outperforms CD with a ratio of 49:1 (since 2006) and 142:1, respectively. In Cambodia this gap is even wider, with the CPP outnumbering the NRP with 1591:0 in terms of municipal control (since 2007) and 7:1 in terms of party membership.[30] For the two more moderately institutionalized opposition parties, the FMLN in El Salvador and the SRP in Cambodia, these ratios are much lower but still significant.

This lack of organizational strength is primarily related to the unequal access to (state) resources between ruling and opposition parties and in some cases poor opposition party leadership in the two respective countries. But what this also shows is that opposition parties in El Salvador and Cambodia have faced similar challenges in building and strengthening their organizational structures and have struggled to expand their political base vis-à-vis the more institutionally entrenched ruling parties.

Party systems: different make-up, similar outcome

The two countries also exhibit a number of commonalities in their overall party systems. Cambodia clearly has all the features of what Sartori calls a dominant-authoritarian party system; a ruling party with an absolute majority of seats, which controls political, economic, media and other institutions in such a way that opposition parties are unable to challenge it.[31] El Salvador's party system is more difficult to classify, however, and the number of politically relevant parties differs per level of governance.

For example, if we focus only at the presidential level, ARENA has been the only party with an absolute majority of votes for 20 years (1989–2009). By contrast, at the level of the Legislative Assembly the seat margins between ARENA and the FMLN are so small that one could easily conclude there is a two-party system. But neither ARENA nor the FMLN has ever held an absolute parliamentary majority necessary for such a conclusion. Moreover, there are two or three other relevant parties with the potential to form or block coalition governments. At the municipal level, with various constantly shifting party coalitions the picture is even more varied. Nevertheless, when we consider the limited number of politically relevant parties and the nature of party competition that is centred around two strong ideological poles, El Salvador can probably best be described as a polarized, pluralist party system.

Looking beyond classifications, however, we can question the different nature of party competition in the two countries. When analysing El Salvador and Cambodia as two distinct cases, the ostensibly more competitive form of party interaction in El Salvador – especially between ARENA and the FMLN – appears to have little in common with the relatively uncompetitive nature of party interaction between the CPP, FUNCINPEC and the SRP in Cambodia. But when we look more closely at how party competition works out in practice, it becomes clear that 'party dominance' is a crucial aspect of both countries' party systems.

In Cambodia, none of the opposition parties can compete with the CPP's access to and use of the state and other resources. Since its emergence in the early 1980s the CPP has relied on elaborate patronage networks to have access to state personnel, equipment and financial resources to support its party activities. In order to retain its dominant position, the CPP has not hesitated to use the security forces and media outlets to attack and undermine the work of political opponents. The CPP has been able to do this not because of its formal position in parliament – where it did not have the necessary two thirds majority to rule until 2008 – but because of its informal, de facto control over almost all state, security and media institutions.[32]

Similarly in El Salvador – where ARENA has not had an absolute majority of seats – the ruling party has dominated the political arena until 2009. Evidence suggests that ARENA's dominant position in the Salvadoran party system at least until 2008 is also more a result of the party's success in exploiting its control over the presidential office, state bureaucracy and the country's media than stemming from its 30-odd seats in the Legislative Assembly.[33] ARENA has tended to use this privileged access to strengthen its position not only during election campaigns but also between different elections. So although it theoretically does not qualify as such, the Salvadoran party system of the past two decades

(1992–2009) has come very close to a (pre)dominant party system. And despite the presence of a much stronger opposition party in El Salvador, the strategies employed by ARENA to maintain its dominance have not been unlike those used by Cambodia's ruling party. This comparative analysis of the Salvadoran and Cambodian party system shows that an exclusive focus on elections and seat shares (as in Sartori's definition) does not tell the full story. Findings from El Salvador in particular indicate that the relative access to and control over state resources among parties have a much greater influence on the degree of party dominance than exactly how many seats the ruling party has.

The influence of international actors

The unbalanced development of party systems in El Salvador and Cambodia has also been made possible because of the relative absence of international pressure on the two ruling parties to stick to the 'democratic rules of the game'. In the early 1990s major powers had a strong desire to reduce their military involvement, to exit and disengage themselves from the domestic politics of the two countries. For a long time therefore the primary focus of international post-war assistance to both countries was on peacebuilding, not on democratization and/or political party development. Only in the context of the peace agreement itself did international actors support various political party-related activities.

After the war in El Salvador, for example, it was the United Nations through its observer mission (ONUSAL) and UNDP that helped ensure the FMLN's participation in the political process. In addition, the National Democratic Institute (NDI), the International Republican Institute (IRI), the Organization of American States (OAS), the Norwegian Centre for Democracy Support (NCDS), the Friedrich Ebert Stiftung (FES), Konrad Adenauer Stiftung (KAS), the Hanns Seidel Stiftung (HSS) as well as Salvadoran diaspora groups have provided a broad range of election observation and party assistance activities, including the training of party leaders, provision of office space and computers, legislative assistance and parliamentary exchange programmes. This benefited not only the FMLN but all main political parties.[34]

In Cambodia, the main international actors that have directly engaged with political parties are UNDP, NDI, IRI and KAS. Their assistance activities have included constituency dialogue programmes, training on how to do public opinion polling, organize election campaigns and election observation by party agents, women leadership training and equal-access radio and TV programmes.[35] Although most of these programmes have been open to all parties, anecdotal evidence suggests that they – often in combination with monetary support from the Cambodian diaspora – have benefited opposition parties in particular and provided them with an important degree of credibility and legitimacy.[36]

But despite these efforts by some international agencies, there has been little attention to the development of a more equitable party system in both countries. Not wanting to jeopardize the fragile political stability, the most important international actors such as the US, EU, France, and Japan, for example, have been reluctant to criticize the partisan use of state resources by ARENA and the CPP and 'tolerated' all but the most egregious limitations put on competitive politics.[37] The channelling of massive international aid packages through party-controlled government agencies seems to have boosted the organizational development of ARENA and the CPP.[38] However necessary for peace-building this strategy may have been, the consequence was that ARENA and the CPP could expand their control over the state, media and other institutions virtually unchecked and thereby strengthen their position vis-à-vis other parties.[39]

The extent to which the ruling parties have been allowed a free hand by the international community has varied per country, however. Despite its public support for ideologically like-minded ARENA governments, the US has made it clear that it wanted El Salvador to become a more democratic state with fair and unrestricted electoral competition.[40] ARENA therefore knew that there were limits to how far it could go. There has been no such unequivocal message from the international actors in Cambodia. Important post-war donor countries like Japan and France have not wanted to interfere in any way in Cambodia's political development. The US has been more critical towards the CPP government, although this position seems to have changed since oil was discovered off the coast in 2005.[41] Generally positive assessments of international election observation missions, which have tended to play down widespread electoral irregularities such as in 1998 and 2003, further contributed to legitimize the CPP's rule. In the absence of a strong, united message from Cambodia's international donors, it is therefore likely that the CPP has felt it enjoys more licence to use and abuse power for its own partisan interests than ARENA has had.

Finally, it is clear that the post-war party systems of the two countries are both not fully institutionalized. Compared to the volatile and at times violent party politics of Cambodia, party competition in El Salvador has certainly been more stable and peaceful in the post-war period. And the remarkable success of the FMLN in the 2009 elections has indeed broken the pattern of ARENA's post-war dominance, at least for now.[42] Yet in both countries opposition parties remain weak, people have little trust in political parties and are becoming more and more disillusioned with elections as the mechanism to change government leadership.[43] This lack of institutionalization in combination with the dominance of the ruling party has in both countries contributed to an uneven form of party competition.

Impact of war...

War-related factors and war itself have proven to be a key missing element in the explanation of the uneven degree of party institutionalization and the unbalanced form of inter-party competition in post-war societies.[44] If we look closer at the situation in El Salvador and Cambodia, we can see that war has had a relatively similar impact on political parties and party systems.

...*On parties*

With regard to individual political parties, war has had three specific effects. First, in both cases the war has provided a distinctive context for party development. Because of continuous violence it was virtually impossible for political parties to organize themselves and canvass mass support during the war. In El Salvador, only the right-wing and centre-right parties (PCN, ARENA and PDC) competed for votes, while the FMLN was excluded from elections. In Cambodia, no competitive elections were held between 1972 and 1993 and only one political party was allowed to exist. Even in the post-war period poor security hindered political parties in building up a local support base, establishing local offices and organizing their electoral campaign. In the run-up to the 1994 elections in El Salvador, dozens of political activists were killed, many more intimidated and party property damaged or destroyed, despite pacts signed by all the main political parties.[45] In the months before the 1993 elections in Cambodia, there were hundreds of allegedly politically-motivated murders and violent attacks against (opposition) party members and property. In some parts of the country artillery attacks by the Khmer Rouge made it almost impossible for political parties to conduct any party activities.[46] Overall therefore, war and its aftermath had a generally negative *environmental effect* on political party development, either by disrupting or stifling the normal growth of already existing political parties or by altogether denying organizations the possibility to become a political party. Because of their long-time incumbent position, ARENA and the CPP are the only two parties in Cambodia and El Salvador that have been less affected by this effect.

Secondly, in both countries war has influenced and shaped the organizational structures of political parties. The highly centralized and disciplined party organization of the PCN in the 1960s in El Salvador, for example, was significantly weakened as a result of the conflict. During the war the party became increasingly dominated by the decentralized paramilitary ORDEN militias that were set up to control the rural population and repress guerrilla activities. As a result, central authority weakened and the party organization became much more militarized.[47] Such a *structural effect* of war on party organization is visible in most parties, but has been greatest for those parties that emerged during the war itself.

In the case of ARENA and the CPP the war has been a primary factor in the establishment of their party organizations in the early 1980s. ARENA was set up to 'defend' El Salvador against the armed resistance of the left-wing guerrillas. The CPP's predecessor, the KPRP, was created to 'liberate' Cambodia from the Pol Pot regime and install a different regime. As their political opponents were either weakened or outlawed, ARENA and the CPP could take over the state administration and security apparatus relatively easily and build up a nationwide network of party cadre and supporters. This required a high degree of formal organization and a hierarchical, tightly controlled party structure to link the local and regional party branches and state institutions to the higher-level central party committee. From this perspective, the war put a premium on political-administrative development of the ruling parties as one of the ways to gain as much control as possible over the state, territory and population. The war provided the 'ideal' conditions for young parties like ARENA and the CPP to grow quickly, to attract and train new people and embed them in the most important state and non-state institutions. As a result, by the time the war ended ARENA and the CPP had highly institutionalized party organizations with a large number of experienced, well-trained party cadre and administrators.

For the FMLN and FUNCINPEC the war gave a similarly strong impetus for organizational expansion. But because they were not allowed to participate in the political and electoral arena, their initial focus was to build up military structures and capabilities. Although political development was certainly part of their activities — for the FMLN even more so than for FUNCINPEC — the development of their political wings was trumped by the focus on the military part of the organization. Both rebel groups had few trained and experienced political staff and their senior leadership was mainly comprised of military commanders. In order to maximize operational effectiveness, the various armed groups that made up the FMLN and FUNCINPEC were united into a single resistance front under a unified command structure based on strict military discipline. But despite this unified structure at the top, during the war the FMLN and FUNCINPEC were by nature relatively loosely organized structures with different (regional) power bases.

When the war ended, the FMLN and FUNCINPEC struggled to make the transformation from an armed rebel group to a political party. Both faced an acute shortage of staff trained and experienced in governance and party administration. In addition, the unified structure that had kept the organizations together during the war disintegrated to a large extent. Old personal and ideological rivalries between groups and leaders quickly re-emerged and translated into a high degree of party factionalism. The FMLN became consumed in an internal power struggle between the ideologically strict *ortodoxos* and the more reform-oriented *renovadores*, which led to a number of splits. Groups united under the FUNCINPEC umbrella first split into different royalist (FUNCINPEC, MOLINAKA) and non-royalist political parties (for example, BLDP). A few years later, FUNCINPEC splintered further into as many as eight different parties. In both cases, the military-oriented, decentralized structures of the FMLN and FUNCINPEC as rebel organizations had a detrimental impact on their post-war institutionalization as party organizations.[48]

The third effect of war on political parties is *attitudinal*, meaning that war influences the behaviour of party leaders. Similar to other post-war societies, leadership has played an important role in the institutionalization of individual political parties in El Salvador and Cambodia. A large part of that leadership is made up of how a particular leader manages political problems and which methods he/she uses to deal with these problems. This leadership style ranges from an authoritarian, confrontational approach to a more consensual, give-and-take approach. If we look at the behaviour of some of the main Salvadoran and Cambodian politicians it is obvious that most of them have a very forceful, confrontational leadership style that leaves little room for dissent. This has partly to do with the authoritarian political culture and tradition of 'strong leaders' common to many Latin American and Southeast Asian countries.[49] But the already existing undemocratic leadership styles of Salvadoran and Cambodian politicians were also exacerbated by the long period(s) of war in these countries.

ARENA's founder and principal leader in the 1980s, Roberto D'Aubuisson, became more reactionary and repressive in his views and tactics when the long-standing conflict between the right-wing government and left-wing guerrillas spilled over into an all-out war in the 1980s. At the same time, prominent FMLN leaders such as Joaquín Villalobos and Salvador Sánchez Cerén also hardened their views and became increasingly intolerant of those who resisted armed struggle. Later party leaders, such as Alfredo Cristiani, Armando Calderón Sol (ARENA) and Facundo Guardado (FMLN), were markedly more moderate but their willingness to compromise with their political opponents remained limited.

The KPRP/CPP's Hun Sen emerged when the country had just been devastated by the extremist Khmer Rouge (KR) regime and was now trying to fend off attacks from an externally-supported armed resistance front that included KR forces. Right from the beginning Hun Sen's leadership was therefore primarily focused on how to defeat his enemies – both outside and inside the party – and how to consolidate a one-party socialist state. Key rebel leaders such as the Khmer People's National Liberation Front's Son Sann and FUNCINPEC's Nhiek Bun Chhay also concentrated on military affairs and were less interested in making compromises with the enemy. Norodom Ranarridh and even Sam Rainsy have continued this winner-takes-all attitude in the management of their own parties as well as in their interactions with political opponents.

Leadership is therefore not an unchangeable constant, but is rather something dynamic that can be influenced by other factors, including war. The uncompromising and confrontational leadership style of most Salvadoran and Cambodian politicians is certainly rooted in the respective country's history of undemocratic, zero-sum politics. But the long period of war seems to have further undermined the limited power-sharing or compromise elements there were and aggravated the authoritarian tendencies in leaders' behaviour. Moreover, it indicates that the main political parties active in El Salvador and Cambodia today should be considered as *hijos de la guerra* (sons of the war) whose organizational structures and leadership culture are to a significant extent a legacy of their war-time origins.[50]

...And on party systems

The long and violent period of war in both countries has also shaped the way in which the various parties interact, or failed to interact. First, war has had a *detrimental effect on the institutional environment* that provides the rules and regulations under which party competition takes place in El Salvador and Cambodia. By establishing extra-legal paramilitary structures to undermine opposition forces (El Salvador) or by banning non-ruling political parties outright (Cambodia) the war further weakened already fragile constitutional and other legal safeguards for free and fair party competition. After the war, new more democratic institutions were adopted, but both countries continued to have a weak regulatory framework with regard to political parties. In El Salvador, there is still no specific law that regulates the formation, functioning and financing of political parties. In Cambodia such a law does exist, but is ambiguous when it comes to crucial areas such as intra-party democracy and party finance. Moreover, because of a biased and extremely weak judiciary – another legacy of the war – the law is just not enforced.

Similar institutional weaknesses exist in the election administrations that in both countries are not considered neutral and independent. In an effort to appease formerly warring parties both countries opted for the establishment of national election committees with party members. However, by basing their membership on party affiliation, the Salvadoran Supreme Electoral Tribunal (TSE) and the Cambodian National Election Committee (NEC) institutionalized old war-time divisions. This has made it very difficult for these institutions to be the neutral organizers and arbiters of elections the law requires them to be. After several changes, the Cambodian NEC now formally consists of independent experts. The Salvadoran TSE has a mixed composition of party-affiliated members and independent experts. In practice, however, both electoral management bodies are still heavily politicized and their decisions generally indicate a bias towards the ruling party.[51]

A second common legacy of the wars on Salvadoran and Cambodian politics respectively is the *hostile nature of party competition*, especially during election campaigns. This is, for example, audible in the insulting, polarizing and abusive language party leaders use to discredit each other and their parties. ARENA and the CPP have commonly branded their political opponents as 'terrorists' whose rule will 'once again lead to instability and anarchy', whereas the FMLN and the SRP have accused the ruling parties of being 'corrupt oppressors' and 'puppets backed or installed by foreign regimes' (that is, the US and Vietnam respectively).[52] Many of these labels are directly associated with the war period, during which parties were each other's military opponent. These rhetorical devices appear to have been effective to some extent as they help cement support among party cadres as well as party supporters. The hostility of party interactions is also visible in the continuation of violent attacks on active party members and ordinary supporters in the post-war period, although this has been worse in Cambodia than in El Salvador. What is clear is that as a result of the war, attempts to undermine, block and attack political opponents by any means have almost become second nature to most parties.

A final, related similarity at the party system level is that the war in El Salvador and Cambodia has *reduced the willingness of parties to cooperate substantively*. As mentioned above, many party leaders have an uncompromising leadership style, which hinders closer engagement of parties. But this lack of engagement is exacerbated by the total lack of trust between party leaders, which can often be traced back to the war or immediate post-war period. Because the war is a relatively recent phenomenon, many politicians still consider their political opponents as 'enemies' and find it difficult to cooperate with them. As a result, plenary and committee debates in parliament in both countries generally result in acrimonious disputes between the ruling party and opposition parties with none of the sides wanting to give way. The concepts of 'accountable government', where the ruling party is held to account by the opposition, and 'loyal opposition', whereby parties agree to set aside their partisan differences for the greater good, seem anathema to Salvadoran and Cambodian party politics.

The only sorts of collaboration that can be found are the patrimonial coalition arrangements between the ruling parties and their junior coalition partners, such as ARENA-PCN in the case of El Salvador and CPP-FUNCINPEC in the case of Cambodia. But these arrangements are usually very unequal and have more to do with political expediency and personal gain than with genuine policy dialogue or team work. Moreover, this lack of cooperation is not only limited to interactions between ruling and opposition parties. Multi-party coalitions or even electoral alliances among opposition parties themselves – which are quite common in established democracies – are extremely rare in El Salvador and Cambodia. When such alliances do occur, as in the joint 1994 FMLN-CD-MNR bid for the presidency or the 2003 Alliance of Democrats between FUNCINPEC and the SRP, they are usually short-lived because leaders do not trust each other and are reluctant to compromise.

Conclusion
Scope of findings

The analysis presented here is primarily based on empirical data from El Salvador and Cambodia. The conclusions drawn are therefore first and foremost pertinent to these two cases alone. But recognizing that the experience of long and violent conflict has not been limited to El Salvador and Cambodia, it is fair to ask whether there is potential to generalize some of the findings and patterns of political party and party system development beyond the two cases studied here.

The three groups of parties found in El Salvador and Cambodia – ruling parties, rebels-turned-parties and new post-war parties – can be found in most post-war countries. Because of similarly devastating and traumatic war experiences, it is therefore probable that the individual parties of countries such as Nicaragua, Ethiopia, Uganda and Sudan, for example, have also been affected by the environmental, structural and attitudinal effects of war as described above. The role of the war in the continuing factionalization of opposition parties and the no-compromise, (semi-)authoritarian leadership styles of many Nicaraguan, Ethiopian and Sudanese politicians are clear parallels.[53] And the wars in Mozambique, Burundi and Rwanda are likely to have had a similarly detrimental effect on the institutional environment of party interaction, and contributed to the hostility of party competition and the unwillingness of parties to cooperate, as in El Salvador and Cambodia. But further studies would be needed to confirm these extrapolations in full.

PROMOTING PARTY POLITICS IN EMERGING DEMOCRACIES

Implications for theory, policy and practice

The findings presented above have a number of implications for academic thinking about parties, party systems, conflict and peace-building as well as for international party assistance. First of all, this study has drawn attention to a gap in knowledge about post-war party development that exists in the party politics literature. The countries deeply affected by long and violent conflict within these new areas have been largely omitted from academic theorizing. This study has shown that that it is possible to collect relevant information from these areas, that war should be treated as an important independent variable, and above all, that there are certain cross-case patterns in post-war party development that merit further systematic analysis. A similar gap in information and analysis exists in the literature on conflict and peace-building. Nowadays there are a few scholars working on post-conflict transition and electoral system design that have highlighted (but not yet fully explored) the important role of parties, their behaviour and interactions for the creation of a sustainable and democratic peace.[54] But this type of research is rare and in the absence of larger systematic comparisons remains tentative.

A second implication of this research is that some of the existing theories of party development and criteria for classifying party systems seem inadequate in certain contexts and therefore need to be revisited. This study has shown that in post-war societies elections are often not free and fair, that parties' access to the media is unequal and that electoral competition does usually not revolve around ideological differences between parties. As a result, the structure of individual party organizations and the overall party system is not influenced by electoral competition in the same manner as in established democracies. Similarly, socio-economic, cultural and other societal cleavages do not translate in the same way into post-war party systems as they have been said to do in many West-European countries at least in the early period of party development.

The findings are also relevant to the design of international assistance policies and programmes that aim to foster stable and democratic parties and party systems. This investigation shows that knowing how and under what conditions political parties emerge is extremely important for understanding their subsequent development and institutionalization. However, when looking at how party assistance programmes are designed in many countries, it is somewhat surprising to see that there is generally little systematic effort to learn about the historical background of individual political parties or to identify the long-term patterns of power distribution within the party or between parties and non-party actors. Yet, to know the origins and early decisions taken by parties makes it easier to understand why, for example, certain parties are so highly centralized (CPP) or particularly prone to factionalization (FMLN, FUNCINPEC). Sensitivity to such knowledge and the related respect for the difficult history of most post-war parties among their international 'partners' would also be appreciated by party leaders; several of those interviewed claimed to be offended by the generic capacity-building programmes of most Western democracy assistance organizations.[55] In addition, a more detailed assessment of parties' historical development can identify the main internal obstacles to change. This in turn can help democracy assistance providers to design better targeted and more realistic assistance programmes, or, even, tell where and when there is not much they do that would make a constructive difference.

In addition, the findings corroborate the conclusions of two other recent studies that the current party assistance approach has had little direct impact on the institutionalization of individual political parties.[56] This is partly a result of the overriding influence of domestic factors and actors that often run counter to international efforts or are aimed at undermining party development. But it probably also has to do with the 'business-as-usual' nature of many international training and capacity-building programmes, which fail to take seriously enough the special organizational and political difficulties many post-war parties face. For example, evidence gleaned from Cambodia suggests that for a party like the SRP efforts to democratize and open up the party to (Cambodian) outsiders might have increased the number of defections and the level of infiltration by opponents.[57] In circumstances such as these, then, an 'automatic' focus by foreign assistance on encouraging greater intra-party democracy might be misplaced and even undermine the prospects for party institutionalization.

More finely targeted programmes that take into account the distinctive post-war conditions are therefore required. Based on the responses of several interviewees in El Salvador and Cambodia, there is an urgent need for more confidence building initiatives in order to address the lack of trust in and between parties after conflict, and to stimulate the necessary measure of inter-party cooperation. Special training and organizational development programmes that cater to the needs of those former armed groups that are genuinely interested in becoming normal (unarmed) political parties is another area of support that merits further attention. Moreover, in El Salvador, Cambodia and undoubtedly also in other post-war countries the institutionalization of opposition parties is negatively affected by a lack of money, unequal access to the media and the pro-ruling party bias of the official election committee. In order to strengthen such parties and help create more stable, representative and balanced party systems, assistance providers should therefore also address the broader institutional environment influencing party competition, especially with regard to party finance, media access as well as the professionalism and neutrality of electoral institutions.

Finally, this study points out that international efforts to support the development of well-organized, representative parties and a democratic party system have often been undermined, not only by domestic governments and party leaders being resistant to change but also by the trade and security agendas of the same donor countries professing support for democratization. Aligning the various agendas of all these actors is not easy and perhaps even impossible. But it is certainly worthwhile to make the conflict between the different agendas more explicit in order to be able to isolate areas where compromise and/or coordination could be possible.

All in all, we have to think about the justification for international actors giving direct and indirect support to political parties. Directly assisting political parties is something that remains highly controversial and can easily backfire, particularly in post-war societies where the political stakes are already extremely high and the risk of a relapse into violence is significant. Findings from El Salvador and Cambodia indicate, however, that indirect assistance such as international election observation and technical assistance to election commissions has done little to counter the pro-government – and by extension pro-ruling party – bias of most bilateral development assistance programmes. If international party assistance is to have a greater and constructive impact on party and party system development it should no longer be offered as an isolated activity. Instead, it should become an integral part of the broader democratic governance agenda.[58]

Final remarks

The cross-case analysis presented here has demonstrated that the wars that El Salvador and Cambodia have experienced have had a significant, lasting impact not only on the formation, development and institutionalization of parties and party systems, but also on the behaviour and interactions of party leaders. Moreover, it shows that post-war international party assistance in these two countries has had some benefits, for example giving smaller opposition parties a degree of credibility and legitimacy. Nevertheless, it has also become clear that international party assistance as such has not fundamentally altered the structures of individual parties nor changed the often violent and one-party dominant nature of party competition. Generalizing these conclusions beyond El Salvador and Cambodia is problematic, but it is plausible that war and war-related factors have had a similarly important impact on the parties and party systems of other post-war countries. The many questions that still remain are an indication that there is much scope for further research that could make a significant contribution to knowledge in this area. To reduce the gap in our knowledge about post-war parties and party systems and make sure that its findings will benefit future assistance programmes, such research should now move forward as soon as possible.

Acknowledgements

This account is based on a PhD thesis completed in the Department of Politics and International Studies at the University of Warwick (UK) and was earlier presented at the Annual European Graduate Conference on Political Parties, University of Birmingham, 16 February 2009. The author is grateful for the comments and suggestions received from participants at that conference as well as from Professor Peter Burnell and two external reviewers.

Notes

1. This article focuses on war situations that are primarily of an internal character (civil or intrastate wars), not of an international character (interstate wars). Following the

widely used definition of the Uppsala Conflict Data Program, *major armed conflict* or *war* is here defined as 'a contested incompatibility, which concerns government and/or territory where the use of armed force between two parties, of which at least one is the government of a state, results in at least 1000 battle-related deaths per year'. See http://www.ucdp.uu.se (accessed February 4, 2009).
2. Mansfield and Snyder, *Electing to Fight*; Jarstad and Sisk, *From War to Democracy*; Reilly, 'Political Engineering and Party Politics'; Bjornlund, Cowan, and Gallery, 'Election Systems and Political Parties'.
3. A notable exception is the work by Carrie Manning, who argues that the internal organizational dynamics of rebel-to-party transformation are affected by the institutional framework in which parties operate in post-war societies. See Manning, 'Party-building on the Heels of War'. However, her work does not look at the impact of war on party organization and party competition per se, which is the focus of this study.
4. Scarrow, 'The Nineteenth-Century Origins of Modern Political Parties', 19–20.
5. Kitschelt, 'Divergent Paths of Postcommunist Democracies'.
6. Salih, 'Introduction'; Sachsenröder, 'Party Politics and Democratic Development'; Diamond and Linz, 'Introduction: Politics, Society and Democracy in Latin America'.
7. Krouwel, 'Party Models'.
8. Randall, *Political Parties in the Third World*.
9. Sartori, *Parties and Party Systems*, 57.
10. For this study the author conducted more than 70 semi-structured interviews (1–2 hours each) in Phnom Penh, Kampot (Cambodia) and San Salvador (El Salvador) with a broad range of political party representatives, academic experts, political analysts, civil society representatives and staff from international organizations. de Zeeuw, 'Political Party Development in Post-War Societies'.
11. War-related factors that received particular attention were the war-time origins of parties, the way in which the war ended (military victory or peace agreement), and the design of post-war electoral, media and other public institutions.
12. This includes both dominant-authoritarian and dominant non-authoritarian systems. Also prevalent in post-war societies are so-called pulverized party systems, found in places such as Afghanistan, Guatemala and Lebanon.
13. By contrast, the processes of post-war peacebuilding, reconstruction and democratization of El Salvador and Cambodia have received much more attention. See, for example, Montgomery, *Revolution in El Salvador*; Call, 'Assessing El Salvador's Transition From Civil War to Peace'; Doyle, *UN Peacekeeping in Cambodia*; Peou, *Intervention and Change in Cambodia*.
14. While some mass-based left-wing political organizations were repressed, others were banned outright as in the case of the Communist Party of El Salvador (PCS). Wade, 'El Salvador: The Success of the FMLN', 34.
15. Baloyra, *El Salvador in Transition*, 35.
16. This included the Nationalist Democratic Organization (ORDEN), an approximately 100,000 strong peasant militia force set up in the 1960s to counter the activities of rural opposition groups. Montgomery, *Revolution in El Salvador*, 54–67.
17. Whereas the FMLN received support from countries such as Cuba and Nicaragua, the Salvadoran military was kept alive by large amounts of technical and logistic military assistance from the United States (estimated at USD6 billion over the 1980–1989 civil war period). Martín-Baró and Cardenal, 'Introduction – Fifteen Years Later: Peace at Last', 4.
18. Chandler, *The Tragedy of Cambodian History*, 79.
19. Peou, *Intervention and Change in Cambodia*, 48–54; and interview with Uk Phourik, 9 July 2008, Phnom Penh.

20. Chandler, *The Tragedy of Cambodian History*, 229.
21. Experts on Cambodia continue to differ in their assessment of the real intentions of the regime the Khmer Rouge established between 1975 and 1979. See Vickery, *Cambodia: 1975–1982*; Kiernan, *The Pol Pot Regime*; Chandler, *Brother Number One*.
22. United Nations, *The United Nations and El Salvador 1990–1995*, 193.
23. For an in-depth analysis of the FMLN's transformation into a political party, see Wade, 'El Salvador: The Success of the FMLN'.
24. Song, 'The Political Dynamics of the Peacemaking Process in Cambodia'.
25. United Nations, *The United Nations and Cambodia, 1991–1995*, 12; Suntharalingam, 'The Cambodian Settlement Agreements', 90.
26. United Nations. *Framework for a Comprehensive Political Settlement of the Cambodian Conflict*.
27. Roberts, *Political Transition in Cambodia 1991–99*, 105.
28. The 19-year post-war dominance of ARENA ended with the resounding win of the FMLN in the parliamentary and municipal elections of 15 January 2009 and the election of the new FMLN candidate and former TV interviewer Mauricio Funes as President of El Salvador on 15 March 2009.
29. For a more detailed analysis of individual party institutionalization in El Salvador and Cambodia, see chapters 4 and 5 in de Zeeuw, 'Political Party Development in Post-War Societies'.
30. In 2006 ARENA won 147 mayoralships against only three by the CD. In 2007 the CPP could nominate the chief of 1591 commune councils against zero by the NRP. See Centro de Información, Documentación y Apoyo a la Investigación (CIDAI), 'Las Elecciones Legislativas y Municipales de 2006'; and National Election Committee (NEC), *Official Results of the 2007 Commune Council Elections*. The numbers of party members are rough estimates provided by various interviewees in San Salvador and Phnom Penh between September 2007 and August 2008. Rather than intending to provide an accurate picture of party membership, these numbers are here only used as an indication of organizational strength.
31. Sartori, *Parties and Party Systems*, 229–31.
32. See chapter 5 in de Zeeuw, 'Political Party Development in Post-War Societies'. See also Un, 'Patronage Politics and Hybrid Democracy'.
33. See chapter 4 in de Zeeuw, 'Political Party Development in Post-War Societies'; and Zamora, *El Salvador*.
34. Wade, 'El Salvador: The Success of the FMLN', 47–8; and interviews in San Salvador with representatives from several of these organizations between September and October 2007.
35. Information from interviews with representatives of NDI, IRI and UNDP between May and July 2008 in Phnom Penh.
36. Un, 'Sam Rainsy and the Sam Rainsy Party: Configuring Opposition Politics in Cambodia'.
37. Roberts, *Political Transition in Cambodia 1991–99*; Peou, *International Democracy Assistance for Peacebuilding*; and Wade, 'The Challenge of Being Left in Neoliberal Central America'.
38. Between 1992 and 2001 El Salvador received approximately USD 3.6 billion in official development assistance. Over the same period Cambodia received slightly more, USD 3.7 billion. Data taken from aid figures reported to the Organization for Economic Cooperation and Development over various years. Available at: http://stats.oecd.org/qwids (accessed February 9, 2009).
39. This view is supported by several interviewees interviewed in El Salvador and Phnom Penh between September and October 2007 and April and August 2008, respectively. See also Roberts, *Political Transition in Cambodia 1991–99*; Peou, *International*

Democracy Assistance for Peacebuilding; and Wade, 'The Challenge of Being Left in Neoliberal Central America'.
40. Holiday, 'El Salvador's "Model" Democracy'.
41. Hughes, 'Cambodia in 2007. Development and Dispossession'.
42. However, the FMLN's recent electoral success has arguably more to do with the nomination of an outsider (non-party cadre) as presidential candidate than with a change in the party's organizational strength. In contrast to the FMLN, FUNCINPEC has always relied on internal candidates, which have paid little attention to strengthening the party's organizational structures.
43. For El Salvador, see Córdova, Cruz, and Seligson, *Cultura Política de la Democracia en El Salvador*. For Cambodia, this view was expressed by Thun Saray, President of the Cambodian Human Rights and Development Association (ADHOC), during a press conference of the Committee for Free and Fair Elections in Cambodia (COMFREL) on 28 July 2008.
44. Research on which this account is based indicates that war-related factors carry at least as much, possibly more weight in explaining the institutionalization of post-war parties and party systems than conventional theories that focus on electoral competition, socioeconomic cleavages and formal political institutions. See de Zeeuw, 'Political Party Development in Post-War Societies'.
45. Montgomery, *Revolution in El Salvador*, 258; Rubio-Fabián et al., *Democratic Transition in Post-Conflict El Salvador*, 22.
46. Doyle, 'Authority and Elections in Cambodia', 54–155.
47. Zamora, *El Salvador*, 97.
48. Wade, 'El Salvador: The Success of the FMLN', 40–4; and Rowley, 'Cambodia'. For a more extensive analysis of the challenges faced by former rebel groups turning into political parties, see the various contributions in de Zeeuw, *From Soldiers to Politicians*.
49. For a more extensive discussion of this issue see, for example, Sachsenröder, 'Party Politics and Democratic Development'; and Diamond and Linz, 'Introduction: Politics, Society and Democracy in Latin America'.
50. The term *hijos de la guerra* was proposed by Jorge Villacorte and Rubén Zamora in separate interviews with the author on 14 September and 24 October 2007, both in San Salvador.
51. Interviews with Roberto Rubio-Fabián, 11 September 2007; Jorge Villacorte, 14 September 2007; and Antonio Cañas, 1 October 2007, all in San Salvador. See also Bartu, 'Cambodia: Tensions Around the National Election Committee'.
52. These descriptions are commonly used in local media reports and were referred to by several interviewees in El Salvador and Cambodia interviewed for this study. See also the various contributions in Artiga-González et al., *La Polarización Política en El Salvador*; and Hughes, 'Parties, Protest and Pluralism in Cambodia', 171.
53. On Ethiopia, see Abbink, 'Discomfiture of Democracy?'; on Nicaragua, see Dye, *Democracy Adrift*; on Sudan, see Young, 'Sudan'.
54. Reilly, 'Political Engineering and Party Politics in Conflict-Prone Societies'; Manning, 'Party-building on the Heels of War'; and Lyons, *Demilitarizing Politics*.
55. Information from several author interviews with party leaders in El Salvador and Cambodia.
56. Carothers, *Confronting the Weakest Link*, 163–6; and Burnell, 'Looking to the Future', 200.
57. Interview with Mu Sochua, 14 June 2008, Kampot.
58. See also Carothers, 'The "Sequencing" Fallacy'; and Hoove and Pinto-Scholtbach, *Democracy and Political Party Assistance in Post-Conflict Societies*.

Bibliography

Abbink, Jon. 'Discomfiture of Democracy? The 2005 Election Crisis in Ethiopia and its Aftermath'. *African Affairs* 155, no. 419 (2006): 173–99.

Artiga-González, Álvaro, Carlos Dada, David Escobar Galindo, Hugo Martínez, Gloria Salguerro Gross, Rubén I. Zamora, and Roberto Turcios. *La Polarización Política en El Salvador*. San Salvador: FLACSO and FundaUngo, 2007.

Baloyra, Enrique A. *El Salvador in Transition*. Chapel Hill: The University of North Carolina Press, 1982.

Bartu, Peter. 'Cambodia: Tensions Around the National Election Committee', in *Electoral Management Design: The International IDEA Handbook*, ed. Alan Wall, Andrew Ellis, Ayman Ayoub, Carl W. Dundas, Joram Rukambe, and Sara Staino, 284–8. Stockholm: International IDEA, 2006.

Bjornlund, Eric, Glenn Cowan, and William Gallery. 'Election Systems and Political Parties in Post-Conflict and Fragile States', in *Governance in Post-Conflict Societies. Rebuilding Fragile States*, ed. Derick W. Brinkerhoff, 64–84. London: Routledge, 2007.

Burnell, Peter. 'Looking to the Future. Practice and Research in Party Support', in *Globalising Democracy. Party Politics in Emerging Democracies*, ed. Peter Burnell, 200–9. London: Routledge, 2006.

Call, Charles T. 'Assessing El Salvador's Transition from Civil War to Peace', in *Ending Civil Wars. The Implementation of Peace Agreements*, ed. Stephen John Stedman, Donald Rothchild, and Elizabeth M. Cousens, 383–420. Boulder, CO: Lynne Rienner Publishers, 2002.

Carothers, Thomas. *Confronting the Weakest Link, Aiding Political Parties in New Democracies*. Washington, DC: Carnegie Endowment for International Peace, 2006.

Carothers, Thomas. 'The "Sequencing" Fallacy'. *Journal of Democracy* 18, no. 1 (2007): 12–27.

Centro de Información, Documentación y Apoyo a la Investigación (CIDAI), 'Las Elecciones Legislativas y Municipales de 2006: Polarización Sociopolítica y Erosión Institucional'. *Estudios Centroamericanos* 61, no. 688/689 (2006): 195–218.

Chandler, David P. *Brother Number One: A Political Biography of Pol Pot*. Boulder, CO: Westview Press, 1992.

Chandler, David P. *The Tragedy of Cambodian History. Politics, War and Revolution Since 1945*. Chiang Mai: Silkworm Books, 1993.

Córdova, Ricardo Macías, José Miguel Cruz, and Mitchell A. Seligson. *Cultura Política de la Democracia en El Salvador: 2006*. San Salvador: IUDOP, 2007.

Diamond, Larry, and Juan J. Linz. 'Introduction: Politics, Society and Democracy in Latin America', in *Democracy in Developing Countries. Volume Four: Latin America*, ed. Larry Diamond, Juan J. Linz, and Seymour Martin Lipset, 1–58. Boulder, CO: Lynne Rienner Publishers, 1989.

Doyle, Michael. *UN Peacekeeping in Cambodia: UNTAC's Civil Mandate*. Boulder, CO: Lynne Rienner Publishers, 1995.

Doyle, Michael. 'Authority and Elections in Cambodia', in *Keeping the Peace. Multidimensional UN Operations in Cambodia and El Salvador*, ed. Michael W. Doyle, Ian Johnstone, and Robert C. Orr, 134–64. Cambridge: Cambridge University Press, 1997.

Dye, David R. *Democracy Adrift: Caudillo Politics in Nicaragua*. Cambridge, MA: Hemisphere Initiatives, 2004.
Holiday, David. 'El Salvador's "Model" Democracy'. *Current History* 104, no. 679 (2005): 77–82.
Hoove, Lotte ten and Álvaro Pinto-Scholtbach. *Democracy and Political Party Assistance in Post-Conflict Societies*. The Hague: Netherlands Institute for Multiparty Democracy, NIMD, 2008.
Hughes, Caroline. 'Parties, Protest and Pluralism in Cambodia'. *Democratization* 9, no. 3 (2002): 165–86.
Hughes, Caroline. 'Cambodia in 2007. Development and Dispossession'. *Asian Survey* 48, no. 1 (2008): 69–74.
Jarstad, Anna. K., and Timothy D. Sisk, eds. *From War to Democracy. Dilemmas of Peacebuilding*. Cambridge: Cambridge University Press, 2008.
Kiernan, Ben. *The Pol Pot Regime. Race, Power and Genocide in Cambodia Under the Khmer Rouge, 1975–1979*. New Haven, CT: Yale University Press, 1996.
Kitschelt, Herbert. 'Divergent Paths of Postcommunist Democracies', in *Political Parties and Democracy*, ed. Larry Diamond and Richard Gunther, 299–323. Baltimore, MD: Johns Hopkins University Press, 2001.
Krouwel, André. 'Party Models', in *Handbook of Party Politics*, ed. Richard S. Katz and William Crotty, 249–69. London: Sage Publications, 2006.
Lyons, Terrence. *Demilitarizing Politics. Elections on the Uncertain Road to Peace*. Boulder, CO: Lynne Rienner Publishers, 2005.
Manning, Carrie. 'Party-building on the Heels of War: El Salvador, Bosnia, Kosovo and Mozambique'. *Democratization* 14, no. 2 (2007): 253–72.
Mansfield, Edward D., and Jack Snyder. *Electing to Fight. Why Emerging Democracies Go to War*. Cambridge: MIT Press, 2005.
Martín-Baró, Ignacio, and Rodolfo Cardenal. 'Introduction – Fifteen Years Later: Peace at Last', in *Revolution in El Salvador: From Civil Strife to Civil Peace*, ed. Tommie Sue Montgomery, 1–9, 2nd ed. Boulder, CO: Westview Press, 1995.
Mohamed, Salih, M.A. 'Introduction: The Evolution of African Political Parties', in *African Political Parties. Evolution, Institutionalisation and Governance*, ed. M.A. Mohamed Salih, 1–33. London: Pluto Press, 2003.
Montgomery, Tommie Sue., ed. *Revolution in El Salvador: From Civil Strife to Civil Peace*, 2nd ed. Boulder, CO: Westview Press, 1995.
National Election Committee (NEC). *Official Results of the 2007 Commune Council Elections*. Phnom Penh: NEC, 2007.
Peou, Sorpong. *Intervention and Change in Cambodia. Towards Democracy?* Singapore: Institute of Southeast Asian Studies and Chang Mai: Silkworm Books, 2000.
Peou, Sorpong. *International Democracy Assistance for Peacebuilding. Cambodia and Beyond*. Basingstoke: Palgrave Macmillan, 2007.
Randall, Vicky. *Political Parties in the Third World*. London: Sage Publications, 1988.
Reilly, Benjamin. 'Political Engineering and Party Politics in Conflict-Prone Societies'. *Democratization* 13, no. 5 (2006): 811–27.
Roberts, David. *Political Transition in Cambodia 1991–99. Power, Elitism and Democracy*. Richmond, VA: Curzon Press, 2001.
Rowley, Kevin. 'Cambodia', revised and updated by Jeroen de Zeeuw, in *Political Parties of the World*, ed. Derek Sagaar, 7th ed, 93–7. London: John Harper Publishing, 2009.
Rubio-Fabián, Roberto, Antonio Morales, Tomás Carbonell, Florentín Meléndez, and Anne Germain Lefévre. *Democratic Transition in Post-Conflict El Salvador. The Role of the International Community*. The Hague: Clingendael Institute, 2004.
Sachsenröder, Wolfgang. 'Party Politics and Democratic Development in East and Southeast Asia – A Comparative View', in *Political Party Systems and Democratic Development*

in *East and Southeast Asia. Volume I: Southeast Asia*, ed. Wolfgang Sachsenröder and Ulrike E. Frings, 1–35. Aldershot: Ashgate, 1998.

Sartori, Giovanni. *Parties and Party Systems: A Framework for Analysis*. Colchester: ECPR Press, 2005. Reprinted edition of *Parties and Party Systems: A Framework for Analysis*. Cambridge: Cambridge University Press, 1976.

Scarrow, Susan E. 'The Nineteenth-Century Origins of Modern Political Parties: The Unwanted Emergence of Party-Based Politics', in *Handbook of Party Politics*, ed. Richard S. Katz and William Crotty, 16–24. London: Sage Publications, 2006.

Song, Jin. 'The Political Dynamics of the Peacemaking Process in Cambodia', in *Keeping the Peace. Multidimensional UN Operations in Cambodia and El Salvador*, ed. Michael W. Doyle, Ian Johnstone, and Robert C. Orr, 68–76. Cambridge: Cambridge University Press, 1997.

Suntharalingam, Nishkala. 'The Cambodian Settlement Agreements', in *Keeping the Peace. Multidimensional UN Operations in Cambodia and El Salvador*, ed. Michael W. Doyle, Ian Johnstone, and Robert C. Orr, 82–106. Cambridge: Cambridge University Press, 1997.

Un, Kheang. 'Patronage Politics and Hybrid Democracy: Political Change in Cambodia, 1993–2003'. *Asian Perspective* 29, no. 2 (2005): 203–30.

Un, Kheag. 'Sam Rainsy and the Sam Rainsy Party: Configuring Opposition Politics in Cambodia', in *Dissident Democrats. The Challenge of Democratic Leadership in Asia*, ed. John Kane, Haig Patapan, and Benjamin Wong, 105–28. Basingstoke: Palgrave Macmillan, 2008.

United Nations. *The United Nations and El Salvador 1990–1995*. The United Nations Blue Book Series, Vol. IV. UN Doc. No. A/46/864-S/23501. New York: UN Department of Public Information, 1995.

United Nations. *The United Nations and Cambodia, 1991–1995*. The United Nations Blue Book Series, Vol. II. New York: UN Department of Public Information, 1995.

United Nations. *Framework for a Comprehensive Political Settlement of the Cambodian Conflict*. Annex 5, Principles for a New Constitution for Cambodia. UN General Assembly, A/46/608, Security Council, S/23177. New York: United Nations, http://peacemaker.unlb.org/doc_view.php?d=475&p=177 (accessed May 28, 2008).

Vickery, Michael. *Cambodia: 1975–1982*. Boston, MA: South End Press, 1984.

Wade, Christine. 'El Salvador: The Success of the FMLN', in *From Soldiers to Politicians. Transforming Rebel Movements After Civil War*, ed. Jeroen de Zeeuw, 33–54. Boulder, CO: Lynne Rienner Publishers, 2008.

Wade, Christine. 'The Challenge of Being Left in Neoliberal Central America', in *After the Peace: Political, Economic and Social Exclusion in El Salvador*. Athens, OH: Ohio University Press (forthcoming).

Young, John. 'Sudan: The Incomplete Transition from the SPLA to the SPLM', in *From Soldiers to Politicians. Transforming Rebel Movements After Civil War*, ed. Jeroen de Zeeuw, 157–78. Boulder, CO: Lynne Rienner Publishers, 2008.

Zamora, Rubén I. *El Salvador: Heridas Que No Cierran. Los Partidos Políticos en la Post-Guerra*. San Salvador: FLACSO, 1998.

de Zeeuw, Jeroen, ed. *From Soldiers to Politicians. Transforming Rebel Movements After Civil War*. Boulder, CO: Lynne Rienner Publishers, 2008.

de Zeeuw, Jeroen. 'Political Party Development in Post-War Societies: The Institutionalization of Parties and Party Systems in El Salvador and Cambodia'. PhD Thesis, University of Warwick, Coventry, 2009.

Problems of party assistance in hybrid regimes: the case of Morocco

Nicole Bolleyer[a] and Lise Storm[b]

[a]*Department of Politics, University of Exeter, UK;* [b]*Institute of Arab and Islamic Studies, University of Exeter, UK*

Like many other transition countries, Morocco is a prime target for democracy promoters. In light of the ongoing democracy promotion efforts in Morocco, this study seeks to analyse the range of measures for political party assistance applied by three major providers, two of which style themselves as non-governmental organizations (NGOs) and one of which is an intergovernmental organization (IGO). To estimate the likely effects of the various measures of assistance, we distinguish between those trying to (a) professionalize party activities in the respective institutional setting, (b) initiate a change of formal-legal rules defining the institutional setting, and (c) establish and intensify party linkages with society. Using these categories to examine political party assistance in a 'hybrid' regime (that combines competitive elections with non-democratic or authoritarian elements) reveals two problems from the viewpoint of provider organizations who apply such assistance as a means of democracy promotion. First, there is a lack of clear incentives, which may result in a failure by the targeted party elites to establish party organizations incorporating citizens in their internal decision-making processes; and secondly, the successful professionalization of the political parties may lead unintentionally to maintaining the hybrid nature of such regimes rather than supporting further democratization.

Measures of political party assistance: democracy promotion by soft incentives and persuasion

Throughout the last decades efforts to promote democracy in transition countries and newly democratized systems have intensified considerably. The success of the various democracy promotion measures, however, has been mixed.[1] Events responding to the 9/11 terrorist attacks complicated the situation further: especially

American initiatives perceived as closely influenced by US government policy have experienced resistance in some of the target countries in which anti-American sentiments have developed.[2]

Evidently, not only the *types of measures* promoting democracy, but which organization, institution or country applies them, i.e. the *measures' origin*, play a role when trying to gauge their impact, whether actual or expected. This study is particularly concerned with party assistance – and therefore democracy promotion efforts – utilizing soft incentives and persuasion. In contrast to national governments, who have a wide range of measures at their disposal, these are often the only tools at the hands of non-governmental organizations (NGOs) as well as a number of inter-governmental organizations (IGOs) seeking to promote democracy in the Middle East and elsewhere. We define NGOs as organizations which claim to operate formally independent from actual government policy.[3] Given that some organizations may be formally independent from actual government policy and at the same time receive most of their funding ultimately from government sources, while being closely tied to a political party (as is the case with the two NGOs at the core of this study), this is undoubtedly a contested definition, not only from an academic perspective. More importantly for our study, their independence might be contested by the inhabitants in the countries receiving the assistance, that is those actors targeted by these measures. Some NGOs, which are formally independent from actual government policy, actually receive substantial amounts of government funding, and they are accordingly perceived by many as agents of that government. This, in turn, might provoke targeted actors to reject assistance.[4]

In face of this difficulty, we need to consider the following possibility: measures of party assistance (as one particular category of measures of democracy promotion) when being employed by American NGOs, might be received differently from those measures employed by other organizations that are similarly limited to soft incentives and persuasion, but due to their intergovernmental nature are less likely to reflect or be associated with one particular government policy.[5] Consequently this study deliberately looks at measures by the following major organizations active in Morocco: two American NGOs, the National Democratic Institute (NDI) and the International Republican Institute (IRI), affiliated with the Democratic Party and the Republicans respectively, and the United Nations (UN) (more specifically the United Nations Development Programme (UNDP)), an IGO, as a (supposedly) more 'neutral' pendant.[6]

It is evident that the question of acceptance by the target actors is particularly crucial for *non-coercive measures* – the focus of this contribution – as they require the cooperation of the recipients in order to be effective. In contrast to governmental actors, who have a much wider range of tools at their disposition, NGOs and some IGOs can employ neither force nor economic sanctions or rewards. They have to rely on soft incentives, naming and shaming tactics or persuasion.[7] This can be considered as their core weakness. Although governmental actors like the US or the European Union (EU) tend to prefer a cooperative approach, thus, avoiding direct economic or military sanctions,[8] governments nonetheless tend to resort to a mix of measures.[9] Yet, the implicit threat of coercive means undoubtedly still plays a role, even though it is used only rarely. This shows that the origin (governmental vs. non-governmental) and the range of available measures are necessarily closely tied, a reality which has immediate repercussions for the effectiveness of party assistance as applied by those organizations having to rely on soft incentives.

Once moving on to *party assistance* as such, the problem is accelerated given the target's nature: political parties as desired by the Western providers are 'voluntary organizations' rooted in society, not elite-dominated, publicly funded bodies closely intertwined with state institutions.[10] To change parties from the latter into the former presupposes the cooperation of party elites, which easily consider such developments as a threat.[11] Moreover, building party linkages to civil society is a long-term process, while democracy promoters are pressed by those who fund them to demonstrate much more immediate success.[12] Finally, party building touches upon the sensitive issue of targeting non-state actors who potentially or explicitly oppose a given regime, a strategy that is therefore less frequently pursued by democracy promoters.[13]

Our study proceeds in the following steps. To analyse the various measures of party assistance employed by the three major organizations, and to assess how these are likely to be received, we first explore the link between parties and democratization. We discuss briefly the extent to which political parties of the mass party format contributed to the development of Western democracies, an observation that has led many democracy promoters to assume that the formation of mass parties is the key to bringing about democracy elsewhere.

In order to systematize the various measures of party assistance that democracy promoters utilize, we introduce, in a second step, a framework that highlights the unit targeted (individual party or the party system), and the type of change that is aimed at (for example merely formal-legal changes or the intensification of party-societal relations instead). It helps us distinguish between measures of party assistance which stabilize parties and support party activities in a system, and measures which actually trigger democratization, two potential effects of such measures which need not necessarily go together. This discrepancy reveals two core problems from the viewpoint of provider organizations inherent in party assistance, particularly when applied in hybrid regimes: first, a lack of clear incentives may result in a failure by the targeted party elites to establish party organizations incorporating citizens in their internal decision-making processes; and secondly, the successful professionalization of the political parties may lead unintentionally to maintaining the status quo of the regime, rather than supporting further democratization.

In a third step we move towards the empirical analysis and justify Morocco as the setting in which the provision of party assistance is studied. It is a regime that holds competitive elections, while executive power remains mainly in the hands of a monarch. It thus falls in the category of hybrid regimes.[14] These regimes are wide-spread and represent settings in which external democracy promoters are very active.[15] The following analysis of party assistance in Morocco draws on the scrutiny of primary documents as well as interviews conducted with target actors in Morocco. It demonstrates that depending on the measure in question, party assistance might not necessarily foster democratization but stabilize the status quo instead,[16] especially when looking at assistance providers that cannot put pressure on targeted actors but depend on the latter's cooperation. This finding is in line with our theoretical elaborations. We conclude with a summary of the findings and a general outlook on the prospects of democracy promotion in Morocco.

Parties and democracy: the mass party as a cure for democratizing countries?

Based on the assumption that political parties have an essential function in established democracies, most prominently as vehicles for citizen representation, the organizational weakness of parties observed in many new democracies and transition countries is considered detrimental to democratization processes. Consequently, political parties are amongst the key targets of democracy promoters – party development is seen as a means to strengthen democracy.[17] Party assistance tries to counter negative organizational tendencies typical for parties in transition countries. These include excessive concentration of power in a small elite, non-transparent party funding and excessive dependence on a few large sources of finance, lack of a coherent policy profile, a virtually non-existent membership organization and, therefore, an absence of stable linkages to citizens.[18]

However, the observation that sufficiently organized parties rooted in society have been essential for the evolution of established Western democracies does not mean that strengthening parties in a democratizing regime that still possesses strong non-democratic elements favours a transition to a fully democratic system. The development of mass parties in Western Europe in the late nineteenth and early twentieth century and the incremental democratization of political systems have been mutually supportive, closely tied, processes. However, the pattern of party development in Western Europe did not 'cause' democratization, understood as a process of regime change from authoritarianism to consolidated democracy, although parties might have been important at certain stages of this process. As Randall and Svåsand[19] emphasize when discussing the role of political parties in democratization processes,

> ...whilst there is a striking consensus on the importance of the actual or potential contribution parties can make to the democratization process and specifically to democratic consolidation, within the relevant literature there is not in fact any extensive body of writing that explicitly seeks to pin this contribution down. Parties are not, typically, expected to feature prominently in early stages of transition, whilst repressive conditions prevail.

The literature indicates that the role political parties can be expected to play is more limited in hybrid regimes, which are still strongly characterized by non-democratic elements, than in systems that face the challenge of developing democratic practices within formally fully democratized structures or, even more so, than in long-lived, fully consolidated democracies.[20] This, in turn, implies that party assistance is more likely to function as an instrument of democratization in regimes already in the process of democratic consolidation, rather than in authoritarian or hybrid regimes that are yet to undergo democratic transition.

A similar problem emerges when looking at the goals of party assistance in greater detail. Here, the mass party emerges as the underlying template which in itself is partially misleading. As Carothers[21] points out, considering that mass parties have tended to decline in Western Europe, such efforts in transition regimes and new democracies are directed 'backwards'. Similarly, parties in new democracies in Central and Eastern Europe tend to be elite-dominated parties with a weak membership organization more dependent on state money than membership fees.[22]

In Western democracies, a strong membership organization (and thus membership fees) played an important role particularly for parties on the left.[23] They developed into what Duverger[24] called mass parties because they were excluded from government. This motivated them to build a strong infrastructure as their main pool of resources. Parties that developed within government institutions could afford to be cadre parties, evolving around a small group of office-holders, either rich themselves or supported by wealthy individuals.[25] In the contemporary Middle East only few, predominantly Islamist, parties have established strong societal networks, often (albeit not always) operating outside and being actively excluded from state institutions or government power.[26] Parties in power tend to be organizationally lighter.[27]

This points to a problem related to the mass party model as a template. The support for opposition parties – all the more if they are Islamist parties to which rightly or wrongly anti-democratic aspirations are often assigned – is a very sensitive issue for external democracy promoters.[28] And, being entirely dependent on the acceptance of and the active cooperation in the target country (be it the cooperation of party elites in government or opposition), this reality makes it all the more difficult for provider organizations involved in party assistance to apply measures effectively. At the same time, those parties which come closest to the party model underlying party assistance, namely Islamist parties, are likely to be ostracized by the established elites exactly due to their links with the general population and their often oppositional character. Carothers[29] argues that these parties developed strong grassroots 'despite the obstacles placed in their path'. In short, the exclusion of some parties from state institutions and resources related to them has created particularly strong incentives for these parties to resort to organization-building strategies associated with the mass party model. This means, in reverse, that those parties that NGOs and IGOs can legitimately target –parties forming part of the accepted elite – are the least likely to be responsive to their measures and therefore unlikely to develop along the lines of their Western counterparts. In other words, it is implausible that these will fully incorporate citizens into their organizations and develop strong ties to society.

Should the application of such measures result in making parties more efficient or in strengthening them organizationally, a second, more fundamental, problem emerges: party assistance – even in apparently successful cases – does not necessarily favour the further democratization of transition systems. Parties which channel citizen demands more effectively could equally lead to the stabilization of not yet fully democratized 'hybrid regimes', where elections take place regularly, while political power is only partially controlled by elected institutions.[30] It is, therefore, crucial to specify which type of change a particular measure is directed towards. This raises the question of whether any kind of party assistance in effect constitutes a useful form of democracy promotion – one that brings about genuine reform of the regime. In fact, such assistance might help to professionalize and strengthen parties without democratizing the regime. This leads us to study party assistance in Morocco which will help us highlight the two problems from the viewpoint of the provider organizations related to party assistance as identified above.

Case selection: party assistance in a 'hybrid regime'

In Morocco, a hybrid regime, the main power-holder is a non-elected monarch, not the parliament or the government. The prime minister, the main executive actor, is appointed by the king. In contrast to one-party states, parties are allowed to compete in legislative elections. Still, the core political power is out of their reach.[31] From the parliamentary parties' perspective, this situation creates conflicting accountabilities –to the king and to the electorate – which given the actual distribution of power is usually resolved in the king's favour.

A system combining elected and unelected institutions with a dominance of the latter helps us to reveal two problems of party assistance by organizations, which are limited to providing support and promoting ideas, and consequently are not in a position to exert pressure on political elites. This is all the more important since in the present century most systems targeted by external democracy promotion are 'hybrid regimes'.[32] A regime which accepts party competition as a legitimate part of the political process – albeit not as its core – might simply function better when run by competent, well-organized (rather than incompetent and unstable) parties. Thus, one needs to examine whether measures of party assistance predominantly help to professionalize party actors (for example, by increasing their competence) and thereby *make democratic institutions within a hybrid regime work better*, while stabilizing this regime in the long run. Systems that mix authoritarian and democratic elements make it difficult to determine the dynamics of a regime. Nonetheless, their analysis can help to specify the contradictory short-term and long-term effects of party assistance for democratization with particular clarity.

A framework for analysing party assistance in transition countries

To improve the working of the democratic components of a regime as compared to the regime's democratization is a crucial distinction with regards to all kinds of democracy assistance, not only party assistance. To allow for a systematic mapping of assistance measures by the NDI, the IRI and the UNDP, the analysis distinguishes between measures targeting the *individual party organization* and those targeting *relations between parties*[33] (for example, towards equality and distinctiveness of parties; open/fair competition; facilitating party cooperation without the collusion of those in power). While the dimensions are connected, it cannot be assumed that changes at the level of the individual parties necessarily generate beneficial effects at the party system level. To capture the contradictory nature of measures stabilizing individual parties while potentially decreasing the chances of regime transformation, we further categorize measures along the *type of change* a measure intends to generate.[34] It is frequently highlighted in the literature that there are different types of conditions and preconditions for achieving not only democratic transition but also democratic consolidation. Most fundamentally, we can distinguish constitutional or formal-legal conditions or preconditions referring to the institutional setting, behavioural conditions or preconditions referring to the actors involved in political decision-making processes within this setting, and finally social conditions or preconditions referring to civil society and the nature of its involvement in politics.[35] Reflecting this three-fold distinction, measures of party assistance can attempt to promote formal-legal change (for example, party funding regulations). Alternatively, they can attempt to improve party actors' performance within existing institutions (for example, through training of parliamentarians) without changing them. Finally, measures can target parties' relations to society (for example, through establishing local party offices). Of course in principle all three can be attempted at once, as well. But while measures targeting the functioning of existing institutions are most direct and one can expect a relatively immediate effect, party–society relations are likely to change only in the long run. Table 1 categorizes the range of measures discussed in the literature along these analytical distinctions.

The categorization along the type of change targeted by measures helps indicate how likely democracy promotion efforts, in our case measures of party assistance, are to achieve their intended effects: actively supporting democratization. The functioning of institutions is easiest to change and the least threatening for (elected or unelected) political elites, since such measures leave the overall power-structure untouched. Changing the legal regulations, in contrast, is problematic if political elites profit from given structures and expect to profit less from new ones. This problem intensifies when organizations employ soft measures only, for these need the active agreement of the targeted elites if they are to be effective. In the following we use this analytical framework to systematically assess and evaluate measures of party assistance as applied by the three major provider organizations, the NDI, the IRI and the UNDP, in the Moroccan context.

Table 1. A categorization of party assistance measures.

Unit targeted by measure towards change		→ Type of change (level/nature of expected effect)
Individual party/intra-party relations	*Party system/inter-party relations*	*Formal-legal incentive structures*
• State regulations of political parties (i.e. requirement for internal democracy) • Political finance regulation (i.e. assuring transparency of party funding) • Institutional resources for party office-holders (i.e. parliamentary staffing)	• Regulations of party foundations • Access to party funding (i.e. restricted to parliamentary parties or based on vote-share • Access to state resources (i.e. civil service structure allowing/preventing patronage) • Access to institutions (i.e. electoral thresholds) • Empowerment of parliament/elected government (i.e. stronger cooperation incentives to form government coalition)	
• Professionalizing party office-holders (i.e. law-making competence)	• Training in campaign organization • Formulate distinct policy platform • Inviting inter-party dialogues (i.e. to avoid ostracism of certain parties, to facilitate inter-organizational learning)	*Functioning of institutions*
• Training office-holders (i.e. building up constituency linkage) • Supporting inter-organizational ties (i.e. between unions and parties) • Set-up party offices • To establish practices of democratic decision-making in parties (i.e. leadership selection) • Support professional recruitment	• Improve media communication of party policy to citizen • Inviting public debates between parties and citizens • Political education of citizens	*Societal relations*

Source: Authors' own construction. Examples derived from, among others, Carothers, *Confronting the Weakest Link*; Carothers, 'Struggling with the Semi-Authoritarians'. Tommasoli, 'Democracy Assistance Trends in the Arab Region; Ottaway and Riley, 'Morocco'.

Party assistance in Morocco

Methods

The following analysis of NGO and IGO party assistance relies on document analysis and in-depth interviews with country experts in Morocco. The majority of documents were reports published by the NDI, the IRI or the UNDP describing their activities in Morocco or the Middle East more generally. Furthermore, interviews were conducted with experts such as journalists looking at political processes from the outside but also with politicians in Morocco, which allowed for the triangulation of the respective information.[36] The combination of document analysis and interviews does not only allow us to gain insights into which type of measures have been used by the three organizations, but also to get an idea about how they have been received in the target country. While the effectiveness of individual types of measures cannot be measured directly, our analysis can give an indication of how target actors have responded to these different measures.

Analysis

Party assistance activities conducted by the NDI, the IRI and the UNDP in Morocco during the past decade cover most of the measures outlined in Table 1, making the international effort in the country seem rather impressive.[37] Providers of assistance – whether the two NGOs or the IGO – usually invite the six largest parties from across the ideological spectrum to attend their activities, and while most of these are generally ready to participate, as of mid-2007, the Islamist PJD (*Parti de la Justice et du Développement*) has boycotted all US-funded democracy promotion efforts as a way of protesting against US foreign policy in the Middle East.[38]

Activities and reports target the need for a change of institutional rules, and usually aim to improve the functioning of existing institutions. To give a few examples, the UNDP has sought to modernize the House of Representatives by making more institutional resources available to office holders, while in the wake of the September 2007 parliamentary elections, the NDI recommended better regulation of – and access to – party funding.[39] The IRI's activities are also aimed at strengthening party structures at the local and regional levels, and improving internal democracy and communication. The organization has also played host to Moroccan MPs during the 2006 US mid-term elections in an effort to provide these with so-called 'hands on experience of competitive campaigning and nonpartisan election administration'.[40] Measures finally seek to motivate parties to create links with citizens at both the individual party and the party system levels. Examples include the UNDP's efforts to promote women's political participation, and the joint NDI/IRI mission aimed at strengthening the societal relations of the country's largest parties.[41] The only measures which appear to have been left out are those targeting institutional resources for party office holders (individual party/intra-party relations), supporting professional recruitment (individual party/intra-party relations), and access to state resources (party system/inter-party relations).

If one takes a closer look at these activities, however, it soon becomes apparent that with regard to a number of measures the NDI, the IRI, and the UNDP are only 'highlighting' shortcomings or 'giving recommendations'. This is less than being able to actually provide assistance which might help alleviate the particular problems that could be targeted via the use of such measures. This is the case, for instance, with measures targeting political finance regulation (individual party/intra-party relations), regulations of party foundations, access to party funding, and access to institutions (all three party system/inter-party relations).[42]

To initiate real change, measures need to motivate political power-holders to change existing formal-legal institutions and the rules under which they operate. As indicated by Table 1, such measures are necessarily indirect. And if existing institutions serve the self-interest of existing elites, recommendations are unlikely to be effective. For instance, in the current political climate, where the political parties are fighting over the limited funding available, it is unlikely that they will potentially diminish their own – albeit restricted – access to state funding.[43]

As far as alternative sources of party funding are concerned, the NDI has highlighted campaign financing as a major problem in Morocco, claiming that 'in some cases candidates are being chosen by parties based less on their history with the party or commitment to party principles and based more on their ability to finance campaigns'.[44] This reality further exacerbates voter apathy and the inability of voters to distinguish the Moroccan parties from each other. This strategy to assure party funding is, indeed, reminiscent of the cadre model emphasizing that parties lack incentives to engage in a strategy of organization-building in society. Referring back to the distinction between intra-party and inter-party relations, it indicates how the internal relations of individual parties can undermine meaningful inter-party competition.

An additional problem is the tendency of the three organizations to spread themselves thinly with regards to initiatives, despite a more concentrated and systematic approach being more likely to be successful. Beginning with the NDI, the organization has activities in no less than four of the six clusters of measures portrayed in Table 1 (functioning of institutions at both levels and societal relations at both levels), and it gives policy recommendations in the final two (formal-legal incentive structures at both levels).[45] The IRI has slightly less coverage as the organization does not have activities that target formal-legal incentive structures, and it also does not have any activities at the individual party/intra-party relations level with regards to the functioning of institutions.[46] Finally, the UNDP has activities targeting formal-legal incentive structures at both levels, the functioning of institutions at both levels, and societal relations at the party system/inter-party relations level.[47]

The reason why activities aimed at reforming the formal-legal incentive structures are far from popular with the different organizations is undoubtedly that this is a very sensitive area. Heads of state tend not to appreciate foreign interference in what they see as domestic matters, particularly when reforms might diminish their hold on power. This reality more than likely explains why the

UNDP's activities in this area are very sparse, and why the NDI and the IRI are only making recommendations.

With regards to measures aimed at improving societal relations, these are the most prevalent amongst the three organizations looked at in this study. It is very probable that their widespread use is related to the fact that measures targeting societal relations are seen as acceptable by all the political parties, the head of state, and the general population. Measures targeting the functioning of institutions are almost equally well-liked by the NDI, the IRI, and the UNDP. These measures constitute somewhat of a middle-ground between activities aimed at improving societal relations and those that seek to change formal-legal incentive structures. They tend to be some of those most popular with the political parties themselves as they usually enhance the political skills of the party elite in particular.

Clearly, these measures add to the efficiency of party actors in their public roles, which might improve the way they are perceived by citizens in the long run. Still, meeting the demands of public office may not be equated with parties' representative function. Governing and representing tend to demand different skills and sometimes even conflict with each other.[48] The former demands neutral expertise and often the willingness to negotiate compromises with the representatives of rival parties, while the latter – from the represented citizens' view point – might be most effective if a party publicly insists on its positions uncompromisingly.[49] Whether party assistance that improves governing supports a regime's democratization depends on the nature of the regime already in place, since such measures tend to stabilize existing structures rather than to initiate change. They might improve the support for a formally democratized regime that still has to develop democratic practices in the longer run, as it negotiates the process of consolidation. In the case of hybrid regimes in the middle of transition, however, they are as likely to stabilize the democratic as the non-democratic elements.[50]

Finally, it is important to highlight the fact that the organizations at the core of this study are not content with simply covering most clusters of measurements as illustrated in Table 1, for they also tend to have several different activities within each cluster, thereby spreading themselves even more thinly. For instance, both the NDI and the IRI have several activities that target societal relations at both levels as well as a number of activities aimed at the functioning of institutions at the party system/inter-party level.[51] Similarly the UNDP has a number of activities in all three clusters at the party system/inter-party relations level.[52]

Implications

The reality that the NDI, the IRI, and the UNDP cover most of the measures outlined in Table 1 has both negative and positive implications. Beginning with the positive, it is clearly evident from the sheer scale of activities that party assistance in Morocco is seen as of crucial importance by the international community. Moreover this is at a time when such assistance is generally under-prioritized by

European and North American NGOs in favour of assistance aimed at improving governance and public institution building. Moreover, in comparison to other Middle Eastern countries, Morocco appears to be a favoured party assistance target state, being the focus of activities by a relatively substantial number of foreign or international organizations.[53]

Apart from the reality that in Morocco virtually all aspects of party assistance – both targeting individual parties and more systemic features – are covered by the NDI, the IRI, and the UNDP, and are reinforced by NGOs such as the German *Stiftungen* (for example, Konrad Adenauer, Friedrich Ebert and Friedrich Naumann), there are not many positive implications of these organizations spreading themselves so thinly. As shall become evident, given the political context in Morocco, what is needed is a concentrated and systematic effort, not only by the individual organization but also by the different NGOs and IGOs in conjunction.[54]

Party assistance and the Moroccan political parties: the lack of attraction to the mass party model

There are two major reasons why a concentrated effort by the organizations providing party assistance is absolutely vital. The first relates to the Moroccan political parties and their lack of interest in party development along mass party lines, while the second concerns the position of the monarchy regarding actual regime change, that is, the transition from what has often been described as an 'executive monarchy' to a democratic regime.[55]

Beginning with the political parties, there is no doubt that while these have generally been keen to take part in democracy promotion activities – and particularly those targeting the political parties – most of the parties, if not all of them, have not done so out of a desire to change. They do so in order to be seen to participate and thereby show good-will, and with the aim of being acknowledged by the provider organizations and the Moroccan population as important actors in the political process.[56]

This reality is hardly surprising given that the voice of the electorate has been far from the most crucial factor in determining access to government power in the post-independence era (1956 onwards). Like the political parties in many other regimes, which have permitted electoral contestation, yet maintained a strong grip on power via various forms of repression and/or electoral manipulation, the Moroccan parties have had to operate in a highly complex environment. The votes cast by the electorate, although imperative, have long been of secondary importance to monarchical favour. Put differently, in order for parties to be taken seriously by the monarchy, they have had to perform well in the parliamentary elections. However, in order to gain access to political power – or indeed to remain legalized – they have to curry favour with the monarchy, essentially proving that they are of no danger to the regime – that is, committed to maintaining the executive monarchy.[57]

Unlike the situation immediately before independence, when popular support for the nationalist movement could be used against the French colonizers, or during the first few years after, when a party's support base could be utilized to pressurize the monarchy, the political parties currently have no use for the citizenry outside of election time.[58] In recent years, one would assume that the parties have come to view the country as more democratic, seeing elections as more important and, hence, finding a large popular support base an essential element of their structure. The adoption of a new constitution in 1996 might be considered particularly significant here, for it awarded the prime minister slightly more responsibility; then there was the inauguration of a new, seemingly more liberal king in 1999; the introduction of proportional representation at the time of the parliamentary elections of 2002; and the promulgation of the law on political parties in 2006, which, among other measures, emphasized the need for party-constituent links.

Yet, the overall effect of these formal changes has not been very great in practice.[59] Save perhaps for the PJD, the parties appear to be rather uninterested in strengthening their links with the citizenry outside of election time. They have been reluctant to hold party congresses, several parties do not have offices in all electoral districts, and most do not contest all of these at election time.[60] Politics in Morocco is essentially elitist, and according to the political elite, there is no need to change this state of affairs.

Party assistance and the Moroccan electorate: evidence of mass party dreams

In contrast to the political parties, which are far from favouring stronger links with the electorate, the citizenry is of a different opinion. According to surveys conducted by Maroc 2020 and the NDI during the time of the September 2007 parliamentary elections, the electorate is strongly disillusioned with the country's political parties, and that owes in part to their lack of linkage. Several statements hinted that the population felt that the politicians did not care about their situation, with one young man stating that 'political parties don't try to make young people interested. They don't organize meetings where they could listen to young people's concerns'[61]; a sentiment echoed by an urban, middle class woman, who told the NDI 'They contact us during elections for their own interests and as soon as they win they disappear. I don't even know where the office of my parliamentary representative is, and I don't know how to contact him'.[62]

As a consequence of weak party-citizen linkages, voter turnout remains low in Morocco despite democratic reforms being introduced over the past decade. In short, despite the electoral system being more proportional, the constitution giving more power to the prime minister, and so on, the electorate simply does not have faith in the parties; voters cannot tell the political platforms apart and, hence, electoral volatility is high.[63] Rather unsurprisingly, very few Moroccans consider themselves party activists or, indeed, sympathizers of a particular party. Only 4% of respondents to a poll stated that they considered themselves to be party activists, and 12% said they sympathized with one or another of the country's many political parties.[64]

To make matters worse, the observed apathy is not simply rooted in a general disinterest in politics or in a more specific disappointment with parties as representatives, rather, both seem to be mutually reinforcing: illiteracy rates are very high in Morocco,[65] which makes it difficult for people to read papers and ballot cards and thereby distinguish between the parties. Another problem is the overwhelming number of political parties: people simply cannot be troubled to try to differentiate between the more than 30 parties available, also because they do not feel they listen anyway. While it is in principle possible to roughly categorize parties as left-wing and right of centre, alliances shift and policies change so much, especially in the right of centre category, that this is a difficult task even for a well-informed observer.

Assistance and prospects for democratization through party change

From the above is obvious that the tendency of the provider organizations of party assistance studied here to focus on the mass party model when putting together assistance strategies, is likely to be welcomed by Moroccan voters who have a strong desire to see the parties making more of an effort to establish a link with them, something which they have failed to do so far. However, the parties themselves are not interested in strengthening their ties with the general population. Also, they do not have much of a desire to change, a reality that became blatantly obvious at the time when the 2006 law on political parties was being debated in parliament – most of the established political parties were against it. While there were a number of reasons why the king's decision to push ahead with the law was unpopular with the parties, a significant proportion of these were simply unhappy with having to hold conferences on a regular basis – something which would undoubtedly make party members feel more empowered, and almost certainly also help attract additional members.[66]

This reality does not imply, however, that the parties will not partake in party assistance activities. In fact, the vast majority of parties – except the PJD at present – are highly interested in such initiatives, as party assistance activities are seen as strengthening the political leadership by increasing its knowledge and efficiency. In other words, the parties are willing to take part, but largely for the wrong reasons. While given such active participation, party assistance activities organized by the NDI, the IRI, and the UNDP will undoubtedly have some effect on party structures and behaviour. But any hopes of seeing the parties developing significantly along mass party lines are highly dubious, given the lack of enthusiasm by the parties themselves and the inability of provider organizations to put any effective pressure on them. However, if these organizations concentrated their efforts, focusing for example on activities relating to societal relations, their ability to put pressure on the parties would be much improved. They would show a united front, and there would be no alternative activities for the parties to pick and choose from. In other words, in a situation where the NDI, the IRI, and the UNDP concentrated their party assistance activities, the parties would be forced to make more of an effort to take the activities seriously. Otherwise they would run the risk of being excluded from future activities. This, in turn, would make them appear to the general population as unwilling to contribute to democratization in the country as a whole, and that perception might then weaken their support at election time.

That said, pressure on the parties to reform in a more democratic direction is only likely to be successful if supported by the key domestic actor: the monarchy. In Morocco, there is a saying that every political process begins with a royal discourse, and although the country has undergone a number of democratic reforms in recent years, this proverb remains very true indeed. It was on the basis of monarchical pressure that the personal status code (*moudawana*) was reformed in 2004, as was also the case with the law on political parties. Both of these were very strongly opposed by several of the dominant political parties, yet once the monarchy put its support behind the proposals, the parties came into line, and both initiatives were subsequently passed though parliament.[67]

The likelihood of the monarchy pushing party reforms beyond what has already been achieved with the adoption of the law on political parties is rather slim. The monarchy undoubtedly would like to see a more politically satisfied population, and would also welcome a better functioning parliament, which would enable King Mohammed VI to concentrate his efforts on bigger political issues, rather than day-to-day politics. However, the monarchy is not interested in the parties being strengthened to the extent that they could actually challenge the current state of affairs. The monarchy is interested in the better working of the regime, not its transformation.

The state of affairs at present, where a number of NGOs and IGOs – such as the NDI, the IRI, and the UNDP – are pouring money into the development of the parties, and thereby making them more effective in the political process, is probably the ideal situation for the monarchy. On the one hand, the monarchy is seen as tolerating, if not encouraging, such activities. On the other, it is well aware that these activities are unlikely to reform the parties into anything that might even remotely threaten the executive monarchy, given the absence of a concentrated effort by the provider organizations, and the blatant lack of interest of the mainstream parties to challenge existing incentive structures. To some, the permission given to such activities may be seen as a sign of a tentative political opening. The willingness of the political parties to engage with the assistance providers could similarly be judged as a sign of political maturity, and the parties may indeed be democratizing somewhat. Taken together, these developments do make the political process in Morocco ever so slightly more democratic than in the past, when foreign involvement and party development were both rather frowned upon out of fear that these might upset the system. That said, the authors of this study are of the opinion that nothing much has changed when it comes to the nature of the regime – the changes made are simply cosmetic.

Conclusion

The case study neatly reflects two problems related to party assistance as a means of democracy promotion from the viewpoint of provider organizations. Given the nature of the Moroccan regime, most party elites face little incentive to adopt a mass party strategy and build up a strong infrastructure to continuously incorporate citizens in their internal decision-making processes. Ironically, among the established political parties, the socially most rooted one, the PJD, has long boycotted all US-funded democracy promotion efforts as a way of protesting against US foreign policy in the Middle East. Looking at the mainstream parties, we found that especially measures trying to improve party actors' performance within the existing institutions are readily accepted by parties and non-democratic actors alike, whether initiated by the two NGOs (the NDI and the IRI) or the IGO (the UNDP). Assessing these measures' likely impact on the political process, we arrive at a second problem. Unintentionally, these measures seem to stabilize a system such as Morocco's, which is not fully democratized, rather than making its democratic transition more likely – a finding in line with our theoretical propositions, which revealed the contradictory effects that measures of party assistance might generate when viewed as an instrument of democracy promotion. This is especially likely in a setting, in which political power is held chiefly by a king and not by elected institutions. For this allows established party elites access to state resources and overall, makes it more rational to rely on wealthy individuals, rather than establishing stable organizational roots in society and rely on small membership fees contributed by wider parts of society, by now distrustful of party elites. This is also the reason why the effectiveness of measures promoting institutional reform towards democratization or stronger linkages between parties and citizens are limited – the key domestic actor, the king, is simply not in favour. There are, in other words, no strong incentives for party elites to engage in such activities given the current institutional setting. Consequently, when it comes to party assistance in hybrid regimes, we need to be careful not to link party assistance and democratization too readily.

Or, to put it differently, we end up with the paradox that the measures most likely to be effective – those improving the functioning of existing institutions – are least likely to trigger faster or deeper democratization. Those measures targeting civil society, which could assist in mobilizing the citizenry, which would then hopefully put pressure on the elites in power – both party politicians as well as non-elected political elites – are the least immediate of the measures categorized and are long-term at best.

All these problems are particularly severe with regards to party assistance and democracy promotion activities provided by organizations that can only rely on soft incentives. While potentially being perceived as more neutral and more trustworthy than foreign government departments (an aspect where intergovernmental organizations may be at an advantage compared to NGOs that are funded mainly by their own government), neither NGOs nor an IGO like the UNDP can put pressure on political actors through economic incentives, sanctions or more coercive means. They are left with trying to educate and support political actors in their activities. Given this restriction, our findings imply that, in the cases where such exist, it may be worthwhile to target societal organizations and political parties outside the established (party) elite, in order to motivate a more effective mobilization of citizen demands in the long run. That, in turn, might create sufficient upwards pressure to motivate formal-legal reform. This, however, brings us back to the sensitive issue of targeting non-state and potentially opposition actors, which NGOs and IGOs tend to be wary of doing.[68]

Concluding with a final remark on the Moroccan case, if more significant steps in the direction of a democratic transition are to be seen, then party assistance activities – just like other democratization efforts – need to come from much higher up. Even large amounts of money and goodwill by the provider organizations analysed here are unlikely to motivate the political parties or, indeed, the monarchy, to embark on serious political reforms. Such pressure can only be applied by governmental bodies which are capable of applying economic sticks and carrots, as Carothers[69] puts it.[70] However, with Morocco's status as a so-called 'friendly' regime in the 'War on Terror', the country is one of the least likely in the Middle East to be the target of such policies.[71]

Acknowledgements

The authors would like to thank the Leverhulme Trust, the ESRC, and the British Academy for their support.

Notes

1. McFaul and Magen, 'Introduction: American and European Strategies to Promote Democracy'; Risse, 'Conclusions: Towards Transatlantic Democracy Promotion?'.
2. Neier, 'How Not to Promote Democracy and Human Rights', 138.
3. Willetts, 'What is a Non-Governmental Organization?'. See also Malena, *Working with NGOs*; Gibbs, Fumo and Kuby, *Nongovernmental Organizations*.
4. Some may argue that such organizations are better described as 'quasi non-governmental organizations', that is, QUANGOs.
5. For a theoretical discussion of the definition of intergovernmental organization, see Baylis and Smith, *The Globalization of World Politics*.
6. UN activities might also be associated with American foreign policy or, more generally, be rejected due to anti-Western, rather than anti-American, sentiments. We would, however, argue that it is more likely that actors associate US government policy with an NGO which is closely linked to one of the two main US parties, such as for example the NDI or the IRI. Please note that the self-proclaimed NGO status of both of these organizations is disputed given their close links to the US government. The two organizations are described as NGOs throughout the paper because they are formally independent from actual government policy, which is our core criterion. For more information on the organization, purpose and activities of the NDI and the IRI, please consult their respective web pages at http://www.ndi.org and http://www.iri.org.

7. Risse, 'Conclusions: Towards Transatlantic Democracy Promotion?'.
8. van Hüllen and Stahn, 'Comparing EU and US Democracy Promotion in the Mediterranean and the Newly Independent States'.
9. Risse, 'Conclusions: Towards Transatlantic Democracy Promotion?'.
10. Randall and Svåsand, 'Introduction'.
11. Carothers, *Confronting the Weakest Link*, 176–9.
12. Carothers, *Confronting the Weakest Link*.
13. Risse, 'Conclusions: Towards Transatlantic Democracy Promotion?'; van Hüllen and Stahn, 'Comparing EU and US Democracy Promotion in the Mediterranean and the Newly Independent States'.
14. Diamond, 'Thinking About Hybrid Regimes'; Levitsky and Way, *Competitive Authoritarianism*.
15. Carothers, 'Struggling with the Semi-Authoritarians'; Ottaway, *Democracy Challenged*.
16. The stabilization of the status quo is not necessarily negative. It might prevent a hybrid regime from regressing to a more authoritarian type of rule by strengthening democratic elements, rather than weakening non-democratic actors and leading to full democratization.
17. Carothers, *Confronting the Weakest Link*; Carothers, 'Struggling with the Semi-Authoritarians'.
18. Carothers, *Confronting the Weakest Link*, 189.
19. Randall and Svåsand, 'Introduction', 3.
20. Randall and Svåsand, 'Introduction'.
21. Carothers, *Confronting the Weakest Link*.
22. van Biezen, *Political Parties in New Democracies*.
23. Gibson and Harmel, 'Party Families and Democratic Performance'; Panebianco, *Political Parties*.
24. Duverger, *Political Parties*.
25. Panebianco, *Political Parties*; Katz and Mair, *How Parties Organize*.
26. Carothers, *Confronting the Weakest Link*, 41.
27. Carothers, *Confronting the Weakest Link*, 41.
28. Risse, 'Conclusions: Towards Transatlantic Democracy Promotion?'.
29. Carothers, *Confronting the Weakest Link*, 41.
30. Note again that, depending on the system, this could be interpreted as a positive achievement, since party assistance could help prevent a regime's regression to a more authoritarian stage.
31. Carothers, *Confronting the Weakest Link*, 40–1; Storm, *Democratization in Morocco*.
32. Diamond, 'Thinking About Hybrid Regimes'; Levitsky and Way, *Competitive Authoritarianism*; Carothers, 'Struggling with the Semi-Authoritarians'; Ottaway, *Democracy Challenged*.
33. For the importance of analytically distinguishing party and party systems as units of reference, see Sartori, *Parties and Party Systems*; Randall and Svåsand, 'Party Institutionalization in New Democracies'.
34. This discussion leads us to the fundamental question of whether the type of parties promoted by party assistance can be viewed as a cause of democratization, or whether they are more accurately defined as a consequence of the latter. The authors of this study argue that parties with strong roots in society can, depending on the setting, be used for very different purposes. On the one hand, parties can, indeed, be forceful instruments in mobilizing and channelling the demands of societal groups into the political process and, if these groups are pro-democratic, this could assist in a regime's democratization. On the other hand, as the literature convincingly

demonstrates, parties can equally contribute to the stabilization of non-democratic regimes (C.f. Brownlee, 'Ruling Parties and Durable Authoritarianism'; Kalyvas, 'The Decay and Breakdown of Communist One-Party Systems'; Solinger, 'Ending One-Party Dominance').

35. See, among others, Diamond, *Developing Democracy*; Pinkney, *Democracy in the Third World*.
36. The twenty interviews were semi-structured with open-ended questions. Detailed written notes, rather than tape recordings, were made as people in hybrid and authoritarian regimes generally feel uneasy about commenting on potentially sensitive issues. For the same reason, interviews were anonymized.
37. When referring to 'the Moroccan political parties' we specifically mean the Union Socialiste des Forces Populaires (USFP), the Parti Istiqlal (PI), the Mouvement Populaire (MP), the Rassemblement National des Indépendants (RNI), the Union Constitutionnelle (UC), and the PJD. These are the parties which have consistently won a significant share of the votes cast in the legislative elections and have a sizeable presence in parliament (Storm, *Democratization in Morocco*).
38. Yacoubian, 'Engaging Islamists and Promoting Democracy', 6.
39. UNDP and Royaume du Maroc, *Programme cadre de gouvernance et de renforcement institutionnel*; NDI, *Voter Apathy in the September 2007 Moroccan Elections*.
40. IRI, *IRI Hosts Elections Observers for U.S. Mid-term Elections*; CEPPS/IRI, *CEPPS/IRI Quarterly Report*.
41. UNDP, *Electoral Assistance*; de Ruyt and Frey, *A Joint NDI/IRI Introduction Mission to Morocco*.
42. NDI, *Strengthening Political Party Capacity for Election Campaigns* and *Voter Apathy in the September 2007 Moroccan Elections*; CERSS, *Workshop on Parliaments and the Reform of Political Party Legislation*.
43. State funding is allocated on the basis of vote share. The minimum qualification threshold is 5% of the valid votes cast at the constituency level. Hence, votes do matter with regards to funding, but not significantly, because the six or seven dominant parties have always passed the threshold (Storm, *Democratization in Morocco*; Storm, 'Testing Morocco').
44. NDI, *Voter Apathy in the September 2007 Moroccan Elections*, 47.
45. de Ruyt and Frey, *A Joint NDI/IRI Introduction Mission to Morocco*; NDI, *Computer Software as a Tool for Political Organizing*; NDI, *Middle East and North Africa*; NDI, *Strengthening Political Party Capacity for Election Campaigns*; NDI, *Final Report on the Moroccan Legislative Elections*; Copley and Baumert, *Workshop on Coalition Building Among Political Parties in the Moroccan Legislature*.
46. de Ruyt and Frey, *A Joint NDI/IRI Introduction Mission to Morocco*; CEPPS/IRI, *CEPPS/IRI Quarterly Report*; IRI, *Moroccan Women Attend Partners in Participation Training*; IRI, *IRI Hosts Elections Observers for U.S. Mid-term Elections*; IRI, *Advancing Democracy in Morocco*.
47. UNDP, *Electoral Assistance*; UNDP, *Projets de développement appuyés par le PNUD au Maroc*; UNDP and Royaume du Maroc, *Programme cadre de gouvernance et de renforcement institutionnel*; CERSS, *Workshop on Parliaments and the Reform of Political Party Legislation*; Club of Madrid, *Club of Madrid Conducts Second Dialogue Mission to Morocco*.
48. Bolleyer, 'The Organisational Costs of Public Office'.
49. Ibid.
50. This supports the argument made by Randall and Svåsand ('Introduction', 3) that parties are usually not expected to play an important role in early stages of transition but rather during a regime's consolidation phase after free elections have been formally established.

51. de Ruyt and Frey, *A Joint NDI/IRI Introduction Mission to Morocco*; NDI, *Computer Software as a Tool for Political Organizing*; NDI, *Morocco*; NDI, *Middle East and North Africa*; NDI, *Strengthening Political Party Capacity for Election Campaigns*; NDI, *Final Report on the Moroccan Legislative Elections*; Copley and Baumert, *Workshop on Coalition Building Among Political Parties in the Moroccan Legislature*; Copley and Deane, *Workshop on the Role of the Groupe Parlementaire*; CEPPS/IRI, *CEPPS/IRI Quarterly Report*; IRI, *Moroccan Women Attend Partners in Participation Training*; IRI, *IRI Hosts Elections Observers for U.S. Mid-term Elections*; IRI, *Advancing Democracy in Morocco*.
52. UNDP, *Electoral Assistance*; UNDP, *Projets de développement appuyés par le PNUD au Maroc*; UNDP and Royaume du Maroc, *Programme cadre de gouvernance et de renforcement institutionnel*; CERSS, *Workshop on Parliaments and the Reform of Political Party Legislation*; Club of Madrid, *Club of Madrid Conducts Second Dialogue Mission to Morocco*.
53. Tommasoli, 'Democracy Assistance Trends in the Arab Region', 5.
54. Please note that the IRI and the NDI seek to complement each other, with the IRI working at the local/regional level and the NDI at the national level. However, because they tend to use similar measures, they often overlap each other as local and national party politics in Morocco are much the same (Middle East Partnership Initiative, *US Policy and Issues*; de Ruyt and Frey, *A Joint NDI/IRI Introduction Mission to Morocco*; Storm, *Democratization in Morocco*; Storm, 'Testing Morocco').
55. Storm, *Democratization in Morocco*; Ottaway and Riley, 'Morocco'.
56. Yacoubian, 'Engaging Islamists and Promoting Democracy'.
57. Storm, *Democratization in Morocco*; Ottaway and Riley, 'Morocco'.
58. In the parliamentary elections of 1963, 1970, and 1977 popular votes were largely unimportant as the elections were heavily rigged by the monarchy, and many parties chose not to contest these or were barred from doing so (García, *Marruecos político*; Storm, *Democratization in Morocco*).
59. García, *Marruecos político*; Storm, 'Testing Morocco'.
60. Following article 40 of the law on political parties, parties that have not held a congress in a five-year period lose the right to apply for state funding. Consequently, party congresses are likely to become more frequent.
61. Maroc 2020, *The 2002 Parliamentary Elections*; *Political Attitudes of the Moroccan Public*; NDI, *Voter Apathy in the September 2007 Moroccan Elections*, 24.
62. NDI, *Final Report on the Moroccan Legislative Elections*, 52.
63. Maroc 2020, *The 2002 Parliamentary Elections*; Maroc 2020, *Political Attitudes of the Moroccan Public*; Storm, 'Testing Morocco'.
64. Maroc 2020, *Political Attitudes of the Moroccan Public*, 5.
65. The literacy rate was estimated at 52% of the population aged 15 and above in 2007 (World Bank, 'Morocco at a Glance', 1).
66. Storm, *Democratization in Morocco*.
67. Storm, *Democratization in Morocco*.
68. Risse, 'Conclusions: Towards Transatlantic Democracy Promotion?'.
69. Carothers, *Confronting the Weakest Link*, 221.
70. That is not to suggest that an end should be put to party assistance and other democracy promotion efforts by organizations limited to soft incentives and persuasion. Such activities can be effective when they also enjoy the support from governmental bodies that have additional (and heavier) measures at their disposal.
71. For more on US democracy promotion in the Middle East during the War on Terror, see Dalacoura, 'US Democracy Promotion in the Arab Middle East Since 11 September 2001'; Storm, 'The Dilemma of the Islamists'; Storm, 'The Persistence of Authoritarianism as a Source of Radicalization in North Africa'.

Bibliography

Baylis, John, and Steve Smith. *The Globalization of World Politics*. 3rd ed. Oxford: Oxford University Press, 2005.
van Biezen, Ingrid. *Political Parties in New Democracies: Party Organization in Southern and East-Central Europe*. Basingstoke: Palgrave Macmillan, 2003.
Bolleyer, Nicole. 'The Organisational Costs of Public Office', in *New Parties in Government*, ed. Kris Deschouwer, 17–41. London: Routledge, 2009.
Brownlee, Jason. 'Ruling Parties and Durable Authoritarianism', *CDDRL Working Paper, No. 23*. Stanford University, 2004, http://cddrl.stanford.edu (accessed April 16, 2010).
Carothers, Thomas. *Confronting the Weakest Link: Aiding Political Parties in New Democracies*. Washington, DC: Carnegie Endowment for International Peace, 2006.
Carothers, Thomas. 'Struggling with the Semi-Authoritarians', in *Democracy Assistance: International Co-operation for Democratization*, ed. Peter Burnell, 210–25. London, Frank Cass, 2006.
Centre des Études et Recherches en Sciences Sociales (CERSS). *Workshop on Parliaments and the Reform of Political Party Legislation: First Working Group Meeting*. Rabat: Centre des Études et Recherches en Sciences Sociales, 2006.
Club of Madrid. *Club of Madrid Conducts Second Dialogue Mission to Morocco*, 2007, http://www.clubmadrid.org/cmadrid/index.php?id=978 (accessed September 18, 2008).
Consortium for Electoral and Political Process Support/International Republican Institute. *CEPPS/IRI Quarterly Report: January 1–March 31 2005. Morocco: Political Party Building*, 2005, http://pdf.usaid.gov/pdf_docs/PDACF989.pdf (accessed September 17, 2008).
Copley, Sarah, and Wendy Baumert. *Workshop on Coalition Building Among Political Parties in the Moroccan Legislature, Rabat, Morocco, July 3 to 4, 1998*. Washington, DC: National Democratic Institute for International Affairs, 1998.
Copley, Sarah, and Arsala Deane. *Workshop on the Role of the Groupe Parlementaire, Rabat, Morocco, February 27–March 1, 1998*. Washington, DC: National Democratic Institute for International Affairs, 1998.
Dalacoura, Katerina. 'US Democracy Promotion in the Arab Middle East since 11 September 2001: A Critique'. *International Affairs* 81, no. 5 (2005): 963–79.
Diamond, Larry. *Developing Democracy. Towards Consolidation*. Baltimore, MD and London: The Johns Hopkins University Press, 1999.
Diamond, Larry. 'Thinking About Hybrid Regimes'. *Journal of Democracy* 13, no. 2 (2002): 21–35.
Duverger, Maurice. *Political Parties. Their Organization and Activity in the Modern State*. London: Methuen, 1964.

García, Bernabé Lopez. *Marruecos político: cuarenta años de procesos electorales (1960–2000)*. Madrid: Siglo XXI de España, 2000.

Gibbs, Christopher, Claudia Fumo, and Thomas Kuby. *Nongovernmental Organizations in World Bank-Supported Projects: A Review*. Washington, DC: The World Bank, 1999.

Gibson, Rachel, and Robert Harmel. 'Party Families and Democratic Performance: Extraparliamentary vs. Parliamentary Group Power'. *Political Studies* 46 (1998): 633–50.

van Hüllen, Vera and Andreas Stahn. 'Comparing EU and US Democracy Promotion in the Mediterranean and the Newly Independent States', in *Democracy Promotion and the Rule of Law: American and European Strategies*, ed. Michael McFaul, Amichai Magen and Thomas Risse, 118–49. Houndmills: Palgrave Macmillan, 2009.

International Republican Institute (IRI). *Advancing Democracy in Morocco: Political Party Building*, 2007, http://www.iri.org/mena/morocco/asp (accessed September 17, 2008).

IRI. *IRI Hosts Elections Observers for U.S. Mid-term Elections*, 2006, http://www.iri.org/mena/morocco/2006-11-30-IRIEO.asp (accessed September 17, 2008).

IRI. *Moroccan Women Attend Partners in Participation Training*, 2004, http://www.iri.org/mena/morocco/2004-09-13-Morocco.asp (accessed September 17, 2008).

Kalyvas, Stathis N. 'The Decay and Breakdown of Communist One-Party Systems'. *Annual Review of Political Science* 2 (1999): 232–43.

Katz, Richard R., and Peter Mair, eds. *How Parties Organize: Change and Adaptation in Party Organizations in Western Europe*. London: Sage, 1995.

Levitsky, Steven, and Lucan A. Way. *Competitive Authoritarianism: Hybrid Regimes After the Cold War*. Cambridge: Cambridge University Press, 2010.

Malena, Carmen. *Working with NGOs. A Practical Guide to Operational Collaboration between the World Bank and Non-governmental Organizations*. Washington, DC: Operations Policy Department, World Bank, 1995.

Maroc 2020. *The 2002 Parliamentary Elections: Attitudes and Expectations of the Moroccan Public*. Casablanca: Maroc, 2002.

Maroc 2020. *Political Attitudes of the Moroccan Public. A Poll by CSA-TMO of Morocco*. Casablanca, Maroc: 2002.

McFaul, Michael, and Amichai Magen. 'Introduction: American and European Strategies to Promote Democracy – Shared Values, Common Challenges, Divergent Tools?', in *Democracy Promotion and the Rule of Law: American and European Strategies*, ed. Michael McFaul, Amichai Magen and Thomas Risse, 1–33. Houndmills: Palgrave Macmillan, 2009.

Middle East Partnership Initiative. *US Policy and Issues: Morocco and MEPI*, 2005, http://rabat.usemebassy.gov/mepi.html (accessed September 17, 2008).

National Democratic Institute for International Affairs (NDI). *Voter Apathy in the September 2007 Moroccan Elections*. Washington, DC: National Democratic Institute for International Affairs, 2008.

NDI. *Computer Software as a Tool for Political Organizing, Rabat, Morocco, September 30 to October 12, 1998*. Washington, DC: National Democratic Institute for International Affairs, 1998.

NDI. *Morocco: National Democratic Institute*, 2001, http://www.ndi.org/ndi/library/1397_ma_women.pdf (accessed September 17, 2008).

NDI. *Middle East and North Africa: Morocco. A Political Overview*, 2005, http://www.ndi.org/worldwide/mena/morocco/morocco_pf.asp (accessed September 17, 2008).

NDI. *Final Report on the Moroccan Legislative Elections, September 7, 2007*. Washington, DC: National Democratic Institute for International Affairs, 2007.

NDI. *Strengthening Political Party Capacity for Election Campaigns*, 2007, http://www.moroccodemocracy.org/en/Associate%20Award%20Program.aspx (accessed September 19, 2008).

Neier, Aryeh, 'How Not to Promote Democracy and Human Rights', in *Human Rights in the 'War on Terror*, ed. R.A. Wilson, 137–42. Cambridge: Cambridge University Press, 2005.
Ottaway, Marina. *Democracy Challenged: The Rise of Semi-Authoritarianism*. Washington, DC: Carnegie Endowment for International Peace, 2003.
Ottaway, Marina, and Meredith Riley. 'Morocco: From Top-down Reform to Democratic Transition?', *Carnegie Paper, No. 71*. Washington, DC, September 2006.
Panebianco, Angelo. *Political Parties: Organizations and Power*. Cambridge: Cambridge University Press, 1988.
Pinkney, Robert. *Democracy in the Third World*. Boulder, CO: Lynne Rienner, 1994.
Randall, Vicky, and Lars Svåsand, 'Introduction: The Contribution of Parties to Democracy and Democratic Consolidation'. *Democratization* 9, no. 3 (2002): 1–10.
Randall, Vicky, and Lars Svåsand, 'Party Institutionalization in New Democracies'. *Party Politics* 8, no. 1 (2002): 5–29.
Risse, Thomas. 'Conclusions: Towards Transatlantic Democracy Promotion?', in *Democracy Promotion and the Rule of Law: American and European Strategies*, ed. Michael McFaul, Amichai Magen and Thomas Risse, 244–72. Houndmills: Palgrave Macmillan, 2009.
de Ruyt, Isabelle, and L. Frey. *A Joint NDI/IRI Introduction Mission to Morocco. Rabat, Casablanca, Meknes, Fez, Marrakesh. October 12–21 1998*. Washington, DC: National Democratic Institute, 1998, http://www.ndi.org/ndi/library/311_ma_jointmission.pdf (accessed September 17, 2008).
Sartori, Giovanni, *Parties and Party Systems: A Framework for Analysis*. Cambridge: Cambridge University Press, 1976.
Solinger, Dorothy J. 'Ending One-Party Dominance: Korea, Taiwan, Mexico'. *Journal of Democracy* 12, no. 1 (2001): 30–42.
Storm, Lise. *Democratization in Morocco. Struggles for Power in the Post-Independence State*. London: Routledge, 2007.
Storm, Lise. 'Testing Morocco: The Parliamentary Elections of September 2007'. *Journal of North African Studies* 13, no. 1 (2008): 37–54.
Storm, Lise. 'The Dilemma of the Islamists: Human Rights, Democratization, and the War on Terror'. *Middle East Policy Journal* 16, no. 1 (2009): 101–12.
Storm, Lise. 'The Persistence of Authoritarianism as a Source of Radicalization in North Africa'. *International Affairs* 85, no. 5 (2009): 997–1013.
Tommasoli, Massimo. 'Democracy Assistance Trends in the Arab Region'. IDEA Meeting on Democracy in the Arab World, The Hague, 25–26 March 2004.
UNDP. *Electoral Assistance*, 2005, http://www.undp.org/women/mainstream/ElectoralAssistance.pdf (accessed September 18, 2008).
United Nations Development Programme (UNDP). *Projets de développement appuyés par le PNUD au Maroc*, 2008, http://www.pnud.org.ma/NosProjets.asp (accessed September 18, 2008).
UNDP, and Royaume du Maroc, *Programme cadre de gouvernance et de renforcement institutionnel – Appui au parlement, chambre des représentants, phase II 1998*, http://www.surf-as.org/Parliament/PDF/Moroccodoc.pdf (accessed September 18, 2008).
Willetts, Peter. 'What is a Non-Governmental Organization?', in *UNESCO Encyclopaedia of Life Support Systems*. Oxford: Eolss Publishers, http://www.staff.city.ac.uk/p.willetts/CS-NTWKS/NGO-ART.HTM (accessed October 13, 2010).
World Bank. 'Morocco at a Glance', 2008, http://devdata.worldbank.org/AAG/mar_aag.pdf (accessed October 8, 2008).
Yacoubian, Mona. 'Engaging Islamists and Promoting Democracy: A Preliminary Assessment', *United States Institute of Peace Special Report*, no. 190. Washington, DC: United States Institute of Peace, August 2007.

Political party assistance in transition: the German *'Stiftungen'* in sub-Saharan Africa

Kristina Weissenbach

Institute for Political Science, NRW School of Governance, University Duisburg-Essen, Duisburg, Germany

Despite the fact that the German *Stiftungen* (political foundations) were the first international institutions to work in the field of political party development, their party assistance has been neglected in political party research for a long time. Remarkably little is known about the approaches, strategies and results of their activities. This contribution explores the role of the *Stiftungen* and their party assistance approaches in the various stages of the democratization process. It explicitly traces the self-declared ambitions of the German *Stiftungen*, and it explores the extent to which their party assistance activities take account of the various stages of the democratic transition process and of the level of party institutionalization, or simply follow abstract, generalized and preconceived ideas. The study develops a 'phase model of party assistance' in the transition process and examines the party assistance activities in two illustrative cases – the Friedrich-Ebert Stiftung (FES) in Kenya and in South Africa – in seven dimensions of party institutionalization: (1) level of organization, (2) internal party democracy, (3) political programme, (4) autonomy, (5) roots in society, (6) coherence, and (7) regional and international integration.

Introduction

For a long time, political party assistance in general and by the German *Stiftungen* (political foundations) in particular, has been neglected in political science research.[1] In turn, political party assistance did not refer to political science. This study argues, however, that political party assistance can learn from a variety of sub-fields of political science, namely democratization research, political party research and party institutionalization research.

In the first section it provides a general overview of party assistance approaches as well as Western organizations working in the field of party assistance and describes the particular position of the different German *Stiftungen* (Konrad-Adenauer-Stiftung, KAS; Friedrich-Ebert Stiftung, FES; Friedrich-Naumann Stiftung, FNS). Secondly, the account advances the argument that these three subfields of political science offer a framework for further development of approaches, as well as measures and instruments in party assistance. Out of the three mentioned research fields the account develops a *phase model of party assistance* capturing the different stages of a country's transition process and a *synopsis of party institutionalization*. Finally, to illustrate that objectives and party assistance approaches found suitable for a specific stage of the transition process in a particular country with a particular level of party institutionalization may be less successful at another stage or in another country, the study examines party assistance activities of the Friedrich-Ebert Stiftung (FES) in Kenya and South Africa along seven dimensions of party institutionalization.

The two cases were selected on the basis that they are suitable to illustrate the theoretical assumptions (transition theory and party institutionalization). The aim of this contribution therefore is not to compare the party assistance activities of KAS and FES but rather to generate the mentioned phase model of party assistance, develop the synopsis of party institutionalization and interrelate the two with qualified cases.[2]

The analysis is based on empirical research the author conducted in Kenya, South Africa and Germany in 2008 and 2009.[3]

'Party assistance tourism' and the German *Stiftungen* in the field of political party assistance

Political parties play an essential role in modern democracies. The relevant literature offers numerous functions of political parties: they function as the central actor between society and government, they aggregate and articulate interests and public opinion, they develop programmes, they recruit people for executive and legislative positions and exercise control over government.[4] This established catalogue of party functions can only be adopted for the African context as long as some modifications are considered: for example the ethnical cleavage model,[5] the need for a stronger inclusion of informal politics, as well as the additional challenges for political parties posed by operating in transitional contexts.[6] However, the implementation of these functions provided by political parties varies significantly in different countries; and young African parties especially are struggling to fulfil their 'consolidation functions'.[7]

To improve the efficiency of political parties as well as their capability to support the democratic consolidation of transformation states and young democracies, numerous Western institutions and organizations are working in the field of party cooperation and party assistance (Table 1). These include the American National Endowment for Democracy (NED), the International Republican Institute

Table 1. Major party assistance providers.

German foundations	Friedrich-Ebert Stiftung (FES)
	Konrad-Adenauer Stiftung (KAS)
	Friedrich-Naumann Stiftung (FNS)
	Heinrich-Böll Stiftung (HBS)
	Hanns-Seidel Stiftung (HSS)
	Rosa-Luxemburg Stiftung (RLS)
International and multilateral actors	Westminster Foundation for Democracy (WFD, Great Britain)
	Netherlands Institute for Multiparty Democracy (NIMD)
	Alfred Mozer Stichting (AMS, Netherlands)
	National Endowment for Democracy (NED, USA)
	National Democratic Institute (NDI, USA)
	International Republican Institute (IRI, USA)
	International Foundation for Election Systems (IFES)
	United States Agency for International Development (USAID)
	Centre for Democratic Institutions (CDI, Australia)
	Swedish International Development Agency (SIDA)
	Olof Palme International Center (OPIC, Sweden)
	International Institute for Democracy and Electoral Assistance (International IDEA, Sweden)
	Norsk Senter for Demokratistøtte (Norwegian Centre for Democracy Support, NDS)
	Foundation Robert Schuman (FRS, France)
	Renner Institute (RI)
	Fundación Pablo Iglesias (FPI, Spain)
	United Nations Development Programme (UNDP)
	Organisation of American States (OAS)
	Organisation für Sicherheit und Zusammenarbeit in Europa (OSZE)
	European Forum for Democracy and Solidarity (EFDS)
International party organizations	Socialist International (SI)
	Liberal International (LI)
	Centrist Democrat International (CDI)
	Global Greens (GG)

Source: Author's compilation. See Erdmann, 'Internationale Parteienförderung'; Wersch and de Zeeuw, 'Mapping European Democracy Assistance'.

(IRI), the National Democratic Institute for International Affairs (NDI), USAID, the Netherlands Institute for Multiparty Democracy (NIMD)/Center for Multiparty Democracy (CMD) and the Westminster Foundation for Democracy (WF). In the words of a Kenyan opposition politician[8] we might even speak of 'party assistance tourism' in sub-Saharan Africa: Western institutions sweep into a given country for a short time to strengthen their party aid, especially when it comes to election time, but rarely consult each other about their party assistance measures and partners.[9] Furthermore, as for example in the Kenyan case, a political party is often only considered as 'serious' by politicians if it is supported by a Western organization.

Out of the various organizations that are funding and assisting political parties, the German foundations can possibly draw on the longest experience[10] – especially in the region of sub-Saharan Africa, where they have been active before most of the countries became independent.

Within the Western organizations working in the field of foreign relations, development policy and political party assistance, the German *Stiftungen* take up a special position: they are neither non-governmental nor governmental organizations and therefore sometimes referred to as 'Quangos' (quasi non-governmental organizations). This status provides unique opportunities in the field of party assistance; while they are nearly as independent as non-governmental organizations (NGOs) in carrying out their projects with resident representatives enjoying a high degree of autonomy, at the same time they are securely state-funded by the German Ministry for Economic Cooperation and Development – and therefore, but only to a moderate degree, subject to ministerial controls.[11]

In the field of party assistance there are the following six major approaches[12]:

- supporting ideologically close parties (partisan approach);
- supporting several parties (multiparty approach);
- supporting supra and inter-party dialogues (cross-party dialogue);
- promoting institutional development (institutional approach);
- supporting transnational cooperation between parties from the same region/ continent (international cross-party collaboration);
- supporting the civil-society environment (civil-society approach).

In comparison to other NGOs or institutions working in the field of party cooperation the German foundations[13] possess unique features: their long tradition within the countries[14] and networking between different branches in the region:

> In the course of their long-term presence abroad, each foundation has managed to create a close-knit network of contacts which it can place at the disposal of its affiliated party.... (T)he foundations' contacts can be instrumental in the creation and maintenance of transnational party cooperation. As such, a political foundation fulfils its international role in the interest of its affiliated party, although this is not its primary concern. The extent to which political foundations and political parties work harmoniously can vary considerably, depending on such variables as the individuals involved and the political role of the respective party.[15]

Even though party assistance has been going on for decades and the German foundations are experts in this field, various evaluations criticize the foundations' strategy and concepts. Carothers complains that within the field of democracy promotion, party cooperation and party assistance is marginal.[16] Even if multiparty elections have spread in sub-Saharan Africa, not in the least because of the pressure 'from a donor community tired of what it perceives as dysfunctional patterns of authoritarian governance in Africa, democracy is struggling in most parts of the region'.[17] In 2006 Erdmann added to this criticism, that

PROMOTING PARTY POLITICS IN EMERGING DEMOCRACIES

none of them [the German political foundations] has compiled a policy or strategy paper which is available to the public, none of them has executives or departments that are responsible for party assistance, none of them has a budget dedicated exclusively to party assistance, none of them states very clearly what party assistance as such consists of, none of their party assistance programmes has so far been examined by political experts, none of them has analyzed its collaboration with political parties in the seventies and eighties and, ultimately, none of them has, as a result of all this, any systematic and institutionalized knowledge of the matter as such.[18]

Mair, in turn, adds that, 'based on the realization that they operate in a very sensitive environment the foundations regard public attention as a potential source of friction',[19] and that therefore literature about democracy promotion and party assistance is limited. As a reaction to increased public interest and – partly – to the criticism based on political science research, foundations like the Konrad-Adenauer Stiftung (KAS) and the Friedrich-Ebert Stiftung (FES) in sub-Saharan Africa are today generally more sensitive with regard to their party assistance concepts. The executives of the 'Party Assistance' and 'Sub-Saharan Africa' divisions of the KAS and the FES in Bonn/Berlin (Germany) developed guidelines or handbooks[20] and are thereby able to define their individual approach, motives and concepts concerning their party assistance. For example, both the KAS and the FES recruited research fellows to conceptualize their party assistance approaches, and the KAS published guidelines on its party assistance worldwide.[21] The FES even published a detailed description about its cooperation with political parties and liberation movements in Africa from the 1970s until the 1990s.[22] In 2006 the FES ran an internal workshop on party assistance measures and edited some relevant papers concerning strategies and methods in political party assistance for all resident representatives. In the course of the alternation of the resident representatives in Kenya and South Africa in 2009, the FES engaged scientific experts for a new round of evaluations.[23]

As illustrated in the above, the German foundations are trying to reprocess and evaluate their party assistance methods and specify their party assistance approaches. But their party assistance approaches rarely reach a level on which precise instruments of party assistance are developed that reflect such aspects as the various stages of the democratization process of a country and the level of institutionalization of the partner party. Consequently, this study argues that party assistance approaches can learn from political science research, especially from the subfields of democratization research, as well as from political party and party institutionalization research. In the following sections, the study will first discuss in what way democratization research offers a useful background for party assistance approaches by developing a *phase model of party assistance*. Then, it turns to political party and party institutionalization research which provide party assistance providers with seven dimensions by which party assistance can be measured. Following this, the study illustrates the suggested phase model and party assistance dimensions with the empirical case of the FES in Kenya and South Africa. Lastly, it will offer some concluding remarks.

What can party assistance learn from democratization and political party research?

This study follows the assumption that party assistance providers can learn from existing research on transition processes by translating the several different phases of a transition into different approaches of party assistance. For example, sometimes democratic transitions do not follow an orderly sequence, but rather follow individual paths including the possibility of a setback, and party assistance providers should include this in their approaches. Furthermore this study assumes that the higher the level of party institutionalization, the higher the impact of political parties on the democratic transition is likely to be.[24] It thereby recognizes that there is certain interdependence between party institutionalization and the level of democratization. Therefore the study considers seven criteria of party institutionalization which reflect the current state of established international party research,[25] to examine the party assistance instruments of the FES in Kenya and South Africa:

- level of organization,
- internal party democracy,
- programmatic,
- autonomy,
- roots in society,
- coherence, and
- regional and international integration.

Before analysing whether party assistance approaches of the German foundations in the past referred to the transition process and if the party assistance instruments included any traces of party institutionalization research, it is important to clarify on what understanding of the 'transition process' the analysis is based and what is meant by 'party institutionalization'.

Learning the lessons of democratization research – a 'phase model of party assistance'

Drawing on Schmitter, O'Donnell and Schmitter, and Przeworski,[26] the 'phase model of party assistance' developed by the author (Figure 1) is based on the distinction between a pre-transition phase and three phases of transition: (1) liberalization (2) democratization and (3) consolidation. For the consolidation process Merkel[27] adopts a maximal understanding of consolidation and distinguishes four sub-levels: (1) 'constitutional consolidation', (2) 'representative consolidation', (3) behavioural consolidation and (4) consolidation of a civic culture. These transition and consolidation phases together are the basis of the 'phase model of party assistance'. Are the approaches of the German foundations in any way related to these phases? Even though the different transition phases identified by the existing research are not selective, and even though sometimes transitional states fall back to a lower level of transition it is useful to classify the

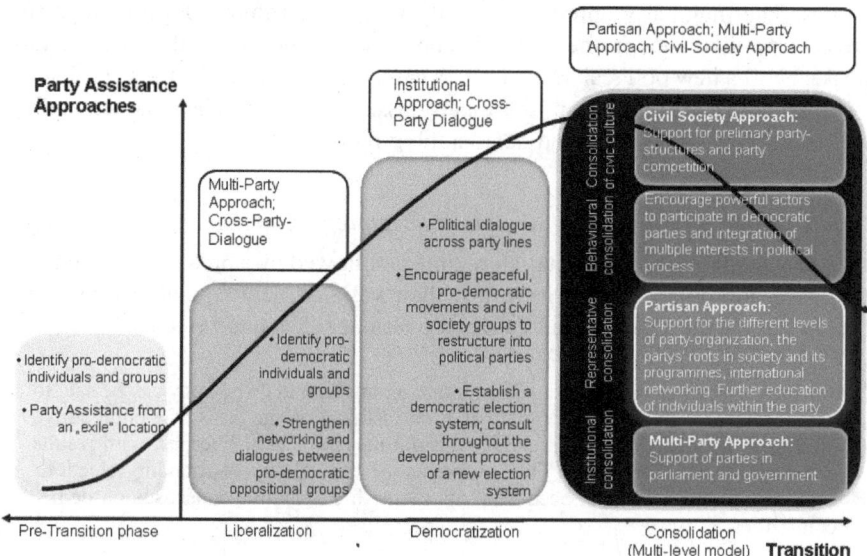

Figure 1. A phase model of party assistance.
Source: Authors' compilation.

different phases of party assistance approaches along the lines of the transition phases (see Figure 1).

Liberalization: authoritarian rulers and violent conflicts

Political liberalization describes the renunciation of a formerly authoritarian regime and the progress towards a political opening. It resembles an intermediate phase of the transition process which appears between a pre-transition phase with authoritarian rulers, protests and civil war situations on the one hand and the emergence of a new democratic regime on the other. In this phase, governments establish rights of freedom which were previously denied or limited:

> Examples of political liberalization include the release of political prisoners, the lifting of government censorship, and the relegalization of banned political parties... [But] political liberalization does not ensure once and for all; it is an ongoing process that happens in a series of incremental steps. Political elites rarely grant all their concessions in one fell swoop, preferring instead to surrender minimum advantage at any one time.[28]

In this phase of the transition process a powerful opposition does not yet exist, or alternatively it is still being suppressed. The challenge for party assistance in this phase then is to establish a basis for a peaceful promotion of the democratization phase, in part by identifying and strengthening pro-democratic individuals and civil society groups which have the potential to establish new democratic political parties. The multiparty approach of party assistance combined with supporting cross-party dialogues is therefore an appropriate concept for the liberalization phase. Until a new political system offers democratic avenues for the participation of a parliamentary opposition, these party assistance approaches may strengthen the networking of peaceful and democratic groups.

Democratization: overcoming an authoritarian regime and institution building

In theory the fall of an authoritarian regime is followed by a phase of democratization. The authoritarian rules have lost their validity, new regulations and institutions have to be designed, and a new government has to be elected.

> According to the definition used throughout, a transition to democracy can be said to have occurred only when a regime has been installed on the basis of a competitive election, freely and fairly conducted within a matrix of civil liberties, with results accepted by all participants. The acceptance of the validity of founding elections by losing parties is crucial because it marks the first tentative consensus on democratic rules.[29]

Nevertheless, at this point of the transition process, civil society will still be sceptical about the newly established institutions and will continue to question the mechanisms of the political decision-making process. Violence and disruption might still be a common phenomenon.

De-escalation and the prevention of conflicts are therefore central approaches in this democratization phase. The strengthening of cross-party dialogues and the institutional approach can encourage trust in new political regulations and in the political parties. Moreover, to cooperate with several political parties is the only practicable assistance concept for the German foundations, as ideologically affiliated parties can rarely be identified at this early stage of the transition process.[30] A selection of several partner parties, difficult as that might be, is nevertheless crucial, as not every party in the newly structured party system can be adequately supported. The aims in this phase are to help civil society organizations to restructure into political parties, to include political parties in the political decision-making process and to support party participation in elections. Party assistance in this democratization phase can help to establish a new party system and to strengthen the political participation of civil society.[31]

During this phase, the new party system may slowly emerge. The underlying logic usually resembles the cleavage between the authoritarian regime on one hand and opposition parties on the other. Nevertheless, empirical research by the author has shown that such cleavages persist only for some time and are followed by a break-up of the formerly united opposition, over the deeper original conflicts of the respective countries, that is, ethnic cleavages as in Kenya. Self-evidently the installed electoral system, which is generally modified in this phase, has a major impact on the configuration of the developing party system. While many students of political science in theory favour majority rule as the ideal type (amongst other things as it leads to robust single party governments and allows for explicit attribution of responsibility), proportional representation including a barring clause concerning the representation of political parties in parliament, has proven to be more beneficial to the consolidation process.[32] Proportional representation reduces fragmentation and polarization in the political culture while strengthening the integration of society and, counterintuitively, governmental stability.[33] When aiming at a party system that supports overall consolidation over the long run it is wise to counsel the establishment of a new electoral system during the oscillating formation phase. The first free elections set the path for the further course of the democratization process. If parties which support democracy and adhere to peaceful conflict resolution mechanisms win, then a deeper consolidation is feasible and probable.[34] If an authoritarian potentate manages to secure power despite the institutional changes, stagnation or a setback in the transition might be the consequence. The legitimacy and value of party assistance at this stage is seen as controversial: some scholars argue that support for certain parties in election campaigns is an unjustifiable external influence and tampers with the election outcome. Others bring forward the argument that short-term campaigning support for pro-democratic parties in this specific historic situation benefits the overall democratization process, and can therefore be accepted as a lesser evil.[35]

Consolidation: institutionalization of democracy and nation-building

Within transformation research definitions of consolidation are frequent objects of discussion. Some scholars such as Huntington have a procedural, minimal understanding of consolidation. Huntington[36] defines a political system as a consolidated democratic regime when 'the party or group that takes power in the initial election at the time of the transition loses a subsequent election and turns over power to the winners of a later election'.[37] Other scholars characterize this understanding as a 'fallacy of electoralism'[38] and follow a broader, maximalist understanding of consolidation. 'In this view, key political institutions, including political parties, the legislature, and the judiciary, need to function effectively and to successfully nurture broad-based pluralism. Some scholars even argue that the emergence of a democratic political culture is an essential component of consolidation.'[39] As noted earlier, Merkel[40] adopts this maximalist understanding of a consolidated democracy and divides the consolidation process into four sub-phases: institutional consolidation, representative consolidation, behavioural consolidation and the consolidation of a civic culture. This maximalist understanding is the reference point of the 'phase model of party assistance' presented here.

Institutional consolidation: democratic decision-making.

When the decision-makers of the political system accept the new institutional norms and structure their actions by them, institutional consolidation is reached.[41] As political parties are founded and establish themselves, they present a channel for political actors to democratically influence decision-making processes. Party assistance can advance institutional consolidation by focusing on multiparty support of parliamentary party groups or parties in government.

Representative consolidation: democratic representation of interests

The representative consolidation phase is a decisive phase for party assistance, as parties become central agents for interest representation. While it is still important to foster a strong multi-party system on the structural level, a window may open for the promotion of single pro-democratic parties, or the partisan approach. Especially in the case of the latter, the level of institutionalization should be focused: questions at the top of the agenda concern party organization, intra-party democracy, party manifestos and programmes, roots in society, links to regional and international party federations and training and education of significant individuals.

Behavioural consolidation: democratic elites

In this third stage the behaviour of powerful actors such as the armed forces, estate owners, entrepreneurs, radical movements, or charismatic leaders is conditioned in such a way that interests are exclusively pursued within democratic institutions and not against legitimately elected representative bodies. Party assistance can therefore ultimately lead to the behavioral consolidation of charismatic party leaders and other high party offices as well as promote the acceptance of basic principles of democracy, establishing a certain degree of decisional autonomy from individual party members and fostering acceptance of intra-party dissent. To obtain these goals it has proven to be decisive that domestic democratic elites do not regard their own interests as threatened by the political institutions.

Consolidation of a civic culture: stabilizing the socio-political foundations and nation building

The last step termed consolidation of the 'civic culture'[42] is reached by stabilizing the socio-political foundations. The 'project of consolidation'[43] can only be regarded as a success if the democratic norms and values accepted by the political elites are dispersed throughout the overall political culture.[44] Party assistance should therefore target the linkages between parties and civic society and support ancillary organizations.

Learning the lessons of political party research: the institutionalization of political parties and political party assistance

While some authors do not distinguish between *party* institutionalization and *party system* institutionalization[45] or else confuse the concepts, the focus here is on *party* institutionalization in the sense of the conceptualization developed by Panebianco, applied to the African case by Randall and Svåsand, and taken as a basis for the 'Index of Institutionalisation' in five African cases by Basedau and Stroh[46]:

> ...the process through which they [political parties] become institutionalised is not identical with the party's development in purely organisational terms. Rather we suggest that institutionalization should be understood as the process by which the party becomes established in terms both of integrated patterns of behaviour and of attitudes, or culture. We suggest further that it is helpful to distinguish between internal and externally related aspects of this process. Internal aspects refer to developments within the party itself; external aspects have to do with the party's relationship with the society in which it is embedded, including other institutions.[47]

Randall and Svåsand take the four elements of systemness, value infusion, decisional autonomy and reification as constituting the core of the process of party institutionalization, that is, the process through which the party becomes established as an institution.[48] But the authors also mention that although 'institutionalization in terms of the four variables will increase the party's prospects for survival, it is certainly no guarantee against regression or *de-institutionalization*'.[49] Basedau and Stroh modified this model of party institutionalization and developed an Index of the Institutionalization of Parties (IIP) along the abovementioned four criteria. They understand 'the institutionalization of political organizations as a process of progress in four dimensions: *roots in society*, *level of organization*, *autonomy*, and *coherence* (emphasis added). In other words, institutionalization is the process of growing external and internal stability as well as value-infusion'.[50]

For the analysis of the German foundations' party assistance instruments and their orientation on the institutionalization-level of the corresponding partner party, the author is extending this understanding of party institutionalization by adding the three criteria *internal party democracy*, *political programme*, and *regional and international integration*, which reflects the current state of established international party research. Each criterion is linked with different indicators (Table 2) which can be directly used to assess the political party assistance instruments of the German *Stiftungen* in Kenya and South Africa.

Party assistance instruments measured in seven dimensions of party institutionalization: the cases of the FES in South Africa and Kenya

Since the dawn of multi-partyism in Kenya and South Africa most of the German foundations have been offering partisan support to more than one political party as well as support for cross-party dialogue and international cross-party collaboration. Nevertheless, they are still focusing on long-term partnerships with ideologically affiliated parties, as, for example, the long-lasting partnership between the South African African National Congress (ANC) party and the Friedrich-Ebert Stiftung in South Africa shows. Based on their *ideological and value-orientated strategy* three of the six German foundations collaborate with a 'partner' or 'sister party'

Table 2. Dimensions and indicators of party institutionalization.

Dimension	Indicator
Roots in society: The party has stable roots in society.	Party age relative to independence. Party age relative to beginning of multiparty period. Changes in electoral support in last and second last elections. Links to civil society organizations.
Autonomy: Notwithstanding its societal roots, the party is relatively independent of individuals within and societal groups outside the party.	Number of alternations in party leadership. Changes in electoral support after alternation in party leadership. Decisional autonomy from individuals and groups. Popular appreciation of particular party.
Organization: There is an organizational apparatus which is constantly present at all administrative levels and acts in the interest of the party.	Membership strength. Regular party congresses. Material and personal resources. Nationwide organizational presence, activities beyond election campaigns.
Coherence: The party acts as a unified organization; the party tolerates a certain level of intra-party dissidence. Tolerance vis-à-vis intra-party dissidence.	Coherence of parliamentary group (no defections or floor-crossing). Moderate relations between intra-party groupings (no dysfunctional factionalism).
Internal party democracy: The internal decision-making process concerning personnel and policy takes place from the bottom to the top of the party. The party represents democratic principles.	Regular party and membership congresses. Bottom-up principle in the internal decision-making process. The internal decisions are transparent. The party finances are transparent. Informal politics are rare.

Regional and international integration:

The party incorporates itself into regional and international party groups and organizations. The party is accepted at the international level.

Integration of the party in regional and international party groups: Socialist International (SI); Liberal International (LI); Centrist Democrat International (CDI); Global Greens (GG).

The Youth League/Women's League are members of the according youth and women's associations (for example, Socialist Youth International; Socialist Women International; International Young Democrat Union; International Women Union).

The party is a member of a regional sub-organization of the international party groups (for example, Democrat Union of Africa).

The Party is involved and accepted by regional African organizations (AU, NEPAD).

Political programme:

The party has an ideological coherence; a transparent positioning concerning its policy, values and ideology

A party manifesto exists; the party is organized around political ideas rather than ethnic, religious or regional identities. No extreme ideologies.[a]

The party develops policies and programmes that represent the party's value-orientation.

Source: Author's compilation; See Basedau and Stroh, *Measuring Party Institutionalization*.

Notes: [a]Ethnic linkage with society and an ethnic identity are not negative per se. The African case especially shows that political parties without a strong organization but based on regional and ethnic cleavages and identity are able to aggregate and articulate interests. Nevertheless the same African examples are proof that, once an ethnic identity is politically mobilized (for example, in election times), it can curb the process of democratic consolidation and become a danger to the public and the political community. (Compare Erdmann, 'Party Research', 74f.)

in South Africa and/or Kenya, and are concentrating on the partisan approach: the Friedrich-Naumann Stiftung (only in South Africa); the Konrad-Adenauer Stiftung; and the Friedrich-Ebert Stiftung[51] (Table 3).

In order to analyse whether party assistance approaches of the German foundations in the past referred to the transition process (Figure 1) and whether their party assistance instruments today include the aforementioned seven dimensions of the institutionalization of their 'partner party' (Table 2), two cases concerning the FES are of particular relevance to review the theoretical assumptions[52]: first, the more or less successful party assistance provided to the African National Congress (ANC) in South Africa – a country in the consolidation phase and with a partner party of FES which in comparison is highly institutionalized,[53] and on the contrary, the failure of the cooperation between the FES and Kenyan Africa National Union (KANU) in Kenya, a country that can be characterized as 'partly free'[54] and has a low party institutionalization.[55,56]

FES party assistance in South Africa

The cooperation of the FES with the ANC in South Africa during the last 40 years illustrates the different phases of party assistance approaches that come close to the developed phase model in this study (Figure 1). The empirical research of the author and the interviews conducted in Germany, Kenya and South Africa demonstrate that the challenge for the FES changed from supporting a liberation movement that could only work in exile in the 1970s and 1980s to an ongoing era of cooperation with the ruling party. Therefore the approaches changed from first supporting democratic civil society dialogues in the 1980s, then following a partisan approach, and later the exclusive funding of one ideologically close party, the ANC. In the 1990s, the FES funded the organizational apparatus and material resources such as office equipment and security services for the ANC. Gradually

Table 3. German foundations and their partner parties in Kenya and South Africa.

German foundations	Partner party
KAS Kenya	Democratic Party (DP)
	National Rainbow Coalition (NARC)
FES Kenya	Orange Democratic Movement (ODM)
	Liberal Democratic Party (LDP)
	United Democrats of Kenya (UNDA)
	Forum for the Restoration of Democracy – Kenya (FORD-K)
FNS Kenya	–
KAS South Africa	Inkatha Freedom Party (IFP)
FES South Africa	African National Congress (ANC)
FNS South Africa	Democratic Alliance (DA)

Source: Author's compilation. Based on interviews by the author with current and former resident representatives of the KAS and the FES in Kenya.

it changed to work not only with the party but also with the ANC parliamentary group. Moreover the FES improved the acceptance of the ANC in the Western hemisphere and strengthened the regional and international integration of the movement. According to the different challenges faced by the FES, the *instruments of party assistance* also changed. First they simply consisted of educational measures concerning the future development of South Africa and scholarships for ANC-representatives in Germany in 1983. Four months after his release, Nelson Mandela visited the FES and the SPD (Social Democratic Party) in Germany to show his gratitude for their support. After the FES established an office in Johannesburg in 1993 it arranged workshops and trainings with the party as well as with the parliamentary group to encourage the ANC to implement a social market economy and a federal state system and to strengthen the unions.[57]

The successful party assistance approach of the FES in South Africa has included the various stages of the transition process, either consciously or instinctively. In the light of today's party assistance instruments, the cooperation is again at a turning point. The FES has a partner party which is performing relatively well in the terms of the seven institutionalization criteria 'roots in society', 'autonomy', 'organization', 'coherence', 'internal party democracy', 'programmatic' and 'regional and international integration'. It is certainly not performing equally well in all seven criteria: as a former liberation movement, the ANC has strong roots in society and still refers to this traditional background, especially in election times. Moreover the ANC does not rely as much on ethnic groups to the extent that Kenyan parties do, but instead focuses on programmatic discussions. The fact that changes in the ANC-party leadership are accepted peacefully, as demonstrated in the relatively smooth transition from Nelson Mandela to Thabo Mbeki to Jacob Zuma, and do not cause a collapse in party structure clearly shows that the party is independent of individual leaders. As we will see later, this is in stark contrast with most of the Kenyan parties.

However, there remain challenges concerning the coherence of the party as well as the internal party democracy. These issues led to the break-away of a new party from the ANC, namely the *Congress of the People* (COPE). Dysfunctional factionalism is still one of the continuing issues within the ANC. ANC-members of parliament stated that a 'higher toleration of intraparty dissidence' is the one topic which partners should strengthen and emphasize when arranging workshops or trainings. They mentioned that the lack of unity within the party organization is 'a challenge the ANC has to cope with at the moment'.[58] As far as internal party democracy within the ANC is concerned, a lack of transparency in party financing remains a problem. Moreover, party assistance has to deal with the fact that power within the ANC has shifted to the executive, that the ANC holds an almost hegemonic position in South Africa and that it also is a leader on the African continent.

Whether the foundations' party assistance in South Africa takes these findings into account and henceforth concentrates on developing instruments that strengthen the coherence of the party and internal party democracy, is a core question for the foundations' party assistance practice and for the professionalization of their party assistance concepts.[59] Possible instruments, amongst others, could be a series of workshops with party officials, stressing the importance of the management of party organization and internal party communication combined with methods for mobilizing party members and civil society. Furthermore, advising the party elites on issues such as the 'decentralization of the internal party decision-making process' or 'ethics and politics' could strengthen tolerance for intra-party dissidence and encourage transparent internal decision-making processes.

FES party assistance in Kenya

In comparison to this relatively successful and ongoing example of party assistance, the cooperation of the FES with the Kenya African National Unity (KANU) in the 1980s illustrates the difficulties that party assistance may encounter in a pre-phase of the transition process. Within this early stage of a transitional process it is often rather complicated to identify a certain group or party as a pro-democratic partner. Hence it is difficult to include the party's special institutionalization-characteristics when designing party assistance approaches and instruments. In the case of Kenya, the FES was confident that KANU represented a Kenyan approach towards the consolidation of democracy and that they would be an influential force for achieving socio-economic development. Later, however, the FES had to come to the conclusion that KANU had in fact reversed the transition process.

Until President Jomo Kenyatta passed away in 1978, KANU had only been an 'election platform' without any stable organizational structures or internal party democracy. The next president, Arap Moi, initiated first contacts with the FES. With the aim of stabilizing the country and supporting the transition towards democracy, the FES developed a consulting-agenda for KANU which in its first phase included issues concerning the organization and autonomy of the party plus links to civil society: the ensuing *Memorandum*[60] was signed by the General Secretary of KANU, Robert Matano, in February 1980 in Bonn, Germany. It consisted of a proposal for the development of a party headquarters, a plan to strengthen the party's organization, plans for the inclusion of a women's league within the party and the education of party cadres. In April 1980 a German graphic designer, who had already contributed to the election campaign for the German SPD, travelled to Kenya to develop a 'corporate identity' for KANU, including schemes for the party's development and for a party newspaper. Furthermore he designed a KANU campaign button. The FES delivered 10,000 campaign buttons, 13,000 calendars, sheets of writing paper and envelopes. They completed the rebuilding of the party headquarters and delivered office and electronic equipment. Nevertheless, the cooperation started with delays and in subsequent years no elections within the party were held. Therefore the FES was not able to install proper 'counterparts' or contact persons inside the organization. In September 1983 Arap Moi rescheduled the parliamentary elections to an earlier date instead of relying on internal party elections. Even though the leadership of KANU effectively aimed at reducing the influence of the party members in the region and opposed regional workshops, the FES was focusing on issues like the 'party at grassroots level'. Because the FES and KANU could not find a common denominator, the cooperation did not develop any further, and Moi transformed the party into a client system which made internal party democratization processes or open debates impossible. The FES therefore broke off the party assistance to KANU and instead focused on workshops with special target groups such as the unions or local councillors.[61]

After the disappointment with KANU the FES was unwilling to cooperate with any of the new parties emerging in Kenya. Only in recent years has the FES identified some new partisan cooperation partners: UNDA, ODM, FORD-K and LDP (Table 3). As a result of the negative experience with exclusively supporting the ruling party, the FES changed its approach from a partisan approach to a multiparty approach. As their level of institutionalization is low, the Kenyan parties pose an increased challenge for the party assistance measures of the foundation.

The partner parties of the FES in Kenya are young (the right to establish parties alongside the ruling KANU party did not exist before 1992)[62] whereas the ANC in South Africa has a much longer political tradition, being established as early as 1912.[63] Therefore the selection of an ideologically close party for the FES in Kenya was, and still proves to be, difficult. A partisan approach and the support for only one affiliated party has proven to be a risk in this context, therefore a multiparty approach and instruments that aim at building up the value-orientation of a party seem to be more appropriate.

In comparison with South Africa, the young multi-party system of Kenya is strongly influenced by ethnic cleavages. Therefore those parties referring to an ethnic group have 'stronger' roots in society than those parties which are organized around political ideas and a political programme. These 'ethnic roots' are not to be considered negatively per se and it would be a mistake to ignore the fact that ethnic cleavages are fundamental to Kenyan political culture. However, ethnic identity becomes dangerous and can weaken a plural civil society and a pluralistic party system, as political leaders exploit ethnic roots in political campaigns and in seeking electoral support.[64] Moreover, the existing youth leagues (for example, of LDP or ODM) only offer weak links between the party and civil society, as all of the youth leagues are organized outside their mother parties' organizational frame and do not have a voice within the party. Personalization and dependence on one powerful political patron, informal politics and non-transparent decision-making processes and party finance systems are the major deficits concerning nearly all Kenyan parties. Likewise there is no evidence of strong membership ties to the parties, regular party congresses, comprehensive material or personal resources or a nationwide organizational presence with party activities beyond the obligatory election campaigns. As for the indicator 'organization', the partner parties of both German foundations (the FES and the KAS) in Kenya are hardly institutionalized. Compared to South Africa this is significantly different. In general the South African partner parties have established an organizational apparatus which is constantly present at all administrative levels and is able to act in the interests of its party. The party system of Kenya, especially since the 2007 elections and the immediately following setback of the country's transition towards democracy, is fragmented. 'Floor crossing'[65] in the National Assembly has a significant impact on the coherence of Kenyan parliamentary groups. Political parties, especially the smaller oppositional parties like the ODM or the DP have lost members of parliament (MPs) and seats as a result of floor crossing. The recently passed Political Party Act of 2008 aims to prevent these developments from continuing.

After the failure of the FES in the assistance of KANU at an early pre-stage of the transition process, the new multi-party system with its weakly institutionalized political parties demands a restructured party assistance approach that addresses its instruments to the needs of the individual 'institutionalization level' of each party. The two cases of South Africa and Kenya which have been presented exemplify that objectives and party assistance approaches that have been suitable at one stage of the transition process in a particular country (the FES in South Africa) may be less successful at another stage or in another country, such as was the case with the FES and the pre-phase of transition to democracy in Kenya. Moreover they strengthen the argument that party assistance instruments could be advanced by referring to different levels of party institutionalization rather than simply follow general, preconceived ad-hoc ideas.

Conclusion

This study argues that the German foundations as 'Quangos' (quasi non-governmental organizations) take a special position within international party assistance providers. They possess both the longest experience and the strongest network in the field of party assistance. Because of their value-orientation they have been able to gain access to ideologically close groups and parties easily. Moreover the foundations have been enhancing their party assistance approaches over the last five years. Nevertheless their approaches could be improved by developing them to a level where precise measures and instruments are prescribed.

By including the various stages of the democratic transition process into party assistance approaches and by shaping the instruments according to each partner party's characteristics, party assistance approaches would not simply follow generalized ideas. Therefore transformation theory and political party research provides appropriate dimensions and suitable indicators to evaluate and refine existing party assistance instruments. Especially party institutionalization research includes approaches that party assistance can build upon. But as is shown by the two cases of party support in Kenya and South Africa, it also needs to involve party characteristics which are not familiar to a Western understanding of party types and functions, like ethnic cleavages, informal institutions or patronage. In other words, it is necessary to include these special characteristics of Kenyan and South African parties into party assistance approaches and instruments. Therefore the account provided a 'phase model of party assistance' which connects party assistance approaches with a pre-transition phase and the three transition phases, liberalization, democratization and consolidation, and then measured party assistance instruments against two African examples (the FES in Kenya and in South Africa) in seven dimensions of party institutionalization: the level of organization, internal party democracy, programmatic, autonomy, roots in society, coherence, and regional and international integration. This can be regarded as an institutionalization-continuum for party assistance that includes conventional Western experiences of party types and functions but is extended by different unique characteristics of African political parties. As Mair[66] states,

> these parties do not have very much in common with political parties in Europe and North America. Many of Africa's parties lack a clear ideological orientation, a firm political programme, internal democratic procedures, accountability, a credible leadership and popular support....Those few parties who enjoy broad popular support and have a committed membership either represent certain region or ethnic groupings or are dominated by a powerful political patron.

Of course, the *phase model of party assistance* that has been introduced here and the suggested enhancements regarding its instruments have now to be tested on other African cases and only then can their applicability and transferability to other regions be discussed in more detail.

Acknowledgements

A first version of this study was prepared for the Academic Workshop of the Department of European Studies, University of Amsterdam: 'The international dimensions of political party (system) development: assessing actors, methods and effects', Amsterdam, 14–15 November 2008. The author appreciated the very useful comments of Peter Burnell, Thomas Carothers, André Gerrits as well as of the other participants of the workshop. For the discussion of the paper and many insights into the problems of transformation research and party research the author thanks colleagues, in particular Christof Hartmann, Karl-Rudolf Korte and the Research Group on Governance of the Institute for Political Science/NRW School of Governance at the University Duisburg-Essen. The author cordially thanks Matthias Bianchi for proof-reading the text. Research for this study was carried out within the dissertation project 'Political party assistance of the German Stiftungen in sub-Saharan Africa', sponsored by the Stiftung Mercator.

Notes

1. Positive 'exceptions' concerning the research field of political party assistance and democracy promotion of the German Stiftungen are: Mair, 'Germany's Stiftungen and Democracy Assistance'; Pinto-Duschinsky, 'Foreign Political Aid: The German Political Foundations and their US Counterparts'; Erdmann, 'Hesitant Bedfellows: The German Stiftungen and Party Aid in Africa'.
2. See for a comparative perspective on party assistance activities of the KAS and the FES in Kenya and South Africa: Weissenbach, *Parteienförderung im Transitionsprozess*.

3. The author conducted qualitative research and interviews with the executives of the 'Party Assistance' and 'Sub-Saharan Africa' divisions of the KAS and the FES in Bonn/Berlin (Germany) as well as with former resident representatives. In Kenya and South Africa interviews were conducted with the resident representatives of the KAS and the FES, party members and members of the National Executive Committees, members of the Parliamentary Groups as well as representatives of the youth and women leagues of the political parties which are supported by the KAS and the FES. Moreover non-governmental organizations (NGOs) and cooperation partners of the German foundations as well as scientific researchers amongst others from the University of Nairobi, the University of the Witwatersrand/Johannesburg and the University of Cape Town have been dialogue partners.
4. See Lipset, 'The Indispensability of Political Parties'; Sartori, *Parties and Party Systems*; Korte, *Politik und Regieren in Deutschland*.
5. As Lipset's and Rokkan's (1967) classic cleavage theory on the relationship between societal cleavages and party formation works for an analysis of Western party system but is not completely transferable to the African context ('Cleavage Structure, Party Systems, and Voter Alignments: An Introduction').
6. These necessary modifications will not be discussed in this study, but for a detailed discussion see Erdmann, 'Party Research: Western European Bias and the "African labyrinth"'; also: Randall and Svåsand, 'Party Institutionalization in New Democracies'; Basedau and Stroh, 'Measuring Party Institutionalization'.
7. Basedau and Stroh, 'Measuring Party Institutionalization'; Weissenbach, 'Konsolidierung ohne Wettbewerb?'
8. Interview by the author.
9. Parties in Kenya get the rent for their headquarters paid by US-organizations while they are undertaking workshops and trainings concerning their political programmes together with the German foundations.
10. Carothers, *Confronting the Weakest Link*.
11. For example, the Ministry for Economic Cooperation and Development assures that none of the German foundations is working together with the partner party of another foundation. But concerning the party assistance measures and instruments, the German foundations are acting relatively independently, in contrast to for example NDI or IRI which are less autonomous as their projects have to conform to guidelines set by the US government. See Mathisen and Svåsand, *Funding Political Parties in Emerging African Democracies*, 6.
12. See Erdmann, 'Internationale Parteienförderung'; as well as the empirical research/interviews with the regional representatives of the German political foundations the author conducted in Kenya and South Africa.
13. Focusing on the KAS and the FES.
14. However there are differences to be acknowledged when comparing the FES and the KAS: 'There are marked differences among the foundations not only in functional concentration but also in regional terms....the FES has permanent offices with field representatives in 21 African countries, 17 Latin American countries, 14 Asian countries and eight Eastern European countries; the numbers for the KAS are 14 in Latin America, 13 in Asia, 10 in Eastern Europe countries, 9 in sub-Saharan Africa, 8 in North Africa/Middle East'. Mair, 'Germany's Stiftungen', 135.
15. Bartsch, 'Political Foundations: Linking the Worlds of Foreign Policy and Transnationalism', 207.
16. Carothers, 'The End of the Transition Paradigm'; Carothers, *Confronting the Weakest Link*.
17. Carothers, *Confronting the Weakest Link*, 35.
18. Erdmann, 'Probleme der internationalen Parteienförderung', 124.

19. Mair, 'Germany's Stiftungen', 128.
20. Hess, *Party Work in Social-Democratic Parties*; and KAS, *Parteienzusammenarbeit und Parteienförderung der KAS*.
21. KAS, *Parteienzusammenarbeit und Parteienförderung der KAS*.
22. Vinnai, *Demokratieförderung in Afrika*.
23. Interviews by the author with the resident representatives of the KAS and the FES in Kenya and South Africa.
24. For a discussion of the role of parties and party systems and their institutionalization in the democratic consolidation see: Beyme, 'Parteien im Prozeß der demokratischen Konsolidierung'; Mainwaring and Scully, *Building Democratic Institutions*; Sandbrook, 'Transition without Consolidation'; Merkel, 'Einleitung'; Randall and Svåsand, 'Party Institutionalization'; Randall and Svåsand, 'Political Parties and Consolidation in Africa'; Basedau and Stroh, 'Measuring Party Institutionalization'. On the basis of a 12-country study in Latin America Mainwaring and Scully came to the conclusion that a high degree of institutionalization of party systems supports democratic consolidation.
25. Huntington, *Political Order in Changing Societies*; Panebianco, *Political Parties*; Dix, 'Democratization and the Institutionalization of Latin American Political Parties'; Mainwaring, 'Party Systems in the Third Wave'; Bendel and Grotz, Parteiensystem und Demokratisierung; Kuenzi and Lambright, 'Party System Institutionalization in 30 African Countries'; Randall and Svåsand, 'Party Institutionalization'; Basedau, 'Do Party Systems Matter for Democracy?'; Basedau and Stroh, 'Measuring Party Institutionalization'.
26. Schmitter, 'Von der Autokratie zur Demokratie'; O'Donnell and Schmitter, *Transition from Authoritarian Rule*; Przeworski, *Democracy and the Market*.
27. Merkel, 'Theorien der Transformation'; Merkel, 'Einleitung'.
28. Bratton and van de Walle, *Democratic Experiments in Africa*, 159–60.
29. Ibid., 194.
30. See interviews by the author with current and former resident representatives of the KAS and the FES in Kenya and South Africa.
31. See interviews by the author with senior researchers and experts in the field of party and democracy assistance, amongst others from the University of Nairobi, the University of the Witwatersrand/Johannesburg, the South African Institute for International Affairs (SAIIA), the German Institute of Global and Area Studies (GIGA) and the Stiftung Wissenschaft und Politik (SWP).
32. Merkel, *Systemtransformation*.
33. Weissenbach and Korte, 'Wahlsysteme und Wahltypen'; Hartmann, 'Paths of Electoral Reform in Africa'. See for a discussion of the choice of an electoral system at the inauguration of a democracy: Giliomee and Simkins: 'The Dominant Party Regimes of South Africa, Mexico, Taiwan and Malaysia'.
34. Burnell, 'Promoting Parties and Party Systems in New Democracies'.
35. See interviews by the author with research fellows in the field of political parties and party assistance, and Grabow, personal communication, 26 June 2008; Saxer, personal communication, 18 December 2008.
36. Huntington, *The Third Wave*.
37. Ibid., 267.
38. Schmitter and Terry Lynn, 'What Democracy Is...', 78.
39. Bratton and van de Walle, *Democratic Experiments*, 235; Hartmann, 'Defekte, nichtkonsolidierte oder gar keine Demokratie?'.
40. Merkel, 'Theorien der Transformation'; Merkel et al., *Defekte Demokratie*.
41. Ibid.
42. Ibid., 39.
43. Distler and Weissenbach, *Konsolidierungsprojekt Südafrika*.

44. Merkel, 'Theorien der Transformation', 39f.
45. See for a distinction: Kuenzi and Lambright, 'Party System Institutionalization'.
46. Panebianco, *Political Parties*; Randall and Svåsand, 'Party Institutionalization'; Basedau and Stroh, 'Measuring Party Institutionalization'.
47. Randall and Svåsand, 'Party Institutionalization', 12.
48. Ibid., 14.
49. Ibid., 15.
50. Basedau and Stroh, 'Measuring Party Institutionalization'.
51. Recently the Rosa Luxemburg Foundation has started dealing with this issue and is considering strengthening its cooperation with the ANC and the unions (traditional cooperation-partners of the FES) in South Africa.
52. For the method of structured, focused comparison see George and Bennett, *Case Studies and Theory Development in the Social Sciences*.
53. Freedom House, *Freedom in the World – South Africa 2009*.
54. Freedom House, *Freedom in the World – Kenya 2009*.
55. Amiri, 'Political Parties in Kenya'.
56. For the according analysis of the KAS in Kenya and South Africa see Weissenbach, *Parteienförderung im Transitionsprozess*.
57. Interviews by the author with the 'party assistance division' of FES as well as with former resident representatives; Vinnai, *Demokratieförderung in Afrika*.
58. Interviews by the author with party members and members of parliament of the ANC.
59. For a detailed analysis see Weissenbach, *Parteienförderung im Transitionsprozess*.
60. Vinnai, *Demokratieförderung in Afrika*, 62.
61. Interviews by the author with former resident representatives of FES in Kenya; Vinnai. *Demokratieförderung in Afrika*.
62. DP was founded in 2002, ODM in 2005, LDP in 2007.
63. And also the partner party of the KAS in South Africa, the Inkatha Freedom Party (IFP), founded in 1975.
64. For a discussion about ethnic parties and ethnic party bans in Africa see: Hartmann, Basedau and Niesen, 'Ethnic Party Bans in Africa'.
65. 'Floor crossing' means to leave one's political party and join another; See Khabele, Shale, and KAS, *The Impact of Floor Crossing on Party Systems and Representative Democracy*; Kotzé, 'The case of South Africa'.
66. Mair, 'Germany's Stiftungen', 134.

Bibliography

Amiri, Jane. 'Political Parties in Kenya. Shared Deficiencies'. *New Path* 2, no. 3 (2007): 4–7.

Bartsch, Sebastian. 'Political Foundations: Linking the Worlds of Foreign Policy and Transnationalism', in *Germany's New Foreign Policy*, ed. Wolf-Dieter Eberwein, 201–19. Basingstoke: Palgrave Macmillan, 2001.

Basedau, Matthias. 'Do Party Systems Matter for Democracy?', in *Votes, Money and Violence. Political Parties and Elections in Africa*, ed. Matthias Basedau, Gero Erdmann, and Andreas Mehler, 105–43. Uppsala: Nordic Africa Institute, 2007.

Basedau, Matthias, and Alexander Stroh. 'Measuring Party Institutionalization in Developing Countries: A New Research Instrument Applied to 28 African Political Parties', *GIGA Working Papers No. 69*. Berlin: GIGA, 2008.

Bendel, Petra, and Florian Grotz. 'Parteiensystem und Demokratisierung. Junge Demokratien in Afrika, Asien und Lateinamerika im Vergleich'. *Nord-Süd aktuell* 15, no. 1 (2001): 70–80.

Beyme, Claus von. 'Parteien im Prozeß der demokratischen Konsolidierung', in *Systemwechsel 3. Parteien im Transformationsprozess*, ed. Wolfgang Merkel and Eberhard Sandschneider, 23–56. Opladen: Leske+Budrich, 1997.

Bratton, Michael, and Nicoals van de Walle. *Democratic Experiments in Africa*. Cambridge: Cambridge University Press, 1997.

Burnell, Peter. 'Promoting Parties and Party Systems in New Democracies: Is There Anything the "International Community" Can Do?', in *Challenges to Democracy. Ideas, Involvement and Institutions. The PSA Yearbook 2000*, ed. Keith Dowding, James Hughes and Helen Margetts, 188–204. London: Palgrave, 2001.

Carothers, Thomas. 'The End of the Transition Paradigm'. *Journal of Democracy* 13, no. 1 (2002): 5–21.

Carothers, Thomas. *Confronting the Weakest Link. Aiding Political Parties in New Democracies*. Washington, DC: Carnegie Endowment for International Peace, 2006.

Distler, Werner, and Kristina Weissenbach, eds. *Konsolidierungsprojekt Südafrika. 15 Jahre Post-Apartheid*. Baden-Baden: Nomos, 2010 (forthcoming).

Dix, Robert H. 'Democratization and the Institutionalization of Latin American Political Parties'. *Comparative Political Studies* 24, no. 4 (1992): 488–511.

Erdmann, Gero. 'Probleme der internationalen Parteienförderung', in *KAS Auslandsinformation, 11/2006*, 123–42. Berlin: KAS, 2006.

Erdmann, Gero. 'Party Research: Western European Bias and the "African Labyrinth"'. *Democratization* 11, no. 3 (2004): 63–87.

Erdmann, Gero. 'Hesitant Bedfellows: The German Stiftungen and Party Aid in Africa. An Attempt at an Assessment', in *Globalizing Democracy. Party Politics in Emerging Democracies*, ed. Peter Burnell, 181–99. London and New York: Routledge, 2006.

Erdmann, Gero. 'Internationale Parteienförderung – neue Agenda und ungelöste Probleme?', *GIGA Focus, 8/2006*. Berlin: *KAS AI*, 11/2006.

Freedom House, *Freedom in the World – Kenya 2009*, 2009, http://www.freedomhouse.org (accessed August 1, 2009).

Freedom House, *Freedom in the World – South Africa 2009*, 2009, http://www.freedomhouse.org (accessed August 1, 2009).

George, Alexander L., and Andrew Bennett. *Case Studies and Theory Development in the Social Sciences*. Cambridge, Massachusetts: MIT Press, 2005.

Giliomee, Hermann, and Charles Simkins. 'The Dominant Party Regimes of South Africa, Mexico, Taiwan and Malaysia: A Comparative Assessment', in *The Awkward Embrace. One-party Domination and Democracy*, ed. Hermann Giliomee and Charles Simkins, 1–45. Cape Town: Tafelberg, 1999.

Hartmann, Christof. 'Defekte, nicht-konsolidierte oder gar keine Demokratie? Systemtransformation in Westafrika', in *Hybride Regime. Zur Konzeption und Empirie demokratischer Grauzonen*, ed. Petra Bendel, Aurel Croissant and Friedbert Rüb, 264–86. Opladen: Leske+Budrich, 2001.

Hartmann, Christof. 'Paths of Electoral Reform in Africa', in *Votes, Money and Violence. Political Parties and Elections in Sub-Saharan Africa*, ed. Matthias Basedau, Gero Erdmann and Andreas Mehler, 144–67. Uppsala: Nordic Africa Institute, 2007.

Hartmann, Christof, Matthias Basedau, and Peter Niesen. 'Ethnic Party Bans in Africa: A Research Agenda'. *German Law Journal* 8, no. 6 (2007): 617–34.
Hess, Hartmut. *Party Work in Social-Democratic Parties. A Practical Handbook.* Düsseldorf: FES, 1996.
Huntington, Samuel P. *Political Order in Changing Societies.* New Haven, CT: Yale University Press, 1968.
Huntington, Samuel P. *The Third Wave: Democratization in the Late Twentieth Century.* Norman: University of Oklahoma Press, 1991.
Khabele, Matlosa, Victor Shale, and KAS, eds. *The Impact of Floor Crossing on Party Systems and Representative Democracy.* Johannesburg: KAS, 2007.
KAS, ed. *Parteienzusammenarbeit und Parteienförderung der KAS. Leitfaden für die internationale Zusammenarbeit.* Sankt Augustin/Berlin: KAS, 2008.
Korte, Karl-Rudolf. *Politik und Regieren in Deutschland.* Paderborn: UTB, 2009.
Kotzé, Dirk. 'The Case of South Africa', in *The Impact of Floor Crossing on Party Systems and Representative Democracy*, ed. Matlosa Khabele, Victor Shale, and KAS, 71–84. Johannesburg: KAS, 2007.
Kuenzi, Michelle, and Gina Lambright. 'Party System Institutionalization in 30 African Countries'. *Party Politics* 7, no. 4 (2001): 437–68.
Lipset, Seymour, and Stein Rokkan. 'Cleavage Structure, Party Systems, and Voter Alignments: An Introduction', in *Party Systems and Voter Alignments: Cross National Perspectives*, ed. Seymour Lipset and Stein Rokkan, 1–64. New York: Free Press, 1967.
Lipset, Seymour Martin. 'The Indispensability of Political Parties'. *Journal of Democracy* 11, no. 3 (2000): 48–55.
Mainwaring, Scott. 'Party Systems in the Third Wave'. *Journal of Democracy* 9, no. 3 (1998): 67–81.
Mainwaring, Scott, and Timothey R. Scully. *Building Democratic Institutions: Party Systems in Latin America.* Stanford, CA: Stanford University Press, 1995.
Mair, Stefan. 'Germany's Stiftungen and Democracy Assistance: Comparative Advantages, New Challenges', in *Democracy Assistance. International Co-operation for Democratization*, ed. Peter Burnell, 128–49. London/Portland: Frank Cass, 2000.
Mathisen, Harald, and Lars Svåsand. *Funding Political Parties in Emerging African Democracies: What Role for Norway?* Bergen: CMI Report, R 2002.
Merkel, Wolfgang. 'Theorien der Transformation. Die demokratische Konsolidierung postautoritärer Gesellschaften', in *Politische Vierteljahreszeitschrift, Sonderheft 26/1995. Politische Theorie in der Ära der Transformation*, 30–58. Opladen: Westdeutscher Verlag, 1995.
Merkel, Wolfgang. 'Einleitung', in *Systemwechsel 3. Parteien im Transformationsprozess*, ed. Wolfgang Merkel and Eberhard Sandschneider, 9–21. Opladen: Leske+Budrich, 1997.
Merkel, Wolfgang. *Systemtransformation. Eine Einführung in die Theorie und Empirie der Transformationsforschung.* Opladen: Leske+Budrich, 1999.
Merkel, Wolfgang, Hans-Jürgen Puhle, Aurel Croissant, Claudia Eicher, and Peter Thiery, eds. *Defekte Demokratie. Band 1: Theorie.* Opladen: Leske+Budrich, 2003.
O'Donnell, Guillermo, and Philippe C. Schmitter. *Transition from Authoritarian Rule: Tentative Conclusions about Uncertain Democracies.* Baltimore, MD: The Johns Hopkins University Press, 1986.
Panebianco, Angelo. *Political Parties: Organization & Power.* New York: Cambridge University Press, 1988.
Pinto-Duschinsky, Michael. 'Foreign Political Aid: The German Political Foundations and their US Counterparts'. *International Affairs* 67, no. 1 (1991): 33–63.

Przeworski, Adam. *Democracy and the Market: Political and Economic Reforms in Eastern Europe and Latin America*. New York: Cambridge University Press, 1991.
Randall, Vicky, and Lars Svåsand. 'Party Institutionalization in New Democracies'. *Party Politics* 8, no. 1 (2002): 5–29.
Randall, Vicky, and Lars Svåsand. 'Political Parties and Democratic Consolidation in Africa'. *Democratization* 9, no. 3 (Autumn 2002): 30–52.
Sandbrook, Richard. 'Transition without Consolidation: Democratization in Six African Countries'. *Third World Quarterly* 17, no. 1 (1996): 69–88.
Sartori, Giovanni. *Parties and Party Systems*. Colchester: ECPR Press, 2005 [1976].
Schmitter, Philippe C. 'Von der Autokratie zur Demokratie. Zwölf Überlegungen zur politischen Transformation'. *Internationale Politik* 50, no. 6 (1995): 47–52.
Schmitter, Philippe C., and Karl Terry Lynn, 'What Democracy Is...and is Not'. *Journal of Democracy* 2, no. 3 (1991): 75–88.
Vinnai, Volker. *Demokratieförderung in Afrika. Die Zusammenarbeit der Friedrich-Ebert-Stiftung mit politischen Parteien und Befreiungsbewegungen in Afrika*, Schriftenreihe der Friedrich Ebert Stiftung. Berlin: Lit-Verlag, 2007.
Weissenbach, Kristina. 'Konsolidierung ohne Wettbewerb? Die Institutionalisierung der politischen Parteien in Südafrika', in *Konsolidierungsprojekt Südafrika. 15 Jahre Post-Apartheid*, ed. Werner Distler and Kristina Weissenbach. Baden-Baden: Nomos, 2010.
Weissenbach, Kristina. *Parteienförderung im Transitionsprozess. Eine vergleichende Studie der parteinahen Stiftungen FES und KAS in Kenia und Südafrika*. Wiesbaden: VS-Verlag, 2011 (forthcoming).
Weissenbach, Kristina, and Karl-Rudolf Korte. 'Wahlsysteme und Wahltypen: Wahlen als Qualitätskennzeichen einer Demokratie', in *Wahlsysteme und Wahltypen. Politische Systeme und regionale Kontexte im Vergleich*, ed. Claudia Derichs and Thomas Heberer, 26–48. Wiesbaden: VS-Verlag, 2006.
Wersch, Jos van, and Jeroen de Zeeuw. 'Mapping European Democracy Assistance', *Working Paper 36*. Netherlands Institute of International Relations. The Hague: The Netherlands Institute of International Relations 'Clingendael', November 2005.

In search of the impact of international support for political parties in new democracies: Malawi and Zambia compared

Lise Rakner[a] and Lars Svåsand[b]

[a]Department of Comparative Politics, University of Bergen and Chr. Michelsen Institute;
[b]Department of Comparative Politics, University of Bergen

Democracy assistance programmes have gradually included support for political parties in addition to support for civil society, parliaments and the electoral process. But, does international party assistance contribute to party and party system institutionalization? This analysis addresses the issue of impact of external support for political parties using the case of one donor, the Netherlands Institute for Multiparty Democracy (NIMD) and the impact of its activities in Malawi and in Zambia. NIMD's stated objectives are to promote party system institutionalization as well as the institutionalization of individual parties. Its funds are spent to support parties in three ways: strengthening inter-party dialogue, strengthening party organizations, and improving party-civil society linkages. This contribution assesses what NIMD hoped to achieve with their party support programmes and how recipient party representatives in Zambia and Malawi evaluate the support provided by NIMD. The analysis suggests that there are significant challenges for international party support. While the political parties indicate a priority for bilateral support, NIMD views such bilateral support as less effective for their overall ambitions. The discussion shows furthermore that enhancement of civil society—party relations through external funding modalities may be particularly challenging.

Introduction

Political parties are considered to be indispensible institutions in a democracy.[1] Yet, in many African democracies political parties are often unstable, with parties appearing and disappearing from one election to another, are often weakly organized and tend to be top-heavy institutions with a weak internal democracy.[2] Moreover, the lack of ideological differences between parties also leads to rapid shifts in coalition patterns. This means that both individual parties as well as party systems are often poorly institutionalized, which may lead to political instability and problems of governing. To promote the development of political parties, democracy assistance programmes have gradually come to include support for parties in addition to support for civil society, parliaments and the electoral process. But, international party support is associated with several problematic aspects, one of which is the problem of assessing its impact: how do we know whether international support for political parties has the intended consequences or not? This contribution intends to address this question, using the case of one donor, the Netherlands Institute for Multiparty Democracy (NIMD). We analyse the impact of NIMD's activities in Malawi and in Zambia and examine to what extent it has succeeded in its objectives, which are to promote party system institutionalization as well as institutionalization of the individual parties.

The analysis is motivated by the fact that most of the literature on party system development in established democracies focuses on the impact of domestic structural factors, like the cleavage pattern,[3] the electoral system[4] or the motivations[5] and resources of the political actors,[6] but does not incorporate an international dimension. At the same time, international actors are often considered to be important for explaining political developments in new democracies. However, international aid efforts, including support for democratization, frequently omit support for political parties. Our study is a contribution to bridge this gap in the literature. The cases of NIMD and of Malawi and Zambia are motivated by the fact that NIMD is active in both countries,[7] operating largely in the same way. It should therefore be possible to identify if this way of assisting political parties has similar types of impact. NIMD was established in 2000 by the Dutch parliament, with seven of the largest Dutch parties as member organizations.[8] Almost all of its funds are spent to support parties in three ways: strengthening interparty dialogue, strengthening party organizations, and improving party–civil society linkages. NIMD support for parties in Malawi and Zambia started in 2003.

In the following, we employ a relatively novel approach to impact evaluation. First, we assess what NIMD hoped to achieve with their party support programmes and to what extent they themselves evaluate the outcomes to be successful or not. We then turn to compare how recipient party representatives in Zambia and Malawi evaluate the support provided by NIMD. The findings show that international party support is a challenging concept. While the political party leadership in both Malawi and Zambia expressed a clear priority for bilateral support, NIMD in turn views this support as less effective for their overall ambitions. The analysis concludes that NIMD's third objective, namely the enhancement of civil society–party relations through external funding modalities, may be particularly difficult to achieve.

Following this introduction, section two examines some of the existing literature on the effects of political party assistance. Section three introduces the NIMD and the contribution proceeds to present the development of the party system in Zambia and Malawi in section four. Section five contains the empirical analysis of NIMD's support for parties in the two countries and a discussion of the impacts. A final section concludes the study by drawing some tentative lessons from NIMD's experiences in Zambia and Malawi.

The development of parties and the rise of international support for parties

It is important to note that we distinguish between *party institutionalization* and *party system institutionalization*.[9] In this context party institutionalization means endurance and routinized organization. In other words, a party becomes institutionalized if it is able to survive across time. Political parties have to be durable institutions in order for them to perform some of the critical functions attributed to them, primarily candidate nomination, interest aggregation, policy orientation, and forming the government or opposition.[10] However, institutionalization understood as ability to survive must be linked to *routinized organization*. This means that parties should have a formal structure and at least partially operate according to the written statutes, with regularized procedures, such as for the election of office holders and nomination of candidates. *Party system institutionalization*, in turn, refers to the continuity among party alternatives competing for votes and the ability of parties to dominate the recruitment process to political offices.[11] Stability across time is necessary in order for voters to hold parties to account from one election to the next, and in an institutionalized party system, the parties become the main channel for political recruitment. Thus, the number of independents running for office should decline as the party system institutionalizes.

The general agreement[12] that parties are needed for democratic governance to function provides the background for the emergence of international party assistance, but the ambiguity about what exactly the qualities of the parties and the party system should be, also make party assistance programmes problematic. As a result, the debates about impacts of party assistance have remained an open and contested question in the literature.[13] The fact that the development of parties in new democracies takes place in completely different contexts compared to more established democracies further underlines the complexities and ambiguities associated with party support activities. Rose and Shin characterize the development of parties in new democracies as a feature of 'democratization backwards': competitive elections based on general suffrage and the availability of mass media are introduced without the presence of basic institutions in a democracy, including well organized political parties.[14] Parties in new democracies, particularly in Africa, are often seen as vehicles for individual party leaders, with ethnically delimited electorates, short existence and unpredictable behaviour.[15] International support for parties often seeks to moderate these deficiencies, but the impact of party assistance seems difficult to trace. Thus, the UNDP *Handbook on Working with Political Parties* states that 'it is widely recognized that political party assistance can take years to bear fruit.... Direct and quantifiable attribution of outcomes to political party assistance is usually impossible', 80.[16] Many studies have problems identifying a clear impact.[17]

The problems of measuring the impact of international party assistance is furthermore related to the fact that the concepts are difficult to operationalize. For example, does the objective of 'strengthening party organizations' mean 'more members' or 'more local party branches', or something else? Problems may also arise if support projects in one context are copied to other contexts, or when the preferences of the donors are not shared by the recipients.[18] Support for political parties has to compete with other objectives of support, such as for civil society. But the potential exists for a similar problem to arise in both cases. Attending to the 'demand side', that is to say the needs of individual parties or civil society actors, can lose sight of the 'aggregation side', that is to say the larger compass of all such actors taken together.[19] The overall objective of democracy support is often to aid the development of a viable party *system* (and the development of a healthy civil society overall), but the precise qualities of such a system tend not to be specified, apart from the belief that it should not be too polarized, too fragmented or too volatile. Moreover too little thought has been given to determining appropriate mechanisms for achieving a viable party system.

NIMD's support for parties

We now turn to our cases, the Netherlands Institute for Multiparty Democracy (NIMD) and its activities in Malawi and in Zambia.[20] NIMD was established in 2000 by the Dutch parliament, with seven of the largest Dutch parties as member organizations. Each of these parties has a representative at the board and two members of the supervisory council. Operationally, NIMD is organized in four regional programmes for Africa, Latin America, Eurasia and new regions. In addition, three cross-regional units deal with knowledge and communication, planning monitoring and evaluation, and office management functions.[21] NIMD became fully operational in 2002 and its budget has doubled from 2003 until 2008. In 2008 its total budget was EUR 10,335,000 of which more than 90% was contributed by the Dutch Ministry of Foreign Affairs.[22] NIMD is currently involved with 150 parties in 17 countries. Table 1 provides information about the changes in NIMD's total budget from 2001 to 2008 and the corresponding size of the budget for its activities in Malawi and Zambia.

NIMD identifies three objectives for its work with political parties in new democracies[23]; strengthening multi-party democratic systems, supporting the institutional development of political parties, and improving the relations between political society and civil society, including the private sector and the media.

In the first objective, the party system is the focus, and the primary mechanism for strengthening the party system is recognized as *dialogue*. To improve the dialogue between parties, NIMD has supported activities where all, or the major parties, of the recipient countries meet. Dialogue between competing parties is seen as a way to build trust among the parties. In the countries where NIMD has operated for some time, such as in Kenya, Ghana and our two countries the dialogue is 'institutionalized' in a national Centre for Multi-party Democracy, a CMD.

Table 1. NIMD budget 2003–2008 (total and for Malawi and Zambia) (in 1000 EUR)*.

Year	Total	Malawi	Zambia
2001	740		
2002	2273		
2003	5117	220	204
2004	7635	299	395
2005	8500	338	350
2006	9075	450	350
2007	10,586	480	502.5
2008	10,335	460	600

Source: *Extracted from NIMD Annual Reports 2002–2008 (due to variations in reporting form, the figures are not entirely equivalent for all years).

The second objective deals with the individual parties, particularly *the strengthening of parties as organizations*, improving internal procedures and internal democracy so that each party may develop into a viable structure. Within this objective it should be possible to identify an effect on the ability of parties to institutionalize, that is, to survive as organizations with established and accepted routines and procedures.[24]

The third element recognizes the significant relationship between the *parties and civil society*.[25] Parties should be engaged with and communicate with the public, develop relationships with the media, but parties are also dependent on the strength of civic education. The development of communication capacity is therefore a central element in the development of a party system. This objective is shared by much of the democratization literature where the prospect for democratic consolidation depends on the development of a robust civil society.[26]

Party system development in Malawi and in Zambia
Malawi

In 1993 the autocratic one-party regime headed by Dr Banda was defeated in a referendum over the introduction of multiparty democracy and Malawi emerged as one of Africa's relatively few countries that saw a return to democracy coinciding with a shift of governing party. The new governing party, United Democratic Front (UDF), emerged from a pro-democracy movement as a response to an increasingly unpopular one-party system of rule. Since then, four multiparty elections have been organized (1994, 1999, 2004, and 2009). A democratic constitution with a strong executive has been in place since 1995. The president and parliament are elected simultaneously for a five-year term. The president (and vice president) is elected in a nationwide vote with simple majority. The presidency is limited to two five-year terms.

Until the run-up to the 2004 elections, a regional based three-party system dominated. The old state party, Malawi Congress Party (MCP), based in the central region, lost the transition election, as well as the following ones, but has survived several subsequent splits and has remained the most institutionalized party in Malawi. The United Democratic Front (UDF), which won the first three presidential elections, is mainly based in the southern region, while AFORD (Alliance for Democracy) had its stronghold in the northern part of the country. Prior to and following the 2004 elections this three-party system fragmented.[27] Before the elections several new parties appeared, as aspiring presidential candidates defected from their 'original' parties after having lost the bid to be nominated[28] while others were formed as a result of frustration with the way the UDF/AFORD coalition government had developed.[29] In the 2004 elections President Muluzi (UDF) was barred from running again, after an unsuccessful attempt to lift the term limitations. Failing to amend the constitution, Bingu wa Mutharika, an outsider to the UDF, was hand-picked by Muluzi to be the party's presidential candidate. Shortly after the election Mutharika resigned from UDF and formed a new party, the DPP (Democratic Progressive Party). Without a single elected official at the local level and with all party officials being appointed by the president the DPP and Mutharika won the 2009 elections with a significant majority. Indicating a precarious lack of party system institutionalization, in the 2004 and 2009 elections a record number of independent candidates stood for election and 'independents' were the third largest 'group' in parliament from 2004–2009. After the 19 May 2009 elections, the group of independents is the second largest after the governing party DPP.

Zambia, in turn, re-implemented multiparty democracy in 1991. Unlike many of Africa's new democracies, there was – as in Malawi – a change of government and the political leadership was transferred from Kenneth Kaunda and the United National Independence Party (UNIP) to the former trade union leader Frederick Chiluba and the Movement for Multiparty Democracy (MMD). The opposition's success in the first multiparty elections has been attributed to the organizational reach and mobilizing success of the trade union structures, the Zambia Congress of Trade Unions (ZCTU).[30] The success of MMD in the 1991 transition elections is also attributed to its ability to incorporate a wide range of societal actors, such as students, churches and business interests. But, over time, rather than institutionalizing, the Zambian party system fragmented with the number of registered parties and independent candidates increasing. As in the case of Malawi, problems of succession and executive dominance appear to drive political party formation. In the 1991 and 1996 elections MMD won the presidency and a dominant position in the parliament. After losing the bid to change the constitution to allow a third term in office, President Chiluba picked Levy Mwanawasa as his successor. The 2001 elections resulted in a much weaker presidential victory (with Mwanawasa securing only 29% of the vote) and a more fragmented parliament.

Uncertainties and conflicts concerning constitutional review processes have characterized the relationship between the MMD government, the opposition parties and civil society in the period after 2001. In 2006 President Mwanawasa and MMD were re-elected with a significantly higher share of the presidential vote (43%) and MMD narrowly gained control of the parliament. However, the 2006 elections also witnessed the emergence of an 'urban protest vote' as a new party, PF (Patriotic Front) under the leadership of an experienced figure in Zambian politics, Michael Sata, won every urban parliamentary seat in the capital Lusaka and the copper belt region. The death of President Mwanawasa in August 2008 led to a new succession crisis. The Zambian constitution states that a vice president is only allowed to serve as acting president for 90 days, pending a presidential by-election. As a result, the death of Mwanawasa resulted in political uncertainty and further fragmentation of the party system. In November 2008 the MMD won a narrow victory and the former vice president Ruphia Banda became the new president of Zambia with 40.6% of the votes in a tight race with Michael Sata of PF with 38.6%.

Zambia and Malawi: the challenges of party institutionalization and executive dominance

Succession, and the political bargaining related to succession, appears deeply damaging in both Malawi and Zambia. As witnessed in 2001 and 2008 in Zambia, and 2004 in Malawi, without an incumbent president running for re-election, many aspiring candidates jockey for the position to be nominated by their party. Those losing the battle for nomination are tempted to break out and launch their own parties. In Zambia, significant splits have occurred in the party in 1993, 1996 and 2001. Similarly, the opposition parties have never managed to institutionalize or create lasting viable coalitions. In Malawi, the three-party system that characterized the first two multiparty elections fragmented in the 2004 election in the absence of an incumbent presidential candidate. Problems of succession and executive dominance clearly also affect the political parties as the strong emphasis on party leadership challenges multiparty dialogue. The political parties function as loose organizational set-ups characterized by fluid membership and lack of public and transparent sources of funding.[31] Similar to many of Africa's new democracies, political parties in Zambia and Malawi are affected by neopatrimonialism and the so called 'big man syndrome' where the party leader is the main fundraiser. There are no provisions for the disclosure of funding and no limits as to how much can be spent on an election campaign.[32]

The impact of NIMD party support in Malawi and in Zambia

Have NIMD's activities in Malawi and in Zambia had any impact that corresponds with the objectives of NIMD? We address this question by looking at the three main objectives of NIMD's programme statement[33]: improving the dialogue between parties, strengthening party organizations, and improving party–civil society relationship. Regarding the first of these objectives, we also look at how parties have been engaged in the constitutional review process in Zambia. For the second objective we identify three important indicators of party strengthening:

the parties' ability to survive over time, the strengthening of party organization, and the ability of parties to conduct nomination processes. Finally, we address the problems involved in working toward the third objective, pointing to the legal challenges as well as the competition between parties and civil society for donor support.

Strengthening the party system through dialogue between parties

Both in Malawi and in Zambia, NIMD's support programme has led to the establishment of an organizational unit, a centre for multi party democracy, that includes representatives from the parties represented in parliament.

Malawi

NIMD became operational in Malawi in 2003 after having sent two missions to the country in 2002. The first mission concluded that due to the political situation[34] plans for cooperation should be shelved. Nevertheless, the second mission advocated running a pilot project 'so as to avoid the potential danger of becoming a "football" in the party political disputes', as the NIMD Annual Report expressed it.[35] In the same report, NIMD perceived the political situation in Malawi as both complex and sensitive and 'decided to take a cautious approach in developing its relationships and programme'. The parties with which the NIMD mission engaged favoured bilateral institutional support, while the international organizations and NGOs advised a cross-party approach. NIMD settled for a combination of the two. From the start, NIMD experienced two kinds of challenges. First, the parties themselves seemed much more interested in bilateral programmes than in the cross-party activities, and secondly, it became a problem to engage the significant players. The first missions noted the importance of personal contacts and when the programme started in 2003 the Annual Report stated 'it has been difficult to identify the right contact persons within the political parties'.[36] This concern was voiced in the NIMD's report for 2003 and then repeated in its 2004 report. Thus, even if the Malawian parties had a formal structure with identifiable office holders, this was apparently not sufficient to secure a party commitment to the programme. The turmoil in the Malawian party system in 2004 led NIMD to suspend its bilateral programmes. In the following year the main emphasis was on the establishment of the Centre for Multiparty Democracy-Malawi (CMD-M), which became formally registered as an NGO in August 2005. Although NIMD funds CMD-M, it is not involved in the operation of the organization, nor is it represented on the board.

CMD-M has functioned successfully with regard to the objective of promoting inter-party dialogue. According to the NIMD Annual Report for 2007 the CMD provides 'an impartial meeting platform for political parties in a very volatile political environment', 33, and is seen by NIMD, as one its key achievements.[37] In a country where there is lack of trust between political actors, both within a party and across parties, getting parties to meet regularly under the same organizational umbrella should be considered a significant contribution to improving the political atmosphere. As an independent NGO CMD-M does not have the image that many domestic institutions have of being allied to, or leaning towards, a particular party.

There are several characteristics of CMD-M that indicate that all of the parties are considered to be equal members. All parties have two representatives on the board, regardless of the size of the parties, and the incumbent party and the opposition have equal formal status. This is important in Malawi: a society in which status and rank normally infuse all social settings. The board meets quarterly and the chairmanship rotates between the parties every sixth months. It was recently decided that the budget for CMD-M (EUR 100,000) should be divided with 85% split on an equal basis and 15% split according to the number of MPs. CMD-M also succeeds in functioning as a forum for debates on issues where all parties seem to have a joint interest, such as the preparations for the 2009 elections, as well as preparations for the local elections scheduled for November 2010. In several board meetings the CMD-M has engaged in meetings with the Malawi Electoral Commission on issues relating the election logistics. Other items for discussion have been how to avoid the election violence in Kenya and Zimbabwe from being repeated in Malawi. Also, the CMD's in Mozambique and Tanzania had requested meetings with CMD-M to exchange views and experiences.

However, there are also some challenges in the relationship between CMD-M and the individual parties. It is not the party chairpersons, but the secretaries-general, or their deputies, who attend the board meetings, and this model of engaging with parties at the top level has some repercussions. On the one hand, it recognizes the realities of the power structure in the parties. Party leaders and their officials, such as the secretaries-general, are the key players in making decisions. They are in effect veto players. On the other hand, NIMD recognizes the reverse side of the coin: 'The top leadership is too entrenched in their conflicts and rivalries, whereas the middle-level politicians are more moderate and willing to pursue reform agendas. Nevertheless, the challenge remains to bring the top leadership into a dialogue as well'.[38]

One of the problems that this model has run into is the relationship between the CMD-M and the way the parties themselves operate. The party representatives report back to their respective parties, but because the parties' national executive committee meets infrequently, the information from the meetings tends to remain at the top level, with the party president or the general secretary. This lack of communication is recognized in the minutes from the board meeting on 8 August 2009: 'The Board appealed to members to report back to party leadership after CMD meetings'.[39] Unless the parties' organizations in general are improved in terms of internal communication, the impacts of CMD may remain isolated. Party leaders also have an incentive not to be drawn too much into this arrangement. By standing outside of the CMD arena they keep their distance from committing their party too much and can block CMD decisions they do not approve of. The 2005, 2006 and 2007 annual reports all point to the problem of engaging the party leaders in the inter-party programme. While the reports indicate that an extensive training programme for regional and local leaders had engaged hundreds of party activists, the top leadership seemed to be keeping a distance from the CMD-M. The need for engaging the party leaders is precisely because it is believed 'that most of the political instability is fuelled by the positions taken by the party leaders'.[40] Party leaders tend to personally dominate their parties, as several events recently exemplify.[41] However, interviews with UDF, DPP and MCP officials confirm that the dialogue function works. Attendance at the board meetings tends to be observed by all the parties. The opportunity to meet with other party officials at a 'neutral location' was mentioned as the most useful aspect of the CMD. Better dialogue between the parties may have contributed to reduced violence during the recent election campaign, compared to earlier elections, but also other institutions, such as MEC (Malawi Electoral Commission), were active in this respect.[42]

Apart from the attractiveness of the 'neutral meeting place' participation in CMD provides other benefits. Only parties represented at CMD can apply to NIMD for bilateral support. This is not only likely to be very attractive for smaller parties, but larger ones can benefit too, as for example was the case for the UDF which after the split in the party in 2005 suddenly found itself in opposition and cut off from the benefits that the incumbent party can enjoy.[43]

Zambia

NIMD's collaborations in Zambia began in April 2002 when an NIMD mission made contact with a number of institutions in Zambia. The aim was to explore whether it would be feasible to investigate the strengths of the political parties through collaborations with central NGOs such as the Zambia Forum for a Democratic Process (FODEP) and the National Democratic Institute. In addition NIMD approached two gender organizations. In the second part of 2003, a NIMD support programme for political parties in Zambia reached its implementation stage. In September 2003, a workshop was organized by NIMD and FODEP with all the political parties participating. It should be noted that during this phase, NIMD worked to support Zambian political parties through some central NGOs (Women for Change, FODEP, NDI), indicating both the perceived weakness of political parties in Zambia, and the potential conflicts associated with external donors working directly with political parties. The sensitivity of international actors supporting the political opposition was particularly challenging in Zambia as the relationship between the donors and the Zambian government had been marked by conflicts in the period after the 1996 elections.[44] NIMD also acknowledged in its Annual Report for 2003 that due to the level of mistrust and conflict between civil society and political parties in Zambia, this was a mechanism that should be reconsidered.

NIMD opened a fully fledged collaboration with political parties in Zambia in 2004 focusing on the institutional strengthening of parties. The goal of NIMD at this stage was to strengthen the internal organization and capacity of Zambian parties. The challenges of international party support to enhance inter-party dialogue is well captured in an evaluation report of the NIMD programme in Zambia: 'Given the profound distrust between parties, NIMD decided not to push the inter-party dialogue too much, but stick to skills-oriented cross-party initiatives, and the funding of bilateral projects'.[45]

According to the NIMD evaluation, cross-party initiatives initiated in 2003–2004 produced tangible results and from 2005 onwards the NIMD programme in Zambia gradually shifted in focus from an almost exclusive one on individual party support (bilateral programmes) to a stronger emphasis on cross-party projects and inter-party dialogue. 2006 represented a marked shift for NIMD's operations in Zambia with the creation of the Zambian Center for Inter-party Dialogue (ZCID). ZCID's mandate and operations resemble that of CMD-M in Malawi and the board of ZCID consists of the secretaries-general of all the parliamentary parties and one representative of the non-parliamentary parties.[46] According to NIMD's own assessment, at the initial stages there was only a modest basis within the parties for this kind of initiative as inter-party tensions were high. However, initiatives such as the MMD-convened meeting for all secretaries-general in 2004 was endorsed by most parties and considered valuable for confidence-building among parties.[47] This and similar party initiated strategies paved the way for a more institutionalized inter-party forum through ZCID. From 2005 onwards political parties increasingly had contact and were able to organize regular inter-party dialogue. In the latter parts of 2006, the Zambian political parties embarked on a process of defining joint priorities.

In the strategic plan the political parties agreed on six common objectives[48] and according to the ZCID's strategic plans, four issues are central to their inter-party dialogue: the constitutional review process; the strengthening of electoral administration; the building of ZCID structures, the creation of a resource centre for political parties; and the intensification of civic education (it is perceived that between elections parties 'hibernate').

The role of dialogue: ZCID and the constitutional review process

Debates over constitutional reviews have dominated the political agenda in Zambia since the turn of the millennium. Zambia has carried out five constitutional reviews since independence. In 2003 President Mwanawasa initiated a new constitutional review commission and the report was submitted on 21 December 2005. However, in early 2006 President Mwanawasa suspended the process of developing a White Paper and its parliamentary passage. He claimed there was not enough time to have a constitution in place before the 2006 elections. In a response Coalition 2005, an alliance between civil society and opposition parties, formed and launched petitions in order to press for amendments to the Electoral Act and the Republican

Constitution before the 2006 elections through a constituent assembly, but the initiative failed.[49]

Until the 2006 elections, the constitutional debates in Zambia were largely driven by civil society and in particular the Oasis Forum. After the elections, the constitutional reform process reached a deadlock as civil society and the MMD government could not agree on the roadmap for constitutional reform.[50] In this situation, Zambian political parties and NIMD agreed that ZCID should facilitate the constitutional review process.[51] ZCID then initiated an agreement between the president of Zambia and the political parties that a dialogue would begin on the revision of the constitution. Thus, after the 2006 elections, the constitutional review initiative shifted to the political party arena as ZCID acquired an important role in this process. In ZCID's own assessments, this shift has enhanced inter-party dialogue and served to build trust and cooperation between Zambian political parties.[52] This view is also shared by external evaluators.[53]

One of the party representatives interviewed argued that perhaps the greatest benefit of ZCID/NIMD funding was that it had enabled the parties to have a forum where issues could be debated and one could in a friendly environment try to convey views to each other. The general secretary of the governing party argued that on a number of issues his views had changed as a result of the inter-party dialogue forum, and he in turn felt he had succeeded in terms of moving the president's (Mwanawasa) position, on the basis of the discussions on the ZCID. While the general secretaries of the main political parties all acknowledged the prerogatives of party leadership/presidents in their various parties, the representatives claimed that a number of party wrangles were solved at the ZCID level. All party representatives consulted reported that they were able to persuade their party presidents to buy into agreements reached at the ZCID board level.

Inter-party dialogue in Zambia and Malawi

In both Malawi and Zambia NIMD appears to have succeeded in improving inter-party dialogue and the support given to parties, collectively as well as individually. It is further evident that this initiative is highly appreciated by the participating parties. As we have seen, in Zambia ZCID functions as a deliberating body on the constitutional reforms. To the extent that such regular dialogue contributes to reduce mistrust and suspicions between the parties, it could also positively affect the interactions between parties in arenas outside of the CMD/ZCID. Dialogue in itself does not create an institutionalized party system in which there is a stable set of alliances between party alternatives, but it may remove obstacles that stand in the way of alliances.

Strengthening individual political parties

The clearest link between NIMD's activities and the concept of party institutionalization is in NIMD's support for individual parties. This type of support has taken several forms, such as organizing training seminars for party activists and providing partial funding for party events, and financial contributions towards organizing national conventions. The bilateral party support was meant to strengthen the parties as organizations and to improve internal party democracy. There are several ways one may think of a successful outcome of this objective: that the parties receiving funding are able to endure, to survive; that the parties are able to function better according to their own statutes (internal party democracy) and general bureaucratic routines; and that the parties are able to implement and gain acceptance among their supporters for decisions, such as nomination of candidates.

Party endurance and the development of organizational routines are two key elements of party institutionalization. Moreover, one of the most important functions of political parties is the nomination of candidates. One would expect therefore that in an institutionalized *party*, the nomination process follows a standardized procedure and that if a party *system* is institutionalized, almost all candidates running for election will run as candidates for parties.

Malawi: party survival

The Malawian party system has changed from a regionally based three-party system prior to the 2004 election, to a fragmented party system from early 2004 to 2009.[54] The total number of parties has increased from eight to almost forty. On the surface, only two of the early formed parties have disappeared, the rest survived in a formal sense of the word: they continue to be registered but it does not necessarily mean that they are active. Very few parties are able to nominate candidates regularly and in several constituencies. The fragmentation of the party system is driven by several factors and it would be incorrect to attribute turbulence to NIMD's programme. NDA was de-registered as a consequence of the party leader's decision to join the Mutharika government after the 2004 elections. Gwanda Chakuamba, president of the Republican Party (RP) attempted the same and for the same reason, but was blocked by the court from de-registering 'his' party. The main reason why the party system fragments seems to be the fight among ambitious politicians to win the presidency or to become a needed player in a coalition game.

Individual party routines in Malawi

From the start the NIMD annual reports noted the organizational limitations of the parties. The 2003 Annual Report announced that for 2004 there would be tailor-made workshops on financial management for all parties 'resulting in more transparent and justifiable financial procedures within the parties', 20. However, these ambitions had to be abandoned in the pre-2004 election turmoil and party finance remains one of the most closely guarded secrets of the parties. In the 2007 NIMD report the lack of financial resources is mentioned as one of the reasons for lack of party institutionalization.[55] Internally, few of the established parties can be said to adhere to their own constitution. Conventions are not organized according to the statutes and even national executive committee meetings seem to be rarely held.[56] Alliances between the parties appear also to be at the initiative of the party leader himself with few people being consulted and in many instances party officials give conflicting statements about which party they are allied with.[57] Parties seem still to be quite distant from being institutionalized with well-functioning structures. The lack of organizational routines is well illustrated by how parties deal with conflicts. AFORD was unable to handle the death of the party president, Chihana, in 2008. Although the party had a vice-president, Chihana's death unleashed a series of conflicts over who was to become the legitimate leader of the party, resulting in party splits and the arranging of rival conventions. Similarly, the emerging of rivals to the entrenched leadership of Thembo, in MCP, and Muluzi, in UDF, resulted in instant dismissals of the critics from their party offices. Moreover, the problems of parliamentary nominations, as outlined below, are part of the lack of organizational routines.

Nominations in Malawian parties

With respect to the third aspect, candidate nomination, the large parties did perform better earlier than today, as AFORD, UDF and MCP were initially able to nominate candidates in a majority of constituencies. AFORD's collapse is reflected in the reduction in the number of candidates, from 159 in 1994 to 29 in 2009. Some of the parties that were originally part of NIMD's support remain marginal in the political landscape or are hardly able to nominate candidates. The greatest problem with nominations however, is the inability of parties to establish and implement routines for the selection process which are acceptable to the participants – including those losing out in the nomination process. In the 2004 election the national centre of the UDF imposed candidates on the constituencies in spite of local resistance, resulting in a number of candidates running as independents. In 2009 the UDF party president unilaterally overturned a party decision requiring all MPs to go through primaries. In the newly formed DPP the primaries were complete chaos due to lacking and/or conflicting understanding of what the rules were and how they should be implemented. Together with the fragmentation of the party system the fight inside the parties over nomination procedures has led to an increase in the number of independent candidates, from 12 in 1994 to 485 in 2009.[58]

Although all parties receiving funding from NIMD do so with an objective to strengthen party structures, it is still a challenge to develop organizational routines that are accepted by the members of top party bodies as well as understood and accepted by the members and supporters of the parties.

Below, we apply the same indicators to assess whether strengthening individual parties has had any success in Zambia: the survival of parties, improving organizational routines and parties' ability to nominate candidates.

Party survival in Zambia

It is not possible to assess what impact, if any, the NIMD programme may have had on party survival, simply because of the short time that has elapsed since the implementation of the ZCID. ZCID became operational in 2006, which was the year of the last parliamentary election; the next one will be in 2011. However, prior to ZCID's formation, the Zambian party system, just as in Malawi, had been struggling with high party turnover before the elections. A major driving force for this is the battle for the presidency, which is possible to win with less than 50% of the popular vote. Hence the party system tends to fragment before the elections.[59] It seems doubtful whether the NIMD programme will have an impact on this. The institutional incentives are the same: executive power concentrated in the presidency, elected on a first-past-the-post basis.

Individual party routines in Zambia

In the initial phases of NIMD support, a relatively large proportion of party assistance was directed to individual parties, but the bilateral programme is currently gradually being reduced and more emphasis is put on the cross-party programme. Funding for consultative tours, party leader conferences, capacity building, membership expansion, communication and media training are examples of projects that NIMD funded at an individual party basis. Tracing the process of individual party support in NIMDs own documents, it is evident that this form of funding was increasingly becoming conflicting as the 2006 elections drew closer. Recognizing that donor resources may become instrumental in the political campaigns, NIMD now enhances the monitoring activities and sanctions the parties who fail to fulfil reporting procedures.[60]

According to NIMD officials, to avoid international support further strengthening strong national party leaders, support for internal party democracy projects (reporting documents) must be signed at regional meetings. Furthermore, annual reports to NIMD should be signed by all National Executive Committee (NEC) members. According to NIMD's own assessments, this requirement has enhanced collaboration between the regional and national level of Zambian parties. The focus on regional leaders has also improved internal party communication. On the other hand, the improved communications have exposed the often diverging policy agendas at the national and local levels.[61] Another important lesson from the first years of collaboration was the need to carefully screen and control local contact persons, as money provided directly to political parties sometimes did not go to parties but to illegal accounts.[62] Suggesting weak internal accounting structures and accountability, NIMD experienced the problem that party officials withdrew funding for personal use.

As we have seen, NIMD now wishes to move away from bilateral support programmes in all its collaborating country programmes. In the case of Zambia, in addition to the administrative burdens of the bilateral programmes, these initiatives were not considered to be working optimally. However, the representatives of the political parties interviewed disclosed that they were not happy about this change, which they perceived to be a unilateral NIMD initiative to move from bilateral support to more inter-party support.[63] According to NIMD, the shift from individual party support to party system strengthening is in part linked to the limited success during the first years of party support. The general secretaries of the parties represented in the ZCID stated clearly that this policy change was not welcomed by the Zambian parties. It was further argued that the problems of reporting and accountability to a large extent were related to the reporting requirements of NIMD that were considered too cumbersome. All participants appeared to agree that NIMD funding was relatively unique, as it comprised direct funding both for parties and cross-party activities. However, confirming the limited effects of international support for party institutionalization, a recent evaluation report of NIMD's work in Zambia noted that beyond the summing up of workshops and meetings, party representatives interviewed could not identify lasting effects resulting from bilateral funding.[64]

Nominations in Zambian parties

With regard to nominations, it is also too early to assess any impact of ZCID, but as in the case of Malawi, the Zambian parties have suffered from problems, with losing candidates showing reluctance to accept the outcome of the nomination process. Thus there have been increasing numbers of independent candidates: 21 (1991), 96 (1996), 84 (2001) and 156 in 2006.[65]

While party representatives emphasized the need for bilateral funding, political parties in Zambia do not disclose information on other sources of funding. It is therefore impossible to assess the importance of NIMD funding in the total budget of parties. However, overall, funding needs are so dire that any actual institutional impact may be some way away. Considering that bilateral funds are closely monitored, and that reports are signed by all members of the recipient parties' national executive committee, efforts to strengthen individual parties through bilateral funding seem to be more successful in Zambia than in Malawi. There are more regular party conventions in Zambia than in Malawi and internal communications seem better. Although there are also a number of independent candidates in Zambia, it is on a smaller scale than in Malawi. Whether these outcomes are *because* of the NIMD programme or because the NIMD programme lends *further support to* processes that are already in place, is difficult to assess.

Party–civil society relationships

A frequent critique of African party systems is that they have shallow roots in society, partly because they do not have a solid membership base, but also because they are poorly linked to broader social movements. Some African parties have grown out of social movements, particularly those that originate in liberation movements, as for example the African National Congress (ANC) in South

Africa or in resistance movements against the one-party state, as for example the Movement for Multiparty Democracy in Zambia. However, many of the newer parties do not have this origin, and instead are splinter groups from existing parties or creations of political entrepreneurs.[66]

Malawi

In Malawi the objective of strengthening parties' societal roots has not really been achieved. Partly an explanation for this is the time it has taken to engage with the political parties as such, but this objective is also difficult to handle due to Malawian legislation. Civil society itself is still rather weak in Malawi; at least in terms of organizations that have a nation-wide coverage, although a number of community-based organizations exist.[67] Civil society organizations are regulated in the NGO Act, and in the NGO Code of Conduct for Malawi (1997) it is stated that 'NGOs shall observe the principal of political non-partisanship in their operations'.[68] Thus NGOs cannot organizationally be linked to political parties and cannot sponsor parties financially. This does not mean that there is absolutely no linkage between parties and civil society. For example, religious organizations play a significant role in Malawian politics.[69] The religious divide in Malawi between the Presbyterian churches and the Muslim societies partially overlap with the strength of the Malawi Congress Party among Presbyterians in the Central Region and Muslim votes and the United Democratic Front in the Southern Region. In addition to the legislative constraints, there are also other reasons why civil society and parties are kept apart. Party politics does not have a high status in Malawi and the parties are among the least appreciated institutions. Civil society organizations are also very much dependent on international support for their programmes. It may therefore be more important for them to establish links to international donors than to political parties. Thus, rather than an alliance between parties and civil society being seen as indispensable, in many instances party and civil society representatives noted that the two compete for political terrain and international resources.[70]

Zambia

During the initial phases of NIMD's programme in Zambia, NIMD worked to support Zambian political parties through some central NGOs (Women for Change, FODEP, National Democratic Institute from the US). However, as noted by NIMD's own evaluation, 'Another important lesson was that we should restrict direct collaboration with NGOs to situations in which political parties indicate a well-defined and highly prioritized need'.[71] The report also acknowledged that the initial anticipation that NIMD's collaboration with civil society organizations would have spill-over effects into the political parties was unfounded. Rather it was suggested that NIMD should aim to play a role to improve the tense relationship between civil society and political parties in Zambia.

The new constitutional initiative that was taken by ZCID after the 2006 elections has pointed towards a conflict of interest between the political parties and civil society. In June 2007, ZCID initiated a summit of parliamentarian party presidents and the president of Zambia that was perceived as a success in terms of bringing the constitutional reform process forward by party representatives and international donors.[72] However, the reactions from civil society were mixed. The Oasis Forum that had led to the initiative on the constitutional reform process for many years did not endorse the initiative. The disagreements between civil society and the political parties relate to provisions in the constitution and also to the ownership or supremacy of the constitutional advising process in Zambia.[73] This conflict in part explains why the three main churches, Women for Change and the main umbrella organization for Zambian civil society organizations, NOCOC (Non-governmental Coordination Council), have opted to remain outside the National Constitutional Committee process (NCC). Popular Front (PF) is the only political party that has opted to stay outside NCC.

Civil society organizations argue that the NCC process has tilted its composition towards government agencies and that there are too many government agencies at the expense of civil society. As a result, the NCC process is boycotted by the Zambia Episcopal conference, the main catholic churches, the council of churches (protestant) and the evangelical fellowship in addition to NOCOC. The Oasis Forum in turn is very critical of the ZCID. In their turn the party representatives interviewed indicated that they regarded civil society as competitors both for public attention and funding. They also saw civil society and media as political actors and argued that civil society regarded political parties as competitors, and this explained their reluctance to take part in the NCC process.[74]

When looking at the model of party system development experiences in older democracies, political party–civil society relations are considered indispensable to the development of viable and institutionalized parties. The NIMD's framework also takes this linkage as a point of departure. As shown in its 2004 Annual Report, it is concerned with how better relations between civil society and parties can both improve the parties' capacity to channel citizens' demands and also improve the link that parties have with civil society.[75] NIMD is particularly concerned with the extent of communication, trust, and collaboration between the parties as distinct from promoting more formal organizational linkage like those between for instance unions and socialist parties in Europe. However, in poor and aid dependent polities such as Zambia and Malawi, collaboration like this is difficult to promote. Political parties are not highly trusted by civil society, and because civil society organizations themselves are often dependent on donors, they see themselves as competing with political parties for scarce resources.

The impact of international party support: lessons from Malawi and Zambia

In terms of the three key objectives – improving party dialogue as a way to strengthen the party system, strengthening individual parties and improving linkages between parties and civil society – NIMD's activities in both Zambia and Malawi seem to have greatest success in the area of inter-party dialogue. From somewhat different points of departure inter-party dialogue has progressed significantly and this should be considered a significant achievement in political systems characterized by limited trust between parties, as well as within parties. In both Malawi and Zambia the party representatives pointed to the role of NIMD and saw the involvement of NIMD as a key factor in the improved dialogue. Compared to NIMD's experiences in Malawi, arguably, the Zambia programme has progressed further since its initiation in 2004. The fact that the ZCID representative board is institutionalized to the extent that it has regular meetings with the same representatives (secretaries-general) signals a more conducive working relationship than the Malawi counterpart. Added to this, through the coordination task of the National Constitution Committee (NCC) ZCID and the Zambian parliamentary parties have acquired an important role in national politics which enhances inter-party dialogue and collaboration. In contrast, in Malawi CMD does not have an active role, nor plans any initiative in the country's constitutional review process.[76]

However, both country cases indicate that there are significant challenges for international party support. First of all, interviews with the political parties indicate a clear interest in – and preference for – bilateral support. This is the form of support that NIMD views the least effective for their overall ambitions as well as administratively the most cumbersome. Secondly, for somewhat different reasons the discussion shows that it will be challenging to enhance civil society–party relations through external funding modalities. It is not entirely clear what improvement of the linkage between parties and civil society means in practice. NIMD's goal is to strengthen communication between the two. But it may not be in the interest of civil society organizations to be perceived as being too close to a particular party. Civil society organizations often portray themselves as being concerned with 'development issues', not 'politics'. In contrast to civil society in established democracies, civil society organizations in African democracies are subject to more bureaucratic oversight.[77] Being too close to particular parties, particularly to opposition parties, may not be conducive to organizations that need permissions and funds distributed by the state. Furthermore, and clearly illustrated by the constitutional reform process in Zambia, civil society and political parties compete for attention, power and funds. The media and civil society are regarded as political players and players that potentially threaten the role of political parties. In Malawi, the civil society–party linkage objective is difficult to handle due to Malawian legislation and the weakness of civil society in Malawi. As in the Zambian case, civil society organizations, like the parties, are very dependent on international support for their programmes. It may therefore be more important for them to pursue their links to international donors than to political parties.

Overall, it cannot be argued that the Zambian or the Malawi party systems have become more institutionalized, nor have the major parties improved the procedures of selecting candidates. But it would be premature to draw a definite conclusion about the impact of NIMD's programme. The time period is simply too short to expect a clear link between the 'input' and the 'output'. But the potential for achieving the aims of organizational improvement is probably limited because of several factors: the overwhelming importance of the presidency combined with the first-past-the-post system is likely to spur further party fragmentation. We argue that the party system will continue to be unstable as long as the presidency is so powerful, combined with the need to attain only a simple plurality to win. Individual parties will also have problems moving towards a more institutionalized internal democracy. Although complete financial information about the parties is lacking, the financial influence and control exercised by a small group of leaders is also likely to restrict progress towards internal party democracy. The volume of financial support coming from the outside, such as that provided by NIMD, is probably too small to break this dependency on the leadership.

To what extent NIMD's experiences and impacts in Malawi and Zambia are different from or similar to other African democracies cannot fully be answered here. However, we should note that NIMD is engaged in other countries where the party systems have completely different trajectories than in the two cases examined here. Tanzania and Mozambique are examples of dominant party systems where the previous single-party regime has successfully continued its dominance, even after multi-party elections have been introduced.[78] Ghana represents another form of party development where most votes are captured by two parties, alternating in power, while Kenya is an example of a competitive party system but without the peaceful outcome of elections as in Ghana. The Centre for Multiparty Democracy in Kenya did make efforts to stem the violence in the post-2007 period, but to no avail. It is likely that it is primarily the national contexts that shape the party systems and the individual parties. Individual external actors like the NIMD can probably aid a process that has already been started and driven by national forces, but cannot change its direction.

Acknowledgements

Previous and more extensive versions of this manuscript have been presented at the Annual Meeting of the American Political Science Association, Toronto and the ECPR General Conference, Postdam, both in September 2009, and at the Norwegian Political Science Conference, Kristiansand in January 2010. We thank participants in those meetings for constructive comments, and in particular Jørgen Elklit, Elin Haugsgjerd-Allern and Elisabeth Bakke. We also thank staff at NIMD for making information available as well as for comments on a previous draft, and the director of the secretariat of CMD-M, Mr Kiziito and the director of the ZDIC Mr Chella Chombe.

Notes

1. Dalton and Wattenberg, 'Unthinkable Democracy'; Lipset, 'The Indispensability of Political Parties'.
2. Caton, *Effective Party Assistance*; Ihonvbere, 'Where Is the Third Wave?'; Monga, 'Eight Problems With African Politics'; Walle, 'Presidentialism and Clientelism'.
3. Lipset and Rokkan, 'Cleavage Structures, Party Systems and Voter Alignments'.

4. Duverger, *Political Parties*.
5. Schlesinger, *Political Parties and the Winning of Office*.
6. Nassmacher, *The Funding of Party Competition*.
7. To our knowledge only two other party supporting institutions have a long-term presence in these two countries: the Friedrich Ebert Foundation in Zambia and the Konrad Adenauer Foundation in Malawi.
8. The NIMD model is only one of several ways of organizing international party support, see Carothers, *Confronting the Weakest Link*.
9. Randall and Svåsand, 'Party Institutionalization in New Democracies'.
10. Dalton and Wattenberg, 'Unthinkable Democracy'.
11. Randall and Svåsand, 'Party Institutionalization in New Democracies'.
12. Dalton and Wattenberg, 'Unthinkable Democracy'; Lipset, 'The Indispensability of Political Parties'.
13. Carothers, *Confronting the Weakest Link*.
14. Rose and Shin, 'Democratization Backwards'.
15. Ihonvbere, 'Where is the Third Wave?'; Monga, 'Eight Problems with African Politics'.
16. UNDP, *A Handbook on Working with Political Parties*.
17. Carothers, *Assessing Democracy Assistance* and *Confronting the Weakest Link*; McGlinchey, *Aiding Political Parties*; McMahon, *The Impact of US Democracy and Governance Assistance*.
18. As for example when a US party assistance project in Kyrgyzstan attempted to promote women and youth within the parties (McGlinchey, *Aiding Political Parties*).
19. Doherty, 'Democracy Out of Balance'.
20. We have interviewed staff members of NIMD in The Hague involved in party assistance in the two countries, the administrative staff of the Malawian and Zambian centres for multi party democracy (CMD) and secretary generals of the major political parties. In addition we have had access to NIMD documents, such as annual reports, an evaluation report on NIMD in Zambia, and documents on CMD in the two countries.
21. NIMD, *Annual Report 2008*.
22. Ibid.
23. NIMD, *A Framework for Democratic Party-Building*.
24. Individual parties may apply to NIMD for direct financial support for specific projects, such as partial funding to arrange a national convention, or to print and distribute a party manifesto.
25. NIMD does not specifically define civil society, but mentions business associations, unions and the media (NIMD, *Annual Report 2004*).
26. Cornwall and Coelho, *Spaces for Change?*; Gill, *The Dynamics of Democratization*.
27. Rakner, Svåsand and Khembo, 'Fissions and Fusions'.
28. This is the case for the National Conservative Party (NCP), Republican Party (RP), National Democratic Alliance (NDA).
29. PPM (People Progressive Movement), PETRA (Peoples Transformation Party).
30. Rakner, *Political and Economic Liberalization in Zambia*.
31. Austin and Tjernstrom, *Funding of Political Parties and Election Campaign*.
32. Simutanyi, *One-party Dominance and Democracy in Zambia*.
33. NIMD, *Annual Report 2004*.
34. The attempt by Muluzi to lift the term limitations on election to the presidency.
35. NIMD, *Annual Report 2002*, 21.
36. NIMD, *Annual Report 2003*, 20.
37. This is confirmed in interviews with party officials in MCP (Malawi Congress Party), United Democratic Front (UDF) and in Democratic Progress Party (DPP). It is also the perception of the CMD secretariat that the parties have a positive view of the organization as a forum for discussion.

38. NIMD, *Annual Report 2007*, 33.
39. CMD, Minutes of the CMD Board Meeting Held at Club Makokola, 8 August 2009.
40. NIMD *Annual Report 2007*, 34.
41. One such example is the re-nomination of Muluzi as UDF presidential candidate for 2009, in spite of the likelihood that his candidature would be blocked by the Malawi Electoral Commission and by the courts – which is what actually happened. Muluzi also unilaterally decided that there would be no primary elections for incumbent MPs, in spite of an announcement by the party for the opposite. A second example is the post-election firing of the MCP's spokesperson Chafukira for arguing that the MCP party leader should resign following the severe defeat in 2009. In the incumbent party, DPP, all office holders have been appointed by the party president, and none were elected.
42. At the CMD board meeting of 29 March 2009 an item on the agenda was 'electoral violence'. It was agreed that CMD should follow up on a tripartite communiqué already signed by DPP, MCP and UDF on efforts to prevent electoral violence. Four steps, one of which was a conference on electoral violence, were agreed upon and the follow-ups should be operationalized within two weeks. At the board meeting of 8 August 2009 the executive director reported: 'The conference was meant to pre-empt this fear. However, things calmed down, violence was sporadic and not widespread' (Minutes, page 10).
43. Interview with UDF secretary general, 13 February 2010.
44. Rakner, *Political and Economic Liberalization in Zambia*.
45. Molenaers, *Evaluation Report*, 16.
46. Representation for parties without parliamentary seats is also being discussed in Malawi.
47. NIMD, *Annual Report 2004*, 50.
48. The objectives were: the development of a code of conduct for political parties in the run-up to the 2006 elections; dialogue on constitutional reforms and the electoral process; examine the issue of funding of political parties; improve the position of women, youth and disabled; build capacity and strengthen political parties; enhance civic education and the public image of political parties; build partnerships and strengthen regional cooperation.
49. Vliet, 'The Politics of Constitutional Reform Processes'.
50. Ibid.
51. Molenaers, *Evaluation Report*.
52. Interview, Chella Chombe (ZCID). This view was shared by the general secretaries of the seven main parties present at a meeting on 9 February 2009, including MMD's representative.
53. Molenaers, *Evaluation Report*.
54. Magolowondo and Svåsand, 'Political Parties'.
55. See the for instance the allegations from the now dismissed MCP treasurer, George Zulu, on lack of financial accountability in the MCP – including funds received from CMD-M. (*Nyasa Times*, 17 January 2010).
56. Svåsand, *Procedural Democracy*. See also acting UDF President Friday Anderson: 'The convention elected people in 2003 and only two people are holding those positions in their originality.... All other people were given those position by the National Executive Committee and National Working Committee'. (*Nyasa Times*, 30 December 2009).
57. Magolowondo and Svåsand, 'Political Parties'.
58. Ironically, the only party in which there is little conflict over nomination is the party with the four mantras: 'loyalty, unity, obedience, discipline', the MCP.

59. Rakner and Svåsand, 'From Dominant to Competitive Party System'. Before the extraordinary presidential election of 2008 there was no fragmentation of the party system, probably linked to the short time span and the absence of simultaneous parliamentary elections. When the two elections are held simultaneously there is a window of opportunity for building a 'national' party based on an alliance between aspiring parliamentary and presidential candidates.
60. NIMD, *Annual Report 2007*; Molenaers, *Evaluation Report*.
61. NIMD interviews, with Jasper Veen, Martin van Vliet and Alvaro Pinto Scholtbach, The Hague, 14 January 2009.
62. Interview with NIMD representatives, The Hague, 2009.
63. This issue was fiercely debated during a meeting of the ZCID board members on 9 February 2009. This perception is not shared by NIMD who in their annual reports (2005, 2006) claim that this decision is based on a joint initiative between Zambian party representatives and NIMD.
64. Molenaers, *Evaluation Report*, 22.
65. Rakner and Svåsand, 'From Dominant to Competitive Party System'.
66. Simutanyi, *One-party Dominance and Democracy in Zambia*.
67. Mwalubunju, 'Civil Society'.
68. NGO-Act, *Non-Governmental Organisations Bill*.
69. Ross, '"Worrisome Trends"'.
70. Perceptions gathered in interviews with civil society and party representatives during 2007–2009.
71. NIMD, *Annual Report 2003*, 42.
72. Vliet, 'The Politics of Constitutional Reform Processes'; Molnaers, *Evaluation Report*.
73. Vliet, 'The Politics of Constitutional Reform Processes'.
74. A main issue of contention is that civil society wants economic and social rights, and a bill of rights that may be judiciable. On the issue of appointing ministers from outside parliament, civil society disagrees with the political parties. This is an issue that is contested heavily by government, ministers and party leaders. Currently the cabinet is bloated: there are 24 cabinet ministers, and 48 vice cabinet ministers of a parliament of 158! The main reason why ministers are against outside appointments is that they consider a minister position an elevation, a first step toward a cabinet position.
75. NIMD, *A Framework for Democratic Party-Building*.
76. CMD board meeting minutes, 8 August 2009.
77. The NGO Act in Malawi requires all NGOs to be members of CONGOMA and failure to do so may exclude an NGO from public funding. Other examples are the recent NGO Act in Ethiopia which prohibits NGOs which receive international funding from engaging in political activities (NGO-Act, *Non-Governmental Organisations Bill*).
78. As of 2010 NIMD is also active in Uganda.

Bibliography

Austin. R., and M. Tjernstrom, eds. *Funding of Political Parties and Election Campaign*. Stockholm: International IDEA, 2003.
Carothers, T. *Assessing Democracy Assistance: The Case of Romania*. Washington, DC: Carnegie Endowment for International Peace, 1996.
Carothers, T. *Confronting the Weakest Link. Aiding Political Parties in New Democracies*. Washington, DC: Carnegie Endowment for International Peace, 2006.
Catón, M. *Effective Party Assistance. Stronger Parties for Better Democracy*. Stockholm: International IDEA, 2007.
Cornwall, A., and V.S.P. Coelho, eds. *Spaces for Change? The Politics of Participation in New Democratic Arenas*. London: Zed Books, 2007.
Dalton, R.J., and M.P. Wattenberg. 'Unthinkable Democracy. Political Change in Advanced Industrial Democracies', in *Parties Without Partisans. Political Change in Advanced Industrial Democracies*, ed. R. Dalton and M. Wattenberg, 3–18. Oxford: Oxford University Press, 2002.
Doherty, I. 'Democracy Out of Balance. Civil Society Can't Replace Political Parties'. *Policy Review* no. 106 (2001): 15–35.
Duverger, M., *Political Parties*. London: Methuen, 1967.
Gill, G. *The Dynamics of Democratization. Elites, Civil Society and the Transition Process*. London: Macmillan, 2000.
Ihonvbere, J.O. 'Where Is the Third Wave? A Critical Evaluation of Africa's Non-Transition to Democracy'. *Africa Today* 43, no. 4 (1996): 343–68.
Lipset, S.M. 'The Indispensability of Political Parties'. *Journal of Democracy* 11, no. 1 (2000): 48–55.
Lipset, S.M., and S. Rokkan. 'Cleavage Structures, Party Systems and Voter Alignments: An Introduction', in *Party Systems and Voter Alignments*, ed. S.M. Lipset and S. Rokkan, 1–64. New York: Free Press, 1967.
Magolowondo, A., and L. Svåsand. 'Political Parties in the 2009 General Elections', in *The 2009 Presidential and Parliamentary Elections in Malawi*, ed. M. Ott and E. Kanyongolo (forthcoming).
McGlinchey, E. *Aiding Political Parties in Central Asia and the Caucasus*. Chicago: International Studies Association, 2007.
McMahon, E.R. *The Impact of U.S. Democracy and Governance Assistance in Africa: Benin Case Study*. Boston, MA: American Political Science Association Meeting, 2002.
Molenaers, N. *Evaluation Report. NIMD-Programme in Zambia 2004–2007*. Antwerpen, Institute of Development Policy and Management, 2008.
Monga, C. 'Eight Problems with African Politics', in *Democratization in Africa*, ed. L. Diamond and M.F. Plattner, 48–62. Baltimore, MD: The Johns Hopkins University Press, 1999.
Mwalubunju, O. 'Civil Society', in *Government and Politics in Malawi*, ed. N. Patel and L. Svåsand, 267–96. Blantyre: Kachere Books, 2007.
Nassmacher, K.-H. *The Funding of Party Competition. Political Finance in 25 Democracies*. Baden-Baden: Nomos, 2009.
Non-Governmental Organisation (NGO)-Act. *Non-Governmental Organisations Bill, 2000* Lilongwe: Government of Malawi, 2000.
Netherlands Institute for Multi-party Democracy (NIMD). *Annual Report 2002*. The Hague: NIMD, 2002.
NIMD. *Annual Report 2003*. The Hague: NIMD, 2003.
NIMD. *A Framework for Democratic Party-Building*. The Hague: NIMD, 2004.
NIMD. *Annual Report 2004*. The Hague: NIMD, 2004.
NIMD. *Annual Report 2007*. The Hague: NIMD, 2007.
NIMD. *Annual Report 2008*. The Hague: NIMD, 2008.

Rakner, L. *Political and Economic Liberalization in Zambia 1991–2001*. Uppsala: Nordic Africa Institute, 2003.

Rakner, L., and L. Svåsand. 'From Dominant to Competitive Party System: The Zambian Experience 1991–2001'. *Party Politics* 10, no. 1 (2004): 49–68.

Rakner, L., L. Svåsand, and N.S. Khembo. 'Fissions and Fusions, Friends and Foes: Party System Restructuring in Malawi in the 2004 General Election'. *Comparative Political Studies* 40, no. 9 (2007): 1112–37.

Randall, V., and L. Svåsand, L. 'Party Institutionalization in New Democracies'. *Party Politics* 8, no. 1 (2002): 5–29.

Rose, R., and D.C. Shin. 'Democratization Backwards: The Problem of Third-Wave Democracies'. *British Journal of Political Science* 31, no. 2 (2001): 331–54.

Ross, K.R. '"Worrisome Trends": The Voice of the Churches in Malawi's Third Term Debate'. *African Affairs* 103 (2004): 91–107.

Schlesinger, J. *Political Parties and the Winning of Office*. Ann Arbor, MI: University of Michigan Press, 1991.

Simutanyi, N. *One-party Dominance and Democracy in Zambia*. FES Occasional Paper. Maputo: Friedrich Ebert Stiftung, 2009.

Svåsand, L. *Procedural Democracy in Malawian Political Parties*. Bergen: Dept. of Comparative Politics, University of Bergen, NUFU Programme on Democratic Consolidation in Malawi, 2008.

United Nations Development Programme (UNDP). *A Handbook on Working with Political Parties*. Oslo: UNDP Oslo, Governance Center, 2006, http://www.undp.org/oslocentre/overview/ogc_political_parties.html (accessed June, 2010).

Vliet, M. van. 'The Politics of Constitutional Reform Processes in Zambia', in *Writing Autobiographies of Nations. A Comparative Analysis of Constitutional Reform Processes*, R. Austin, C. Irahola, P. Lumumba, L. Narváez-Ricaurte, A. Sachs, and M. van-Vliet, 39–60. The Hague: NIMD Knowledge Centre, 2009.

Walle, N. van de. 'Presidentialism and Clientelism in Africa's Emerging Party Systems'. *Journal of Modern African Studies* 41, no. 2 (2003): 297–321.

Political party assistance and political party research: towards a closer encounter?

Gero Erdmann

GIGA German Institute of Global and Area Studies, Hamburg, Germany

Generally speaking the effects of international political party assistance are viewed negatively or at least controversially. This study attributes some of the shortcomings of political party aid to the poor relationship between assistance providers and political science party research. They simply operate in different worlds. Party assistance lacks clear-cut concepts and strategies in practice, which makes it difficult to evaluate it adequately. At issue is its 'standard method', with its 'transformative' intention to change the party organization of the assistance receivers. At the same time, the scholarship on political parties can provide only limited help to assistance providers due to its own conceptual and methodological restrictions, such as the Western European bias of its major concepts, the predominance of a functionalist approach, and the scant empirical research on political parties outside Europe and the US. Taking a cue from recent political party research, we could begin to question the overarching role of political parties in the transition and consolidation process of new democracies. Other research findings emphasize the co-existence of different types of party organizations, and the possibility of different organizational developments, which might all be consistent with consolidating democracy. All this suggests abandoning the controversial transformative aim of political party aid.

Introduction

Political party assistance and research on political party assistance are both very new topics. As a particular component of international democracy assistance, support for political parties was 'discovered' surprisingly late, after the assistance of civil society and democratic institutions. In the literature on democracy assistance the term 'political party assistance' was used by Thomas Carothers for the first time as a chapter heading only in 1999. His controversial critique of the 'transition paradigm' in democracy promotion in 2002 came along with a strong plea for political party assistance.[1] Despite the fact that it was generally agreed that political parties were 'indispensable' for democracy, and that some sort of international support for political parties took place before 1999, as a conceptual part in its own right political party assistance remained marginal and even controversial within the wider framework of democracy promotion.

The academic literature on political party assistance is even younger. Only since 2004 has the number of publications on the topic started to increase. Most of the publications were basic systematic explorations of the issues involved, such as: What is party assistance? Who are the major actors? What are their instruments, concepts and strategies?[2] However, as pointed out by Peter Burnell, the practitioners of party assistance and the established research on scholarship on political parties and party systems remained in two different worlds.[3] While some political scientists with an expertise in Western political parties and party systems were providing advice and background information to political party assistance agencies, the contacts are poorly documented and research on the topic was basically non-existent. Our knowledge of political party assistance and its effects was based initially on commissioned reports and evaluations of donor agencies, and on the insights of researchers collecting the evaluations. Only recently, as indicated by the contributions in this collection, has systematic research on political party assistance started that takes the findings of research on political parties in non-Western societies into account. In fact, some of the problems of political party aid-providers might be attributed to the advice they took from established political science research on political parties with its particular Western European bias. And again only recently, following Thomas Carothers' critique of international political party assistance as the 'weakest link'[4] and some paradoxical experiences and controversial results of the kind well illustrated in this collection, have some party assistance agencies started to consult political scientists with research experience on non-European political parties, in order to reconsider and possibly reshape their approaches.

This raises the question of what political science research on political parties can offer to political party assistance, in order to help solve its problems. Related to this question are a number of additional questions such as: What do we actually know about the functioning of non-Western European political parties. An example is the 'clientelistic parties'[5] that operate in non-industrialized societies in which the majority of the population often lives in poverty and with a very small middle class, whose professionals usually perform the role of organizers? What do we know about the institutional development of these parties? Is it possible to transform, for example, an 'ethnic congress party'[6] or a 'clientelistic party' into a traditional mass or a modern electoralist party, and how can that be achieved?

The issues involved in bringing international political party assistance and political party research closer together will be approached here in four main sections. The first section describes the major actors in international political party assistance and the problems they experience. The second section examines the extant research on political party assistance, which remains very limited in scope. The third section then explains the particular importance of political science research, focusing on its contribution to our understanding of the role of political parties in the transition from authoritarian rule and in the consolidation of democracy, while identifying a significant knowledge gap in existing research in our understanding of political parties and of political party systems in non-Western societies. Finally the main arguments are summarized in the conclusion. In attempting to explain the problems and failures of political party assistance, our contention is twofold. First, political party promoters lack sound policy strategies and do not have adequate evaluation policies. Secondly, it is problematic not only that practitioners and political scientists work in isolation from each other, but also that political science research currently lacks the appropriate systematic knowledge about political parties outside the Western world.

Promoters and policies

Promoters of political party assistance are, above all, political party foundations in Europe and the United States that are usually engaged in democracy assistance in general.[7] There are also a number of small foundations in various European countries that are exclusively engaged in political party assistance (not necessarily financial assistance), for example the Alfred Mozer Foundation in the Netherlands; since the late 1990s party assistance has furthermore been provided by some multilateral organizations such as the International Institute for Democracy and Electoral Assistance (IDEA), the Organization for Security and Co-operation in Europe (OSCE), and the United States Agency for International Development (USAID).[8] Most of the European foundations were formed only in reaction to the events in and around the German Democratic Republic in 1989. The same applies to the three US institutes that operate in the democracy assistance field. They started with political party aid only during the 1990s: the National Democratic Institute (NDI), the International Republican Institute (IRI) and the National Endowment for Democracy (NED). The first two receive funds from the NED as well as from the United States Agency for International Development (USAID), the US Department of State and other sources; the NED too calls itself a non-profit, non partisan, nongovernmental organization. It was founded as a result of an initiative by the US government during the presidency of Ronald Reagan and receives its funds from the government with the approval of the US Congress. The various organizations' experience with political party assistance is limited, because most of their activities started only in the early 1990s. Only the older German political foundations, well known for their close affiliation with German political parties and for their partisan approach, have experience in party assistance that spans over four decades. However, this particular knowledge has not been documented or analysed – it is lost.[9]

Closely related to this problem is that hardly any of the political party promoters operate with what can be called a proper concept or strategy. Many claim, of course, that they have one, but usually they cannot provide any written source for such a claim; or if they have an outline for their operations, then 'strategy' does not deserve the name[10] – that is, if the understanding is that a strategy should consist of a clearly defined goal, a reason why this goal has been chosen, clear instructions for target-oriented action, and, perhaps, what sort of action should be avoided. The absence of clearly articulated concepts and strategies also leads to a lack of criteria to evaluate the success or failure of the assistance – or it at least makes it difficult. At the same time, the writer's own conversations with practitioners suggests there is no total agreement on what political party assistance includes and what it excludes: for example, should the training of members of parliament be included under the umbrella of party assistance, given that most of them are members of political parties and the parliamentary caucus of the parties might benefit? Or is that rather part of the assistance to parliament as the legislative branch of government?

In general, political party assistance aims at political parties and party systems that stabilize, sustain and consolidate democracy; this may include supporting the efforts of political parties to democratize electoral authoritarian and hybrid regimes. Because political parties in young democracies and hybrid regimes are perceived as 'weak' and therefore rather 'dysfunctional' for democracy, the external assistance aims to change these parties into 'strong' parties which are 'functional' for (consolidating) democracy.[11] The aim of party assistance can also comprise a change in the party system, not only by changing the parties as parts of the system, but also changing how they interact with each other; hence a polarized party system, which might endanger democratic development, ought to be changed into a moderate competitive system in which parties interact in a less confrontational manner. Carothers has termed these envisaged changes the 'transformative impact' of party assistance.[12]

As 'outsiders', political scientists provided some order for the different approaches and methods applied by the various assistance agencies; and it is interesting to note that none of them has a strong background in traditional political party research. They suggested useful distinctions, for example, between 'party-to-party relations' (the 'partisan approach'), the 'multi-party approach', 'cross-party dialogue', the 'institutional approach', and international cross-party collaboration, to which I would add the 'civil society approach'.[13] Also, commentators like Carothers have made a distinction between the 'standard method', which targets political parties directly and includes some of the approaches just mentioned, and the wider 'party system aid' which addresses the institutional framework for the operation of political parties (electoral system, party law, party financing, and so on).[14] Most of the party assistance providers rely on a combination of approaches, not on one main approach as might be suspected in the case of the German foundations, which are often identified with the partisan approach. In fact, some of the German foundations started to refocus on political parties only over the last couple of years, while in the 1990s their focus was rather more on civil society than on political parties, and some do not even support political parties at all.[15]

At the same time, it remains unclear how much time and how many funds these agencies spend in support of political parties; political party assistance is – apart from organizations such as the Netherlands Institute for Multiparty Democracy (NIMD) – only one field within their wider framework of democracy assistance. For some of the German foundations, party assistance is estimated to be at most 25% of the 'efforts' of their overall international assistance; almost all agencies are unable to provide exact figures. They usually do not run specific budget lines for party assistance, as it is often integrated into other projects; hence, available figures are based on guesswork.[16]

The actual activities of party assistance providers are characterized by the following 'standard method', as Carothers put it:

> Organizations that implement party aid start by getting to know the parties in a new or struggling democracy, find that the parties do not conform to the ideas that the aid groups have about what constitutes a good political party, and design assistance programs to try to reshape them along those lines. This is done primarily by transferring knowledge through training on topics like party building or electoral campaigning. Although training efforts are diversifying over time, they have long relied on very conventional methods typified by the two or three-day workshop, seminar, or conference led by a few experts flown in from the sponsoring country. Other common party assistance tools include exchange visits and advice.[17]

In general there is also very little information available on which particular field and approach the party assistance is focused on within its own framework. A study by van Wersch and de Zeeuw on the major political European foundations provides some rough estimates.[18] These indicate that a variety of different issues are addressed, among which the strengthening of party organization figures prominently, covering one third of project expenditure (Table 1). For the implementation of the approaches, about 56% of the expenditure is spent on 'training', 14%, on 'advice and technical assistance', 12% on 'seminars and conferences', and about 18% on a variety of other, unspecified activities.[19] These general figures suggest that if the support for party organization, the participation of women, and the political parties in parliament are taken together, a major push towards institutional

Table 1. Types of political party assistance.

Strengthening of	%
Party organization	33
Electoral campaigning	15
Women's participation	12
Parliamentary role of parties	11
Party system	9
Party poll watchers/electoral staff	8
Others	12

Source: Van Wersch and de Zeeuw, 'Mapping European Democracy Assistance', 16.

assistance or what might be termed as 'institutionalizing political parties' can be identified. However, this is no more than a rough speculation, because we do not have solid knowledge about the exact figures, attributions, and aims of the particular projects and programmes; also, the categories used for the analysis are very broad – for example, party programmes and the party–society linkage are not mentioned.

The knowledge we have about political party assistance is not based on systematic political science research projects. Such knowledge is only slowly being compiled, as in the collection of which this study is a part, but even here the provision of hard statistical data is only patchy. Most of the evaluation reports and commissioned studies of assistance agencies are not available to the public. Our knowledge is largely based on critical assessments of political scientists who were in one way or the other involved in the evaluation or implementation of political party assistance projects, or were conducting their own small research projects.[20] From these studies a number of conceptual and practical problems of political party assistance can be summarized:

- The assistance guidelines and policies are based on a Northern European party model – regardless of whether the assistance agency is in the US or in Europe.
- This is a 'mythic model', as Thomas Carothers has termed it, because it is the out-of-date model of the mass party of the first half of the twentieth century in Western Europe. It is not only outdated, but reflects only in parts the bygone reality of political parties in European democracies; it is remarkable that US agencies apply this model as well, although they have a different tradition and reality today.
- Applying the mass party model implies also that party assistance is based on a particular model of party sequences, which is derived from the historical development of political parties in industrialized Western Europe – from the elite to the mass party, to the catch-all, electoral-professional, cartel and, perhaps, to the evolution of new movement parties. However, this particular sequencing cannot be expected to occur in other parts of the world in the same way as already indicated by the example of the US.
- The overall implication is that political party assistance comes with a concept that has very little or even nothing to do with the societal context in which it is supposed to function.

Consequently, there are a number of practical weaknesses in the implementation of party assistance, summarized by Carothers as stale techniques of institutional modelling[21]:

- Too short and ill-conceived training workshops isolated from day-to-day concerns of the participants.
- Frequently ill-chosen participants with no real interest in the training (cronies of party leaders).

- 'Fly-in' experts (political consultants, parliamentarians or professors) without substantial knowledge of the local context.
- Workshop topics chosen by aid providers, reflecting rather 'Western' instead of local needs.
- Repetitive training programmes without deepening the subject.

Noting the conceptual and practical shortcomings of political party assistance, it is surprising that the evaluation of its effects does not come to negative conclusions only. For assistance providers are usually convinced that their work has a positive impact. Independent observers share a more critical assessment. Carothers sees hardly any evidence for 'transformative effects', while others observe modest, marginal or mixed effects at best.[22] Based on the evaluation of USAID party assistance in Middle and Eastern Europe, Krishna Kumar found positive effects in organizational development, but poor results regarding the role of parties in parliament.[23]

Carothers' critique addressed the heart of the problem: political party assistance aims –although not explicitly stated, but implicitly it is quite clear– at an institutional transformation of political parties which do not show the characteristics of the mythic mass party model. He observed what is difficult to disprove: that after years or even a decade of party assistance, the political parties in the post-communist and non-European world still show the same deficits as before – deficits that were perceived as the cause for party assistance. He also refers to the ongoing crisis of political parties in Latin America. The party assistance from German political foundations during the 1970s and 1980s seemed unable to prevent it.[24] This critical assessment could be judged overdone, based on criteria that are unjustified and too demanding, and one could argue that political party assistance was, in terms of funds, too marginal. However, such a refutation of the critique cannot deny a major shortcoming of political party assistance, which is that it provides no strategic goals that might serve as criteria for a more appropriate assessment of its impact. This brings us to the question of what political science can offer for a better assessment and design of political party assistance.

Research on political party assistance

As indicated above, political party assistance is a new agenda and political science research on the topic is scant. Even within the wider agenda of democracy promotion, party assistance remained 'marginal, or...too invisible' to be the subject of controversy.[25] There are basically no publications or publicly accessible works that date back beyond 2004,[26] while a few older publications on democracy promotion made just cursory references to party assistance.[27] There are and were, of course, a few political scientists involved as experts in political party assistance, as far back as the 1970s and 1980s, but although involved in giving advice and training they did not conduct any research on the topic, which was unknown as a field of its own in development assistance until the turn of the twenty-first century. As mentioned in the introduction the literature on the topic has been little more than a systematic stock-taking of the new field. One reason for this state of affairs is that until recently there has been only a handful of political scientists interested in this particular and marginal field, and it was not their only or major academic concern. At the same time, none of them had a background in the established political science sub-discipline of party research, although a few had research experience with non-European political parties. Hence, our accumulated body of knowledge about political party assistance is small. Even what we seem to know about political party assistance is very general and undiscriminating and not based on systematic empirical research but rather on 'thick' empirical experience and evidence from a few selected cases. Carothers in his *Confronting the Weakest Link* draws on much more than most: his cases are drawn from several countries in Latin America, Africa, Europe and Asia, and range from Morocco to Guatemala, and from Russia to Mozambique. Even the cases discussed in this collection of studies comprise but a small fraction of the total number that could be investigated.

Although the lack of research is clearly a major reason for this unsatisfactory state of affairs, three further points can be made. One is the general causation or attribution problem in political science. It is generally difficult to relate particular provisions of democracy assistance to specific effects within a political system; external democracy promotion is only one factor among many others within a system that might contribute to changes in the political system. To 'measure' the impact of external democracy assistance on democratization processes has proven an extremely difficult undertaking. Secondly, some of the difficulties spring also from the fact that there is usually not one 'homogeneous' external actor, but a multitude of them, whose actions can even contradict each other. Moreover, political party assistance is usually only one component of democracy assistance, a marginal one, and the local political parties are, again, only *one* internal factor that impacts on political development. This indicates the magnitude of the challenge to identify beyond plausible guesswork the effects of political party assistance.

Apart from this general observation related to political science research, there are two other issues for which the assistance agencies are responsible. One is that the assistance agencies have commissioned only a limited number of studies and evaluation reports on political party assistance; the numbers are increasing now but the 'evaluation culture' has long been underdeveloped in this particular field of democracy assistance.[28] The other reason rests in the lack of clear, conceptual and strategic orientation of party assistance, which in turn leads to a lack of success or impact criteria. The same usually applies to the terms of reference, which are often too general to allow for a plausible estimate of causes and effects.[29] The many small 'items' of party assistance – training workshops, seminars, exchange visits, and so on – make an impact analysis even more difficult, if not impossible. The problems can be summed up by saying that evaluating the performance of party assistance is probably inherently difficult, because of the various conceptual and methodological issues, and because too little attention has been devoted to addressing these issues as they apply to the study of party assistance.

Political party research

The question of what the scholarship on political parties and party systems can offer to international party assistance has closely related theoretical, conceptual and empirical dimensions. The two issues to be addressed are: (1) the role of political parties in the transition process and the consolidation of democracy, and (2) the lack of an empirical overview of our knowledge on political parties, their organization and organizational development, as well as on political party systems outside Western Europe (we know relatively more about parties in Eastern Europe and Latin America than in much of Africa and Asia).

Controversial roles

According to the literature on political parties and on democratization, political parties play a key role in democratization and in the democratic polity; a role that no other institution can perform. Bartolini and Mair emphasize the integration of various institutional orders and political processes and identify five core processes: (1) the electoral process, (2) the channelling of organized or corporate interests, (3) the legislative process in parliament, (4) the formation of the executive, and (5) policy-making. Other scholars have identified more functions, but these five can be considered to be the 'core' functions acknowledged by most scholars.[30] The crucial point here is that the core processes are not only attributed to political parties in functioning democratic polities but also to parties in the process of democratization and democratic consolidation. The implication is that while political parties and party systems are not institutionalized and consolidated themselves, they are expected – theoretically – to perform a crucial additional role or 'service': to be the driving force for the consolidation of other partial regimes of democracy or at least for the 'systemic integration' of a 'wide-ranging set of institutions and processes'.[31]

This proposition about the overarching role of political parties in consolidating democratic polities can be questioned from two angles, one theoretical and one empirical. First, can we expect political parties within young democracies to not only drive the institutionalization of themselves, but also the consolidation of the party system, and to contribute to the consolidation of other partial regimes even when they are weak and lack institutionalization themselves? Under authoritarian rule, political parties usually suffer just like other organizations and institutions and either have to 'rebuild' or completely reorganize during and after democratization; at the same time, some of the former 'state parties' might have survived the transition to democracy and proceeded to act in ways that are unhelpful to further democratic advance. The role-ascription of the overall consolidating function of political parties seems to be related to well-developed and functionally differentiated (social democratic) 'super parties' of established democracies of Western and Northern Europe, where these 'super parties' already perform all the core functions in one measure or another. But this ascription could be too ambitious and misleading.

In fact, the claim that political parties play the crucial role in the consolidation of democracy has been challenged by Philippe Schmitter,[32] who argues his point using evidence from Eastern Europe and Latin America. In both these contexts, he finds consolidated democracies with weakly institutionalized parties and party systems which also exhibit a very high degree of volatility. The empirical evidence about the parties and party systems, particularly for Eastern Europe, has been largely confirmed by other scholars.[33] They, however, differ about the state of the democracy: some qualify the Eastern European democracies as 'consolidated',[34] others argue that because there are 'floating' (not institutionalized, highly volatile) party systems, the democracies cannot be viewed as consolidated.[35] Meanwhile, Schmitter's view on the Latin American cases as consolidated democracies has been challenged; some are regarded as 'delegative democracies' and a few even as having become authoritarian regimes – and apart from the Chilean democracy, all the other cases are linked to weak political parties and even collapsed party systems, as in Venezuela and Peru.[36] Beyond this debate about the third wave democracies, there are cases of old democracies, too, such as the US and India, which suggest that consolidating democracy is possible with something other than the Western European 'super parties' and party systems.

Regardless of which argument one follows about the state of democracy, the role of political parties and party systems in the process of democratization and consolidation remains a puzzle for scholars. It underscores the question above about whether young political parties and party systems can perform the overall consolidating function for democracy. To raise this question is not to say that political parties can be neglected or that they do not play a role; political parties and party systems certainly contribute to the consolidation of democracy, but their importance might have been overestimated, and the issue should be addressed in more specific terms. For example, there might be a 'minimum' or particular degree of party or party system consolidation required, and, perhaps, only a small or core number of political parties are necessary; or a particular type of political parties might be important for providing the overall consolidating performance; or the consolidating effects of parties and party systems might be dependent on a specific combination or interplay with other institutions – for example, a well-organized and articulated civil society. All in all political party scholarship currently cannot provide a satisfying and empirically based answer to the question of what the role of political parties is, or what their most effective pattern is along with other institutions for democratization and consolidation. In general, it cannot be expected that the political parties that emerged during the third wave of democratization within a societal context different from that of Western Europe will develop the same features and capacities as in the history of old democracies.

Before turning to the accumulated knowledge on political parties, two further issues must be addressed. One is the Western European bias, the other the dominant functionalist approach in political party research. Neither is a moot point, but rather they are closely related to political party assistance approaches – for example, to the choice of the 'mythic' reference model mentioned above, which directly affects the aims and designs of assistance approaches. Only more recently has the established scholarly literature of political party research acknowledged that it takes its terms of reference and models primarily from Western European historical experience, in short that its concepts are determined by a Western European bias.[37] For example, the traditional inventory of political party types, most of which are related to a particular era, comprised the 'elite party' of the nineteenth century; the 'mass party' or 'cadre party' dated from the late nineteenth century up to the 1960s. Finally there is the 'catch-all party', which emerged after World War II, and the 'cartel' and the 'electoral-professional parties' or 'cadre parties' that have been developing since the 1970s.[38]

After the experience of political parties and party systems which evolved during the third wave of democratization, especially in Southern and Eastern Europe, the conceptual limitations changed.[39] For example, a whole range of new party types were 'invented' by Richard Gunther and Larry Diamond, who explicitly aimed to classify political parties in Africa, Asia, Eastern Europe, and Latin America and include them in the established repertoire.[40] With the traditional Western European party types it was not possible to capture the different features of political parties in other parts of the world. Gunther and Diamond's proposal is a most ambitious one, and it deals with different dimensions of party life – for example with 'thin' and 'thick' organizations. In fact, altogether, they cover a time span back to the nineteenth century and categorize five 'genera' of party types – elite-, mass-, ethnicity-based parties, and electoralist and movement parties – which are comprised of 15 subtypes or 'species' of parties.[41]

Interwoven with this conceptual issue is a methodological one. Political party scholarship is largely dominated by functionalist analysis.[42] The functionalist approach is indispensable in political party research, but it has its own particular research questions and perspectives which do not seem to be very helpful for determining the requirements of political party assistance. Functionalist analysis does not seek to explain 'why' something happens or comes into being and 'how' it develops and changes – these are historical questions. With the help of the functionalist approach, we can establish whether a particular party and party system is 'functioning' or not as a maintainer and consolidator of the democratic polity. The reference frame of what is functioning or not is provided by the 'standard' party models, which were designed using Western Europe as a basis: this means there should be well-organized party structures with strong societal linkages that also provide clear ideological or programmatic profiles without being polarized. So we end up with a comparison that results in deciding whether a party or party system in Africa, Asia or Latin America conforms to these models. The conclusion is that a party or party system is – in most cases – dysfunctional. However, the perspective on what is functional and dysfunctional is narrowed down to the specifications of these models and tends to exclude other possible patterns of functionality for democracy; at least theoretically, we should not exclude others. This issue has been highlighted by the puzzle with the 'unconsolidated' party system and the consolidation of democracy seen in Eastern Europe.

The problem with the functionalist analysis is not only related to the bias of its models, but it is also not very interested in the historical evolution of particular types of parties and how they are reproduced. Yet, historical-institutionalist analyses of party and party system development, which could provide some insight, are scant, apart from a few notable exceptions. And even within these exceptions some focus on very broad societal issues and party systems rather than on single party development and change.[43]

Concluding the theoretical and conceptual discussion, the specific Western bias, along with the functionalist approach, makes it difficult to reach a differentiated understanding of how non-European political parties operate. And that the functionalist perspective is also prevalent in political party assistance is evidenced by the application of the mythic party model in the various background papers in which questions about party development and about the genesis of a particular party type are not discussed.[44]

Unknown political parties

With the third wave of democratization, and particularly after 1989, the interest of political party research shifted to Eastern European and non-European areas. As indicated above, this shift had some impact on the conceptual discussions within the sub-discipline. However, the new knowledge that emerged on the basis of systematic empirical studies is unevenly distributed and ambivalent. Among the different research areas, Eastern Europe and Latin America both figure rather prominently compared to research on political parties in Africa and Asia, which is more scant. Moreover, the systematic interest, and with that our accumulated knowledge, focused much more on party systems (rather than on party organization); how the various types develop; and how parties link up with society and perform in parliament, which relates to the core functions of political parties.[45] To make it quite clear: there is almost no empirical research on party organizations outside Europe.

Nevertheless, there seems to be a general understanding about some particular characteristics of political parties that emerged in hybrid and democratic regimes during the third wave, especially outside Europe: weak organizational structures; weak institutionalization, lack of linkages with society; lack of inner-party democracy; little ideological or programmatic differences between the parties; dominance of informal, personalistic and clientelistic relationships; and high electoral volatility. Three points should be noted however:

- First, this list is based on more or less casual observations, not on systematic empirical research, and most scholars, experts and party assistance providers working on African, Asian or Latin American parties – and probably those working on Eastern European parties as well – would concur.
- Secondly, most of these observations describe deficits or 'dysfunctions' related to the established model of the 'mythic' party. Only the references

to the 'informal relationships' provide a general hint of how these parties might operate in practice.
- Thirdly, most of the deficits relate to two of the three crucial facets or 'faces' of political parties: (a) the organizational structure and (b) the linkages into society, while (c) the party in parliament (and government) seems not to be that problematic.[46]

The three party 'faces' are also of major concern for political party assistance, hence the issue is crucial for this discussion.

The established scholarship about the party organization as a bureaucratic structure, its development and change is not yet very elaborated and differentiated. It has not been taken beyond the issues discussed by Maurice Duverger, Leon Epstein and Angelo Panebianco.[47] What can be drawn from Duverger's and Epstein's scholarship is the distinction of two or three basic organization models, which are the organization 'thick' – the branch-based, mass membership – party; the 'thin' – the decentralized, cadre-based caucus – party; and a hybrid model which combines elements of the branch and the caucus models. With different historical backgrounds in Europe and the US respectively, Duverger in his *Political Parties* (1995) and Epstein in his *Political Parties in Western Democracies* (1967) both explain the development and change of these party organization models by referring to the electoral competition for votes and either a 'contagion' of the 'left' (Duverger for Europe) or the 'right' (Epstein for the US).[48] As Alan Ware has pointed out, however, their causal models do not survive an empirical test.[49] Moreover, Ware goes on to point out that the once-different party organizations do not necessarily converge and become the dominant form for the future as Duverger and Epstein assumed, but instead may continue to coexist and even be re-invented at a time when the caucus model appears not to have survived. The timelessness of the two models and explanations of their change might also indicate that the categorizations are too parsimonious.

Panebianco's institutional approach, more limited because of its narrow focus on Western Europe only, but at the same time more sophisticated than the two previous approaches, does not provide a useful alternative. He includes in his 'genetic' party model the organizational origins of the parties under analysis such as 'territorial penetration' and 'diffusion', the existence of external 'sponsors', and the involvement of a charismatic leader; the different origins are then linked to different patterns of institutionalization which implies the 'degree of autonomy' in relation to its environment and the 'degree of systemness'.[50] Again, this institutional approach provides a more sophisticated framework for understanding the organizational development of parties, but according to Ware seems to fail in its empirical analysis even for some of the Western European cases.[51]

The discussion of the approaches for the analysis of the organizational structure of political parties, what the types of organization are, and why and how they change, illustrates that the whole issue is still highly controversial and at the same time under-researched. This applies not only to European parties, but actually even more so to non-European political parties. Despite this gap in knowledge, three conclusions seem to be important: first, at the same point in time and within one party system 'a wide variety of party organizations' can exist; secondly, there is no 'uniform direction of change' across countries; and thirdly, the general explanation for this phenomenon is that organizational weaknesses as well as the 'reforms they initiate' differ from party to party.[52]

Regarding the knowledge generated by political party research, we can conclude several points that are relevant for political party assistance. First of all, there is – apart from some generalized observation of deficits and dysfunctions – little systematic empirical knowledge about the various new types of political parties that emerged during the third wave of democratization outside Europe. This ignorance applies in particular to political parties in terms of how they organize (type of organization), how they operate, and why and how they develop and change over time.

Secondly, the organizations of these parties are different from those of the mass or professional electoral parties of industrialized or post-industrialized societies. It is very likely that Bartolini and Mair's cautious suggestion will be true, especially for non-European societies – that is, these parties will vary 'according to the circumstances of their initial formation and development'.[53] This might entail that these parties may not perform all the functions or will perhaps perform them in a different way than the ways ascribed to the classical functions of political parties by the mainstream political party scholarship. In addition, parties in new and emerging democracies might perform different political functions from those mentioned in the standard list, some of which might have an indirect effect on the consolidation of democracy, for example, on social and national integration.

Thirdly, the established sequencing of different party eras might suggest not only a fixed historical development pattern based on the Western European experience (elite, mass, catch-all, etc.), but also that there was one particular party type during each era. However, nothing could be more misleading. Apart from the dominant type of an era, there have always been different political party types at the same time and most often even within the same party system. For example in Germany, just as in many other Western European countries, the branch- and mass-based social democratic party co-existed from the late nineteenth century with various elite-based and caucus-structured liberal parties up until the *Freie Demokratische Partei* (FDP) of the 1970s. For another example, nowadays in Tanzania, the branch-based, catch-all ruling party, *Chama Cha Mapinduza* (CCM) exists along with a small (probably) religious-cum-region-based party, the *Chama Cha Wananchi* (CUF), and a clientelistic (perhaps even ethnic) party, the United Democratic Party (UDF). It can therefore be safely assumed and also observed that this kind of variation applies to political parties and party systems in young democracies and hybrid regimes inside and outside Europe as well. So we might have small ethnic parties next to parties which resemble the catch-all type, and the same party system might include a religious party as well.

To phrase the challenge differently, we have little knowledge about how an ethnic congress party or a clientelistic party organize (they might have different organizational structures even within one 'general' type), how they are rooted in society, how they perform in parliament, and how they develop and change over time. The last in particular is of major importance for political party assistance, because we do not know, for example, whether an ethnic congress party can be developed into something that resembles the mass- or catch-all party, or conversely whether its fate will be to split into a number of pure ethnic parties each based largely on one ethnic group and destined to become more ethnically radicalized. Moreover, with the impact of modern mass media the development of an ethnic congress or a religious-based party into a 'professional-electoralist' party is a real possibility; for example, this seems to be the trend of the Indonesian *Partai Amanat Nasional* (PAN) or *Partai Kebangkitan Bangsa* (PKB) in recent years.

At the same time, one should not forget what the era-model of the European party development tells us as well: the development and change from one party type dominating one era to the party type dominating a different era seems not to be a short-term process. Instead it is a long-term process that might unfold over an entire decade or perhaps even several decades. Furthermore, the parties themselves might have helped shape this movement and bear some responsibility for the outcome. These processes of change are usually linked to profound socio-economic and political developments that have affected the electorate and to which political parties have reacted in different ways. The change or transformation of political parties was the outcome of at least one of two different approaches; it was related either to (1) a reform process consciously directed by the party leadership (for example, the German conservative party during the late nineteenth century organizing a mass base linkage through the Agrarian League (*Bund der Landwirte*) and the Christian Democratic Union (CDU) in the early 1970s organizing an enlarged and stronger membership), or to (2) a piecemeal process of various, more or less erratic adaptation policies, for which there are many examples, for instance during the transformation from the era of the ideologically committed mass- to the catch-all and professional-electoralist party type.

Conclusion

Political parties are difficult partners for assistance providers, as Peter Burnell and André Gerrits have pointed out in the opening contribution to this collection.[54] They identify three major reasons for the limited success of international party assistance: first, the 'specific method of party aid'; secondly, the 'unfriendly political environment'; and thirdly, the strong local 'ownership' of political parties that makes external influence so difficult. These are valid points but as an explanation they do not go far enough. I would argue that the lack of clear concepts of and strategies for international party assistance are contributory factors that cannot be ignored. An adequate strategy needs to take into account the particularities of the object it is aiming at, and to include these particularities into the strategic design. It might sound paradoxical, but larger political parties represented in parliament are usually much more independent from external assistance and influence than the government of the country they are operating in. This is simply because 'official' external party assistance (apart from perhaps in the case of some Eastern European countries) is often marginal compared to parties' income from private sources. These private sources can be local 'well-wishers', international corporations, or other countries' governments involved in offering 'unofficial', direct party-funding.[55] Hence, the parties can ignore the 'pressure' or possibility of conditional support of assistance providers – which might differ quite markedly from their own country's government which does have to concede to donor demands because its budget is often dependent on major official aid contributions. The implication of this observation deserves more detailed analysis and discussion. The many practical shortcomings of the party assistance programmes, described as the 'standard method',[56] are the side-effects of having goals that are rather vague, which connects with the lack of clear concepts and feeds into weak strategies. As such, one has to draw the conclusion that these weaknesses are partly to blame for the fact that international political party assistance is not always successful and in some cases even fails.

Another contributory factor to the problems in party aid is the lack of collaboration between political scientists and practitioners. However, as outlined above, established political party scholarship has its own theoretical and conceptual shortcomings, which make giving profound advice to aid providers difficult. One issue is the controversial view on the role played by political parties in democratization and consolidation processes, and particularly that their contribution might have been overestimated. The other major issue is the lack of systematic empirical knowledge on the type of political parties outside Europe, how they operate and organize, and how and why they develop and change. This requires not only modified concepts, but also, above all, the accumulation of additional knowledge through empirical research, which takes time. Regarding the issues here, the dominant functional approach of political party research should be complemented by historical-institutional analyses in order to get a better understanding of party development.

Despite the comparatively 'weak' scholarship on the organization of political parties outside Europe, the discussion of problematic issues within the current scholarship on political parties has revealed some insights. First, the mythic party model should be abandoned; apart from it being unrealistic to assume that this model could emerge in other parts of the world in the same way as it has in Europe, the major point is that democracy is possible with other types of political parties as well. Secondly, often different political party types operate next to each other in the same party system; they pose different organizational challenges to assistance providers and therefore require different strategies or approaches. So not only does each country with its own party system as a whole require a special approach, but each party probably requires such an approach as well, depending on its organizational structure and on views about what would constitute improvement – views that may differ somewhat between the providers of party assistance, the party leaders, and political analysts in academia.

Finally, the brief references to the historical development of political party types in Western Europe have suggested another crucial insight: political party development is related to and probably conditioned by broader and deeper societal change and usually takes place over a period of one, two or three decades. However, my impression is that political party aid providers tend not to conceive their programmes and projects with perspectives as long as these. Indeed, the magnitude of such an organizational transformation of political parties should cause us to discuss more frankly the strategic goals of political party assistance. The result might include deciding to abandon the 'transformative' aim, replacing it with less ambitious strategic goals that are clearly defined, more likely to be achieved, and whose effects can be more easily appraised. The relative autonomy of political parties from external influence should be a major component in such a reassessment.

Acknowledgements

I would like to thank the two editors of this collection for their very helpful and stimulating comments, which have helped me to improve this contribution; for all remaining flaws I alone am responsible.

Notes

1. Carothers, *Aiding Democracy Abroad*; Carothers, 'The End of the Transition Paradigm'.
2. An example is Burnell, *Building Better Democracies*.
3. Burnell, 'Party Development and Party Aid'.
4. Carothers, *Confronting the Weakest Link*.
5. A clientelistic party is formed by a group of ('modern' or 'traditional') notables each with its own personalistically-based support built on loyalty and linked with the direct exchange of services and material benefits; Gunther and Diamond, 'Types and Functions', 14–5; Kitschelt, 'Formation of Party Cleavages'; Kitschelt et al., *Post Communist Party Systems*, 47–53.
6. An ethnic congress party is formed by an elite coalition of distinct ethnic groups; it is different from an ethnic party, which is based predominantly on one ethnic group only; Gunther and Diamond, 'Types and Functions', 22–5.
7. See for example Carothers, *Confronting the Weakest Link*; and Van Wersch and de Zeeuw, 'Mapping European Democracy Assistance'.
8. A full list is provided by Van Wersch and de Zeeuw, 'Mapping European Democracy Assistance', 39.
9. Erdmann, 'Hesitant Bedfellows', 197–8.
10. Erdmann, 'Hesitant Bedfellows'; Carothers, *Confronting the Weakest Link*.
11. On the concept of hybrid regimes see Karl, 'The Hybrid Regimes'; the conceptual discussion in Bendel, Croissant, and Hüb, *Hybride Regime*; Diamond, 'Thinking about Hybrid Regimes'; see also the contribution by Bolleyer and Storm ('Problems of Party Assistance in Hybrid Regimes: The Case of Morocco') in this collection.
12. Carothers, *Confronting the Weakest Link*, 163.

13. Burnell, *Building Better Democracies*, 9–15; the civil society approach means support for particular civil society organizations which are close to political parties, such as trade unions that are often affiliated with social democratic parties.
14. Carothers, *International Assistance*.
15. Erdmann, 'Hesitant Bedfellows', 188–9.
16. Van Wersch and de Zeeuw, 'Mapping European Democracy Assistance', 13–15; Erdmann, 'Hesitant Bedfellows', 191–2. Different information is available: while Van Wersch and de Zeeuw estimate that the European political foundations spent about 72% of their budget on political party assistance, the German political foundations, which have by far the biggest budget, told me that they were unable to specify the 'political party budget'; they preferred to talk about 'efforts' they directed at parties.
17. Carothers, *International Assistance*, 7.
18. Van Wersch and de Zeeuw, 'Mapping European Democracy Assistance'.
19. Ibid., 16.
20. For example ibid.; Burnell, 'Party Development and Party Aid'; Carothers, *Confronting the Weakest Link*; Kumar, 'International Political Party Assistance'; Kumar, 'Reflections'; Erdmann, 'Hesitant Bedfellows'; Mair, 'Germany's Stiftungen'; Mair, *Parlamentskooperation*.
21. See Carothers, *Confronting the Weakest Link*, especially 120–7.
22. Ibid.; Burnell, 'Looking to the Future', 200–1; Erdmann, 'Hesitant Bedfellows'; Kumar, 'Reflections', 508–11; Mair, *Parlamentskooperation*.
23. Kumar, 'International Political Party Assistance'.
24. Carothers, *Confronting the Weakest Link*, 164–5.
25. Burnell, 'Party Development', 5.
26. Burnell, 'Promoting Parties and Party Systems'; Burnell, *Building Better Democracies*; Burnell, 'Party Development and Party Aid'; Burnell, 'Political Parties, International Party Assistance'; Burnell, 'Globalising Party Politics'; Carothers, 'Political Party Aid'; Carothers, 'Examining International Political Party Aid'; Carothers, *Confronting the Weakest Link*; Erdmann, 'Hesitant Bedfellows'; Kumar, 'Reflections'; Kumar, 'International Political Party Assistance'; Van Wersch and de Zeeuw, 'Europe in Democracy Assistance'; Van Wersch and de Zeeuw, 'Mapping European Democracy Assistance'.
27. Carothers, *Assessing Democracy Assistance*, for example devoted around 10 pages to party assistance in Romania.
28. Carothers, 'Political Party Aid', 169; this observation can be confirmed for the German political foundations.
29. See for example Mair, *Parlamentskooperation*, iii.
30. Bartolini and Mair, 'Challenges to Contemporary Political Parties', 339; for example, Schmitter identifies four core 'functions': structuring electoral competition, providing symbolic identity, forming governments, aggregating interests and passions (Schmitter, 'Critical Reflections', 479–91; Schmitter, 'Parties Are Not What They Once Were', 72–3; he also mentions a number of other 'functions' parties can perform).
31. Bartolini and Mair, 'Challenges to Contemporary Political Parties', 339; Merkel, 'Einleitung', 13; Biezen, *Political Parties*, 6.
32. Schmitter, 'Critical Reflections'; Schmitter, 'Parties Are Not What They Once Were'.
33. For example Ágh, 'East-Central Europe'.
34. Merkel, *Systemtransformation*, 418.
35. Rose and Munro, *Parties and Elections*, 47–57.
36. Merkel, *Systemtransformation*, 254–9.
37. Bartolini and Mair, 'Challenges to Contemporary Political Parties', 338; Kitschelt, 'Formation of Party Cleavages'; Kitschelt, 'Divergent Paths'; see also Erdmann, 'Party Research: Western European Bias'.

38. Katz and Mair, 'The Evolution of Party Organizations in Europe'; Panebianco, *Political Parties*. There are, of course, many other typologies as well; this one seems to be the most heavily acknowledged one.
39. It is interesting to note that an article 'Approaches to the Study of Parties and Party Organization in Contemporary Democracies', based on a paper presented at a prominent conference on political parties in 1994, but published only in 2002, did not even discuss problems related to political parties and party types outside the northern hemisphere; see Wolinetz, 'Approaches'.
40. Gunther and Diamond, 'Types and Functions', 9–30.
41. Gunther and Diamond, 'Types and Functions'.
42. Wiesendahl, *Parteien und Demokratie*; Almond and Powell, *Comparative Politics*; Beyme, *Parteien im Wandel*; Gunther and Diamond, 'Types and Functions'; Randall and Svåsand, 'Introduction'.
43. Ware, *The Democratic Party*; Ware, *The Breakdown*; Ware, *The American Direct Primary*; Lipset and Rokkan, 'Cleavage Structures'; Shefter, *Political Parties*; Daalder, 'The Rise of Parties'; Panebianco, *Political Parties*.
44. See for example Norris, 'Building Political Parties'.
45. Biezen, *Political Parties*, 6; Kitschelt et al., *Post Communist Party Systems*; Mainwaring, *Party Systems*; Mainwaring and Scully, *Building Democratic Institutions*; Bendel, *Parteiensysteme in Zentralamerika*; Bendel and Grotz, 'Parteiensysteme'; Erdmann and Basedau, 'Party Systems'; Bogaards, 'Counting Parties'.
46. The three facets resemble, although not exactly, the 'three faces' of Katz and Mair ('The Evolution of Party Organizations'): 'party in central office', 'on the ground', and 'in public office'.
47. Duverger, *Political Parties*; Epstein, *Political Parties*; Panebianco, *Political Parties*.
48. Duverger, *Political Parties*, 17–8, 67; Epstein, *Political Parties*, 126–9, 257–60.
49. Ware, *Political Parties*, 101–2.
50. Panebianco, *Political Parties*, 50–5, 63–8.
51. Ware, *Political Parties*, 102–5.
52. Ibid., 102.
53. Bartolini and Mair, 'Challenges to Contemporary Political Parties', 329.
54. Burnell and Gerrits, 'Promoting Party Politics in Emerging Democracies'.
55. For example, for various reasons a number of political parties in Africa, in power and in opposition, get 'unofficial' funds from other African governments, from Asian governments, and most likely from Western governments as well; these funds exceed official party aid by far: the 'rumoured' figures suggest in some cases a multiplier factor of at least ten.
56. Carothers, *Confronting the Weakest Link*.

Bibliography

Ágh, Attila. 'East-Central Europe: Parties in Crisis and the External and Internal Europeanisation of the Party System', in *Globalising Democracy*, ed. Peter Burnell, 88–103. New York: Routledge, 2006.

Almond, Gabriel A., and Bingham G. Powell. *Comparative Politics. A World View*. Boston, MA: Little, Brown & Company, 1984.
Bartolini, Stefano, and Peter Mair. 'Challenges to Contemporary Political Parties', in *Political Parties and Democracy*, ed. Larry Diamond and Richard Gunther, 327–44. Baltimore, MD: Johns Hopkins University Press, 2001.
Bendel, Petra. *Parteiensysteme in Zentralamerika: Typologien und Erklärungsfaktoren*. Opladen: Leske+Budrich, 1996.
Bendel, Petra, and Florian Grotz. 'Parteiensysteme und Demokratisierung. Junge Demokratien in Afrika, Asien und Lateinamerika im Vergleich'. *Nord-Süd-Aktuell* 15, no. 1 (2001): 70–80.
Bendel, Petra, Aurel Croissant, and Friedbert W. Rüb, eds. *Hybride Regime. Zur Konzeption und Empirie demokratischer Grauzonen*. Opladen: Westdeutscher Verlag, 2002.
Beyme, Klaus von. *Parteien im Wandel. Von den Volksparteien zu den professionalisierten Wählerparteien*. Wiesbaden: Westdeutscher Verlag, 2000.
Biezen van, Ingrid. *Political Parties in New Democracies. Party Organization in Southern and East-Central Europe*. Basingstoke: Palgrave Macmillan, 2003.
Bogaards, Matthijs. 'Counting Parties and Identifying (Dominant) Party Systems in Africa'. *European Journal of Political Research* 43 (2004): 173–97.
Bolleyer Nicole, and Lise Storm. 'Problems of party assistance in hybrid regimes: the case of Morocco'. Democratization 17, no. 6 (2010): 1202–24.
Burnell, Peter. 'Promoting Parties and Party Systems in New Democracies: Is there Anything the "International Community" Can Do?', in *Challenges to Democracy. Ideas, Involvement and Institutions. The PSA Yearbook 2000*, ed. Keith Dowding, James Hughes, and Helene Margetts, 188–204. Basingstoke and New York: Palgrave, 2001.
Burnell, Peter. *Building Better Democracies. Why Political Parties Matter*. London: Westminster Foundation for Democracy, 2004, http://www.wfd.org/upload/docs/WFDBBD5_noprice.pdf (accessed 16 October 2010).
Burnell, Peter. 'Party Development and Party Aid'. Paper presented at the conference 'Die Institutionalisierung politischer Parteien in Afrika, Asien und Lateinamerika'. GIGA u. KAS, Konrad-Adenauer-Stiftung, Berlin, 6. Juni 2006.
Burnell, Peter. 'Political Parties, International Party Assistance and Globalisation', in *Globalising Democracy. Party Politics in Emerging Democracies*, ed. Peter Burnell, 16–45. London: Routledge, 2006.
Burnell, Peter. 'Globalising Party Politics in Emerging Democracies', in *Globalising Democracy. Party Politics in Emerging Democracies*, ed. Peter Burnell, 1–15. London: Routledge, 2006.
Burnell, Peter. 'Looking to the Future. Practice and Research in Party Support', in *Globalising Democracy. Party Politics in Emerging Democracies*, ed. Peter Burnell, 200–9. London: Routledge, 2006.
Burnell, Peter, and André Gerrits. 'Promoting party politics in emerging democracies'. Democratization 17, no. 6 (2010): 1065–84.
Carothers, Thomas. *Assessing Democracy Assistance: the Case of Romania*. Washington, DC: Carnegie Endowment for International Peace, 1996.
Carothers, Thomas. *Aiding Democracy Abroad. The Learning Curve*. Washington, DC: Brookings Institution Press, 1999.
Carothers, Thomas. 'The End of the Transition Paradigm'. *Journal of Democracy* 13, no. 1 (2002): 5–19.
Carothers, Thomas. 'Political Party Aid'. Paper prepared for the Swedish International Development Agency, Washington, DC, 2004, http://www.idea.int/parties/upload/Political_Party_Aid_by_Carothers_Oct04.pdf (accessed 16 October 2010).

Carothers, Thomas. 'Examining International Political Party Aid', in *Globalising Democracy. Party Politics in Emerging Democracies*, ed. Peter Burnell, 69–85. London: Routledge, 2006.

Carothers, Thomas. *Confronting the Weakest Link. Aiding Political Parties in New Democracies*. Washington, DC: Carnegie Endowment for International Peace, 2006.

Carothers, Thomas. *International Assistance for Political Party Development*. Bergen: U4 Anti-Corruption Resource Centre, Chr. Michelsen Institute, 2008, http://www.cmi.no/publications/file/3015-international-assistance-for-political-party.pdf (accessed 16 October 2010).

Daalder, Hans. 'The Rise of Parties in Western Democracies', in *Political Parties and Democracy*, ed. Larry Diamond and Richard Gunther, 40–51. Baltimore, MD: Johns Hopkins University Press, 2001.

Diamond, Larry J. 'Thinking About Hybrid Regimes'. *Journal of Democracy* 13, no. 2 (2002): 21–35.

Duverger, Maurice. *Political Parties*. London: Methuen, 1995.

Epstein, Leon D. *Political Parties in Western Democracies*. London: Pall Mall, 1967.

Erdmann, Gero. 'Party Research: The Western European Bias and the "African Labyrinth"'. *Democratization* 11, no. 3 (2004): 63–87.

Erdmann, Gero. 'Hesitant Bedfellows: The German Stiftungen and Party Aid in Africa', in *Globalizing Democracy: Party Politics in Emerging Democracies*, ed. Peter Burnell, 181–99. London: Routledge, 2006.

Erdmann, Gero, and Matthias Basedau, 'Party Systems in Africa: Problems of Categorising and Explaining Party Systems'. *Journal of Contemporary African Studies* 26, no. 3 (2008): 241–58.

Gunther, Richard, and Larry Diamond. 'Types and Functions of Parties', in *Political Parties and Democracy*, ed. Larry Diamond and Richard Gunther, 3–39. Baltimore, MD: Johns Hopkins University Press, 2001.

Karl, Terry Lynn. 'The Hybrid Regimes of Central America'. *Journal of Democracy* 6, no. 3 (1995): 72–87.

Katz, Richard S., and Peter Mair. 'The Evolution of Party Organizations in Europe: Three Faces of Party Organization', in *Political Parties in a Changing Age*, ed. William Crotty. Special issue of *American Review of Politics* 14 (1994): 593–617.

Kitschelt, Herbert. 'Formation of Party Cleavages in Postcommunist Democracies'. *Party Politics* 1, no. 4 (1995): 447–72.

Kitschelt, Herbert. 'Divergent Paths of Postcommunist Democracies', in *Political Parties and Democracy*, ed. Larry Diamond and Richard Gunther, 299–326. Baltimore, MD: Johns Hopkins University Press, 2001.

Kitschelt, Herbert, Zdenka Mansfeldova, Radsoslaw Markowski, and Gábor Tóka. *Post Communist Party Systems*. Cambridge: Cambridge University Press, 1999.

Kumar, Krishna. 'International Political Party Assistance. An Overview and Analysis', *Working Paper 33*. The Netherlands Institute of International Relations 'Clingendael', The Hague, 2004.

Kumar, Krishna. 'Reflections on International Party Assistance'. *Democratization* 12, no. 4 (2005): 506–28.

Lipset, Seymour M., and Stein Rokkan. 'Cleavage Structures, Party Systems, and Voter Alignments', in *Party Systems and Voter Alignments. Cross-National Perspectives*, ed. Seymour M. Lipset and Stein Rokkan, 1–64. New York: The Free Press, 1967.

Mainwaring, Scott. 'Party Systems in the Third Wave'. *Journal of Democracy* 9, no. 3 (1998): 67–81.

Mainwaring, Scott, and Timothy R. Scully. 'Introduction: Party Systems in Latin America', in *Building Democratic Institutions. Party Systems in Latin America*, ed. Scott

Mainwaring and Timothy R. Scully, 1–36. Stanford, CA: Stanford University Press, 1995.
Mair, Stefan. 'Germany's Stiftungen and Democracy Assistance: Comparative Advantages, New Challenges', in *Democracy Assistance. International Co-operation for Democratization*, ed. Peter Burnell, 128–49. London and Portland: Frank Cass, 2000.
Mair, Stefan. *Parlamentskooperation der Friedrich-Ebert-Stiftung in Afrika. Vergleichende Studie Ghana, Namibia, Simbabwe, Südafrika*. München: Gutachten für die Friedrich-Ebert-Stiftung, 2000.
Merkel, Wolfgang. 'Einleitung', in *Systemwechsel 3. Parteien im Transitionsprozess*, ed. Wolfgang Merkel and Eberhard Sandschneider, 1–21. Opladen: Leske+Budrich, 1997.
Merkel, Wolfgang. *Systemtransformation*. Wiesbaden: VS Verlag, 2010.
Norris, Pippa. 'Building Political Parties: Reforming Legal Regulations and Internal Rules'. Report for International IDEA, 2005, http://www.hks.harvard.edu/fs/pnorris/Acrobat/Building%20political%20parties.pdf (accessed 16 October 2010).
Panebianco, Angelo. *Political Parties: Organization and Power*. Cambridge, Melbourne and New York: Cambridge University Press, 1988.
Randall, Vicky, and Lars Svåsand. 'Introduction: The Contribution of Parties to "Democracy and Democratic Consolidation"'. *Democratization* 9, no. 3 (2002): 30–52.
Rose, Richard, and Neil Munro. *Parties and Elections in the New European Democracies*. Colchester: ECRP Press, 2009.
Schmitter, Philippe. 'Critical Reflections on the "Functions" of Political Parties and their Performance in Neo-Democracies', in *Demokratie in Ost und West*, ed. Wolfgang Merkel and Andreas Buch, 475–95. Frankfurt: Suhrkamp, 1999.
Schmitter, Philippe. 'Parties Are Not What They Once Were', in *Political Parties and Democracy*, ed. Larry Diamond and Richard Gunther, 67–89. Baltimore, MD: Johns Hopkins University Press, 2001.
Shefter, Martin. *Political Parties and the State. The American Historical Experience*. Princeton, NJ, and Chichester: Princeton University Press, 1994.
Van Wersch, Jos, and Jeroen de Zeeuw. 'Europe in Democracy Assistance: Facts and Figures'. Background Research Paper: A European Profile in Democracy Support; Conference Reader: Enhancing the European Profile in Democracy Assistance, The Hague, 5–6 July 2004. Democracy AGENDA: Alliance for Generating a European Network for Democracy Assistance, 2004.
Van Wersch, Jos, and Jeroen de Zeeuw. 'Mapping European Democracy Assistance', *Working Paper 36*. Netherlands Institute of International Relations 'Clingendael' The Hague, 2005.
Ware, Alan. *The Breakdown of Democratic Party Organization, 1940–80*. Oxford: Clarendon, 1985.
Ware, Alan. *Political Parties and Party Systems*. Oxford: University Press, 1996.
Ware, Alan. *The American Direct Primary: Party Institutionalisation and Transformation*. New York: Cambridge University Press, 2002.
Ware, Alan. *The Democratic Party Heads North. 1877–1967*. New York: Cambridge University Press, 2006.
Wiesendahl, Elmar. *Parteien und Demokratie. Eine soziologische Analyse paradigmatischer Ansätze der Parteienforschung*. Opladen: Leske+Budrich, 1980.
Wolinetz, Steven B. 'Approaches to the Study of Parties and Party organization in Contemporary Democracies', in *Political Parties. Old Concepts and New Challenges*, ed. Richard Gunter, José Ramón Montero, Juan J. Linz, 136–65. Oxford: Oxford University Press, 2002.

Index

Page numbers in *Italics* represent tables.
Page numbers in **Bold** represent figures.

abbreviations: glossary of 89–90
accountability 100, 128, 200
Afghanistan 16
African National Congress (ANC) 171, 174; South Africa 201–2
Agrarian League 225
aid recipients: electoral performance **57**; suspicious 59–60
Akhmetov, Rinat 32
Albania 47
Alfred Mozer Foundation 213
Alliance for Change 71, 96
Alliance for Democracy (AFORD) 191, 199
Alliance for the Future of Kosovo (AAK) 97
Alliance of Independent Social Democrats (SNSD) 72, 73, 87, 95, 100
American National Endowment for Democracy (NED) 162
anti-communist nationalism 119
Antonic, S. 58
ARENA (Nationalist Republican Party) 115, 118–28
armed forces 170
Armenia 36
Ashdown, Paddy 101
Ashkali 97
assistance 3–4; Carothers 211, 212, 214; failure 13; or manipulation 48
authoritarian rulers: liberalization 167–8
authoritarianism 125; democracy 143
autonomy 171, 175

Bader, Max 10, 11, 13, 14
Balkanism 73
Balkanization 103
Banda, Ruphia 190, 192
Bartolini, Stefano 3, 219, 224
Basedau, Mattthias 171
Bastian, S. 93
Batkivshchyna 30, 35
behavioural consolidation 166; democratic elites 170
Benjamin, Rob 51
big man syndrome 192
Bolleyer, N. 10, 11, 13, 14
Bosnia: party system *71*
Bosnia and Herzegovina 12, 15; accountability 101–3; conclusion 82–3; Election Law 98; ethnopolitical electoral contexts 76–8, *79*; international administrations and political systems 93–4; international intervention 74–6; introduction 68–70; non-nationalist voters voting nationalist *80*; non-nationalist voting 78; non-nationalist/nationalist ticket splitting 78–82; party competition 70–3; patterns of party competition 73–4; political parties 94–6; Social Democratic Party 70; WLS regression of ticket splitters *81*, *see also* post-conflict countries
Bosniaks 70, 76–7, 97
Buddhist Liberal Democratic Party 118
Bulgaria 47
Bulldozer Revolution 45
Burnell, Peter 48, 212, 225
Burundi 128
Bush, George W. 57
Bussey, Jane 55

INDEX

cadre party 221, 223
Caldéron Sol, Armando 126
Cambodia 12, 13; early party development and war 116–17; findings 128; impact of war on parties 123–6; impact of war on party systems 126–8; implications 129–31; influence of international actors 122–3; introduction 112–13; methodology 113–15; National Democratic Institute (NDI) 122; parties and institutionalization 119–20; party members 120; party systems 120–2; peace and party development 117–19; State of 117
Cambodian National Election Committee 127
Cambodian People's Party 117, 119
campaign finance: Morocco 147
campaigning 4, 53
Cantonal Assembly 77
capacity-building 129–30
Carothers, Thomas 4–7, 48, 142, 154, 164; *Confronting the Weakest Link* 218; mythic model 6, 216, 217; political party assistance 211, 212, 214; standard method 6, 215
cartel party 221
Catholic Church 95
Central and Eastern Europe (CEE) 21
Centre for Free Elections and Democracy (CeSID) 54, 56, 59, 60
Centre for Multiparty Democracy 189; Kenya 205
Centre for Multiparty Democracy-Malawi (CMD-M) 193–6
Centrist Democrat International 97
Chakuamba, Gwanda 198
Chama Cha Mapinduza (CCM) 224
Chama Cha Wananchi (CUF) 224
Chapultepec Accords 117
Chihana 199
Chile 9, 220
Chiluba, Frederick 191
China 116; US Democratic Party 57
Christian Democratic Party 115
Christian democrats 8
Christian-Democratic Union: Germany 24
Christiani, Alfredo 126
citizens: decision-making 140
Citizens' Union: Georgia 24–6, 30, 32, 34
civic culture: consolidation 166, 170

civil conflict 10
civil rights 31
civil society 187; approach 164, 214; parties 190
civil war: political party development 112
coalitions 128, 186
coherence 171, 175
Cold War: party support 5
colonial administration: party development 113
Commonwealth of Independents States (CIS) 21–2
communism 119; fall of 48
Communist League of BiH 96
Communist Party 26, 33; Ukraine 23, 26, 31, 35
competition: party 74; party politics 25
competitive authoritarianism 49
conflict prevention 168
Confronting the Weakest Link (Carothers) 218
Congress of the People (COPE) 175
conservatives 8
consociationalism 69, 76
consolidation 166; institutionalization of democracy 169; project of 170
constitutional consolidation 166
constitutional review 196; process 196–7
controversial roles 219–22
corporate identity 176
corruption 31, 72, 95, 101, 102
Covic, Dragan 101
Coyne, C.J. 104
Croatia 48
Croatian Democratic Union (HDZ) 71–3, 92, 95, 96, 100, 101
Croats 70
cross-ethnic competition 76
cross-party assistance 5
cross-party dialogues 164, 168, 214
cross-party initiatives 196
culture: democracy 100

database: voter targeting 54
D'Aubuisson, Roberto 126
Dayton constitution 76
Dayton Peace Agreement (1995) 69, 72, 73; implementation 93, 94, 95
de Zeeuw, J. 10, 11, 12, 16, 215
de-institutionalization 171
de-nationalizing politics 68
decentralization 176
decision-making: citizens 140

INDEX

democracy: authoritarianism 143; culture 100; denunciation of 3; designing 93; hybrid regime 143; and parties 141–3; qualifying as 48; soft incentives 138–41
democracy assistance 5, 211; measuring 218
democracy building 94
democratic decision-making: institutional consolidation 169–70
democratic elites: behavioural consolidation 170
Democratic League of Dardania (LDD) 97
Democratic League of Kosovo (LDK) 96, 97
Democratic Opposition of Serbia (DOS) 50, 51, 52
Democratic Party of Kosovo (KLA) 91, 97
Democratic Progressive Party 191
democratic representation of interests: representative consolidation 170
democratic rules 122
democratization 10, 37, 92, 130, 166; backwards 188; institution building 168–9; institutionalization 166; party change 151–2; political parties 141
democratization research: phase model of party assistance 166–7
demographic analysis 53
Demokratieunzufrindenheit 8
Denmark: Ministry of Foreign Affairs 6
Department for International Development (UK) 6
dependence 177
dependencies: creating 60
dialogue 196–7; party system 189
Diamond, Larry 221
diffusion 223
Dinkic, Mladjan 59
disbanding parties 28
dissent 175, 176; intra-party 170
Djindjic, Zoran 51, 52
Dodik, Milorad 72, 95
dominant authoritarian party system 120
Draskovic, Vuk 59
Duverger, M. 142, 223; *Political Parties* 223
dysfunctional parties 221
dysfunctions 222

Egypt 97

El Salvador 12; early party development and war 115; findings 128; impact of war on parties 123–6; impact of war on party systems 126–8; implications 129–31; influence of international actors 122–3; International Republican Institute (IRI) 122; introduction 112–13; methodology 113–15; parties and institutionalization 119–20; party systems 120–2; peace and party development 117–19
election campaigns 215; funding 192; support for 169
election observation 131
elections 92, 94; legitimate 48; non-competitive 119
Electoral Act and the Republican Constitution (2006) 196–7
electoral capacity building 4
electoral institutions 130
electoral manipulation 149
electoral meddling 55–7
electoral performance: aid and non-aid recipients **57**
electoral process 219
Electoral Revolution 44
electoral systems 29; design 99–100; mixed 29
electoral volatility 74, 150, 222
electoral-professional parties 221
electoralism: fallacy of 169
elite party 221
elitism 150
entrepreneurs 28, 170
environmental effects 124
Epstein, Leon 223; *Political Parties in Western Democracies* 223
equal access 122
Erdmann, Gero 6, 14, 15, 16, 164–5
estate owners 170
Ethiopia 128
ethnic allocations 76
ethnic census 78
ethnic cleavages 168
ethnic congress party 212
ethnic identity 177
ethnic minority representation 49
ethnic nationalism 48
ethnic parties: studies 75
ethnic tribune 78
ethnical cleavage model 162
ethnicity: politics 69

INDEX

ethnopolitical electoral contexts 76–8, 77
EU accession 8; Bosnia 75
European Serbia: ZES 58
European Union (EU) 4, 139; Bosnia 68; conditionality 75; enlargement 7; integration 58, 90
European Union Special Representative (Bosnia) 74–5
exchange visits 215
exclusion 119
executive dominance 192
executive formation 219
exit strategy 102

façade democracy 31
factionalization 128
Farabundo Martí National Liberation Front 115
Federation and BiH Assembly elections 79
floor crossing 178
Foreign and Commonwealth Office (UK) 6
foreign contributions 57
foreign donations: political parties 57
foreign interference 147
fragmentation: party system 74, 198, 199
Freedom House 31
Freedom Party 30
Freie Demokratische Partei (FDP) 224
French colonizers 149
Friedrich Ebert Stiftung (FES) 24, 30, 34, 122; Kenya 176–8; Serbia 47, 50–1, 61; South Africa 174–6
Friedrich Naumann Stiftung 47
Fukuyama, F. 93
funding: election campaign 192; illegal accounts 200–1
fundraising 192

G17 Plus 59
gender balance 6
Georgia 11, 14, 48; Citizens' Union 24; conclusions and implications 35–7; introduction 21–2; parties in aftermath 34–5; party assistance 21–2, 22–4; party characteristics 24–7; response of party assistance 29–31; undemocratic politics and party assistance 31–4; USAID 23; volatility 27–9
Georgia's Way 30

German Federal Ministry for Economic Cooperation and Development 24
German foundations: partner parties Kenya and South Africa *174*
Germany 5, 9; Christian-Democratic Union 24; Socialist Party 24
Gerrits, André 225
Get-Out-The-Vote (GOTV) campaign 44, 54, 60; USAID 56
Ghana 189, 205
globalization 7, 8
governance: improving 148; reliable 48
Green Party: Ukraine 27
Grzymala-Busse, Anna 74, 75
Guardado, Facundo 126
Guatemala 218
Gunther, Richard 221

Handbook of Party Politics 2
Handbook on Working with Political Parties (UNDP) 188
Hanns Seidel Stiftung 47, 122
Haradinaj, Ramush 97
Heinrich Böll Stiftung 47
Herzegovina-Neretva canton 101
Hulsey, John W. 10, 11, 12, 15
human rights 48, 94, 102
Huntington, Samuel P. 169
hybrid regimes: democracy 143; political parties 142

ideology 24, 113, 129, 171
illiteracy 151
incentives 140; party development 28
independence 150
Index of the Institutionalization of Parties (IIP) 171
Industry Will Save Georgia 27, 30
Innes, A. 75
institution building: democratization 168–9
institutional approach 164, 214
institutional consolidation: democratic decision-making 169–70
institutional dimension impact 97–8
institutionalization 119, 162, 166, 170; democratization 166; dimensions and indicators of *172–3*; executive dominance 192; lack of 123; party system 187; political parties 170–1
institutionalization of democracy: consolidation 169
institutionalizing political parties 216

INDEX

inter-party dialogue 196; Zambia and Malawi 197
internal communications: parties 194
internal decision-making 176
internal democracy 6
internal party democracy 175
international administrations: impact on political culture 100–1
International Criminal Tribunal for the Former Yugoslavia (ICTY) 56, 58, 95, 98
international cross-party collaboration 164, 214
International Institute for Democracy and Electoral Assistance (IDEA) 213
international intervention: Bosnia and Herzegovina 74–6
international networks: political parties 8
international party support 203–5
International Republican Institute (IRI) 4, 23, 146; El Salvador 122; Morocco 144, 146–9, 151–3; Serbia 55, 56, 58, 60
international support: intrusiveness and effectiveness 4–9
Iraq 16
Islamist PJD 146
Islamists 142
Izetbegovic, A. 72

Jarstad, Anna K. 93
Johannesburg 175

Karadzic, Radovan 95
Katz, Richard 3
Kaunda, Kenneth 191
Kenya 11, 12, 13, 189, 194; Centre for Multiparty Democracy 205; German foundations and partner parties *174*
Kenya African National Unity (KANU) 174, 176, 177, 178
Kenyatta, President Jomo 176
Khmer People's National Liberation Front 126
Khmer People's Revolutionary Party (KPRP) 116
Khmer Republic 116
Khmer Rouge 116, 120, 124, 126
King, Charles 31
Komsic, Z. 71, 78
Konrad Adenauer Foundation 35
Konrad Adenauer Stiftung (KAS) 23, 24, 35, 47, 122; Africa 162, 165, 177

Kosovo 12; accountability 101–3; international administrations and political systems 94; National Democratic Institute (NDI) 97; political parties 96–7, *see also* post-conflict countries
Kosovo Assembly 97
Kosovo Objective Party (KOS) 97
Kosovo war 50
Kostunica, Vojislav 51, 59
Kuchma 31
Kumar, K. 48, 217
Kyrgyzstan 36

Labour Party: Georgia 30, 33
Lagumdzija, Zlatko 71
leaders 24; charismatic 170
leadership 127, 194, 223; style 125–6, 126
legal reform 147
legislative process: parliament 219
legitimacy 3, 26
Levitsky, S. 49
liberalization 166; authoritarian rulers 167–8
liberals 8
local ownership 90, 102
loyal opposition 128
Luckham, R. 93

Mair, Peter 3, 219, 224
Mair, Stefan 165, 179
majority rule 168
Malawi 13, 15; impact of NIMD support 192–5; inter-party dialogue 197; nominations 199; party routines 198–9; party survival 198; party system development 190–2; societal roots 202
Malawi Congress Party (MCP) 190, 202
Malawi Electoral Commission (MEC) 194, 195
Mandela, Nelson 175
manifestos 170
manipulation: or assistance 48
mass parties 142, 221, 223
mass party model: Morocco 149–50; mythic model 216
Matano, Robert 176
maximalist understanding 169
Mbeki, Thabo 175
media: access 129, 130
membership 192
meritocracy 101

INDEX

Merkel, Wolfgang 166, 169
militarization 124
military juntas 115
military stabilization 94
Milosovic, S. 44–61, 72
Ministry of Foreign Affairs: Denmark 6
mixed electoral systems 29
Mohammed VI (King of Morocco) 152
Moi, Arap 176, 177
monarchy: executive 149
money 130; parties 142
mono-ethnic contexts 77
Montgomery, William 49
Morocco 10, 11, 13, 218; campaign finance 147; citizens view of parties 150; conclusion 153–4; constitution (1966) 150; friendly regime 154; hybrid regime 143; implications of assistance 148–9; king 143, 152; law on political parties (2006) 151; mass party dreams 150–1; mass party model 149–50; National Democratic Institute (NDI) 139; party assistance analysis 146–8; party assistance measures *145*; study methods 146; United Nations Development Programme 144, 146–9, 151–3
Moroz, Oleksandr 33, 35
moudawana 152
Movement for Multiparty Democracy (MMD) 191; Zambia 202
moveon.org 57
Mozambique 128, 194, 205, 218
multi-party approach 164, 168, 214
multi-party elections 164, 190
multi-party support 5
Muluzi, President Elson Bakili 191, 199
Mutharika, Bingu wa 191, 198
Mwanawasa, Levy 191, 192, 196
mythic model 216, 220; Carothers 6, 216, 217
mythic party 222

naming and shaming 139
nation building 169, 170
National Conciliation Party 115
National Constitution Committee (NCC) 203, 204
National Democratic Institute (NDI) 4, 23, 30, 48, 51, 213; 2004 Quarterly Report 54; Bosnia 75; Cambodia 122; Kosovo 97; Morocco 139, 144, 146–53; Zambia 195
National Democratic Party 30

National Endowment for Democracy (NED) 4, 213
National Liberation Movement of Kampuchea 118
nationalism 8, 13; divisive ideology 103
Nationalist Republican Alliance 115
Nenadovic, Maja 10, 11, 12, 13, 14
nepotism 101
Netherlands 9
Netherlands Institute for Multiparty Democracy (NIMD) 4, 10, 14, 24, 30, 47; Africa 163; Annual Report 193; budget (2003–2008) *190*; Malawi and Zambia 186–205; support for parties 189–90
New Kosovo Alliance (AKR) 97
New Rights Party 30
NGO Act 202
NGO Code of Conduct: Malawi (1997) 202
Nhiek Bun Chhay 126
Nicaragua 128
Nikolic, Tomislav 50, 53, 54
Nol, Lon 116
Non-governmental Coordination Council (NOCOC) 203
non-nationalist voting: Bosnia and Herzegovina 78
non-partisanship 47
Nordlund, P. 92
Norodom Ranarridh Party 120
Northern Ireland 78
Norwegian Centre for Democracy Support 122

Oasis Forum 197, 203
O'Donnell, Guillermo 166
Office for Democratic Institutions and Human Rights (ODIHR) 24
Office of the High Representative 72, 74, 93
office-seeking 27
oligarchic parties 27
one-party dominance 29
Open Society Foundation 101
opposition: undermining 126–7
opposition parties: weak 123
Orange Revolution *see* Ukraine
organization 175
Organization of American States (OAS) 122
Organization for Security and Co-operation in Europe (OSCE) 4, 94, 97–100, 213

INDEX

organizational weaknesses 224
organized crime 101
Orientalism 73
ortodoxos 125

Pacolli, Behgjet 97
Panebianco, Angelo 171, 223
paramilitary structures 126
Paris Peace Accords (1991) 117
Paris, Roland 92
parliament: legislative process 219
parliamentary training 144
Partai Amanat Nasional (PAN) 225
Partai Kebangkitan Bangsa (PKB) 225
partisan approach 5, 164, 214
partisanship 13
Party for Bosnia and Herzegovina (SBiH) 72, 95, 100
Party for Democratic Action (SDA) 71, 72, 73, 78, 82
party members: Cambodia 120; El Salvador 120
party politics: competition 25
Party of Regions 31, 32, 33, 35
party-citizen linkages 150
party-to-party relations 214
Patriotic Front 192
patronage networks 114
Pavlovic, D. 58
peace: political parties 92, 99
People's Democratic Party 26, 30
People's Party Work for Betterment (NSRzB) 96
People's Republic of Kampuchea (PRK) 116
People's Union Our Ukraine 24, 30, 34, 35
personality politics 28
personalization 177
Peru 220
phase model: party assistance 162, 165, **167**
Phnom Penh 116
Pinochet, President Augusto 9
Pol Pot regime 124
polarization 57; exacerbating 57–9
policies 213–17
policy making 219
policy seeking 27
political culture: impact of international administrations 100–1; term 91
political elites 141
political entrepreneurs 202
political finance regulation 147

political liberalization 167
political parties: aid 4; aid arsenal 47; building 140, 215; civil society 140, 190; civil society relationships 201–2; colonial administration 113; competition and exclusion 119; competition and hostility 127; crisis 2–3; and democracy 141; democratization 141; development 188–9; development after civil war 112; dominance 12; endurance 198; financing 104, 175; foreign donations 57; funding 146; funding regulations 144; hybrid regimes 142; ills of development 22; incentives to develop 28; institutionalization 170–1; international assistance 3–4; international networks 8; international support 188–9; law on 127; legitimacy 3; list voting 34; localising 144; membership 113; organization 144; peace 92, 99; of power 7, 26; regulation 92, 98–9; strength 28; strengthening 190, 197–8; too many 151; turnover 23; unknown 222–5; weak link 2
Political Parties (Duverger) 223
Political Parties in Western Democracies (Epstein) 223
political party: definition 114
Political Party Act (2008) 178
political party assistance 114, 129; approaches 164; conclusion 225–7; framework for countries in transition 144–6; instruments 171–4; introduction 211–13; measures in Morocco *145*; Morocco 146–8; persuasion 138–41; phase model 162, 165, **167**; problems of 216; providers *163*; reasons for limited success 225; research 166; research on 217–18; texting 55; types of *215*; weaknesses of implementation 216–17
political party research 219–25
political party system: aid 214; development in Malawi 190–2; dialogue 189; fragmentation 74, 198; institutionalization 170, 187; knowledge 131; theories 7
political pluralism: promoting 48
political polarization: exacerbating 57
political processes: core 219
political profiling 4
political recruitment 188

INDEX

politically motivated murder 124
Polt, Michael 52
Popular Front (PF) 203
popular mass movements 115
popular support 3
popularity 3
populism 13, 24
post-conflict countries: conclusion 103–4; introduction 90–1; political parties 91–2; political system design 92–3
Potemkin democracy 31
power sharing 69
Presbyterians 202
presidency: Bosnia 76–7
presidential regimes 28
programmatic integration 175
promoters 213–17
proportional representation 29, 150, 169
Przeworski, Adam 166
public institution building 149
public opinion polling 47
puppet regimes 127

radical movements 170
Radical Party 61
radicalism: fear of 58
Rainsy, Sam 126
Rakner, L. 10, 14, 15, 16
Ranarridh, Norodom 126
Randall, V. 14, 141, 171
Reagan, President Ronald 213
Reformist Party ORA 97
refugees 72
regime change 44
regime strength 26
Reiily, B. 92
renovadores 125
representative consolidation 166; democratic representation of interests 170
Republican Party 30
Republika Srpska 74, 79, 95
resources 26
Revolutionary Party of Democratic Unification 115
Rights Party: Georgia 27
Roma 97
Rosa Luxemburg Stiftung 47
Rose, R. 188
Rose Revolution *see* Georgia
Rugova, Ibrahim 96
Rukh for Unity Party 26, 30
Russia 218
Russian Federation 7

Rwanda 128

Saakashvili, President Mikheil 24, 25, 34, 36
Said, Edward 73
Salvadoran Supreme Electoral Tribunal (TSE) 127
Sam Rainsy Party 118
Sanchez Cerén, Salvador 126
Sangkum Reastr Niyum 116
Sann, Son 126
Sartori, G. 114, 120, 122
Sata, Michael 192
Schedler, Andreas 100
Schmitter, Philippe C. 166, 220
security 130
semi-authoritarianism 44
Sen, Hun 126
September 11th terrorist attacks 138
Serbia 12; consequences of party aid 55–60; national question 58; party aid (1997–2000) 50; party aid (2001–2003) 50–2; party aid (2004–2009) 52–5; party aid and partisanship 46–50; US SEED spending **51**; USAID 56
Serbian Democratic Party (SDS) 71, 72, 73
Serbian Progressive Party (SNS) 50
Serbian Radical Party (SRS) 49–50, 52–6, 58–9, 61
Serbian Renewal Movement 59
Serbs 70
Seselj, Vojislav 52
Shevardnadze, Eduard 24, 25, 31, 32
Shin, D.C. 188
Sihanouk, King Norodom 116, 118
Silajdzic, H. 72, 73, 95
single-member districts (SMDs) 29
Sisk, Timothy D. 92, 93
Slovakia 48
Social Democratic Party: Bosnia and Herzegovina 70, 71, 96; Ukraine 27, 31
social democrats 8
Socialist Party 30, 35; Germany 24; Ukraine 33
Socialist Party of Serbia (SPS) 49, 55, 58
societal networks 142
societal relations 148
socio-political foundations: stabilization 170
sofa parties 48
soft incentives: democracy 138–41

INDEX

South Africa 11; African National Congress (ANC) 171, 201–2; FES party assistance 174–6; German foundations and partner parties *174*
Soviet Union 26
Special Representative of the Secretary General (SRSG) 94
splinter groups 202
Spoerri, M. 13
spoiler parties 26
stability 188
stabilization: socio-political foundations 170
standard method 24; Carothers 6, 215
Stiftungen 10, 47, 149; conclusion 178–9; introduction 161–2; party assistance tourism 162–5
Storm, L. 10, 11, 13, 14
Stroh, Alexander 171
Strom, K. 27
structural effects 124
succession 192
Sudan 128
Svasand, Lars 10, 14, 15, 16, 141, 171
Sweden 57

Tadic, Boris 50, 53, 60
Tanzania 194, 205
territorial penetration 223
texting: party assistance 55
Thaçi, Hashim 97
Thembo, G.W. 199
thick organizations 221, 223
thin organizations 221, 223
third wave world 22
ticket splitting: Bosnia and Herzegovina 78–82
Titoist symbolism 70
trade 130
training 215
transition process 166
transparency 6; party financing 175
trust 127, 130, 193
Tudman, Franjo 72, 73
turnout 54
turnover 28
Tuzla Canton 71, 78
Tymoshenko, Yulia 24, 30, 35

Uganda 128
Ukraine 11, 13, 14; Communist Party 26; conclusions and implications 35–7; Green Party 27; parties in aftermath 34–5; party assistance 22–4; party characteristics 24–7; response of party assistance 29–31; Social Democratic Party 27; undemocratic politics and party assistance 31–4; volatility 27–9
unconsolidated party system 221
United Democratic Centre 118
United Democratic Front (UDF) 190, 202
United Democrats 30
United Kingdom (UK) 6, 9
United National Independence Party (UNIP) 191
United National Movement 24, 25, 30, 32, 34
United Nations (UN) 4, 117
United Nations Development Programme (UNDP) 139; *Handbook on Working with Political Parties* 188; Morocco 144, 146–9, 151–3
United Nations Mission in Kosovo (UNMIK) 94
United Nations Observer Mission in El Salvador 117
United Nations Security Council Resolution (UNSCR) 94
United Nations Transitional Authority Cambodia (UNTAC) 117
United States Agency for International Development (USAID) 7, 213; Africa 163; Bosnia 75; evaluation of 217; funding for US party institutes **53**; Georgia 23; GOTV campaign 56; Serbia 56
United States of America (US): foreign policy in Middle East 146
United States of America (USA) 213; Cambodia 123; Democratic Party 57, 139; foreign aid spending 52; government 4; Republican Party 139
unknown political parties 222–5

value-infusion 171
value-orientated strategy 171
values 24
Van Wersch, Jos 215
Venezuela 220
veto rights 69
Villalobos, Joaquín 126
violence 127, 167–8, 168, 205; non 48
virtual parties 32
vision 24
vote-seeking 27
voter targeting 53–4, 56, 60

INDEX

voter turnout 150

war criminals 72
Ware, Alan 223
Washington Agreement (1994) 73, 74
Way, Lucan 49
weakest link: political party assistance 212
Weichert, Michael 51, 61
Weissenbach, K. 10, 11, 13, 47
Western European bias 220
Westminster Foundation for Democracy (WFD) 47, 163
Wheatley, J. 25, 31
Wolinetz, Steven 27
women 4, 53, 146
Women for Change 195, 202, 203

Yanukovich, Viktor 24
youth 4, 53

Yushchenko, Viktor 24, 30, 35

Zajedno 50
Zambia 14; impact of NIMD support 192, 195–7; inter-party dialogue 197; party nominations 201; party routines 200–1; party survival 200; societal roots 202–3
Zambia Congress of Trade Unions (ZCTU) 191
Zambia Episcopal conference 203
Zambia Forum for a Democratic Process (FODEP) 194
Zambian Centre for Inter-party Dialogue (ZCID) 196–7
ZES: European Serbia 58, 59
Zimbabwe 194
Zuma, Jacob 175

Space & Polity

EDITOR:

Ronan Paddison, *University of Glasgow, UK*

Space & Polity is a fully refereed scholarly international journal devoted to the theoretical and empirical understanding of the changing relationships between the state, and regional and local forms of governance. The journal provides a forum aimed particularly at bringing together social scientists currently working in a variety of disciplines, including geography, political science, sociology, economics, anthropology and development studies and who have a common interest in the relationships between space, place and politics in less developed as well as the advanced economies.

To view free articles please visit **www.tandf.co.uk/journals/cspp** and click on News & Offers.

To sign up for tables of contents, new publications and citation alerting services visit www.informaworld.com/alerting

Register your email address at www.tandf.co.uk/journals/eupdates.asp to receive information on books, journals and other news within your areas of interest.

For further information, please contact Customer Services at either of the following:
T&F Informa UK Ltd, Sheepen Place, Colchester, Essex, CO3 3LP, UK
Tel: +44 (0) 20 7017 5544 Fax: 44 (0) 20 7017 5198
Email: subscriptions@tandf.co.uk
Taylor & Francis Inc, 325 Chestnut Street, Philadelphia, PA 19106, USA
Tel: +1 800 354 1420 (toll-free calls from within the US)
or +1 215 625 8900 (calls from overseas) Fax: +1 215 625 2940
Email: customerservice@taylorandfrancis.com

View an online sample issue at:
www.tandf.co.uk/journals/cspp